Dear Jim Ryan —
Best Wishes.

Joe Cronin '57
Faculty 65-71

REFORMING BOSTON SCHOOLS,
1930 TO THE PRESENT

Barriers to educational
opportunity in Boston

PALGRAVE STUDIES IN URBAN EDUCATION

Series Editors: Alan R. Sadovnik and Susan F. Semel

Reforming Boston Schools, 1930 to the Present

Overcoming Corruption and Racial Segregation

Joseph Marr Cronin

First published in hardcover in 2008 by
PALGRAVE MACMILLAN®
in the United States—a division of St. Martin's Press LLC,
175 Fifth Avenue, New York, NY 10010.

Where this book is distributed in the UK, Europe and the rest of the world,
this is by Palgrave Macmillan, a division of Macmillan Publishers Limited,
registered in England, company number 785998, of Houndmills,
Basingstoke, Hampshire RG21 6XS.

Palgrave Macmillan is the global academic imprint of the above companies
and has companies and representatives throughout the world.

Palgrave® and Macmillan® are registered trademarks in the United States,
the United Kingdom, Europe and other countries.

ISBN: 978–0–230–11145–5

Library of Congress Cataloging-in-Publication Data

Cronin, Joseph M.
     Reforming Boston schools, 1930 to the present : overcoming corruption
and racial segregation / Joseph Marr Cronin.
       p. cm.—(Palgrave studies in urban education)
     Rev. ed. of: Reforming Boston schools, 1930–2006. 2008.
     ISBN 978–0–230–11145–5 (pbk.)
      1. Schools—Massachusetts—Boston—Case studies.
2. Educational change—Massachusetts—Boston—Case studies.
3. Discrimination in education—Massachusetts—Boston—Case
studies. 4. School integration—Massachusetts—Boston—Case studies.
5. Educational equalization—Massachusetts—Boston—Case studies.
6. Education, Urban—Massachusetts—Boston—Case studies. 7. African
Americans—Education—Massachusetts—Boston—Case studies.
     I. Cronin, Joseph M. Reforming Boston schools, 1930–2006. II. Title.

LA306.B7C76 2011
379.2'60973—dc23   2011017643

A catalogue record of the book is available from the British Library.

Design by Newgen Imaging Systems (P) Ltd., Chennai, India.

First PALGRAVE MACMILLAN paperback edition: August 2011

10 9 8 7 6 5 4 3 2 1

Printed in the United States of America.

Transferred to Digital Printing in 2011

Mentors: Owen B. Kiernan,
Herold C. Hunt, H. Thomas James

Former Doctoral Students: <u>William Leary</u>,
<u>Charles Glenn</u>, Diana Lam, Steve Leonard,
<u>Charles Leftwich</u>, Robert <u>Schwartz</u>, Thomas Payzant

Passed Students
65-71

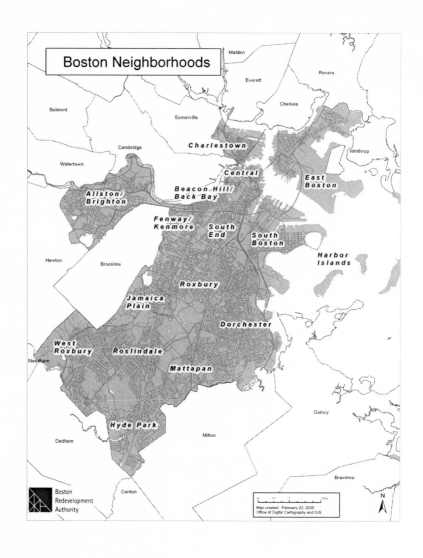

Boston Neighborhoods

Malden
Revere
Everett
Chelsea
Belmont
Somerville
Winthrop
Cambridge
Charlestown
Watertown
Central
East Boston
Allston/Brighton
Beacon Hill/Back Bay
Fenway/Kenmore
South End
South Boston
Newton
Brookline
Harbor Islands
Roxbury
Jamaica Plain
Dorchester
West Roxbury
Roslindale
Needham
Mattapan
Quincy
Hyde Park
Dedham
Milton
Braintree
Canton

Boston Redevelopment Authority

Map created - February 22, 2005
Office of Digital Cartography and GIS

N

Contents

ACKNOWLEDGMENTS

This book grew out of the 1968–70 Danforth study of schools in five major American cities. New discussions began in 1985 with James Fraser, dean of the Northeastern University School of Education and a historian of American education. Ralph Edwards provided insights from research on the selection of Boston's first black superintendent and the campaign to appoint the Boston School Committee. Richard Hailer, Sam Tyler, Patricia Graham, Ken Rossano, Kathleen Kelly, Ed Doherty, Steve Coan, Larry DiCara, Susan Moore Johnson, Kim Marshall, Betty Power, Sylvia Simmons, James Buckley, Charlotte Harris, Robert Consalvo, Robert Dentler, and Robert Binswanger reviewed portions of the manuscript. The cover photo was by Tim Cronin.

Other support came from former state Commissioner of Education Owen B. Kiernan, H. Thomas James of Stanford University, Luvern Cunningham of Ohio State University, Allan K. Campbell of Syracuse University, Herold Hunt of Harvard University, Don Davies of Boston University, and Blenda Wilson of the Nellie Mae Education Foundation. Sources of ideas included Michael Usdan, Frank Lutz, W. Deane Wiley, Jay Scribner, Dick Hailer, Peter Horoschak, Robert Peterkin, David Tyack, Theodore Sizer, Frank Keppel, Jeff Raffel, Brook Derr, and Larry Iannacone. The research and editorial assistance of Gina Sartori of Northeastern University and help offered by James Burnham of Harvard were especially valuable. Marie Cronin and our children were very supportive of my work.

The following leaders provided interviews on developments from 2006 to 2011: Superintendent Carol Johnson, Ellen Guiney, Neil Sullivan, Sam Tyler, John Mudd, and Hubie Jones. These readers critiqued drafts: Paul Reville, Ellen Guiney, John Mudd, Bob Peterkin, Bob Gittens, Maritta Cronin, Charles Glenn, Sam Tyler, and Larry DiCara.

SERIES EDITORS' PREFACE

The Palgrave Series in Urban Education is dedicated to the examination of important issues related to the history, sociology, economics, philosophy, and politics of urban education and schools. Over the past century, urban education has been the subject of significant controversies with policies aimed at urban school improvement vigorously debated, especially over the last forty years. Since the 1960s, as cities became increasingly poor and populated by minority groups, urban schools have reflected the problems associated with poverty. Although rural and many suburban schools have similar problems, urban schools represent the most serious challenges.

As urban areas became increasingly poor and segregated, their school systems exhibited many problems, including low student achievement, high student mobility, high dropout rates, and high levels of school failure. Since the 1960s, the achievement gaps based on social class, race, ethnicity, and gender have been the focus of educational policy, especially in urban areas.

The reasons for the differences in achievement are complex, including factors both outside and inside the schools. Despite these problems, there are also numerous examples of highly successful urban schools and some successes at district-wide reform. Improving entire school systems has nonetheless proven difficult. Over the past two decades, a variety of educational policies have been implemented to replicate these schools and reforms and to improve urban schools and entire districts. These include school finance litigation, comprehensive whole school reform programs, effective school models, school choice, including charter schools and private school vouchers and state takeover of failing urban districts.

These educational reforms have the potential to improve urban schools and districts; however, many argue that by themselves they are limited in reducing the achievement gaps unless they also address the factors outside of schools responsible for educational inequalities. Given these issues, the Palgrave Series in Urban Education is dedicated to understanding the complex nature of urban education and school improvement.

Reforming Boston Schools, 1930 to the Present: Overcoming Corruption and Racial Segregation by Joseph Marr Cronin provides an important historical analysis of one city's struggles to improve its school system over the past eighty years. Cronin provides a complex and compelling history of protests, reforms, politics, and racial and ethnic conflict, all part of the story to improve the Boston schools. His history examines the roles of students, teachers, parents, politicians, the business community, universities, and the courts. It chronicles the school desegregation wars that began in the 1970s and the struggles of low-income families and families of color to make the schools help their children realize the American dream through schooling. He looks at white flight and why some parents chose to leave the system and others chose to stay. As Cronin notes, Boston's award from the Eli Broad Foundation Award for the nation's most improved urban school in 2006 represented significant progress from the violence of the 1970s. Most importantly, Cronin shows that such improvement is the result of long, complex struggles and that school improvement must address issues both inside and outside the schools.

ALAN R. SADOVNIK
SUSAN F. SEMEL

BOSTON SUPERINTENDENTS OF SCHOOLS

Name	Years in Office	Total Years
Nathan Bishop	1851–56	5
John D. Philbrick	1856–78	22
Samuel Eliot	1878–80	2
Edwin P. Seaver	1880–1904	24
George H. Conley	1904–05	6 months
Stratton D. Brooks	1905–11	6
Franklin Dyer	1911–18	7
Frank V. Thompson	1918–21	3
Jeremiah E. Burke	1921–31	10
Patrick Campbell	1931–37	7
Arthur Gould	1937–48	11
Dennis Haley	1948–60	12
Frederick Gillis	1960–63	3
William Ohrenberger	1963–73	9
William Leary	1973–76	3 — *MCSEd*
Marion Fahey	1976–80	4
Robert C. Wood	1980–83	2
Robert Spillane	1983–87	4
Laval Wilson	1987–91	4 ½
Lois Harrison-Jones	1991–95	4 — *MCSEd*
Thomas Payzant	1995–2006 *2012*	11
Carol Johnson	2007–	*6*

Paul Kennedy served as acting superintendent in 1980–81. Joseph McDonough in 1981, 1985, 1990–91, Arthur Stellar in 1995, and Michael Contompasis 2006–07.

Source: Boston School Committee Reports and Boston *Globe*, November 26, 2000.

INTRODUCTION

EXIT, VOICE, AND LOYALTY: LEAVE, SPEAK UP, OR STAY

Boston schools won the Eli Broad Award in 2006 as the "most improved urban school system" in the nation. This was an impressive comeback from the negative publicity attending the burning of six Boston public schools in the 1960s and the stoning of Boston school buses in 1974 and 1975. How did Boston schools become revitalized? The scope of urban school reform includes the removal of corruption, abuses, and excesses, along with deliberate campaigns to treat more appropriately students, teachers, and other employees. New Massachusetts laws enacted in one key year, 1965, authorized two radical reforms, collective bargaining for teachers and the "elimination" of racial imbalance, two measures that in time generated traumatic conflict for school parents and union members. Over four decades, parents, teachers, and principals, elected officials, corporations, unions, universities, and foundations generated the ideas and energy needed to pursue serious school reform. Very rarely did they learn from predecessors about how or how not to help urban students succeed.

Once, Boston schools were judged best in the nation, especially from the 1830s into the 1930s. However, during the 1970s headlines screamed about the racial and ethnic violence in Boston. Actually, in every decade Boston struggled to update and reinvigorate the public schools. The issues depended on who spoke up, whose voices prevailed, how seriously teacher views mattered, and how parents, universities, and employers expressed their views about public schools. Most history books are written chronologically. This book examines the perspectives of different stakeholders, specifically Boston parents, high-achieving alumni, teachers, universities, business corporations, and reviews controversies from several points of view—biographically, demographically, and politically.

The Carnegie and Danforth Foundations supported my 1960s studies on how Boston schools either defied or accepted change, why and how. Vantage points over four decades included those of Stanford doctoral researcher, Harvard professor, state agency consultant, Massachusetts state education secretary, college president, Boston Chamber of Commerce Education Committee chair, and senior fellow with the Nellie Mae Education Foundation and later with Eduventures. Important influences included Glazer and Moynihan's *Beyond the Melting Pot*, which discredited the notion that American immigrants were easily assimilated into one great stew.[1]

Albert Hirschman's essay on *Exit, Voice and Loyalty* posed useful questions on how consumers respond to declines in quality in public services either by leaving, speaking up, or trying to save the organization from within. Hirschman quoted Erik Erikson, "You can either actively flee or actively stay put."[2] Hirschman suggested how important it is to watch who leaves a public school system as well as who stays around to articulate dissatisfaction and make managers uncomfortable.

Hirschman drew both from the fields of economics (where competition encourages "exit") and political science (which defines "voice" as interest group articulation). He examined how public institutions try to recover from scandal, corruption, and complaints about ineffective operations. He recognized that public schools appeared to be monopolies, except when unhappy clients placed children in private schools or moved to other communities, which are two exit routes. Hirschman also explored the functions of boycotts, strikes, and other ways of voicing discontent. His inquiry provided a useful backdrop for investigating efforts to "reform" the Boston schools, especially in the twentieth century.

Boston's court-ordered desegregation orders in 1974–75 attracted many writers. The most widely read book, *Common Ground* by Anthony Lukas, described how the decision affected families.[3] But it failed to document at all how hard black parents fought for equal opportunity within the system for a full decade prior to the court decision. Also, the book criticized the Catholic Church whose leaders in fact strongly supported school desegregation. This study provides a second opinion on the parent voice, documented through the published papers of Ruth M. Batson, Boston NAACP leader in the 1960s and 1970s.[4]

Unpublished doctoral dissertations and theses on Boston public schools made possible a panoramic review of education reform initiatives. Collectively they provided windows on many specific reform proposals, and allow the subsequent critique that hindsight makes possible. Another quest was for expressions of loyalty to Boston schools from significant alumni, donors, and neighborhood advocates.

What emerges is an assessment of Boston schools as possibly too severe for staunch loyalists, too moderate for radical reformers. Certainly Boston still must raise the achievement of all youth to meet the expectations of the

U.S. Congress, state leaders, higher education, employers, and parents. As the historian David Tyack suggested, the quest for "one best system" might be utopian. Children and families need educational choices, some of them already in place. Many educational remedies for education were proposed for decades or even a full century before acceptance. Some reform solutions do not survive. The junior high school, a reform of the 1920s, is losing loyal supporters in Boston and elsewhere. Perhaps no reform format is permanent.

Individuals and reform groups struggled hard for many decades to perfect the schools of Boston, to root out the inequities, the bigotries, and the inefficiencies that held the schools in check. How did they pursue their goals, and with what effect? This is the central question explored in this study.

The Hirschman categories of Exit, Voice, and Loyalty require further definition. Boston schools in each generation spawned loyalists, outspoken critics, and those who voted with their feet and chose a school elsewhere. In Boston, parents and citizens either

- Exit, resign from, defect, or depart to choose another school, such as the Catholic schools founded in the 1800s, or the Yankee departures from the Latin School by the 1920s, or departure of black students from city to suburban schools in the mid-1960s, or
- exercise their Voice, speaking up, complaining, agitating, marching, and even litigating for what they feel they need, a safer school, new textbooks, and a better education. Examples included black parents boycotting and petitioning for integrated schools in the 1850s and 1960s, teachers campaigning for benefits and pay increases, or white parents marching against the Racial Imbalance Law, or
- show Loyalty, staying with the public schools and quietly supporting either the status quo or working inside the system for incremental improvements. The highpoint was the 130,000 students attending Boston schools in the 1930s, or hundreds of Boston's teachers in the 1960s defending the concept of racial integration.

It is useful to listen to those who criticized Boston's public schools. But Boston school graduates periodically acknowledged that their schooling worked, even identifying teachers who helped them succeed. Alumni biographies helped explain "Loyalty" to Boston's public schools.

Hirschman's framework helped raise these questions: Did families voice complaints, fail to get an appropriate response, and then exit the schools? Why do organizations such as public schools not make necessary corrections from within? Why is there the need for so much intense agitation and raising of voice?

Each chapter outlines the tensions and pressures that drove thousands of individuals to speak up, fight for change, and then dramatize their discontent by assemblies, marches, boycotts, walkouts, strikes, political action, or the withdrawal of their children from the schools—the "exit" decision. Meanwhile large numbers of satisfied or inert parents kept their children in Boston's schools. Many teachers, despite dissatisfactions, remained loyal employees of the schools for decades and some of them were public school parents as well.

Schools became important in new ways in each of the past four centuries, once to prepare the ruling elite, and then for the masses seeking a new life, good jobs, and financial opportunities. Not every group in power wanted the next group to use education to climb the ladder of success and fortune. Therefore, many of the specific reforms provoked opposition by those who earlier won control over the decision-making system.

It has become fashionable to label public schools as a monolithic monopoly, impervious to change or new direction. True, many families feel they have few choices, but tens of thousands of parents in each generation left the city or rejected the city schools (while remaining in the city) to find the education their children needed. Many did not leave without expressing their educational preferences, sometimes very loudly. When they found alternatives to their local public schools, their choice refuted the monopoly argument. How and why does the "exit" option accomplish the pursuit of parent values?

The purpose of this book is to examine closely the last eighty years of Boston school history through several lenses in order to understand how schools respond to severe criticism, and to examine what happens and who benefits if they change or do not change.

CHAPTER 1

BOSTON SCHOOLS: THE HEIGHT OF LOYALTY AND ETHNIC EXITS (1920–40)

The Boston Latin School from 1635 on was the flagship of the academic fleet, the ultimate public preparatory school sending graduates mainly to Harvard College for a century. The schools taught only young Puritan boys until the 1680s, then adding white Protestant males of other denominations.[1] Boston schools for the first 200 years declined to enroll women, blacks, or Catholics. Public school policies of exclusion or inferior treatment often elicited cries of protest (voice) along with a quest for alternatives (exit or "choice").

From 1629 to 1822 Boston remained a small town, a series of hills on the modest peninsular jutting into Boston harbor, the schools of the 1820s serving 7,000 children. The nineteenth-century city grew larger by filling in docklands and the Back Bay, acquiring five suburban towns (Brighton, Dorchester, West Roxbury, Charlestown, and Hyde Park), and accepting tens of thousands of immigrants from Canada, Ireland, Italy, Poland, and Russia. Boston in the nineteenth century grew from a placid village to a dynamic city with 700,000 inhabitants (almost half of Irish ancestry) and 100,000 schoolchildren.[2]

Boston schools in the 1830s appeared to enjoy a wonderful reputation. Alexis de Tocqueville, the French visitor, said about New England education: "Every citizen receives the elementary notions of human knowledge;...his religion, the history of his country, and the leading features of its constitution...and a person wholly ignorant of them is a phenomenon."[3]

An impressive expression of loyalty came from Harvard Professor George Ticknor who said, "The best proof of the excellence of the public schools was the fact that the rich could find no better."[4] He wrote this tribute just prior to the major Irish immigration to Boston in the 1840s.

Boston schools from 1850 on demonstrated a remarkable capacity to accommodate new clientele, beginning with the new Girls High School in 1850 (paired with the all boys English High School) and Girls Latin School in 1876, after refusing to allow girls to study at The (all-male) Latin School. Boston established schools for blacks and briefly desegregated them during the 1850s when Know Nothing legislators responded to black aspirations while fighting Catholic immigrants.[5] Philanthropists financed the first public kindergartens in the 1870s and supported trade school and manual training, ideas imported from Germany. Pushed by the reformer Horace Mann, the Boston schools hired its first superintendent of schools, reduced student whippings, and required academic examinations for students and teachers.

After tens of thousands of Irish children flooded the city in the 1840s, followed by Jewish, Italian, and other ethnic groups in the 1880s, the Boston schools changed dramatically. Affluent Yankees, the Brahmin merchant aristocracy, looked down upon the shabby, uncouth immigrants, choosing for their own sons private instruction at George Washington Copp Noble's school, or Volkmann's, Stone's or Hopkington's, all on Beacon Hill or the Back Bay. Famous Nobles graduates included Henry Cabot Lodge and future Admiral Samuel Eliot Morison, who studied the same classical curriculum offered by the Latin School but in small classes with their social peers.[6] Yankees were the first ethnic group to exit Boston's public schools, in large numbers after 1900.

Despite these losses, Boston public school enrollments soared from 100,000 students in 1900 to a high of 133,339 in 1932, expanding by a full third in only one generation. The mid-1930s were the height of parent loyalty to Boston's public schools, at least for the offspring of immigrants. Although many Yankee families and some Catholics left, why did Boston schools become so popular? Why could not that impressive loyalty persist? Several autobiographies of successful Boston graduates and the field notes of urban sociologists help answer these questions.

First of all, both city population and school enrollments continued to grow until the Great Depression deepened (see table 1.1).

Boston's expanding populace cried out for more public schools, playgrounds, libraries, transit systems, and other urban amenities. The law did not permit the Boston School Committee to raise taxes or float bonds for

Table 1.1   Boston Population (1920–40)

Year	Total Population	School Enrollment
1920	748,060	113,000
1930	781,188	130,000
1940	770,000	120,000

Source: U.S. Census, 1940 and School Committee Reports 1930, 1940.

new or expanded school facilities. The mayor and Council were the key decision-makers. Of the new breed of Irish American mayors, none was a greater builder than James Michael Curley. Curley was a demagogue whose speaking talents were honed at Boston's public Dearborn School and the Boston Evening School where he often read Shakespeare aloud.[7]

Curley was elected mayor of Boston first in 1914 and a second time in 1922. The prospect of his domination troubled Governor Calvin Coolidge so much that the Yankee legislature passed a law in 1918 prohibiting Boston mayors from serving two successive terms. But Mayor Curley, in his four years through 1926, built new schools, subway tunnels, added wings to the City Hospital, and raised taxes to support the additional facilities.[8] Curley negotiated with Republican campaign managers to nominate in 1926 a pliable successor who would keep many of his staff. Even while out of office, 1927–32, half of Republican Mayor Malcolm Nichols's appointees were Curley men, and the school contractors remained loyal Curley contributors.[9]

Curley dominated Boston politics from 1914 well into the 1940s. It is useful to see how the schools of his city served Boston's children, especially newcomers. All the high schools attracted more students, but the two Latin Schools remained the "jewels in the crown," the most prestigious public schools in New England. The key questions about 1920–40 were as follows: Who attended, why, and who graduated? How loyal were they to the teachers who taught or encouraged them? Who controlled the teacher selection and administrative promotion process?

Of all the immigrant newcomers, many Boston Jewish boys worked very hard to make the public schools their escalator out of poverty. Jews most of all were committed to "the book," to scholarship, disputation, and academic studies. Their goal was to pass the Latin entrance exam, the others attending English High or the Hebrew Industrial Schools.[10] Yankee and Irish teachers recognized and often encouraged Jewish talent. The evidence flows from autobiographies of three Latin School graduates. Theodore White attended Boston schools from 1920 to 1932, Nat Hentoff from 1929 to 1941, and Sumner Redstone one year ahead of Hentoff. They provided a clinical view of the Latin School rigors, and acknowledged the Irish takeover of Boston schools. They also explained why Jews so often voted for Irish American candidates for Mayor and School Committee.

Theodore "Teddy" White was the son of a Russian Socialist lawyer coming to Boston in 1891. White attended the Endicott and Gibson Schools in Dorchester. "The Irish had replaced the Yankee schoolmarm," he noted. "The police were all Irish...the schools were just as Irish. Irish teachers dried our tears, kissed and coddled us, and taught us what their Yankee overlords in the Boston Public Schools directed them to teach."[11]

He took the exam for the Latin School, "a cruel school but it might have been the best in the country." How tough was the exam school? "It accepted students without discrimination and it flunked them—Irish, Italians, Jewish, blacks—with an equal lack of discrimination."[12] He understood how the Irish captured power and used it to help other immigrants.

> Only the Irish spoke English at home, and more than that (knew) the Anglo-American courts, law, and officialdom.... They acted as intermediaries between government and the bewildered immigrants. They could drop a word in a judge's ear; intercede with the school board to get, say, a girl into the city's teachers college. Their fee was gratefully and willingly paid, and might be as high as a dozen sure votes.[13]

White won a scholarship to Harvard where he studied Chinese. His brilliant career included *TIME* magazine coverage of China and the Making of the President series.

Nat Hentoff, another Boston boy, felt he would never have attended Latin School "if it had not been for Miss Fitzgerald, my sixth grade teacher at the William Lloyd Garrison school where nearly all the children were Jewish and nearly all the teachers were Irish. Miss Fitzgerald expected everyone to learn what had to be learned in her class, and without excuses."[14] Why should Nat's mother allow Nat to take the Latin School entrance exam? "He will be a sure success," Fitzgerald told Mrs. Hentoff. Nat was then ten years old, and became a famous New York jazz critic and commentator on civil liberties.

Hentoff agreed with White about the Latin School. "There were masters so cold that a kind word from them seemed to be a terrifying trap." And, "even today, when old graduates reminisce, you will rarely hear them say of any teacher, 'He really understood me.' They're more apt to say, 'He certainly taught me trigonometry and the (Latin) ablative absolute.'"[15]

Like other Jewish students at the Latin School, Hentoff studied seven hours at the Latin school, and then two hours each evening for Hebrew school. But in certain ways, Latin remained a "common school." For "Under the purple and white flag of Boston Latin School, we were all united: the Irish, the Italians, the Jews, the Greeks, the Scots, the Armenians, the relatively few Yankees who were still there (the others no longer applied because all the rest of us were there) and the far fewer blacks."[16]

A third Latin School alumnus (1940) was billionaire Sumner Redstone, owner of Viacom, CBS, Simon and Schuster (which published his memoirs). Redstone's mother was the key influence. He described the Latin School as one that was "run like a private academy" and that demanded "an obsessive driving commitment to excellence from everyone." Afterward, Harvard was "a terrific letdown, until the Law School."[17]

The departure of the Yankee students was essentially complete by 1930, the decade when Irish faculty took over the Latin School as they had the primary and intermediate schools earlier. Jewish students emerged as the most diligent students at Latin School during its third century, and their memoirs verify their loyalty.

Phillip Marson, an outspoken Boston Latin School master teaching English, wrote two books about his work. A Tufts graduate, himself Jewish, he was stoutly loyal to the Latin School and especially proud of its alumni, the five signers of the Declaration of Independence, the many governors, U.S. Senators, the numerous authors and educators including Emerson, Santayana, and Harvard President Charles William Eliot. Marson described the major changes he saw in Boston schools from the 1920s through the 1950s.[18]

Marson confirmed that "outnumbered and outmaneuvered Yankees" turned away from Boston Latin School after three centuries of loyalty. "Boys from the first families of Boston appeared in the public school in ever-decreasing numbers; and by 1925 had become almost extinct." The exceptions were "a very few Yankees, mostly from families either too poor to send their boys to private schools, or from staunch alumni who democratically believed in the mingling of races and classes."[19] Still, the Latin School kept growing, to a peak of 2,500 students, including every race and creed "but in greater numbers the sons of Irish and Italian Catholics, and of Russian and Polish Jews" with a few Chinese, Scandinavian, Germans, and Lithuanians.[20]

The faculty and administrative leadership at this most conservative of schools began to change. Marson picked 1920 as the important changeover year, when Patrick Campbell, the first Irish American "but a Harvard man" came on as headmaster. This ended the "ancient tradition of the Boston School Committee in restricting the selection for the post to native New Englanders" (Yankee Protestants) such as Moses Merrill, Latin School head from 1871 to 1901, Arthur Irving Fiske, 1901–10, or Henry Pennypacker, headmaster from 1910 to 1920, who left to supervise Harvard College admissions.

Patrick Campbell himself attended Boston Latin, then Harvard College graduating with the Class of 1893. He taught Latin and Greek at suburban Medford High School until 1897. He served as a junior master at Latin for eleven years, then another eleven as head of the History Department. He worked his way up the ladder, loyal to the system of which ultimately he became superintendent.[21]

A series of headmasters of Irish ancestry, graduates of Boston College, followed Campbell, an even more dramatic shift from three full centuries of Harvard hegemony. These were new men such as Joseph L. Powers from

1929 to 1948 and George McKim from 1948 to 1954. The journalist Peter Schrag counted hundreds of Irish names in the Boston school directory in the 1960s, but at the Latin School the takeover began in the 1920s.[22]

Marson thought Campbell and Powers "continued to adhere to the principles and practices established by their predecessors," holding the line against anti-intellectualism, religious interference, and political compromise. Of course, he noted ruefully that the old Yankee masters at the school "retired one by one, resigned to the irreversible changes in leadership."[23]

The Latin School remained uncompromising in its allegiance to traditional Classical standards. Although Harvard President Eliot, a Latin School graduate, opened his college to electives and eliminated Latin and Greek admission requirements, his secondary school alma mater never changed its traditional curriculum. What was the consequence? Marson, while loyal to his school, noticed that many boys were intelligent but linguistically inept in the classic languages. He bemoaned the "tragedy of wasted minds," creative citizens lost under the unyielding rigor so vividly described by White and Hentoff. Marson estimated that only one-third of entering students actually graduated, then achieved "unfair success in college entrance examinations" and went on "to distinction in national life." These winners included scholars, doctors, and lawyers but also the composer Leonard Bernstein and the art expert Bernard Berenson.[24]

Those students who dropped out generally transferred to English High or district high schools such as Dorchester or Roxbury, taking a less demanding curriculum, certainly not the three hours of Latin translations and math homework each night. Was Marson's dismay about Latin School failures justified? One was Joseph Gerard Brennan, born in 1910, who attended the Latin School briefly in 1922. Number two in his class at St. Joseph's parish school in Roxbury, he passed the Latin School entrance exam with ease, his mother's idea. "Although she was...respectful towards Cardinal O'Connell's views on the importance of Catholic education, it was not her plan for me to jog peacefully along with the nuns of St. Joseph's forever. I must go to Boston Latin School. How else was I to get to Harvard and be a doctor?"[25]

It did not work.

> I was lost in the big new (Latin School) building on Louis Pasteur Street near Harvard Medical School....Most hopelessly, I was lost in the classroom. Accustomed to the nun's intense interest in their pupils, I was puzzled by the dry detachment of the Latin School masters. I tried half-heartedly to keep up with the driving competitiveness pace of class and homework, but soon fell behind..."[26]

He transferred to English High School.

... a gloomy pile of red brick sprawling the length of a bare street in Boston's seedy South End. So I joined the sons of Italians, Syrians, Jews, Armenians, Chinese, blacks and Yankees who crowded by thousands into the disinfectant-smelling corridors at eight in the morning....It wasn't a bad school. I had an excellent physics course and a couple of good English teachers. For my exertions in literary composition I won a couple of prize books (one of them *Moby Dick*).[27]

Brennan graduated from Boston College, took his master's degree at Harvard, and earned a Ph.D. at Columbia. He taught philosophy for thirty years at Barnard College, a witty Latin School dropout whose mind, contrary to Marson's gloomy assessment, was hardly "wasted."

The popularity of the Latin Schools, one for boys, one for girls, grew steadily during the 1920s. Catholics and Jews in growing numbers passed the sixth grade Latin School admissions exams. The two schools swelled in size, from 966 boys and 745 girls in 1919–20 to 1925 boys and 924 girls as of 1926. Boys Latin, by 1935, enrolled 2505 students, and Girls Latin 1905 students, a 250 percent growth in fifteen years. Seven hundred students a year graduated from the Latin Schools ready for college.[28]

So many Jews graduated from Boston Latin School, and from classical schools in other cities, that they made up 21 percent of the Harvard freshmen class, up from 7 percent in only two decades. What an accomplishment for an immigrant group to achieve such recognition in less than a generation; this is deserving of accolades for the public school teachers who prepared them! However, Harvard President A. Lawrence Lowell worried (as did Yale and Princeton presidents) about whether Harvard could assimilate them and whether non-Jewish college students would go elsewhere which, he rationalized, might incite (or increase) anti-Semitism at Harvard. Although Jewish alumni, faculty, and Harvard's Board of Overseers protested, Lowell's national student-recruiting policies held that percentage to 20 percent through World War II.[29]

Boston high school students in the 1920s divided themselves, half attending the city specialty schools (Latin, English, Commerce, Trade, etc.) and half attending the neighborhood or district high schools (Brighton, Charlestown, Dorchester, etc.). They attended senior high schools because their parents in the 1920s could feed and clothe families without sending their twelve-year old-children to sell newspapers on the street or work in sweatshops.

Graduates of Boston's prevocational high schools rarely wrote autobiographies about their lives, teachers, or curriculum. Boston students chose either a citywide vocational school, or an auto mechanics or carpentry program in a district high school. Total high school enrollment grew by 50 percent, from 19,461 in 1921 to 30,000 by 1936, the peak year prior to World War II.[30] This accounts for one-third of the total Boston public school increase between 1920 and the mid-1930s. What explains this new loyalty to high schools?

First of all, until the 1920s few students in any eastern city remained in school through grade twelve. Working-class adolescents after eighth grade went to work in factories and stores. In the prosperous 1920s the number of Boston students persisting in high school almost doubled. The percentages of sixteen- to eighteen-year-olds remaining in high school rose from 43 percent in 1920 to 77 percent in 1940.[31] More dramatically, while the city population grew by 41 percent between 1900 and 1928, the school population grew by 62 percent and the high school enrollment rose by 335 percent.[32]

In 1920 only 892 males remained in school through graduation, compared to 1,441 female students or 2,334 high school graduates in all. Prior to World War I, few employers required a diploma or expected new employees to complete high school. Two-thirds of the 1920 graduates were college-bound from the Latin or English High Schools; the remaining third were district high school students. As late as 1920 fewer than 1,000 district (neighborhood) high school diplomas were awarded—278 to boys (see table 1.2).[33]

Hundreds of women stayed in school an extra year so they could become teachers. In 1920 sixty-five students graduated from Boston's Normal School, all of them female and most of them interested in elementary school teaching. The total Normal School enrollment grew dramatically from 301 in 1921 to 722 in 1927.[34]

Table 1.2 Total Graduates (June 1920) from District High Schools in Boston

High School	Boys	Girls
Charlestown	3	37
Brighton	29	73
Dorchester (of 1,900 students)	112	252
East Boston	46	87
Hyde Park	28	66
Roxbury (of 2,035 students)		198
South Boston	35	85
West Roxbury	25	116

Source: Boston Public School Document Number 10, 1920, 32.

Table 1.3 Increases in District High School Enrollments (1920–35)

Boston High Schools	1920	1935
Brighton	554	1,565
Charlestown	480	869
Dorchester	1906	1,860 (Boys)
New school (1925)		1,975 (Girls)
East Boston	682	2,022
Hyde Park	738	1,502
Jamaica Plain	797	1,264
Roxbury High	2,035	
for Boys		1,241
for Girls		1,812
South Boston	815	1,326
West Roxbury	866	1,884

Source: Boston Latin and High Schools, Boston Public Schools, *Tercentenary* Report, 1935.

District high schools served the outlying neighborhoods, the semirural suburbs annexed after the 1860s. In 1920 most district high schools, except Roxbury and Dorchester, enrolled only 500–900 students. During the next twenty years, the school population of Dorchester and Roxbury grew so large that those high schools were divided in two, one for boys and one for girls, to house the surging demand. Table 1.3 shows how Boston district high school enrollments all over the city doubled or tripled.

Boston's district high schools expanded once they installed practical vocation specialties, which enhanced their holding power. Each high school added an attractive prevocational specialty. Brighton High offered auto mechanics, Dorchester High woodworking, Charlestown electricity, East Boston machine shop, and Jamaica Plain High School a choice between agriculture and commercial subjects. Hyde Park High offered printing and drawing.

These specialties competed with the newer Boston's citywide vocational schools such as Mechanics Arts High School (1894) that offered machine shop, forging, pattern making, woodworking, and drawing. The Boston Trade High School (1910) offered electrical, painting, and decorating, auto mechanics, carpentry courses while Girls Trade (1909) offered dressmaking, millinery, and costume design.

In fact, all but the Latin Schools then allowed students a choice among practical subjects. English High offered mostly college preparation courses but also bookkeeping, drawing, and other commercial subjects. Girls High, the counterpart, offered a choice of a precollegiate course or bookkeeping and secretarial tracks.

Boston's High School of Practical Arts (secretarial) provided typing, shorthand, and other office skills and bookkeeping. Commerce High School offered merchandising and commercial courses. Memorial High School in Roxbury offered dressmaking courses less advanced than Girls Trade. All of these programs attracted students who were intent on avoiding the lowly housekeeping jobs that their immigrant aunts and mothers endured a generation earlier.[35]

The smorgasbord of career education choices was attractive, and helped secondary school enrollment soar by 10,000 students. The vocational specialties over time pleased union members since older apprentices commanded higher wages. Meanwhile, employers valued the extra years of employee maturity, and wasted less time explaining basic tools and standards. So the increased high school enrollments accounted for much of the expanded membership in Boston schools. The prosperous economy allowed working-class children to remain in high school through eleventh or twelfth grade—as many as 20 percent pursuing college but the vast majority still preparing for immediate employment.

At the lower-grade levels, Boston school enrollments also grew. Kindergarten classes, first established in the 1870s in Boston, became very popular. From an enrollment of 7,000 in 1915 then 8,179 in 1921, kindergarten grew to serve 9,000 pupils up until 1932. After that Boston experienced a gradual decline as the production of little children slowed down during the hard times of the Depression. The major depressant was the restrictive immigration legislation passed first in 1917, 1919, and then 1924 that choked off the flow of European families into Boston and other cities.

Finally, Boston expanded special schools for the hard of hearing and physically handicapped. The Massachusetts legislature in 1920 for the first time required public schools to provide special education classes. Special school enrolments almost quadrupled, from 904 in 1915 to 1,317 in 1921, and 3,500 by 1941. Parents who previously kept their children with disabilities at home overcame fears of ridicule from other children and discovered that Boston teachers could be protective and effective.[36]

Competition from Catholic Schools

America's Catholic bishops meeting in Baltimore in 1829 recommended that Catholics build parish schools to preserve their faith in Protestant America, avoiding public schools requiring prayers from the King James Bible and teaching history that glorified British kings and denigrated Rome. But Boston's Bishop John Fitzpatrick was a Latin School graduate who believed in immigrant assimilation to New England values; he built many more churches than schools, and accepted a Harvard honorary degree in 1861. His successor, Archbishop John Williams (1866–1906), also attended public schools and built hospitals, orphanages, convents, and enough parochial schools to educate 40 percent of Catholic youth, following the second Baltimore Council (1870) mandate to require Catholic schooling.[37]

Cardinal William O'Connell after 1907 aggressively built Catholic schools, complaining about enduring the biased English history books and the antipathy public school teachers conveyed to Catholic immigrant children in Lowell, his home city.[38] However, Boston built parish schools much later than Buffalo or Rochester, New York.

By 1930, 28,000 Catholic youth attended parochial elementary schools and 200 attended Catholic high schools. The largest parish school enrolments were in Dorchester (5,000 students), South Boston and Roxbury (more than 3,400 students in each community). Four parochial schools each enrolled more than 1,000 students. Cardinal O'Connell doubled the numbers of Boston students attending Catholic schools. He encouraged the growth of private Catholic high schools including Boston College High School in the South End, Mount St. Joseph's Academy in Brighton, and two Notre Dame Academies, one in Boston and one in Roxbury.[39] Still, only 40 percent of Catholics attended Church-sponsored schools; 60 percent remained in the Boston public schools.

Rarely did Catholic parents refuse to use the public schools. Parochial schools did not offer kindergarten, so many Catholic families used the public schools for that first year, patronized parochial schools for the next eight, and often returned to four-year public high schools, which were free, numerous, and, for nonacademic students, more practical. A Catholic family could, therefore, display loyalty to the public schools for as many as five of the thirteen grades. Or, if a studious child passed the Latin School entrance exam, he or she studied six years in a parochial school and then six years at the public Latin School—a mixed-use pattern that continued for the rest of the twentieth century, the alternating use of public and church schools. So much for the notion of public schools as a monopoly, at least for Boston's Catholics.[40]

When immigration was curtailed, and child rearing was deferred, the elementary schools suffered first. The massive elementary school numbers rising from 85,000 in 1915 to 90,000 in 1921, peaked at 94,470 in 1926 and began to fall during the 1930s. During the Depression years elementary enrollments dropped to 72,623, a decline of 20,000 or 22 percent from the mid-1920s. Catholic school enrollment suffered as well. At least one parochial school, St. Peter and Paul's in South Boston, closed in the 1930s for lack of students and a shortage of funds. With employment uncertain, marriages and children were often postponed.[41]

Boston's Italian School Experience

Not all of Boston's ethnic groups appreciated the overwhelmingly Irish teaching force and the way Italian immigrant children were treated in Boston's public schools. The Harvard sociology graduate student William Foote Whyte interviewed men who attended Boston schools in the 1920s. From 1936 to 1938 Whyte observed "Cornerville," the densely populated North End of the city that once housed Paul Revere, then the Irish, then Italian immigrants. He described this neighborhood as "the home of racketeers and corrupt politicians, of poverty and crime, of subversive beliefs and activities."[42]

Whyte interviewed Italian boys who completed public school and attended college. Chick Morelli (a pseudonym for Christopher Iannella) was born in a small Italian town near Naples.

> I took an academic course in (English) high school.... I always liked those studies. At that time, I didn't think that I would be able to go to college, but I don't know what I would have done if I couldn't have gone.... In my uncle's store (a bootlegging shop, during Prohibition), I was associating with the lowest of the low, the bums and the drunks.[43]

His mother saved money so he could attend college.

Chick was sensitive about his ethnicity. "In grammar school we were all Italians. In high school the races were mixed. At St. Patrick's College (Boston College) there were only about a hundred Italians out of 1400 students. About 1200 were Irish, and the other hundred were of different races.... An Italian lawyer suggested Ivy Law School (Harvard) which admitted him."[44]

Whyte described the subsequent lives of both college students and workers of the North End. After graduation Chick stayed in Cornerville and organized an Italian Community Club, recruiting his old friends from the ninth grade. The college men, preparing to move up in medicine, business, politics, were saving money and considering home ownership in the future. Cornerville at that time faced a serious Depression. Both the professional ambitions of Chick's friends, and also the willingness of college graduates to help the old neighborhood were laudable. They were loyal to their corner of Boston, and gave back what they had gained through education, a manifestation of loyalty.

A very different Cornerville group, the Norton Street Gang, attracted high school dropouts, seasonal workers, quarrymen, baseball players, and unloaders of fruit and vegetable trucks. Gang members spent their paychecks freely, and were unlikely to move away. They resented Irish domination of their schools. The gang leader "Doc" voiced strong feelings about his schooling: "You go the first grade—Miss O'Rourke. Second grade—Miss Casey. Third grade—Miss Chalmers. Fourth grade—Miss Mooney. And so on. At the fire station it is the same. None of them are Italians.... When an Italian boy sees that none of his own people have the good jobs...it makes him feel inferior."[45] He argued that at least half of these professionals including teachers and settlement house workers should be Italian.

North End Italian Americans relied on public schools extensively in the 1920s and 1930s. Unlike the Jews, whom Irish teachers encouraged, many Italian boys felt alienated and marginalized. The most studious entered college and the professions, and during the 1930s some of them pursued electoral politics. Chris Iannella (Chick) became a Boston city councilor and later ran for mayor, unsuccessfully. A son, with the same name, became governor's councilor from Jamaica Plain. Not until the 1930s were teachers with Italian names hired, and at first to teach only music. In the 1990s Boston elected its first mayor of Italian ancestry, city councilor Thomas Menino, one hundred years after the Italian immigration to Boston began.[46]

Exodus from Old Neighborhoods

Another famous section of Boston suffered serious depletion and population dispersion beginning in the 1920s and lasting the rest of the century. South Boston boasts of a national reputation as the proud Irish section of the city, partly because the incumbent state senator each year hosts a lively political breakfast on St. Patrick's Day, March 17, just before the parade celebrating the British evacuation from Boston Harbor. However, as native son Patrick Loftus explained, South Boston's total Irish actually population peaked in 1915 at 48 percent of the neighborhood and declined for the rest of the century. In 1910 the total population of "Southie" topped off at 71,703 then dropped to 54,661 in 1920. The population fell slowly to 50,000 in 1950 and by 1980, down to 30,372 people, losing approximately 500 citizens a year. By then the descendants of Irish immigrants declined to only 40 percent.[47] Many Irish families found their way out, moving to less congested Dorchester or the leafy suburbs.

Some of the reasons were economic. The South Boston iron works and the foundries of the early 1900s lost out to competition from Pennsylvania and the Great Lakes. While the Irish population dropped, so did other recognizable groups dwindle almost as fast including the Poles, Albanians,

Lithuanians, Italians and a few Germans, Greeks, Chinese, and Jews. Another factor was the old stereotype of South Boston as the locale for less fortunate citizens. South Boston, Loftus complained, suffered from an old reputation as a dumping ground for Boston's undesirables. In the 1820s South Boston hosted the City Insane Asylum, the House of Corrections, the House of Industry (the poor house for indigents), the Home for Feebleminded Youth, and the Institution for Homeless Juveniles.[48] These institutions helped make certain South Boston neighborhoods a place from which you left when you had a choice.

During the 1930s the federally assisted Boston Housing Authority cleared away the most congested South Boston slums to build two, then three, large public housing projects. This action, thought progressive at the time, obliterated the entire parish of St. Monica's, requiring 300 Lithuanians to find alternative lodging. It was a precursor to the urban "removal" policies of the 1950s that displaced large blocs of ethnic families.

South Boston earlier fought to get its own district high school, a request initially denied by the twenty-four-member School Committee in the 1890s. When 1,000 citizens signed a petition to express their voice, South Boston High School opened in 1901 with 500 students, requiring an addition in the 1920s to accommodate higher enrollments.

Heavily Catholic South Boston was fertile ground for new parochial schools. Even so, the city constructed a total of twenty-two public school buildings, primary and grammar schools (many built in the Curley years), to accommodate heavy demand from South Boston's traditionally large families. Families scrimped for enough money to buy textbooks and uniforms so some of their children might attend Catholic schools, but many families used both public and parish schools.[49]

Within the city the migration was from the old city out to rural and suburban neighborhoods annexed in the last third of the nineteenth century,

Table 1.4 Population Growth in Boston's Neighborhoods (1900–30)

District	1900	1910	1920	1930
Dorchester	77,000	111,500	155,000	185,000
West Roxbury	37,000	45,000	62,000	86,000
Brighton	19,000	25,000	42,000	56,000
Hyde Park	12,000	15,000	18,000	23,900

Source: Boston School Committee Reports 1931.

Note: West Roxbury numbers probably included Jamaica Plain and Roslindale, according to Larry DiCara, a former City Council president.

Brighton, Dorchester, West Roxbury, and Hyde Park. Boston's efficient school statistician kept excellent records on which sections grew rapidly during the first third of the century (see table 1.4 here).

The old congested immigrant neighborhoods lost population. The Central City (Beacon Hill, North End, and South End) dropped from 195,000 to a more habitable 151,000. Charlestown, another overcrowded section, thinned out from 40,000 to 26,000 residents over the same thirty years. The second generation moved from tenements housing ten or more people per floor to three-decker houses where one family purchased the building, renting out one-floor apartments to two other families. Roxbury and East Boston, serving families of Jews and Italians, grew but not as rapidly.

The high-growth Boston neighborhoods were three to six miles out from the State House and the core city. They were "streetcar suburbs," in contrast to the walking neighborhoods of Charlestown and lower Roxbury that housed less-educated workers who could not afford streetcar fare.[50]

School Spending Exonerated

In 1926 James Michael Curley completed his second term as Boston's mayor. The business leaders voiced anger about the growing municipal payroll, the rumors about payoffs and corrupt practices, the probable waste and extravagance in many corners of the municipality. Malcolm Nichols was elected as mayor.

The state-appointed Finance Commission (created to study such issues in Boston) proposed a $60,000 study of school expenditures and practices, but this was hooted down as extravagant. In 1928 the "Fin Com" launched a less expensive, more focused study on the following questions:

1. Why had the Boston public school budget soared since 1918 from $7.5 million to $19.5 million in only nine years?
2. Why were there 200 portable school classroom buildings since funds had been made available for new school construction?
3. Were the schools overstaffed, or properly organized?
4. Why wasn't the increase in parochial school enrollments taking pressure off the public schools?

Judge Michael Sullivan led the nine-member School Survey Committee. Sullivan was a former chair of the Boston School Committee and then of the Finance Commission, and was thought by all factions to be a man of the highest integrity. Other appointees represented the Chamber of Commerce, the Boston Real Estate Exchange, and the Central Labor Union and, at the last moment, a woman from the Home and School Association, Boston's Parent Teachers Association.

The most famous member of the 1928–30 Survey Committee was A. Lawrence Lowell, president of Harvard, returning to the public school arena thirty years after losing a Boston School Committee election. His biographer explained that Lowell was pleased to participate and had kept himself informed about Boston's schools even while doubling Harvard's square footage and handling weighty university issues in Cambridge.[51]

The Survey Committee found that Boston's cost of living rose by 60 percent in the 1920s, that the number of Boston's students increased dramatically, and, therefore, most of the increased operating costs were justified. However, they sharply criticized the school construction system—the Boston Schoolhouse Commission, three men appointed by the mayor, that tolerated waste, allowed "unwarranted delays," and worse, and should, therefore, be replaced by a newly established Board of Commissioners of School Buildings with better planning and spending habits. The School Committee, legislature, and Boston voters in 1929 approved this latter reform by a vote of 110,000 to 57,000.[52]

The Survey also challenged the allegedly corrupt practice of allowing school custodians a "lump sum" payment to hire staff to clean the school buildings. Head custodians, accountable only to a city chief schoolhouse custodian, reported directly to the School Committee (not the superintendent), and hired helpers without any qualifications or any annual reports of net compensation. The Committee declared this practice "unbusinesslike," called for custodial civil service exams, and recommended that principals supervise their own school's custodians.

The Survey Committee verified that Boston's parochial school enrollments grew dramatically, from 16,000 in 1907 to 28,000 in 1928, by 70 percent, but that the public school enrollments increased by comparable numbers.[53] So Harvard's president, and a respected judge, the Chamber of Commerce delegate, and other luminaries acknowledged that Boston public school attracted tens of thousands of new students and that the school expenditures were mainly justifiable, other than certain school construction and custodial contracts. In effect, this report confirmed increased family loyalty to Boston's public schools.

The Impact of the Depression on Boston Schools

Boston during the 1920s had enough wealth to pay for building new schools and hiring more teachers. Among major cities Boston registered the highest per capita retail sales, the highest blue-collar wages, and enjoyed the third largest wholesale volume and the fourth largest banking assets among major U.S. cities.[54]

The Great Depression ended Boston's century of growth, and along with it, the resources to replace Boston's obsolete school facilities. To accommodate the additional students many ancient Boston schoolhouses continued in use from the 1860s and 1870s well into the 1960s, especially in older sections of the city. The economic problems included declining employment. Certain industries, already weakened in the 1920s, began an accelerated slide, shoes and leather goods losing 50 percent of market volume and employment, textiles by 25 percent. These traditional Boston enterprises would never recover. Wages of Boston employees dropped by 37 percent between 1929 and 1937. The Boston Chamber of Commerce lost 3,000 dues-paying members, dropping from 5,000 to 2,000. By 1930 unemployment was so severe that 3,000 men marched on the State House demanding jobs. The percentage of workers on welfare grew from 6 percent in 1929 to 35 percent in 1933. Property valuations fell by 25 percent between 1930 and 1940.[55]

As a Depression mayor, Curley, between 1930 and 1934, reluctantly reduced city payrolls and salaries by 10 percent. Personally, he opposed putting out-of-work males on "the dole," feeling that unemployment "relief" payments undermined self-respect. Curley preferred putting men to work on new public schools, branch libraries, roads, tunnels, beaches, and the city hospital. When he overspent, he threatened the banks in order to get loans in anticipation of tax receipts.[56] He was not without critics. A Jewish School Committeewoman Jennie Loitman Barron charged that Curley "saw the schools primarily as a way to reward his pet contractors."[57] The contractors in turn rewarded Curley, contributing to his campaigns and personal fortune.

Yet, during the depths of the Depression, Massachusetts' citizens elected Curley as governor, recognizing his eloquent compassion for the poor and unemployed. This political side effect of the Depression completely destabilized state-imposed protection for Boston taxpayers and schools. State Republicans had restructured Boston's governance to limit damages any mayor might impose. During the 1920s state law allowed the governor to appoint the Boston Finance Commission to investigate waste or corruption, and could set limits on school spending and the maximum tax rate, subject to legislative approval.

As soon as Curley became governor, he appointed a new chairman of the Boston Finance Commission, narrowly averting a damaging investigation of his own mayoral contracts. He installed as state education commissioner an Irish Catholic superintendent from North Adams who enforced Curley's wishes to impose a loyalty oath on every teacher lest Communists contaminate the minds of schoolchildren.

Curley as governor so overplayed his role that he fractured the Democratic Party and ended any chance to become U.S. senator. Once Curley captured the Boston Finance Commission, Boston's business leaders in 1932 immediately established a private fiscal watchdog agency. The new Boston Municipal Research Bureau would monitor agency spending, administrative practices, tax policy, and advise the mayor, City Council, school officials, and others on budgets, agency efficiency, and financial issues. Curley's spending habits generated intense corporate taxpayer anxiety. Curley's biographer Joseph Dinneen called Curley "the last of the political buccaneers...irrepressible, incorrigible...."[58]

Mayors after Curley tried to reduce public school payrolls. While Curley was governor, Frederick Mansfield (a Democrat) won the mayor's office. He cut the city workforce and paid down the debt from Curley's public works programs. For the most part, Mansfield left the schools alone. In his 1937 annual address he urged the School Department to "train those on relief as compensation for the almost complete breakdown of the apprenticeship system during the Depression." But without new private jobs or a new stream of public revenue, nothing happened.[59]

Curley in 1937 ran for mayor again. His opponent this time was Maurice Tobin, former Boston School Committee member and chairman (1931–36). Tobin graduated from the High School of Commerce and presented himself as a handsome, businesslike, honest politician who would free the city of scandal and noisy investigations. Curley personally felt betrayed, for Tobin had been once been his aide and speechwriter. Furthermore, other Curley campaign loyalists including State Senator Michael Ward and John B. Hynes (a future mayor) defected to help Tobin. Republican leaders including Henry Lee Shattuck (founder of the Boston Municipal Research Bureau) also supported Tobin, who won West Roxbury and other middle-class wards where tolerance for Curley's antics had evaporated. Cardinal O'Connell stopped short of endorsing Tobin but was quoted on Election Day as saying, "Anyone who votes for a person they know to be dishonest, or otherwise unfit for office, commits a sin."[60]

Even after Mayors Mansfield and Tobin reduced the city payroll, Boston's per capita expenditures for police, fire, welfare, health, and hospitals remained the nation's highest. Federal New Deal work programs employed an additional 300,000 Bostonians between 1930 and 1940, dropping unemployment rates for Italians to 25 percent, 21 percent for blacks, 18 percent for Irish, and 6.5 percent for white Anglo Saxon Protestants.[61]

Boston's Irish and Anglo Saxons fared better than other groups. Inequities in hiring were visible and the unequal treatment caused a vocal outcry. Italians from the North End felt strongly "that the Irish received all the administrative plums" and that "green power invariably won" even menial positions. They rebelled and in the 1930s finally elected their own Italian state legislators, after forty years of Irish political domination. Jewish workers accused Irish and Italian supervisors of prejudice. Jews increased their political organizing, electing two Jews between 1933 and 1937 to the Boston City Council, still outnumbered by the thirteen Irish on the twenty-two-member council.[62]

Boston schools suffered during the Depression, but the school budget still remained above average for American cities. Baltimore, with more students, spent only half as much money on students and teachers as Boston.[63]

Several high schools suffered enrollment losses in the late 1930s, especially the two Latin Schools, English High, and High School of Commerce. The cause may reflect less the stagnant economy than the inevitable effects of congressional immigration restrictions from the 1920s.

Boston's curriculum remained constant, even in the face of criticism. At certain Ivy universities, especially Columbia, professors denounced the dramatic failures of capitalism. Professors urged that education might reshape society and the schools. Historian Patricia Graham examined the impact of radical Progressive Education ideologies and found that urban teachers rarely discussed or implemented these ideas. The idea of schools trying to "reconstruct the social order" during the Depression did not challenge the established regime in Boston. The old models of teacher-centered instruction and conservative values persisted and prevailed.[64]

The Boston School Committee in the 1920s abided by an informal agreement that two Catholics, two Protestants, and one Jew would represent appropriately the needs of the schoolchildren. This consensus evaporated after 1930. Earlier in the century businesses posted signs "No Irish Need Apply." Suddenly it seemed that for the Boston School Committee "Only Irish Need Apply," electing a Tobin, Hurley, Mackey, Lyons, and two Sullivans. Jeremiah Burke, Patrick Campbell, Arthur Gould, all insiders and all Catholics, took turns as superintendents of schools.[65] Chapter 2 reveals how corrupt several School Committee members became, imitating the worst hiring practices in place a few blocks away at City Hall.

During the 1930s, because of the Depression, almost all working-class Jews and Catholics stayed in the city. The major migration of 70,000 Jews was within the city limits, south from Roxbury to Dorchester and then to Mattapan. Approximately 4,000 Jews moved out of the congested West End to better housing in the less densely populated Brighton (13,000 by 1950), a pleasant neighborhood of Boston adjacent to the suburbs of Brookline and Newton. Jews strongly supported public schools and decided against building their own religious schools. The one exception was the Moses Maimonides School, on Columbia Road in Dorchester, founded by Lithuanian Rabbi Soloveitchik in 1937. Successful Jewish business leaders such as Louis Kirstein of the Filenes Department Store believed in public schools and felt that assimilation into mainstream America and competition with other Boston youth was desirable.[66] The Maimonides school served only several hundred students.

However, Jewish middle-class migration out of Boston began during the 1920s. Brookline, the nearest Yankee suburb (surrounded on three sides by the city of Boston), hosted one small temple founded in 1911. In 1920 Brookline welcomed 1,000 Jews (only 2 percent of the town), increasing to 8,000 by 1930 (17 percent of Brookline). After World War II the numbers soared to 19,000 by 1950, 33 percent of the Brookline population.[67] Brookline remained an attractive suburban town committed to excellent schools.

Newton, calling itself "the Garden City," a few miles west of Boston, welcomed 200 Jews in 1920, then 1,400 in 1930, and 8,000 in 1950, the newcomers establishing temples, synagogues, and educational centers.[68] Five years after World War II one-third of Boston's Jews had exited to Brookline and Newton, eroding the staunch Jewish loyalty to Boston's public schools.

The 1937 Report of Hecht House, the Jewish settlement House serving Dorchester and Roxbury, included this candid explanation of exit. The report concluded, "There are few families of wealth in Dorchester. It is a stopping place for the Jews, who as soon as they are financially able move on to Brookline and Newton."[69] Rabbi Rubenovitz of Miskan Tefila, the Conservative Jewish temple built in 1925, complained in 1940, "The wealthy Jewish families who lived in this area and helped build this large and costly temple have moved out of the district."[70] His temple later became the Elma Lewis School for black artists and musicians.

Gamm cites the classic work of Glazer and Moynihan, *Beyond the Melting Pot*, to point out that "whenever studies have been made, Jews have been found to be moving out of the working class into the middle-class at a surprising rate."[71] Stephan Thernstrom explained that Boston Jews opened shops and small industries, moving quickly into the middle class, and sent 44 percent of their children to college, compared with 27 percent of the equally well-educated English middle class.[72]

Many upwardly mobile Jewish students expressed gratitude to Boston Schools, especially Latin School, but showed little intention of staying around once their own education was complete. The first 10,000 Jews moved to middle-class Brookline and Newton before World War II.

Loyalty to the city and to Boston schools did not mean raising their children in three-decker homes on congested streets when there were other options. The exodus of ambitious pro-education Jewish families to nearby suburbs would weaken the base of support for Boston schools after 1940.

Boston's black community, in stark contrast, was allowed no such exit option. The African American population of 11,300 in 1910 expanded gradually to 23,000 by 1940, still less than 3 percent of Boston's population. Most lived in a confined rectangle of streets in the South End and lower Roxbury, half a mile wide and a mile long, in old housing units once occupied by the Irish, then Jewish immigrants. A few African Americans by 1920 moved from the South End to Elm Hill or "Sugar Hill" in upper Roxbury, near Franklin Park to spacious homes and streets with trees. By 1930 there were 3,200, and by 1940 some 5,700 black residents lived in Roxbury. The new residents established their own stores, funeral homes, and a few taught in the schools. Some families had lived in Boston since the 1800s; others had migrated to Boston from Virginia, Barbados, or other West Indian islands.

The larger Boston factories, banks, and agencies rarely employed blacks. Essentially, black Bostonians had to work for themselves and help each other. After the Civil War, freedmen became retail merchants, barbers, musicians, realtors, railroad porters, and doctors. In fact, two black medical doctors served on the twenty-four-member Boston School Committee toward the end of the nineteenth century. Another doctor, William Munroe Trotter, Harvard educated, published a newspaper called *The Guardian*. Trotter organized the Equal Rights League and the Boston Committee to Advance the Cause of the Negro, which became the National Association for the Advancement of Colored People (NAACP).[73]

Black women during the Depression complained that Works Progress Administration (WPA) officials restricted their subsidized employment to household work, excluding them from federal sewing, singing, and writing programs. In 1936 the Boston chapter of the NAACP formed a youth council of fifty-eight members to learn how to express their voices. The Boston NAACP membership rose from eighty-eight members in 1929 to 2000 in 1937.[74] The NAACP held a mass meeting in 1937 protesting educational inequality in the Boston public schools. Black parents complained about junior high school counselors who told minority youth to attend only the trade schools. This was the largest collective expression of critical black voices since the 1850s. However, no public official responded with remedies.

The Catholic Church expressed an interest in black newcomers. Cardinal O'Connell reached out to a small black Catholic population, several-hundred strong, and brought to Boston teaching nuns of the Order of the Blessed Sacrament to provide instruction to black students before World War II.[75]

However, Boston blacks had little choice but to remain in Boston and stay loyal to Boston schools. Hardly any bank would sell or finance houses outside of a restricted area within Boston. Medford and Cambridge traditionally hosted small black communities, but Boston remained the major black population center, and public schools the only realistic option, then and for the next quarter century.

In summary, Boston's public schools, kindergarten through high school, enjoyed tremendous popularity in the 1920s, extending well into the 1930s. This was accomplished by the comparative prosperity that allowed families to keep their children in school through the upper grades. Also, the specialized high schools and the district high schools created magnetic occupational programs leading to good jobs.

However, the depth and durability of "loyalty" to Boston schools differed for each ethnic and racial group. The Yankees whose ances-tors built the schools turned to private schools and suburban schools, perceiving accurately that they had lost control over the management and teacher selection. Jews seized every opportunity to pursue academic studies, pushing Latin School enrollments to record numbers, even as middle-class Jewish families began to move to Brookline or Newton. Their stated appreciation was eloquent, especially to the Latin School. But their loyalty to Boston itself was transient. More Italians aspired to go to college, but many resented the lack of Italian American role models in the schools or police force. Theirs was a limited loyalty. Many blacks moved out of the South End to Roxbury, to better housing, but voiced concern about discriminatory school and WPA policies relegating them to trade schools and domestic work. Moreover, few could buy homes outside of Boston or even think of attending other schools. Their loyalty was involuntary.

The Great Depression injured Boston as it did so many American cit-ies. The elementary schools declined first, as fewer immigrants came to Boston and families deferred having babies. Then the high schools began to lose enrollment in the five years prior to World War II.

Many Catholics, even as parish schools multiplied, continued to use public schools for kindergarten, for special programs, and both academic and career high schools through graduation. Irish used public schools both for educating many, but not all, of their children but enthusiastically pursued employment, electing representatives to the School Committee, who then chose teachers and principals who transmitted Yankee values of academic discipline and order to newcomers. Forty percent of their chil-dren attended parochial or citywide Catholic schools. When middle-class

Catholics left the city for the suburbs, the cardinal organized new parishes and suburban Catholic academies.

The Yankees, retreating from city politics and school attendance, left their distinctive imprint on the public schools. Boston's Irish leaders, with the exception of Superintendent Jeremiah Burke (who created new junior high schools), loyally continued most of the academic programs and standards inherited from the Yankees, especially the Latin school curriculum and career high schools. The Irish paid highest attention to filling School Department jobs and expanding educational employment opportunities. This preoccupation with jobs remained a challenge for future reformers well into the federal court case of the 1970s. The debate would continue not only over "who governs" the schools but who captured instructional and administrative positions. Chapter 2 reviews the serious professional challenges facing teachers in the decades before public employee collective bargaining was legalized.

CHAPTER 2
BOSTON TEACHERS EXPRESS
THEIR VOICES (1920–65)

December 1935 was a low point for Boston teachers when Boston newspapers reported that new teachers had to pay a bribe to get a job in the schools. That same year the School Committee assigned teacher trainees called "cadets" to regular positions to save on salaries. Teachers were in no position to protest, for they never agreed on a single teacher organization that might articulate their concerns. Over the centuries Boston teachers spoke up for better working conditions and the right to select textbooks for children. Elected officials occasionally listened to their voices. But not until the 1965 public employee bargaining law could teachers collectively negotiate their compensation, teaching conditions, and professional rights.

What were the critical issues? Which reforms did teachers favor? What held Boston schoolteachers back from building dignity and adequate compensation for the teaching profession? Why could a network of teacher clubs or a professional "teacher alliance" not overturn outmoded policies? Who supported and who thwarted teacher reforms?

During the first half of the twentieth century, teacher leaders fought to reduce class size, sometimes as high as sixty and usually forty or more students in elementary classrooms. Boston women teachers, paid less than men, objected to discrimination in both pay and title. Classroom teachers fought for years to gain a voice in designing the curriculum and choosing textbooks and instructional materials. Why did they have to request this presumably obvious consultation?[1]

Boston teachers were considered hired hands not professionals but lowly civil servants, workers with few occupational rights and no job protection. Stagnant pay scales and overcrowded conditions, especially in decades of high enrollment growth, never became public issues until teachers spoke up. The challenge for teachers was achieving unity, learning to speak with one voice, and getting the men in leadership positions to listen.

Becoming a Boston Teacher

One reason for the lower status of women was the superior status of male teachers in the upper grades, a tradition carried over from the old seventeenth-century grammar school days. The Boston Latin School was essentially a college prep school, the ultimate in academic rigor. Boston hired college-trained "masters" (instructors) for their ability to teach secondary school Latin, Greek and English, and sometimes German. Harvard College was the exclusive source of male schoolmasters for Boston's first two centuries. Boston College, offering classical language study after 1863, slowly emerged as a source of Catholic teachers. Next came Boston University (then under Methodist sponsorship), Tufts College, and a few small liberal arts colleges.[2]

However, as of 1920, 85 percent of Boston's teaching jobs were in the lower grades. Boston employed several thousand women teachers to instruct young children, many for only a few years until a woman teacher married. Prospective elementary teachers studied at the Boston Normal School, a legacy of pedagogical reform efforts by Horace Mann and his ally Catharine Beecher who was an articulate advocate for women teachers in the 1840s. The Normal School program slowly expanded from one year of preparation to two years in 1892, three years in 1913, and only became a four-year baccalaureate program after 1922.[3] In 1924 Boston's Normal School became the Boston Teachers College, offering master's degrees in education as well. Well after 1922, high school masters who earned classical bachelor's degrees felt academically superior to the presumably lesser-educated elementary school women who studied how to teach arithmetic, basic geography, and penmanship.

At the turn of the century new teachers earned less than $100 a year in wages. From 1895 to 1911 teacher salaries in Boston remained at this level. The rationale for this pay plateau was the "unlimited supply of partly educated young women who act temporarily as teachers. They have no family to support and do not look upon teaching as their life work."[4]

Obtaining a job teaching in Boston took time and patience. Boston initially placed a normal school graduate on trial for two years as a "permanent substitute" teacher. Then she became eligible for appointment as an "assistant teacher." In 1919, once a young woman survived two years as a "sub," the starting pay rose from $500 to $690 a year. Boston paid men teachers $300–$600 more than women, even those several dozen women teachers working at Boston's girls' high schools.

The status of all Boston female employees in the early 1900s was comparatively low. Most women worked in factories, stores, the telephone exchange, as stenographers and clerks, and still as domestic and personal servants. Of 100,000 single women aged between twenty-five and forty-five in 1910,

32 percent were employed, of whom only 4 percent were Boston teachers. Although working in a school was cleaner than factory work, city teachers endured serious health and safety hazards including typhoid-ridden neighborhoods, poorly lit facilities, buildings without fire escapes, late deliveries of low-quality coal, and dangerous ventilation.[5]

Occasionally a public official championed the cause of Boston schoolteachers, addressing their inadequate pay and pensions. One was Mayor John F. Fitzgerald who helped Boston teachers win pension rights and a sizeable increase in wages in 1911.[6] These improvements required School Committee approval, a favorable vote by the legislature, the governor's signature, City Council ratification, and the School Committee ratification once again. Political action was complicated and time consuming, and sometimes required a strong champion outside the ranks of teachers.

The most effective advocate among the teachers was Cora Bigelow, a well-organized and articulate Boston teacher, who led the Elementary Teachers Club. She managed the 1911 and 1918 teacher pay-raise campaigns, organizing rallies of teachers to pursue teacher salary increases in 1911. She was from the powerful Bigelow family who for centuries contributed prominent Yankee lawyers, investors, tea and textile entrepreneurs. She later used her presidency of the Teachers Club (1917–19) to build a coalition of support for women's suffrage with the School Voters League (precursor to the League of Women Voters), which earlier won the right of women to vote in school elections.[7]

Would political action be enough to sustain the gains? 1918 was another crucial year when teachers worked together to fight for higher salaries. After much debate, the School Committee raised the pay of elementary assistants by 8 percent or $96, to a new maximum of $1,368. The president of the Boston Principals Association wrote Cora Bigelow that "the outcome demonstrates the essential solidarity of the teaching force and the value of worthy cooperation."[8]

Beginning in July 1918, the Boston Teachers News Letter proposed forming a union for teachers. The rationale was the pursuit of "voice" for teachers in decision-making. The Boston "Letter" quoted Professor John Dewey of Columbia University who suggested that the movement to federate teachers could only be understood as part of the larger campaign to give "members of the teaching staff of educational institutions . . . a voice in the control of the institutions."[9]

Boston workers understood well the potential usefulness of trade unions. Massachusetts union leaders effectively challenged the excessive workdays in mills (reduced from seventy-two hours to fifty-eight for women and children by 1900), and what today would be issues of air quality and workplace safety. The 1912 Bread and Roses strike in Lawrence attracted 30,000 marchers, including Bostonians who sympathized with striking workers. Boston women formed the Boston Women's Trade Union League early in the twentieth century. Thousands of female garment workers went out on strike.[10] Even so, women teachers with a year or two of collegiate education resisted joining a labor union for the longest time. Women teachers thought they had joined a profession, and professional teachers did not unionize.

Following World War I, 1919 was a spectacular year for labor union protest. Steel workers and coalminers in the heartland of America went out on strike. Boston streetcar and elevated train operators struck in June, followed by the fishermen of Boston Harbor. The Boston Police voted to strike, frightening the public and elevating Governor Calvin Coolidge, who denounced the strike, to national prominence and eventually the White House.[11]

The American Federation of Teachers that year organized Massachusetts, recruiting ten teachers at Boston's High School of Practical Arts (the school that prepared office clerks). They recruited male teachers from Boston English High and a few radical faculty members from Harvard, Wellesley College, and from the Brown and Nichols School, a private academy in Cambridge.[12] This union was designated AFT Local 66, the numeral the Boston Teachers Union still uses. Forty elementary women teachers applied for their own AFT charter, Local 88. Thirteen women high school teachers organized another union, Local 85. Fifty male high school teachers organized Local 100. So Boston educators formed not one but four unions, which continued the confusion of multiple voices for teachers. There was no clear "community of interest" around which to mobilize support and consensus. Meanwhile, headmasters and principals advised against joining any union, most men remaining active in the antiunion Schoolmen's Economic Association.

Public opinion on worker strikes after World War I reflected trepidation about the Russian "Red" Revolution and the prospect of either anarchy or Communism imported from Europe. Boston's Sacco-Vanzetti murder case conviction and legal appeals lasted from 1921 to 1927. New York City anarchists blew up J.P. Morgan's bank. Attorney General Mitchell Palmer conducted highly publicized raids in pursuit of subversives and broke the influence of the Industrial Workers of the World (the Wobblies). Strikes, and even union membership, grew unpopular as company owners and employees feared for their personal safety. By January 1921 members of Boston locals 66, 85, and 100 voted to turn back their Federation charters. Nationally, the American Federation of Teachers membership dwindled by two-thirds—victims of hysteria over European radicalism and violence in the isolationist postwar era.[13] *The Boston Globe* reported that the cost of living rose almost 100 percent after

World War I. The postwar surge of prices in effect canceled the value of the 1918 teacher wage increases. At a School Committee meeting on October 15, 1919 Cora Bigelow led teachers requesting another $600 increase for all teachers. Boston teachers rented a Boylston Street office from which to coordinate their campaign, asking churches, parent, and civic associations to vote for supportive resolutions. On November 18, 1919 teachers held a mass meeting at Tremont Temple, the large Baptist hall at the foot of Beacon Hill, where 2,500 of the 3,000 Boston teachers rallied to the cause. They denounced as totally inadequate the School Committee offer of a $384 raise. Teachers filed legislation to increase the School Committee appropriations power. Despite Mayor Andrew Peters's threat to veto the bill, teachers finally won the raise they sought in February 1921.[14]

What became clear to Boston teachers was that political action could be one effective way to express voice. The positive intervention of the state legislature, and a teacher-friendly governor, were major assets. Voice could be expressed through mass meetings, petitions, and election campaigns. What was not at all clear was whether there was a role for organized collective bargaining for teachers in unions, not with such great antipathy to public employees threatening to use the strike weapon and withholding services to children. Teacher leader Cora Bigelow used union-organizing tactics to build support among the 3,000 teachers and principals for overdue wage increases.

Teachers Advocate "Voice," Industrialists "Efficiency"

Teachers sought a voice in professional decisions made about educational programs, the choice of textbooks, reference materials, and other classroom furnishings. If the school was an engine for promoting democracy, Cora Bigelow asked why the adults working in schools practiced so little of it? Might not teachers be consulted about textbook and curriculum choices, or would schools be run as autocracies, on the factory superintendent model that emerged from the nineteenth-century industrial revolution?

Business executives, meanwhile, urged school boards to study the examples of industry and apply "scientific management," testing, and statistics to school management issues. A few vocal university professors expressed outrage over campaigns to turn schools into factories, mainly turning out efficient clerks and technicians for employment in industries and counting houses. Chief among the academic critics was John Dewey, the Columbia philosopher who created the Laboratory School at the University of Chicago where the "whole child" was the focus of attention and the library the central place within each school, hardly the factory model. He deplored the movement to make employees appendages to machines, concerned that "the worker has had no opportunity to develop his imagination...."[15] Dewey's voice rose in protest to the industrial efficiency model described in Raymond Callahan's *Education and the Cult of Efficiency.*

Boston's Bigelow and other teachers listened to Dewey's Chicago lab school colleague, Ella Flagg Young, later Chicago's school superintendent. She denounced the excessive reliance on "close supervision" of schoolteachers (industrial style visitations and critiques of classroom minutiae by superintendents), a practice unknown in colleges and universities. Young urged every school system to create "school councils whose membership in the aggregate should include every teacher and principal" but with a smaller working group to delineate school improvement issues. Each school would "elect delegates to a central council to meet with the superintendent and his assistants and supervisors." Teacher rights to express their ideas should be recognized as an "intrinsic part of this democracy."[16]

Margaret Haley of Chicago, the forceful leader who organized the Chicago Teachers Federation, in 1904 addressed the National Education Association, then dominated by male superintendents of schools. She outlined the fundamental conflict in values:

> "Two ideals are struggling for supremacy in American life today: one, the industrial ideal, dominating through the supremacy of commercialism, which subordinates the worker to the product and the machine; the other, the ideal of democracy, the ideal of educators, which places humanity above all machines, and demands that all activity shall be the expression of life...." She justified teacher unions as enabling democracy, and said, "Democracy is not on trial, but America is."[17]

Boston's Bigelow in 1919 worked to turn her teachers' club into an effective teacher union. She embraced Haley's idea that teacher councils could replace school autocracy with democracy. President Woodrow Wilson's World War to "make the world safe for democracy" created the backdrop for her continued criticism of the industrial model of supervision then blanketing the schools.[18]

Stratton Brooks, Boston's business-oriented superintendent from 1906 to 1911, felt teachers had no legitimate role in making decisions, that they simply carried out policy and imposed law and order in the classroom. Franklin Dyer, coming from Cincinnati to be the next Boston superintendent (1912–18) was more inclined to listen to teachers. He appointed working groups of teachers to advise him on the curriculum. The peppery Cora Bigelow scolded him for appointing rather than allowing election of teacher advisors. She complained that "the councils are called upon (established) by school authorities and therefore not strictly representative of the teachers.... A more democratic way would be for the teachers group to appoint a certain number to each council." She reminded him that "we in America preach democracy but, after all, we are last to practice it in many ways."[19] Bigelow won a few more victories. Dyer's final superintendent's report (1918) boasted that "scarcely a textbook has been adopted and no course of study written without consultation and advice from the teachers concerned."[20]

Frank V. Thompson rose from the ranks of Boston teachers to follow Dyer as superintendent. He let teachers choose a broadly representative council voicing ideas "both with regard to questions affecting the education outlook and the economic welfare of the various ranks of teachers." Bigelow thought Thompson's creation of that Teachers Council one of her finest accomplishments. Three pro-labor members of the School Committee supported her, two of them close allies of working-class Mayor James Michael Curley, Fitzgerald's successor. Bigelow was the last of the Yankee teacher leaders, whose ranks thinned during the 1930s.

Dyer and Thompson relied on supervisors who found ways to advance the status of teachers. One was Mary Mellyn who taught at the Boston Normal School, and after 1916 served as assistant superintendent for two decades. Active in the National Education Association, she was an outspoken advocate for equal pay for equal work. She admired John Dewey and promoted his ideas such as "learning by doing" through the project method, an alternative to the often sterile recitation method employed in most Boston classrooms. She felt children learned more through "problem-solving exercises." She believed in practicing democracy in the classroom, a novel idea for most teachers, and advocated more classroom discussions and group work.[21] She asked classroom teachers to help her revise the curriculum and select textbooks and teaching materials. This participatory reform of allowing a voice in educational decisions lasted into the 1930s.

Organized labor traditionally voiced strong support for public education. As early as 1885 Samuel Gompers and the American Federation of Labor passed policy resolutions favoring compulsory education and a longer school day for children, so many of them still competing with adults for jobs. In 1917 the American Federation of Teachers (AFT) formally advocated awarding tenure for permanent teachers, calling for no dismissals without full and fair hearings. The AFT also recommended self-governing councils of teachers to have a voice in shaping and carrying out school policy. Boston superintendents and teacher leaders in the 1920s agreed that teachers could participate in decisions about textbooks and the curriculum. Teachers won a limited voice at the table under two Boston school superintendents willing to listen to their educational ideas.

Teacher Growth in the 1920s, Stalled in the 1930s

Boston's teaching staff expanded dramatically during the 1920s. Students stayed in school longer than in prewar decades. Labor leaders agreed to this because dropouts at age fourteen flooded the job market, depressing wages for adults. Employers meanwhile preferred to hire graduates with bookkeeping and clerical skills, or the basics of machine work or welding. Teachers and parents shared the conviction that students learned more if classes were smaller and if teachers met fewer students during the day. Class size was reduced from as high as sixty students in elementary schools to an average of forty-three in elementary schools over the years 1900–30. High school class size was reduced to thirty, with even smaller classes in advanced or elective subjects. Between 1920 and 1930 Boston public school enrollment increased from just below 80,000 students to 130,000 in 1930, a 60 percent increase. The number of teachers increased by 133 percent, from 1,904 teachers (in 1900) to 4,475 (in 1930).[22] The number of female teachers over this thirty-year span more than doubled, from 1,669 to 3,516. The number of male teachers tripled, from 235 to 959. Male teachers as a percentage of the teaching workforce rose from 12 percent to 21 percent, most of them assigned to high schools.

One explanation was the changing workforce requirements as the Boston economy changed. Banking, retail trade, and electrical manufacturing replaced the declining semiskilled garment and shoe trades, which moved south.[23] Trucks and autos overtook railroad transportation, which began to decline in Boston and all of New England. The expansion of the new, more practical Boston public high schools was a factor in explaining the increase in males teaching at the high school level. Surging enrollments at the High School of Commerce (1906), the Boston Trade School (1910) and the growing neighborhood high schools (Dorchester, Hyde Park, Brighton) required more men teachers.

The Boston Normal School was the most important source of new female teachers. The Normal School enrolled 301 students in 1921, and more than doubled to 722 in 1926. Women competed with each other to work in Boston's schools. Theodore White's memoirs explained how Irish ward leaders helped get young women admitted to the Normal School and prepare for a teaching position. This was possible while school employment was increasing (1890–1933) but became extremely difficult in the mid-1930s once enrollments stabilized and declined.

The Depression abruptly ended the growth of new teaching positions. Too few jobs, too many applicants. A Boston School Committee order prevented nonresidents from taking the Boston teacher examination. The Boston Finance Commission, the state-appointed fiscal watchdog group, complained in 1930–31 that Boston required new teachers to reside in the city and gave hiring preference to Boston Normal School graduates. The "Fin Com" charged that the Boston schools had become an employment system for the daughters of local residents.[24] Of course the Normal School, later the Boston Teachers College, remained under the control of the Boston School Committee until well after World War II.

The Depression of the 1930s hit Boston with the force of a hurricane. In 1931–32 some 90,000 Bostonians lost their jobs. By 1939 Boston's workforce earned 37 percent less than in 1929. The School Committee devised several ways to reduce costs. One technique was to appoint no new teachers and hire only substitute teachers working at $5 per day. Another economy was assigning apprentice teachers, called cadets, who were paid only fifty cents a day to cover classrooms for other teachers.[25] In effect such a policy exploited trainees still learning how to teach. Qualified teachers who completed a degree were frozen out of applying for vacant teacher positions. The one teacher union remaining strongly protested these cost-saving methods. The Committee discussed additional economies including raising class size, reducing kindergarten teacher pay, and even closing down the Normal School because of a backlog of qualified teachers without job openings. The Normal School admitted no new students during the worst Depression years.[26]

Pressure to obtain a teaching position in the Boston schools grew extremely intense. On December 11, 1935 *The Boston Globe* described a private meeting between ten young teachers seeking permanent teaching appointments and a bagman (broker of bribes) who promised them jobs in return for a $1,250 fee.[27] Boston School Superintendent Patrick Campbell denounced this accusation, saying it was "absurd for anyone to think that an appointment as a teacher in the Boston's schools could be fixed." He conducted a hurried five-day investigation, and reported finding "no truth to the charges." Suffolk County District Attorney William J. Foley challenged Campbell's conclusion and requested a special grand jury investigation. He criticized Campbell's failure to hold hearings and suggested that the "bagman" might even be working for the School Committee. Dr. Charles J. Mackey of the Boston School Committee on December 21 complained of personal "betrayal" when two of his closest friends, both of South Boston, were indicted on nine counts of "solicitation to gain a bribe" to help a candidate win the necessary three votes for a teaching appointment.[28]

Next, an unsuccessful candidate for a music director administrative position complained that he was pressured to pay $2,000 to assure his selection for that position. Two other men were indicted for trying to sell that particular job. The Grand Jury praised District Attorney Foley for his work, denouncing how school appointments were made. The Jury reported "irregularities" including Committee members sharing personnel information to "their privileged friends."[29] Boston School Committee Chairman Frederick Sullivan branded the allegations as "grossly unfair." Incredibly, no one in Boston was convicted.[30]

Had the Boston Schools turned to auctioning teaching positions to the highest bidder? Two years later Henry Smith, a new School Committee chairman, declared, "We must impress both those within and those without the educational system of Boston that the school department is not an employment agency."[31] The grand jury findings confirmed the dire predictions of Yankee reformers thirty years earlier—that without reform teacher qualifications and hiring on merit were no longer paramount.

Philip Marson, after retiring as a Latin School teacher, described the way the School Committee made their decisions in the 1930s and early 1940s. Boston high schools, he charged, had become closed to all but the graduates of (Catholic) Boston College and Holy Cross. To get a promotion, "personal opinions, prejudice, or politico-religious affiliates" were the most important factors," he observed. To move to a higher position a teacher was rated on a scale of 1,000 points, of which the first 600 points were for academic degrees and school experience. The remaining 400 points were subjective judgments and opinions from higher administrators. Bitterly, Marson reported, "No Protestant or Jewish candidate during the preceding twenty-five years (1934–59) seems to have been able to overcome the handicap of being an alumnus of Harvard, Massachusetts Institute of Technology, or other 'inferior' institutions. Objective evaluation had little to do with where one landed on the lists."[32]

Marson disparaged Boston's school committeemen as "well meaning fools or scheming politicians" who appointed to administrative posts "conformists, mediocrities, and joiners." In fact, the School Committee's public reputation sank to new lows. School Committeeman Charles Mackey, a former Suffolk county sheriff, was shot dead by his brother in South Boston. Joseph Hurley, another 1930s school committeeman, was found dead on a city street. Only Maurice J. Tobin, a one-time Curley protégé, led a charmed life, rising from school committeeman to mayor, governor, and secretary of labor under Harry Truman. The use of the Boston School Committee to advance one's elected political career was rampant, beginning in the 1930s, and did little to enhance the reputation of the schools.[33]

Individual Bargaining: The Consequences

The polar opposite of collective bargaining is individual teachers or specialists negotiating for themselves or a small group of peers. In 1944 George

Strayer, a retired Columbia University professor of school administration, reviewed the personnel policies of the Boston schools. Strayer described how "members of the School Committee invite individuals and groups, within the school and out, to come to them with their grievances and demands."[34]

Strayer criticized the incredibly complicated school personnel structure, one reflecting individual or small group requests for special consideration, resulting in ninety-one different categories of teaching positions, thirty-five different salary grades, and fifty different administrative titles and salary grades.[35] Generally no city school system needed so much customization of instructor roles.

How did this work? A group of teachers would approach three School Committee members and suggest that their specialty (e.g., teaching electricity, or sheet metal) was more demanding, and, therefore worthy, of a higher pay classification than other teachers. This was small "interest group" bargaining and in no way resembled collective bargaining. It fractionated and atomized the Boston's school employee classification scale. Strayer's report eventually helped focus teacher discontent on a system that pitted one department and school specialists against each other. Out of this chaos the post–World War II Teacher Alliance arose, unifying Boston's teachers around salary equity issues.

Women teachers suffered from a series of gender inequities. Boston's women schoolteachers, well into the 1940s had to resign from teaching once they married, and, elementary school teachers, virtually all female, were paid less than high school teachers, mostly male. World War II disrupted the normal balance of tensions between the sexes. When millions of men went to war, women took their places as assembly line workers, riveters, drivers, and accountants. Married teachers presumably might, therefore, fill teaching vacancies. The Boston Federation of Teachers in 1943 outlined a "Program for Victory," which included letting married women teach during the war. The Massachusetts Civil Liberties Union along with the Massachusetts Congress of Industrial Organizations (CIO) supported this change, but to no avail at least not in Boston. The superintendent and School Committee majority found it difficult to accept the idea of letting married women come back as teachers. Only Joseph Lee, the eccentric Yankee, argued that it was bad policy to force young women to make an "absolute choice" between teaching and marriage.[36]

One married teacher case went to court. Grace Lonergan Lorch was a former teacher whose new husband, Private First Class Lee Lorch, was transferred overseas. She filed a case over her loss of her teaching position. Mrs. Lorch had been offered work as a substitute teacher for $500 a year, dramatically less than her regular $2,300 salary prior to her marriage.

Attorneys for the Massachusetts Federation of Teachers, supported by the state labor federation, argued that this pay reduction was unfair, but did not prevail.[37] Not until 1953 did Massachusetts enact a new statewide teacher tenure law allowing women to continue teaching after marriage. The Massachusetts League of Women Voters, many of them former school-teachers, helped make this policy change a state priority.[38]

The campaign for equal pay for women teachers faced strong opposition for many decades. The School Committee would not relinquish separate pay scales, and the Schoolmen's Economic Association exerted a powerful reactionary force to maintain higher salaries for men. Their arguments mirrored those of New York City males opposing similar equal pay pro-posals in New York City, that men usually command more money in the marketplace. Men asserted that boys needed male role models, and also, that if women were paid the same as men, it might discourage their will-ingness to marry and raise a family.[39] Presumably male teachers thought equalizing pay between the sexes would potentially reduce the future sup-ply of children for the schools.

Boston was comparatively late in winning gender equity for teachers. California female teachers won equal pay in 1870, eighty years before Boston. New York teachers in 1911 won salary parity after only two decades of advo-cacy. Progressive California discovered gender equity much earlier than the old East Coast cities. The Nineteenth Amendment to the Constitution sig-naled a national commitment to recognize women as voters, and by 1925 most American communities paid women and men teachers the same sala-ries for comparable roles. Boston women raised their voice loudly but a coali-tion of Yankee and Irish Catholic conservatives postponed by three decades the end to gender pay discrepancies. Cardinal O'Connell told legislators to kill one proposal to let married women teach; the traditional Catholic view was that women should marry, stay home, and raise children.[40]

The women certainly spoke up often and clearly. The Boston Women Teachers Club tried in 1922 to put an initiative for equal pay for equal work on the state ballot, was blocked, but then obtained a favorable court ruling. The statewide referendum won by a narrow majority of 3,000 votes, 70,900 to 67,780. However, Boston citizens were also required to approve the measure on the ballot scheduled on December 11, 1927. Boston's women teachers won support from the National Education Association, the American Federation of Labor, local Boston unions, and the state Commissioner of Education. Helen Keefe, a leader in the 1919–20 pay-raise campaign, led AFT Local 88 and was president of the High School Women Assistants Club. Arguing for fairness in compensation matters, she pointed out that many women teachers provided financial support to parents and other family members.

The Latin School Masters led the opposition, especially Patrick Campbell who was then the Boston Latin School Headmaster. The Schoolmen's Economic Association behaved as though this proposal was Armageddon, the brink of disaster for mankind. They asked Henry Holmes, dean of the Harvard Graduate School of Education, to criticize the referendum in public, citing the law of supply and demand as though women would flood the teacher marketplace and depress wages. The Boston Chamber of Commerce and Boston's realtors warned of possible property tax increases if the measure was enacted. Mayor James Michael Curley publicly sided with opponents of equal pay.[41] The overwhelming 1927 defeat at the ballot box, 51,556 no votes (62 percent) to 29,318 in favor, revealed major gaps in popular support for Boston women teachers.

The Depression and World War II provided no new openings for gender pay parity. After the war, women advanced a novel argument, that male high school teachers should not be forced to compete with female teachers who were paid less. This was unfair to the men! Women teachers again sought a referendum that prevailed this time—the legislation was passed, and Governor Robert Bradford, scion of the Puritan Bradfords, signed the equity measure into law. Unfortunately for elementary teachers, this statute only helped women high school teachers achieve comparable pay, at best a partial reform. Not until 1957 did Massachusetts authorize a single salary scale for all teachers, regardless of sex.[42]

What became clear is that equal pay for women could not be won within the Boston city limits but required state approval, as was true earlier with several of the earlier pay raises. Nor could labor unions alone muster enough support for women teachers. A series of School Committee members and mayors listened to the conservative coalition that insisted that men deserved to be paid more. The Boston bias against married teachers was just as difficult to break. Gender discrimination was deeply rooted in both the old Yankee and new Catholic immigrant Boston culture. Boston teachers themselves remained sharply divided over pay equity, although women teachers outnumbered men five to one.

Birth of the Boston Teacher Alliance

After each of the two world wars, Boston teacher organizations assessed their weaknesses and tried to work together. The old Boston Teachers Club continued both as a social and professional organization well into the 1960s. Unofficially, it connected Boston to the National Education Association, still considered a professional group and in no way a labor union.

The School Committee, mostly Irish Bostonians all through the 1930s and 1940s, became highly critical, even disparaging, of teachers. School Committee Chairman Clement Norton was an especially harsh critic, in 1946, calling teachers "careless and overpaid." Teachers demanded a meeting with him, ostensibly protesting a discipline case where the Committee ruled against a teacher. After a three-hour stormy session, 2,000 Boston teachers walked out of the meeting assailing Norton's interference with school discipline and his assault upon teacher's "professional dignity."[43]

The Elementary Teachers Association, the Schoolmen's Economic Association, and the principals then agreed to form a new organization, The Boston Teachers Alliance. The Alliance became an umbrella group linking nonunion teachers and administrators in a quest to restore dignity to a demoralized teacher workforce. The greatest postwar triumph for Boston teachers was the 1947 defeat of Clem Norton at the voting booth, a year when 3,200 of the 4,000 teachers belonged to the Alliance, the high watermark of loyalty to their new coalition. In 1947 teachers supported an energetic Jewish reformer Isadore H.Y. Muchnick who sympathized with teacher concerns. Muchnick openly criticized the corrupt School Committee patronage practices, urging that the superintendent be the sole source of recommending appointments and salary adjustments. He advocated promotions based on merit and voiced sharp criticism of the promotional rating system.[44]

The Boston Teachers Alliance in 1948 advocated a single salary scale for all levels, and opposed raises for high school teachers until wage parity was achieved. This principled stand cost them 1,000 members, mostly high school teachers.[45] The Alliance took the School Committee to court protesting a decision to raise salaries for principals, headmasters, and department heads, almost all of them male. In August 1956, when the School Committee granted higher salary increases for high school teachers, the Alliance worked to defeat the three School Committee members who so voted. Five candidates endorsing a single salary scale won the 1957 election, the Alliance winning their case after more than a decade of hard work. Alliance activism, however, slowly ebbed away in 1959, 1961, and 1963.[46]

The Revival of Teacher Unions

Mary Cadigan, Boston Teachers Union president after 1945, emerged as a caustic critic of the Alliance. She dismissed the Alliance as a "company union" and a tool of the administration.[47] The evidence does not support this charge. The Alliance spoke up for three paid sick days per year for teachers. In 1946 the Alliance fought for raises from $600 to $1200, the latter amount going to lower-paid elementary teachers. The Alliance in 1957 coordinated the fight for a single salary scale. These were hardly the initiatives of a captive, administrator-controlled faction. In fact, the Alliance defeated Clem Norton after he was so harshly critical of teachers.

Cadigan was a forceful, feisty teacher union leader of approximately 300 teachers. She was a thorn in the side of the School Committee, which punished her by reassigning her from a high school English position to a health education class. She refused the new assignment, citing her lack of relevant qualifications and training. The Committee accused her of insubordination and "conduct unbecoming a teacher" and initiated dismissal proceedings. Unions all over Massachusetts protested, forcing the Committee to cancel her reassignment. This was in 1948. She fought for another five years. In 1953 a conservative male teacher faction forced her out as union president because of her support for a single salary scale. Thereafter, the union carried on with new leadership.[48]

The Boston Teachers Union worked closely with the Massachusetts Federation of Teachers on several other fronts including placing Boston schoolteachers under the 1947 state tenure law, winning the right to appeal teacher dismissal cases to the Superior Court, acknowledging the right of teachers to join a union (1958), and in 1960 recognition of public employee collective bargaining rights.

Boston Teachers Union, once again Local 66, in the 1950s signed up 400 teachers, fewer than 10 percent of the total city teacher force, but emerged as the key faction in the 1960s. The highly visible 1960 New York teacher strike and election stimulated considerable interest in Boston. In New York City, The United Federation of Teachers (the AFL-CIO affiliate) after a strong campaign defeated the Teacher Bargaining Organization (the NEA affiliate) decisively, by 20,045 to 9770 votes, empowering them to negotiate with city officials.[49]

Boston teachers watched the New York teachers pursue bargaining power with great fascination. President John F. Kennedy, strongly supported by public employees in 1960, had issued an executive order authorizing federal employees to be represented by unions. During 1964–65 northern industrial states such as Wisconsin, New York, and Massachusetts enacted comprehensive public sector collective bargaining laws. The new statutes, modifying the industrial model, outlined an orderly process beginning with employee requests for an election for union representation, banned public employee strikes, specified conflict resolution measures including mediation and arbitration, and defined in broad terms what was negotiable.[50]

The dramatic developments in other cities pushed the Boston teachers toward the AFT union model. Many New York and Boston teachers perceived the National Education Association membership as mostly suburban and rural, and opposed to any aid for Catholic schools, a cause popular with many Boston teachers. The Federation also welcomed minority teachers, and the 1960s were the decade of rising support for African American rights to equal access to education and jobs. The victories and setbacks facing the Boston Teachers Union are detailed in Chapter 6.

Massachusetts Governor John A. Volpe, a moderate Republican, signed legislation in October 1965 requiring School Committees to engage in teacher collective bargaining. Also that year the Massachusetts Racial Imbalance Law was passed, as was the Willis-Harrington education reform act that placed state teachers colleges under a new Board of Higher Education. The year 1965 was a watershed year in Massachusetts education, providing new opportunities for both teachers and black parents to voice their grievances. On November 9, 1965 the Boston Teachers Union in a special employee election won the right to represent Boston teachers at the bargaining table with school and city officials. A new era began, one recognizing a union as the voice of classroom teachers, and a potentially unified force.

How much respect did Boston teachers enjoy prior to collective bargaining? Not much, because until the 1960s, teachers were a fragmented, fractious lot, underpaid and denied rights now considered fundamental to educators. School Committees and superintendents did not have to listen to teachers, could freeze their wages for a decade, and could pay women lower salaries than men. The 1920s were exceptional, for two Boston superintendents listened to teachers who advised on curriculum and text materials. For Boston teachers to win on most issues, they had to build statewide coalitions to win political support, a difficult task to sustain. This was political action, not professional negotiations. Perhaps once in ten years teachers won good raises and could celebrate a temporary victory. Their champions included a few progressive elected officials, Mayor John F. Fitzgerald in the early part of the century, and Governors Robert Bradford and John Volpe in the middle decades. Their opponents included James Michael Curley, most Boston business leaders, and Dean Holmes of the Harvard Graduate School of Education.

Teachers as professionals earnestly sought to participate in educational decision-making. For a brief shining decade, the 1920s, Boston teachers were given a voice in curriculum and textbook selection. This activist, professional role for teachers did not survive the Depression. Teachers again became marginalized and demeaned when the economy worsened, and teaching jobs were sold to the high bidders. Men had the voice, the higher pay, and status, retained with powerful support from Harvard, corporate leaders, the Catholic hierarchy, and James Michael Curley. The behavior of male teachers and male elected officials at keeping women in a lower place today seems reactionary and reprehensible. Yet the struggles, for men to retain economic superiority, and for women to achieve salary parity, consumed tens of thousands of hours by women teacher advocates over five decades. If Cora Bigelow was the heroine for women and elementary school teachers in these battles, then Patrick Campbell might qualify as the villain. As Boston Latin School headmaster he led the opposition to equal pay for women. As Boston's school superintendent, he scoffed at the blatant sale of school jobs during the Depression. His career marked the transition from Yankee headmasters to Irish inheritors of a system that protected men and high school "masters." His was the stand pat voice of an unusual coalition, Mayor James Michael Curley and his spoilsmen, Boston's corporations, and Harvard University, whose leaders appointed him to overseer visiting committees. His defense of unequal pay and of the corrupt School Committee signaled a sordid downward turn for Boston schools. His name was for thirty years attached to a junior high school, later renamed after the Reverend Martin Luther King, Jr. after 1968.

The Depression and weak support for articulate citywide educational reformers in the 1930s and 1940s took a heavy toll on the conditions under which teachers were hired, promoted, and paid. The Boston schools in the 1930s well into the 1970s became vulnerable to the worst types of corruption and job-selling, religious and ethnic discrimination. Boston school politics for decades reinforced the status quo, excessive internal employee loyalty to the way schools had for so long been managed. The inequities cried out for systemic reform. But male administrators and the patronage-oriented School Committee blocked virtually all the school reform measures proposed during and after World War II, as it becomes clear in chapter 3.

CHAPTER 3
SCHOOL REFORM POSTPONED
(1940–62)

The Boston Public Schools, after 1935, began to slide into mediocrity, suffering irreparable losses in family loyalty to the schools. The School Committee rejected all proposals for school reform. Anyone who thought Boston schools were terrific before the 1974–75 desegregation court orders must review the Boston school situation during and after World War II. The oldest wooden school buildings became fire hazards. The calcified curriculum and antiquated teacher personnel system resisted any and all suggestions for a thorough overhaul.

Once again in 1943 the Boston Finance Commission called for a comprehensive review of city school costs and efficiency. Business leaders voiced complaints about the School Committee failing to cut costs or close school buildings, despite serving 30,000 fewer students than in 1934. Mayor Maurice Tobin, former chair of the School Committee, approved a $75,000 study of all aspects of the Boston schools, including the curriculum, facilities, governance, personnel system, planning and finance.

The "Fin Com" recruited Professor George D. Strayer of Columbia University, the most respected university analyst of American city schools, who for thirty years coordinated dozens of city and state education surveys. Teachers College, Columbia, was the Mayo Clinic for educational pathology, and Strayer the leading authority on school facilities and planning. He compiled an 1100-page report on Boston schools, twenty-two chapters describing an inbred, ultra-conservative, out-of-date school system. His report indicted a city school system grown lax and complacent.

Strayer reported that the 198 elementary school buildings operated at 79 percent of capacity, so 35 of the worst schools could be closed. This alone would reduce operating costs by 15 percent, exactly the economies the Finance Commission sought. He criticized wholly obsolete, and "inefficiently small" buildings. He criticized the old wooden structures, the floors saturated by flammable cleansing oil, schools that were potential tinderboxes.

He described a thoroughly incoherent grade structure. Forty-one schools housed kindergarten through grade six, seventeen provided kindergarten through grade eight, and four of them kindergarten through grade nine. One building housed only grade four. One school omitted a few grades, offering kindergarten, grades one, five, six, and eight. Eight schools housed only boys, and eight of them only girls. The sixty-two principals each supervised between two and four buildings with no help, each day counting milk money, handling discipline cases, routine messages and serving, he thought, as "glorified office boys."[1]

The high schools employed contradictory grade patterns. The two Latin Schools offered grades seven to twelve. Ten high schools offered grades nine to twelve and seven offered grades ten to twelve. Seven served boys only, seven girls only, and seven served both. Fourteen high schools remained sex segregated into the early 1970s.

Strayer's team of university specialists sharply criticized the curriculum. The only system-wide examinations were of reading, with no assessment of mathematics, science, history, geography, or citizenship. Military drill had been instituted in 1863 during the Civil War (as preparation for combat) and took up student time that other cities provided for physical and health education. Only two elementary schools housed libraries (both serving as branch public libraries). Strayer scolded the Boston Teachers College for using fifteen-year-old textbooks and hiring only their own graduates as instructors, an extreme case of academic inbreeding. No new students were admitted after 1939 because of a great backlog of certified graduates and so few teacher vacancies. Chicago, St. Louis, and Kansas City closed their teachers colleges, which in Boston would save $100,000 a year.[2]

After 1933 only Boston residents were hired as teachers, a restriction even the superintendent protested. The Boston teacher exam was given only during Christmas vacation when non-Bostonians were away with their families. Strayer recommended use of the National Teachers Examination. The Boston school administrative structure looked far too bureaucratic to Strayer, with a Board of Examiners to review teachers and administrative qualifications, a Salary Board adjudicating ninety-one discrete staff categories, and a Board of Apportionment parceling out equipment and textbooks. A "Trial Board" heard complaints about custodians, bypassing the principals because janitors reported directly to the Chief Schoolhouse Custodian who reported only to the School Committee (which approved all staff reassignments, promotions, pay, and retirements). Strayer also thought the Board of Superintendents (consisting of the six assistant superintendents) was unnecessary, and he urged folding the autonomous Board of Commissioners of School Buildings into the school department, as had other cities.

Boston's School Committee members, he observed, recognized two kinds of loyalty, first to their own political careers, and then to those seeking jobs, contracts, or other benefits from the schools. Where was loyalty to education, to the schoolchildren? Strayer concluded that school committeemen "regard membership as a stepping stone to political advancement." School Committee members invite individuals and groups to present grievances and "demands for favors," exchanging them for votes and political support. He concluded that the elected School Committee was not working. He recommended the mayor appoint the Boston School Committee from nominees recommended by a panel of university presidents, business, and civic leaders. If necessary, perhaps the electorate might vote to confirm these appointees after two years of service.[3]

It is important to review the reasons why Boston's population and school enrolments dropped during the 1940s and 1950s. One factor was national policies that encouraged suburban migration and denied federal funds to help Boston do other than tear down old tenements and build housing projects. The erosion of public school enrollments, and shift to Catholic schools was another indicator of something going wrong with city schools (see table 3.1).

The peak year for Boston school membership was 1934, despite a drop of 100 students in the lower grades. By 1937 the schools lost 4,500 students, half in the early grades. What contributed to this decline? First of all, European immigration had been severely curtailed by Congress and President Coolidge in the 1920s, and fewer immigrant children were in the schools. Statewide the numbers dropped by 70 percent, from 98,456 in 1930 to 27,350 in 1940. Few new immigrants replaced those adults who died.[4] The 1920 and 1924 federal immigration restrictions on European newcomers worked extremely well to reduce the flow of "huddled masses."

Second, fewer couples married and produced children during the "hard times" of depression and war. In 1915 Boston recorded 38,045 marriages, a number that dropped to 22,817 in 1932, the year the Depression deepened. The 45 percent drop in nuptial commitments was reversed very

Table 3.1 Public School Enrollments (1935–60)

Year	Public School Membership	Parochial School Enrollments
1935	134,288	28,000 (est.)
1940	110,448	29,090
1945	94,820	30,000 (est.)
1960	86,792	43,264

Source: Boston Public Schools, Annual Statistics 1940, 1960; Archdiocese of Boston: Catholic School Directory 1962.

briefly in 1940, and then lagged while so many young men were away on military duty. Most of all, the drop in Boston's live births 1920–40 was the crucial choke on the child supply line. There were 19,573 infants born in 1920, 18,000 in 1930, 16,582 in 1940, and only 13,700 in 1945.[5] The loss of almost 6,000 new students each year, when multiplied by thirteen years of schooling, left dozens of Boston school buildings half empty. Also, while Boston schools shrunk to 86,000, Boston's Catholic school population expanded to 43,000, to exactly half of the public school enrolment. If schools were companies, surplus facilities would be sold and staff reduced. The leaders of the Boston public schools, instead, fought any retrenchment and opposed most reductions in schoolhouses and jobs.

How did Boston miss the national post–World War II prosperity? The old industries—shoes, leather, textiles—left Massachusetts for nonunion states, the textile industry alone losing 200,000 jobs in the two decades after the war. Wage rates declined between 1947 and 1964, especially for semiskilled and unskilled workers. Massachusetts labor union membership dropped to 525,000 in the 1960s, then to 250,000 in the 1970s.[6] Boston's population peaked around 1950 at just over 800,000, then began to fall. The city began to look old and tired. There was little new construction 1935–50, explained by the exigencies of Depression, then war. Boston built a new public high school in 1934, just for Dorchester girls. Named after former superintendent Jeremiah Burke, that would be the last Boston high school constructed for forty years.

Boston's downtown office vacancy rate ballooned to 25 percent. Retail shops closed, a few moving to the suburbs. Railroads cut back commuter trains to Boston. After World War II the number of Boston nightclubs dwindled from twenty-six to four. *The Boston Globe* in 1950 concluded that "Boston was a dead city, living in the past" and urged young people to "seek their fortunes elsewhere."[7]

Federal Policies Affecting Boston

Federal housing and tax policy played a major role in encouraging families to exit the Boston schools for the suburbs.[8] The gasoline tax earmarked for highways financed new roads but not urban trolleys or subways. Boston's transit system (The T) instead competed for the general tax dollar against all other public services. Two Federal housing policies kept poor families trapped in the city, penalizing racial minorities in particular. The Federal Housing Act (Wagner-Steagall) of 1937 enabled city housing authorities to clear slums and build public housing projects. The program resulted in new segregated all-white or all-black low-income family projects in Boston, Chicago, St. Louis, and elsewhere, effects lasting well into the

1970s. Boston built federal housing projects on Mission Hill, in the South End, Jamaica Plain, Brighton, and an ill-fated Columbia Point project between Dorchester and South Boston.[9] These projects concentrated low-income families, usually of one race, in nearby elementary schools. The other discriminatory housing practice was called "redlining." Areas colored red on the city map, much of Boston, signified potential danger and warned mortgage bankers about neighborhoods that might pose an investment risk. Loan underwriting manuals allowed restrictive covenants in home sale documents, so that new housing developments emerged all white and sometimes all Christian. Although the U.S. Supreme Court in 1949 declared these covenants illegal, the FHA did not revise its regulations until 1951. Realtors continued discriminatory marketing practices against black families until the U.S. Congress banned covenants in the 1960s. In the meantime, hundreds of all-white suburbs with new schools flourished around Boston while blacks were locked into the central city.

The racial restrictions on housing were extremely effective. Few black families were able to purchase homes in suburbia in the 1940s, 1950s, and early 1960s. As late as 1980, Boston's black suburban population totaled only 34,000, or 1.6 percent of the total suburban population. Boston black families had little choice but to remain connected to Boston and its schools. Their loyalty was involuntary, their only option.[10]

Strayer's study team struggled with racial issues in Boston. The report recognized racial prejudice, suggesting that, for example, "the boys may notice that Negroes do not play on major league ball clubs."[11] Black students "were largely concentrated in a relatively few elementary school districts such as the Everett in the South End and the Dillaway, Dudley, Higginson, Hyde, Julia Ward Howe and Sherwin in Roxbury...the Hyde and Sherwin elementary schools are nearly 100 percent Negro."[12]

However, in 1944 Strayer offered few constructive remedies. In fact, Strayer recommended merger of the Hyde and Sherwin schools, although each was 100 percent minority. He sharply criticized one school, the Frances Willard Center for ninety girls (seventy-seven of them black)

> situated in the most unwholesome part of the South End in a wretched, antiquated building....The school should be condemned...the school houses many disciplinary problems. Such cases as sex misdemeanors and illegitimate childbearing are common among the group.... But they should not...see and hear so many vicious things as they travel back and forth to school. They should be educated in a school where beauty is present....[13]

This was Strayer's strongest voice of moral indignation, raised against a mostly black school serving women with problems in the red-light district of Boston. He lacked visionary suggestions on how Boston might combat racial isolation.

There was in 1944 no agreed-upon remedy for northern school racial segregation. The military, the professions, the unions, hotels, sports teams, and neighborhoods were all segregated. The Strayer team, however uncomfortable, was unable to articulate a racial integration strategy to accompany their school consolidation or curriculum reform strategies.

Neither Superintendent Arthur Gould nor the School Committee visibly repudiated the Strayer Report. Instead, they dodged the bullet, and called upon the Board of Superintendents to conduct a thorough review and prepare a response. The assistant superintendents criticized the recommended closing of thirty-five schools, asserting that Strayer did not understand Boston road traffic patterns and, besides, five buildings had recently closed. Perhaps another eleven buildings could close but nineteen should remain open. They voiced support for keeping the old wooden buildings, although six of them later burned down. The Board of Superintendents defended their special tribunal, abolition of which (they pointed out) had been a standard recommendation since an earlier 1916 Fin Com report. The School Committee members ordered their critique of Strayer printed and distributed to anyone interested.[14]

Republican legislators filed bills to implement the Fin Com Strayer survey recommendations. Alexander Sullivan, business manager of the Boston Public Schools, wrote the legislature in the spring of 1945 opposing legislation placing his position under the superintendent. He recommended that he and his successors continue to report directly to the elected Committee.[15]

School Committeeman Clem Norton, a former legislator, urged Boston teachers (those living in the city as well as the other half) to express their "honest opinion" to legislators about Strayer Report bills coming up in mid-March 1945.[16] Whatever teachers thought about Strayer's ideas, and many had won jobs and promotions under the current system, few were inclined to support major changes. The bills to implement Strayer's reforms languished in the legislature. Support was scanty for those educational and structural changes for Boston schools, despite the prospects of saving millions of dollars. The city undoubtedly was diverted by great efforts to win a major world war. No organized citizen group advocated a more effective or efficient school system, at least not in the next five years 1944–48. Thus the Strayer Report languished on the shelf, victim of complacency and loyalty to a system that worked quite well for insiders and career politicians.

A new citizen group emerged in 1949, ashamed of the fact that Boston's famous mayor James Michael Curley was serving time in a federal prison in Connecticut. Working-class neighborhoods in 1945 had elected Curley to his fourth term, hoping he would find ways to make up for the loss of shipbuilding and military defense jobs. But Curley was convicted of mail fraud, misusing his federal franking privilege to help an engineering firm. Governor Bradford appointed City Clerk John B. Hynes as acting mayor. Five months later South Boston Congressman John McCormack persuaded President Truman to pardon Curley. When Curley was released, Hynes held back 30 millions in contracts for Curley to sign on his first day back. Curley bragged that he accomplished more in one day than Hynes had in five months. Hynes, stung by Curley's ingratitude, challenged Curley for mayor in 1949.[17]

Voters elected Hynes Mayor mainly because third- and fourth-generation descendants of immigrants agreed with him that "we can't afford the city bosses anymore" and "it is possible to have a better city." Boston taxes were highest in the nation and the ratio of city employees 45 percent higher than the average of the eight largest cities. Boston's City Hospital had become a patronage haven and the fire and police departments a "virtual employment bureau."[18]

The City Council in 1948 squabbled over the scandalous practice of demanding bribes for city licenses. City Councilor Isadore Harry Yaver Muchnick announced in a public meeting that approval of a water-taxi license had been deferred until other councilors were paid bribes.[19] Muchnick, graduate of Harvard College in 1928 and Law School 1932, was a very tough and feisty councilor from the old Ward Fourteen, mostly Jewish neighborhoods. Muchnick was fearless on matters of principle. He hated corruption, waste, and any form of discrimination. He delayed the Council from allowing the Boston Red Sox to play Sunday baseball until the team agreed to let a black ballplayer (Jackie Robinson) try out for the team.[20] He became an advocate for the Strayer recommendations and a School Committee critic of the status quo.

Plenty of Bostonians wanted to be proud of Boston, including its schools, but only under new and honest political leadership. Jerome Rappaport, a recent graduate of Harvard Law School, mobilized the many citizens ashamed of Curley's style and mistakes. He recruited to the New Boston Committee an army of young people to campaign for John B. Hynes. Hynes, a mild-mannered bespectacled career municipal worker, promised better management of the city. A record-high vote in the newer middle-class neighborhoods (West Roxbury, Roslindale, Jamaica Plain, Hyde Park) gave Hynes 138,000 votes to Curley's 126,000. Curley won in the older working-class neighborhoods—the North End, South End, West End, East Boston, and South Boston.

That year, 1949, voters elsewhere dismissed the political bosses of Jersey City, Memphis, and Chicago. Boston historian Thomas O'Connor concluded, "Many young Irish Catholics were tired of the steady diet of ethnic rivalry, clan animosity, and religious antipathy."[21] Enough third- and fourth-generation Bostonians "grew ashamed of Honey Fitz, of Knocko McCormack (a Curley campaign manager), even of silver-crowned younger pols like ex-Mayor Tobin."[22] The stylish new postwar Irish American model politician would be John Fitzgerald Kennedy, the new congressman. But in 1949 John B. Hynes was considered honest and decent enough to be mayor of Boston.

The New Boston Committee in 1949 also endorsed four of the five successful candidates for School Committee, and three winners in 1951. This would be the only School Committee between 1940 and 1962 to try to change the way school decisions were made and to propose reallocating funds to meet critical school needs. The Boston Teachers Alliance also backed the outspoken city councilor Isadore H.Y. Muchnick moving to the citywide School Committee in 1949. In 1951 the New Boston Committee helped elect Mrs. Alice Lyons and Dr. Patrick Foley who elected Muchnick chair of the 1952 School Committee. He immediately proposed ending committee preoccupation with personnel details (employee transfers and sick leave) and proposed instead a new emphasis on educational policy-making. He scolded the school administration for "favor-doing, which resulted in decreased educational benefits for our pupils."[23]

Muchnick's eighteen suggestions to the superintendent and Committee resurrected Strayer's old recommendations: school consolidations, reduction of superfluous supervisory and custodial positions, elimination of boards, and exclusive reliance on the superintendent for salary recommendations. Muchnick also proposed investigating the allegedly impartial "rating" system for promotions, which seemed to promote mostly Catholics with Boston College or Holy Cross degrees.[24]

After considerable debate, the School Committee majority voted to close seventeen elementary schools and two senior high schools, and transfer the Boston Teacher's College to the State College system. These actions would eliminate hundreds of redundant jobs. The proposal upset school employees and the Muchnick household received 270 phone calls in protest one evening. At a public meeting at Dorchester High School an irate worker caned Isadore Muchnick with a furled umbrella.[25] Superintendent Dennis Haley, product of the system, did nothing to help Muchnick. Haley's power as superintendent rested largely on support from career employees and his well-placed brother in law, editor-in-chief of the once influential Boston *Post*. Haley leaked negative stories about his chairman, provoking a Muchnick lawsuit for slander against Haley and the *Post*.

The New Boston Committee detected a bitter backlash to Muchnick proposals, much of it by affected employees, from principals to custodians, whose schools would close and their jobs ended. Although NBC again endorsed Muchnick and Mrs. Lyons, a Curley protégé, Mike Ward, former city councilor and Register of Deeds, topped the 1953 School Committee ticket. Ward won 80,000 votes, 30,000 more than Muchnick. This election served as a public referendum on the Strayer Report, whose reform recommendations voters "loyal" to the old system decisively rejected.

The new School Committee elected William Carr as chairman in January 1954, an incumbent who supported none of Muchnick's proposals. He called for a new era of cooperation, predicting dire consequences when "the voters were bypassed and the School Committee members pretend to think for themselves.... "[26] The majority of voters who were either related to or friendly with school employees rejected efforts to achieve savings by closing schools and reducing excess school employee headcounts.

"Izzy" Muchnick was an extraordinary public servant, energetic, demanding, and impatient with the Boston school culture of exchanging mutual favors. His was the strongest voice for reform in the 1950s. Howard Bryant later concluded, "There was something about Muchnick, something both admirable and self-destructive about his unfailing adherence to a high personal code which often conflicted with Boston's insularity. He did not play the game."[27] George Strayer concluded nine years earlier that "politics had dealt a paralyzing blow to progress in Boston's schools.[28] The only loyalty that triumphed surrounded keeping school jobs. Boston schools the next thirty years remained unchanged and any major school reforms were deferred.

Meanwhile, Mayor Hynes initiated planning for a Boston Common underground garage, a Central Artery to handle traffic, "a new Government Center to replace seedy Scollay Square, and the Prudential insurance center over abandoned railroad yards."[29]

Hynes responded to corporate voices clamoring for a rejuvenated core city whereas Curley had neglected downtown and built neighborhood health centers, schools, and beaches for his supporters. Hynes was reelected in 1951 and 1955.

One postwar remedy for blighted communities was urban redevelopment, tearing down slum housing, and erecting bright new buildings for the middle class. The city cleared homes in one part of the South End, dubbed the New York Streets (around Albany Street) in 1954 and 1955. The 13 acres, then developed commercially, displaced 858 families.[30] For these South End families, exit was not a voluntary option.

Such was also the fate of Boston's West End in the 1950s, a neighborhood with substandard housing, "declining population, (low) standards of school and community services, and play spaces far below a desirable level."[31] The neighborhood surrounded the Massachusetts General

Hospital, affiliated with the Harvard Medical School. The West End population, once Irish, then Jewish, had declined from 23,000 to 12,000 between 1910 and 1950. Jews as late as 1926 accounted for three-quarters of the neighborhood, until they found better housing in Brighton or Brookline. By 1942 Italians accounted for more than 50 percent, Jews only 10 percent with smaller numbers of Albanians, Greeks, Poles, a few Irish, Ukrainians, Gypsies, hospital orderlies, artists, and transient students. Most West End residents lived in low-rent apartment buildings with quirky plumbing, makeshift heating, and rodents.

Both parochial and public schools in the West End lost enrollment after the 1930s. The local parochial school once filled sixteen rooms but needed only eight by the 1950s. This school remained popular because Catholic nuns imposed such strict discipline. Graduates attended public high school elsewhere in the city. Most families viewed college generally as "a playground for the idle rich."[32]

What was the status of the West End neighborhood schools? The two public schools lacked parental involvement, even an active Home and School Association, and student performance was lackluster. Principals complained, "Neither children nor teachers get much help from parents" and "the majority of children displayed little interest in learning." Truancy was common. Peer criticism often discouraged the best students. Only half of the students completed high school. One principal explained that only the third-generation students were likely to continue in school.[33]

Gans described the emotional tensions many West End children faced in schools. He observed, "Educational achievement depends largely on the ability to absorb and manipulate concepts, to handle the reasoning powers embedded in the lessons and the texts, and to concentrate on these methods to the exclusion of other concerns. West End children are adept at none of these." Their skills were often more social than scholarly, and their interests inclined to action. They resembled the New York Italian children who found that academic values taught in school conflicted with those of family, home, and village. "Do not make your child better than you are!" was a Southern Italian admonition.[34]

One Boston principal looked back nostalgically on the once predominately Jewish school, an era when assigning library research "was much easier, before the Jews moved out of the West End." One of the last Russian Jewish families was that of actor Leonard Nimoy (Dr. Spock of Star Trek) who, son of a barber, grew up in the West End. He found his greatest satisfaction not in school (his two autobiographies never mention his attending English High School 1944–48) but at the Elizabeth Peabody Playhouse, named after the nineteenth-century philanthropist. His parents were "grief-stricken" when he left Boston not to attend college but to study drama.[35]

In 1953 the city declared the West End a slum. In 1958 the City Council approved contracts to raze properties, two-thirds of costs assumed by the federal government and one-third by the city. The Catholic archbishop and business leaders voiced their support of this decision, which presumably would transform a rundown neighborhood to resemble the Upper East Side of New York City. A feeble neighborhood protest, supported by School Committeeman Joseph Lee, a Beacon Hill neighbor, failed to stop the bulldozers.[36]

Jerome Rappaport of the New Boston Committee served for a while as a City Hall assistant, learning how city decisions were made. As a private attorney, he fashioned a West End plan featuring high-rise luxury apartment units, attracting "good shoppers" to a new mall near the hospital and luring affluent residents to a new indoor tennis club. The city evicted 2,600 West End families and more than 4,000 schoolchildren, who had to scramble for other homes and schools, often outside of Boston. This was another case of school exclusion, an involuntary departure more severe than exit.[37]

Gans and other urban-planning experts subsequently denounced this as a crime perpetrated upon the neighborhood. Hynes's successor John Collins and his Development Director Ed Logue learned not to trifle with other ethnic neighborhoods, most of them on full alert for the next invasion by profit-seeking developers. The other neighborhood affected was Chinatown where 300 families lost homes for the Southeast Expressway and lost land for the expansion of the Tufts New England Medical Center.[38]

How important was it to keep these poor neighborhoods viable, or upgrade their public schools? Were the senior Boston decision-makers themselves that loyal to public schools? H. Thomas James of Stanford University visiting Boston in the early 1960s remarked that the mayor, the superintendent of schools, and the school business manager all sent their children to parochial or private schools. Lawrence O'Connell, then a Syracuse University doctoral candidate, made the same comment a few years later about Mayor Collins and top school officials.[39] This, of course, was their personal choice but it spoke volumes about their divided loyalty, their own limited confidence in the quality of Boston's public schools for their own children at that time.

The Strayer Report on school facilities was not a complete loss. Mayor Hynes selected university experts to update the assessment of facilities. Nine years after Strayer, a 1953 school evaluation by Harvard Professor Cyril Sargent urged the closing of sixty-three school buildings by 1960. The city shut down thirty-two buildings, most of them very old and small. The mayor following Hynes was John Collins, a World War II veteran and conservative lawyer, who won strong business support for his pledges to reduce property taxes and rebuild the city. His major advisor was Edward Logue, an accomplished urban planner recruited from New Haven. Collins and Logue asked Professor Sargent to update the school building plan as of 1962. The second Sargent report recommended closing an additional twenty-seven schools. Boston's two oldest schoolhouses (photographed for the Sargent report) were built in 1867 and 1889, the Josiah Quincy School in Chinatown being almost one hundred years old. The report casually mentioned that fire safety and prevention became a major priority after 1945, a delayed tribute to the crusade Strayer waged against the old wooden tinderboxes.[40]

Sargent analyzed the 1962 enrollment low of 89,000 students, by that time 45,000 students fewer than in 1934, a massive decline. White flight of Protestants, Jews, and Catholics from Boston to the suburbs was in full cry well before busing, a phenomenon totally forgotten in the turmoil of the 1970s. One-third of Boston's former school enrollments, all white, had either exited or their siblings were born in other communities. Sargent, however, optimistically projected an increase in public school enrollment back to 94,000 by 1965 and to as high as 106,000 by 1970. He outlined a strong case for a new citywide campus high school (5,000 pupils) and for as many as 55 new elementary school buildings or school additions. He exuded confidence that city neighborhoods would bounce back and bring an increasing school population. These predictions fit the optimistic Collins-Logue expectations that the city would grow again, and the reality that state and city school construction funds could be used as a match for federal development dollars.

Harvard planners during the 1960s typically recommended larger high schools in order to combine ethnic groups and combat racial segregation. The Ford Foundation supported several such Harvard School of Education urban school-planning studies.[41] Foundations over the decades presented a megaphone to university professors, amplifying their educational recommendations to city leaders.

The New Boston Committee and Isadore Muchnick advocated the Strayer reforms from 1949 through 1954. A second school reform group rose out of the 1959 failed election campaign of a Beacon Hill "Yankee Grandmother," Mrs. Dorothy Winsor Bisbee, former president of the League of Women voters. A well-educated Brahmin, her family had founded the Winsor School for Girls in Boston. Her late husband taught at the elite Middlesex School in Concord. She cared so much about school quality that she ran for the Boston School Committee. John F. Collins graciously allowed her to speak at his rallies for mayor that year. After she lost the election, she invited supporters to join a "Boston Public School Association," later renamed Citizens for the Boston Public Schools in 1960.[42]

Mrs. Bisbee paid for a small Citizens office on Beacon Hill, took notes at every School Committee meeting, and distributed her own candid minutes on what really happened at each meeting. Volunteers, including interested college students, helped Mrs. Bisbee. The Citizens in 1960 announced four school reform objectives, to assist in the improvement of the Boston public schools, study the changing needs of Boston schools, stimulate public concern for the best education of Boston children, and recruit and support qualified candidates for the Boston School Committee.

This was an era of national enthusiasm for better public schools. Americans in the late 1950s became visibly upset about Soviet scientific superiority when the Russians launched the spacecraft Sputnik. Supported by the Carnegie foundation, former Harvard President James B. Conant wrote a series of books about high schools, junior high schools, teacher education, and then *Slums and Suburbs* to raise awareness of the disparities between city and suburban schools.[43]

Boston School Superintendent Dennis Haley resigned in 1960 to assume the presidency of nearby Suffolk University, two blocks away. The Citizens called for fresh talent at the top and new thinking about the schools, winning editorial support from *The Boston Globe* for a nationwide superintendency search. The Committee instead appointed the oldest assistant superintendent, veteran Boston educator Frederick Gillis, age sixty-seven. Members named William Ohrenberger as deputy superintendent, and presumed heir apparent (since Gillis's retirement at age seventy was compulsory).

The Citizens, now numbering 350 members, decided the School Committee itself must change. They spoke out and voiced strong member concerns in 1961. To create attention, the Citizens publicly criticized the lack of Boston school budget discussions contrasted with extensive attention to personnel appointments and employee issues. They scolded the School Committee for always starting meetings late, an hour or two after the scheduled time, so that members might line up votes among themselves to decide which friend, supporter, or relative might win a promotion or pay increase. Older teachers advised new and ambitious teachers that their best hope for advancement was through buying tickets to fund-raising receptions for School Committee incumbents who voted on promotions.[44]

The Citizens tried to build a stronger coalition for school reform. The Boston Municipal Research Bureau in 1961 sharply criticized the school budgetary process; so the Citizens found Bureau members (mainly companies and Boston law firms) logical allies. A Boston Latin School parent group calling itself Spotlight on Schools (SOS) was critical of the decline of the Latin School, and decided to endorse candidates in 1961. SOS became an important partner in the 1961 Citizens campaign effort.[45]

The Citizens Board interviewed School Committee candidates and endorsed the following four: Arthur Gartland was a Latin School and Harvard College graduate, an insurance executive who moved back from the suburbs so his son could attend the Latin School. He was a leader in the SOS movement to restore the reputation of the Latin School. William O'Connor was a professor of business at Suffolk University and former Boston schoolteacher. Melvin King was an articulate and energetic black social worker from the South End Settlement House and Nathaniel J. Young was a Republican lawyer who had attended Boston schools and lived on Beacon Hill. Three of the nominees were Catholic and the fourth, a black Protestant. The search to recruit a fifth candidate, preferably Jewish, failed. The likely successors to Muchnick were moving to Brookline and Newton. Also, some Citizens preferred not to oppose Joseph Lee, a maverick Beacon Hill Brahmin who styled himself as an independent. He thoroughly enjoyed political campaigns, running once against John F. Kennedy for Congress and against Curley for mayor.

The Citizens campaign hired a professional campaign organizer, recruited twenty-two ward captains and precinct volunteers, and raised campaign contributions totaling $13,500. The four candidates each collected 2,000 signatures and ran well enough to qualify among the ten finalists in the November election. Mayor Collins helped Citizens candidates by denouncing incumbents for refusing to trim the School Committee budget. He warned the dollar shortfall meant teachers might not be paid for their Christmas vacation, and reminded everyone that all five Committee members were seeking reelection. Meanwhile, the Boston Teachers Alliance endorsed Arthur Gartland and other four non-Citizens candidates.

In the final election, two Citizen-endorsed candidates, O'Connor and Gartland, both won as did Joe Lee, the only incumbent. The other new members were Boston attorneys with well-recognized surnames, Thomas Eisenstadt (nephew of Judge Eisenstadt) and Louise Day Hicks (former teacher and daughter of Judge William Day of South Boston).

The two Citizens Committee members elected Mrs. Hicks as chair. The Citizens for the first year hoped that Mrs. Hicks might be open to new ideas and might earn the Citizens endorsement in 1963. However, as chapter 4 explains, the issues of racial inequality in the schools came to the fore during 1963 and ended chances for a Citizens majority on the School Committee. The school department felt under siege in 1963, and four of the five members took the side of teachers, principals, and the board of superintendents against external critics.[46]

Meanwhile, the exodus of Boston families from the city, which had begun during the 1920s and accelerated after World War II ended, was continuing. What would persuade native Bostonians to leave the city of their birth? What forces pulled the returning veteran or the ambitious young engineer to a suburb that only a few years ago featured apple orchards, farms, or sand and gravel pits?

After World War II Massachusetts marriage- and birthrates soared, creating a pent-up demand for new housing. Sixteen million veterans became eligible for favorable home mortgage rates; often with little or no money down if they bought new homes. Builders responded by developing new suburban subdivisions offering Cape Cod style homes or split-level ranches. The land most readily available was outside Boston. Furthermore, suburban zoning laws and real-estate covenants excluding certain races or religious groups kept out "undesirables."[47]

Interstate highways, built with state and federal gas taxes, whisked former Bostonians, including veterans recently educated under the GI Bill, to new jobs, often in a suburb. The numbers of automobiles licensed in the United States grew to 50 million by 1955. Production of trucks liberated manufacturers from railroad spur lines and allowed the "deconcentration of employment from congested city to satellite suburbs."[48]

Route 128, the new highway circling three sides of Boston, attracted the new industries of Massachusetts. Route 128 intersections spawned industrial parks catering to the start-up electronic enterprises, smokeless industry, and "a burgeoning high tech mecca."[49]

Gerald Blakely, a land development executive, expressed pride in what he had done to liberate inner-city dwellers: "It was easy to see that we took people out of the Somervilles and the Dorchesters and the Chelseas into the suburbs...and their whole life style changed. It was exciting to me that this was changing the face of Boston."[50] Blakely, son of an MIT professor, foresaw the promise of high technology and grew wealthy enough to buy the company for which he worked (Cabot, Cabot, and Forbes). Returning veterans and educated city dwellers took new jobs in the new growth industries, abandoning the city and Boston schools in great numbers.

Why was school reform postponed? The Strayer Report had provided a detailed blueprint for modernizing Boston's public schools. Boston voters instead elected School Committees that denied the need for reform, especially school closings and changes in the promotional system. Two new school reform groups organized, one in the 1950s and one in 1960. Whenever reform looked likely to occur, the opposition of Boston voters, including school employees potentially disrupted by change, generally blocked it.

The major demographic trend was the sharp decline in Boston inhabitants, including children enrolled in the Boston public schools, from the high of 134,000 to the low of 86,000, a drop of almost 50,000 white students in twenty-five years. The key reasons include the immigration restrictions during the 1920s, low birthrates, the postwar incentives to build highways and homes in the suburbs, aggravated by FHA restrictions on urban home rehabilitation that promoted suburban relocation.

Over and over again, the explanation surfaces that Boston schools provided respectable employment for thousands of teachers and indoor work for custodians who defended their jobs even at old and underinhabited school buildings. As the Boston schools shrank, the defenders mobilized relatives and friends to vote against those who might consolidate facilities and trim jobs. The voices for reform were outnumbered. Too many of those who might stay and fight took flight, the Jewish families to Brookline and Newton, the Irish and Italian middle class to many suburbs. The exit option prevailed so that suburban communities built new schools while Boston held on even to old, outmoded school buildings.

Boston was not strong economically in the 1950s and 1960s. The booming wartime economy concealed temporarily the loss of textiles, shoes, and leather jobs. The new "tech" industry located elsewhere, taking advantage of subsidized highways and suburban locations. The educated workforce moved out of the old city, away from the rundown housing, the ancient school buildings, and the obsolete nineteenth-century curriculum that troubled Strayer and his team of professors. The choice of a sixty-seven-year-old veteran school superintendent in 1960 rewarded loyalty to the old regime and signified comfort with an increasingly outmoded school program. Thus "loyalty" within Boston was a force for preserving the status quo, keeping jobs and careers intact, rewarding longevity not innovation. Those loyal to saving the Latin School or restoring a great national reputation for Boston schools could not elect a majority to the School Committee.

The Fin Comm chose George Strayer to articulate a reform agenda for the schools. He did so with impressive documentation and an expert team. What Boston lacked was a mandate for change, a strong popular commitment to modernize a proud but obsolete system of education. Strayer could describe it and Muchnick, then Bisbee, and Gartland could denounce it, but those who benefited by steady employment out-shouted critical voices. The reform of Boston schools would eventually require litigation and court intervention since political action by itself failed to achieve visible progress.

The one group that would not stop speaking out for reform was black parents, whose growing concerns and frustrations with Boston Public Schools are described in chapter 4.

CHAPTER 4

BLACK VOICES FOR EQUAL EDUCATION, AND THE WHITE RESPONSE (1960–74)

Ruth Batson, a young black parent, thought well of the Strayer Report, especially the recommendations that all Boston schools should have lunchrooms, libraries, and gyms. In the late 1940s she was invited to join the Parents Federation, a mostly white group committed to parent education. She learned that the black neighborhoods had the oldest schools and were often unsafe. She met with Mayor Hynes who "denied the validity" of the Strayer Report, defended the schools, and abruptly terminated the meeting. Hynes later proposed a new public school in Hyde Park to serve a growing population. The Parent Federation challenged Hynes, complaining that Boston's busy South End was "hardly a ghost town."[1] This was the beginning of Ruth Batson's political education and the birth of her personal protest against racial discrimination toward black children in Boston. Her story is missing from the annals of the Boston desegregation story, as is the long struggle to achieve racial equality for Boston's black students.

For a while, in the 1850s, the Massachusetts legislature and governor, most of them Know Nothings, voted to allow black children to attend any Boston public school.[2] This early "Open enrolment" option did not survive the backlash against the post–Civil War reconstruction. William Monroe Trotter, M.D., Harvard Phi Beta Kappa and publisher of Boston's black newspaper, the *Guardian,* fought for the abolition of lynching and desegregation of schools in the early years of the twentieth century. Trotter formed a committee that later merged with the National Association for the Advancement of Colored People (NAACP). The NAACP in Boston already had an education committee designed to raise funds for college scholarships. The NAACP in 1950 did not place the racial integration of schools high on the Boston agenda.

Ruth Batson did not accept the Hynes verdict on Strayer's findings and ran for School Committee in 1951. She advocated cost of living increases for teachers, new schools, and hot lunches for all students. She won 15,000 votes in the primary, finishing sixteenth out of thirty-six candidates, not high enough to qualify among ten finalists for the November runoff election. She attracted the attention of the NAACP whose leaders asked her to organize a new education committee that would focus on improving the Boston schools.[3]

Not all black students were denied access to the best Boston schools. Sylvia Quarles was elected president of the Girls Latin senior class in 1951–52 and won a scholarship to Manhattanville, a New York Catholic College on whose trustee board she later served. Later in life Sylvia Q. Simmons became a Harvard-Radcliffe financial aid officer and president of the American Student Assistance Corporation that financed the education of college students. However, she was only one of only three black girls at Girls Latin her senior year. Melvin Miller was at the Boston (Boys) Latin School, 1 of 4 black seniors out of the 125 admitted to Harvard College in 1952. A lawyer (Columbia Law School), he became publisher of the *Bay State Banner*, Boston's black newspaper, ran for Congress, and served as a Boston University (BU) trustee for three-and-a-half decades.

While these future leaders were in college, the U.S. Supreme Court in 1954 declared school segregation illegal in the Topeka, *Kansas Brown v. Board of Education* decision. The old "separate but equal" school doctrine was thrown overboard.

Boston's black community, approaching 50,000 in numbers (8 percent of the city), assumed prematurely that the Brown decision and subsequent Little Rock, Arkansas integration would also apply to Boston public schools at some point.

Mrs. Batson took Miller, a Harvard senior, to a national conference on civil rights where he recalls "lynching" was one of the topics along with schooling.[4] The Massachusetts Democratic State Committee invited her to serve as a member, the year that Lincoln Pope became the first black Democratic state representative. The black community began to voice concerns about the inadequate schools to which their children were assigned.

The racial integration of schools was not necessarily the only remedy for Boston families. American blacks even before the Civil War argued about racial solutions other than integrating with mainstream white America. The radical alternatives to integration included abandoning either the United States, or Christianity, or capitalism.

The most dramatic exit option for blacks was migration out of America, such as "Back to Africa"; when freed slaves in the 1820s moved to Liberia. Marcus Garvey later advocated Black Nationalism, an ideology that attracted support from thousands of blacks including the father of Malcolm X. Within the United States, black separatism meant setting aside a section of a state or city for minorities only, or seeking total control over a predominately black school, its curriculum, teachers, principal, and staff. Black nationalists argued that white teachers could never become appropriate role models for black students. As early as the 1840s dissenters expressed this view when Boston's parents sought equality for the all-black school on Beacon Hill. This separatist perspective would be voiced again in Boston during the 1960s (and for New York City schools) through the invention of black-run community schools and proposals to make Roxbury an autonomous black community renamed Mandela.[5]

Another choice was Islam, the outright rejection of Christianity, a religion that outspoken critics thought kept blacks subordinate. Elijah Muhammed and his Nation of Islam advocated a color-blind religion with African roots, carrying the promise of personal liberation and salvation. Malcolm X, reading extensively in a Massachusetts prison, became convinced that white Christianity was hopeless, and joined the Nation.[6]

Still another option was an alternative economic system, socialism or communism. After the 1917 Russian Revolution and especially during the 1930s Depression, both black and white intellectuals discussed the option of rejecting capitalism. The black poet Langston Hughes and singer Paul Robeson were impressed with the Russian Communist program. They and others thought the free enterprise system failed the lowest classes, especially those deprived of educational opportunities. If communism was not the answer, then perhaps state socialism? Black labor leader A. Phillips Randolph and his Railroad Porters union kept these discussions alive, financing Socialist publications such as the *Messenger*. Of course the discussion of Marxist solutions by educators or union leaders terrified mainstream political leaders. White leaders advocated exporting radicals and imposed loyalty oaths on all Massachusetts schoolteachers to protect impressionable schoolchildren from dangerous subversives.[7]

In the end, the strong NAACP preference for racial integration prevailed in Boston. Demonstrations, law suits, and new federal civil rights statutes opened up previously all-white Southern restaurants and schools during the 1950s and 1960s. The Gandhi-like stance of Martin Luther King Jr., protesting Southern race discrimination, inspired Bostonians to adopt the techniques of boycott, peaceful demonstrations, and, when needed, lawsuits. Also, the moral Christian advocacy of the Reverends King, Ralph Abernathy, Jesse Jackson, and others inspired Boston's black ministerial leadership to speak on secular issues.

The NAACP, in the early years of the Depression, enrolled 50,000 members nationally. After World War II the NAACP enlisted 450,000 members, becoming the major Boston advocacy group for black educational opportunity and mobility. The Urban League was the other moderate black organization, aggressive in the quest for job opportunities.[8]

The most acceptable vocal strategy in Boston was political, supporting black candidates running for School Committee, state office, or mayor so that city schools might educate black children to their full potential. After Mrs. Ruth Batson ran in 1951, Mel King, a black social worker, ran for Boston School Committee in 1961 and 1963, but was not elected. He ran successfully for Massachusetts state representative in 1972, 1974, 1976, and 1978, and then ran for mayor both in 1979 and 1983.

King was born and raised in the South End, adjacent to Chinatown, in a multiracial neighborhood of blacks, Hispanics, Syrians, Jews, and a dozen other ethnic groups. As a young adult, he could not believe that the larger Boston community was so full of distrust, even hatred toward persons of color. After college he returned to work in community agencies such as the South End Settlement House, founded in the 1880s to assist immigrant families. He saw clearly both the possibilities and the limitations of political action. King described a three-stage theory of black political development:

The service stage. Black people from the 1940s into the early 1960s, he felt, were subservient to whites, dependent on their "good will" for access to goods, education, services, jobs, and housing.

The organizing stage. Blacks in this stage acquired the skills to lead themselves. "Our collective voice began to be heard more clearly than our timid, individual pleas for entry, and the political implications for working together became more obvious." The voices in this stage became evident in the 1960s, first in the South.

Institution-building. Blacks invented new organizations, such as private community schools, black banks, community agencies, and action groups to control their futures, politically and economically. King himself organized the Black Political Assembly and, when five blacks from Boston became state legislators, formed a legislative Black Caucus.[9]

What followed in Boston was an escalation of voices, a migration from accepting charity to organizing for action and the building of black-controlled institutions, including schools. At the same time, black leaders experimented with other exit options to achieve equal access to the presumably better schools serving white children.

Black parents protested conditions at one of the worst buildings, the old Sherwin School, the stench from whose urinals poisoned the air of nearby streets. The Henry Lee Higginson School parents protested conditions at the David Ellis School, one of the nearby schools. Then the Boston NAACP asked the Massachusetts Commission against Discrimination (MCAD) to collect data on school facilities, public school quality, curriculum and teaching, and school transfer policies. The NAACP was concerned that Girls High and Girls Trade School were becoming all black, partly because the Hyde Elementary School (grades kindergarten to eight) had become a feeder school to one-race black high schools. Batson and other black parents voiced their complaints.

Black Bostonians faced several setbacks in 1961, beginning with Mel King's defeat for School Committee. Two NACCP meetings with Superintendent Gillis on overcoming "de facto segregation" or racial isolation were totally unproductive. Gillis thought it highly objectionable, possibly even illegal to record the race of any student or teacher. Instead, Nancy St. John, a Harvard doctoral student, collected student data showing that seven Boston schools were at least 90 percent black, eight schools 80–85 percent black, serving 12, 800 black students in all. In October the Massachusetts Commission against Discrimination, the state agency that pursued complaints about inequality, informed the Boston NAACP that "only colored teachers were employed at the colored schools and that white teachers refused appointments to these schools." This only confirmed the deliberate racial separatism black parents suspected.[10]

One of the Southern protest tactics adopted was the boycott, the shunning of a person, company, or school to signal intense displeasure with existing practices. The Montgomery, Alabama, boycott of segregated public buses back in 1956 demonstrated the potential of nonviolent action. In 1960 black Bostonians joined the Northern Students Movement, NAACP, and the Congress on Racial Equality (CORE), in boycotting Woolworth stores that refused to allow Negroes to sit at lunch counters in the South. In 1962 a black citizen Boston Action Group boycotted Wonder Bread stores for twenty-nine days until store managers agreed to hire black workers. The civil rights victories learned first in the South migrated north and began to show promise. These positive outcomes confirmed the promise of peaceful boycotts as a potentially useful form of voice.[11]

The year 1962 began with Boston suburban schools supporting racial justice and black students in a prophetic precedent. Virginia's Prince Edward County closed public schools rather than complying with a desegregation order. The American Friends Service Committee (Quakers) asked the Boston NAACP to accept black Virginia students to live with Boston-area families. Seven students came north, some to Boston and others to Medford, Newton, and Cambridge where host families lived. This was the earliest form of suburban racial outreach. Few realized that it suggested how Boston's suburbs might host Boston's black children in the future.[12]

Massachusetts in November of 1962 elected a black Republican Attorney General Edward Brooke. Royal Bolling, newly elected black state legislator, Democrat from Roxbury, filed a one-sentence bill outlawing racial imbalance in Massachusetts schools. This was the origin of twentieth-century efforts to outlaw the racial concentration of black students in city schools. The battle, temporarily successful in the 1850s, had to be waged again in the 1960s.[13]

Governor Endicott Peabody in 1963 appointed a twenty-person commission to study the condition of all of Massachusetts education. The NAACP raised a question, "Where was the black member?" Later, the Boston NAACP protested hiring Chicago School Superintendent Benjamin J. Willis as director of the study commission, because Chicago blacks severely criticized Willis for renting portable classrooms (called Willis Wagons) rather than integrating their children in adjoining white-neighborhood schools. The NAACP requested the Willis-Harrington (Kevin Harrington was state senator from Salem) Commission to study the issues of school segregation and possible educational enrichment for Negro students. This did not happen.[14]

The year 1963 was one in which Boston black leaders expressed their strong dissatisfaction with the schools, voicing the most specific demands to date. The Higginson parents protested overcrowded first grade classes and the shortage of substitute teachers when older children sometimes filled in for absent teachers. Furthermore, they complained that there were not enough textbooks. They requested education funds from the Action for Boston Community Development, the agency formed by Ed Logue to manage urban relocations and disburse federal community program funds. On April 5 black parents sent Mayor John Collins fourteen specific complaints about treatment of black students, asking him to support equal educational opportunity for their children.[15]

The Civil Rights movement began to attract Northern supporters. In May of 1963, 10,000 blacks marched on Boston Common protesting the attack dogs unleashed by Birmingham Alabama Police Chief Bull Connor. Birmingham merchants opened lunch counters to all citizens rather than endure protests and the backlash of national opinion. What happened in the South (the Freedom Riders, the breakthroughs in lunch counters, and public bus desegregation) made a strong impact on Boston, stimulating popular resolve to seek the blessings of justice for Boston as well.[16]

Meanwhile, the leadership of Boston schools was about to change. Superintendent Gillis had to retire by the end of September 1963 when he turned seventy. Mrs. Louise Day Hicks was elected chair of the Boston School Committee in January, 1963. Her inaugural remarks called for new schools recommended in the Sargent Report and a higher school expenditure limit, especially since school enrollment, as Sargent had forecast, increased from 88,000 to 93,000.

The new Citizens for Boston Schools president, Beacon Hill attorney Herbert Gleason, wrote Mrs. Hicks in February asking her to give time to spelling out the qualifications, and organizing the search for a new superintendent of schools. Mrs. Hicks replied that the city's April budget deadline took precedence. On March 17, the Citizens asked the School Committee to solicit candidate ideas on the following four problems confronting Boston schools: the need for a teacher-recruitment program with local colleges, the drafting of imaginative programs for the disadvantaged students, effective advocacy of school priorities before the state and city, and shaping a great school-building program.

The Citizens briefed education reporters and publishers on how other cities conducted superintendency searches. Within weeks the *Globe* and the *Traveler* announced special series on the quest for a new superintendent. Arthur Gartland won a 4–1 vote authorizing Mrs. Hicks to launch a full search, and suggested an advisory committee of education deans from Boston College and Harvard. Joseph Lee was the committeeman least enthusiastic about a formal search. He believed Boston should select someone from the Board of Superintendents who already knew the schools. Committeeman Thomas Eisenstadt, a young attorney, felt Mrs. Hicks could not speak for him and sent out his own invitations to apply, one to Admiral Hyman Rickover. *The Boston Herald* branded his letters "scattergun tactics."[17]

Mrs. Hicks on May 20 announced that, after consultation with university presidents and national associations, she became convinced of the usefulness of a national search. She defined minimal qualifications for the post (at least the Master's degree and fifteen years of teaching and administration) and "an unusual ability to live with a high pressure job." Her suggested search procedures passed unanimously. Gartland's motion to hire a consultant to aid in evaluating candidates passed 3–2. He proposed Harvard Professor Herold C. Hunt as consultant.[18]

Herold Christian Hunt was the former superintendent of Kansas City and Chicago public schools, invited to Harvard in 1953 to lead a program preparing future school administrators. Hunt had been president of the American Association of School Administrators, which published a pamphlet on searching for a new superintendent. Urban school reform and executive talent searches were two of Hunt's professional specialties. Hunt wondered whether School Committee Members would even consider outsiders, other than Arthur Gartland, who hired one of Hunt's doctoral students as a research assistant. He knew from the 1960 search that Joe Lee thought Boston educators possessed an inherent advantage from growing up in the system.[19]

Mrs. Hicks, chairing the Boston School Committee in 1963, at first appeared willing to listen to the voices of black parents. She was a mother, a former teacher, daughter of a respected South Boston judge, and had gone back to earn her own law degree. By 1965 she became, Peter Schrag said, "a symbol, a spectre... the North's leading representative opposed to school desegregation, its outstanding defender of neighborhood schools...."[20] This was not her initial stance. Mrs. Hicks agreed to attend a Roxbury parent meeting at Freedom House on May 22, 1963. Paul Parks, a black engineer originally from Indiana who was both vice president of the Citizens and a member of the NAACP Education Committee, presided. Paul Parks introduced her, reading a four-page statement on the plight of Negro students, citing thirteen outmoded schools that Sargent recommended for abandonment, the lower per pupil expenditure for Negro students, and the need to look outside for a superintendent to cope with these problems.

Mrs. Hicks expressed surprise and concern. "Why hasn't someone told me about these problems?" she asked. Paul Parks drove her home that evening and four decades later remained convinced of her sincerity at that meeting. He believes Superintendent Gillis later warned her she would lose every teacher's vote if she listened to such criticism, especially about school segregation.[21]

Two weeks later, on June 4, 1963, the NAACP asked the Boston School Committee to respond to fourteen grievances. The Committee agreed to hear the complaints on June 13, 1963, with Ruth Batson chosen to speak for all black parents. Three hundred supporters including clergy, labor leaders, and the American Civil Liberties Union, joined her. "Our goal is first class citizenship, and we will settle for nothing less," she began. She quoted President John F. Kennedy who the previous week acknowledged "de facto segregation" as a problem in northern cities. Mrs. Batson denounced stereotypes such as the following: "Negro students are lazy, stupid and inferior." She called for an end to Boston school segregation. The first step would be acknowledgment of the problem by the School Committee.[22]

Next, she requested teacher training on how to work more effectively with Negro children. She urged appointment of permanent not temporary teachers, lower class sizes, and the purchase of books portraying all races. She asked for better school buildings, employment of more counselors, appointment of Negro principals, and a review of IQ tests biased against minority children. Finally, she asked that she, Paul Parks, and Mel King meet with Dr. Hunt of Harvard about the superintendency search. The NAACP urged selection of an educator "experienced in dealing with the problems of an urban community, who is sensitive to the needs of minority youth, and who sees the community as an ally...."[23]

Boston's black ministers rejected her moderate negotiating stance and on June 12 proposed a "Stay Out for Freedom" boycott to protest de facto school segregation. Three days later the NAACP met for seven hours with the School Committee, making little progress. The next day NAACP leaders met with Attorney General Brooke who warned that a school boycott violated compulsory school attendance laws, a meeting Mrs. Batson recalled as "rancorous."[24]

Mrs. Hicks met with city principals to seek their perspectives. They denied any discrimination and reminded her how strongly Bostonians felt about their neighborhood schools. She proposed her own advisory committee on racial matters, but key black leaders declined to serve. She referred the NAACP complaints to the Board of Superintendents, the panel of assistants whose predecessors rebutted Horace Mann, George Strayer, and other critics over the decades.

On June 18, 1963, 3,000 black high school students boycotted the schools under the banner "Stay Out for Freedom." Churches hosted Freedom Schools, with black ministers and other volunteers teaching black history and music. This boycott deeply offended Boston school officials but persuaded state officials to become involved.

Hunt met with the School Committee three times in May and early June, offering to review the qualifications of insider candidates and identify other experienced city school superintendents. The superintendency interviews took place from June 20 through the first week of August. One member leaked the names of seven finalists to the Boston *Traveler* on July 10, with Mrs. Hicks refusing any comment. She announced that a decision would be made within a month and that candidates were being questioned about teacher recruitment, programs for the culturally deprived, the segregation issue, and administrative organization. This statement acknowledged that both the Citizens and the NAACP helped define questions for the candidates, a modest triumph for voice.[25]

On July 9 the Board of Superintendents responded to the NAACP complaints. The most important concession was that transfers to schools with open seats were possible, but only if approved by the principal. Certainly permanent teachers should be assigned to schools in "culturally deprived" areas. The state agreed to provide race relations materials presented to teachers at Boston State College. Boston would ask ten area colleges to assign their student teachers to disadvantaged neighborhood schools. Publishers would be invited to submit books with illustrations of all races. The Ford Foundation and the Agency for Boston Community Development (ABCD) were asked to help with developmental reading programs. Finally, Boston would review intelligence tests to eliminate any racial bias.

Boston, the Board suggested, could appoint more counselors from the approved candidate list, but only when more funds became available. The

Board asserted that race, color, or creed had no bearing on principal selection, although all Boston principals were white. The Board was not authorized to arrange a meeting with Professor Hunt (and at least one of their members was an active inside candidate). The Board decided not to comment on the matter of acknowledging "de facto" school segregation.[26]

The Boston NAACP, frustrated by the Boston School Committee, reached out for National help. Roy Wilkins, the national president, sent senior attorney June Shagaloff to Boston on July 15. Boston NAACP President Ken Guscott, Mrs. Batson, and five Boston attorneys, several from the American Jewish Congress, listened carefully to Miss Shagaloff's advice. Mrs. Batson took careful notes, never published until 2000. Shagaloff said that the Boston school boycott made a dramatic national impact. The protest against Ben Willis as state consultant was much less important than the focus on Boston issues. Busing was, in her opinion, the least effective policy solution compared to redrawing school attendance boundary lines within the city.[27]

When asked, "Should the NAACP file suit against Boston schools?" Shagaloff responded cautiously. The NAACP had already initiated seventeen cases before various courts, many focused on intentional school segregation (such as New Rochelle, New York). The side effect of a lawsuit included freezing any other positive actions, she said, and could take many years to settle. The Boston attorneys present at that meeting offered to research the litigation option.

Mrs. Batson meanwhile prepared a detailed rebuttal to the Board of Superintendents. Mrs. Hicks denied Batson's request for another meeting with the School Committee. On July 29 the Boston NAACP and the Northern Student Movement picketed School Committee headquarters at 15 Beacon Street, white and black demonstrators forming a human chain to block the entrance. After ten days of headlines and bitter charges, Mrs. Hicks agreed to hold a meeting on August 15 not to exceed one hour. However, Mrs. Hicks said that any mention of "de facto" segregation would automatically signal adjournment. When Mrs. Batson cited the New Rochelle court ruling outlawing "de facto segregation," Mrs. Hicks abruptly ended the meeting.[28]

The *Herald* on August 24 asked whether the search was "an empty gesture of deference to reform groups like the Citizens for the Boston Schools." The *Globe* published the qualifications of seven outsider nominees, most of them holding doctorates from Columbia, Harvard, or New York University, comparing them to three insiders, two with honorary degrees from Calvin Coolidge College and only one with an earned doctorate.[29]

The leading insider was William Ohrenberger, deputy superintendent, former math teacher and coach at English High School. A large and energetic man, he excelled both in academics and football at Boston College, and while a Boston teacher, played semiprofessional football for the Pere Marquette Knights of Columbus team in South Boston. Although of German extraction, he mixed well with Boston's Irish. One of six assistant superintendents, his duties included curriculum revision and legislative representation for the Boston public schools. In 1960 he was designated "deputy superintendent," both a consolation prize and portent of "favorite son" status next time. As heir-apparent, Ohrenberger had three years of lead-time to prepare his candidacy.

Ohrenberger during the early 1960s regularly attended national conferences of the Research Council of the Great Cities Program for School Improvement and built a list of educational innovations tested in other cities, often with Ford Foundation funds. He summarized his program for Boston schools in a twenty-four-page working paper. He shared his "Boston Plan" with committee members and Dr. Hunt during his late summer interview.[30]

Ohrenberger's plan included hiring additional guidance counselors for junior high schools serving disadvantaged students, lowering class sizes, and adding teachers and tutors for schools in congested areas. He advocated a longer school day and salary increases for teachers working in difficult areas. He proposed a new Vocational Institute to train qualified technicians at the post–high school level. He would name a special assistant for teacher recruitment, publicizing the teacher exam more widely. He favored expanding libraries and reading, dropout prevention strategies, team teaching, and other innovations for all Boston schools. Committeeman Joseph Lee said he was impressed. "He had a plan. He wasn't just telling us what he had done."

Herold Hunt presented credentials of superintendents from other cities to show the Committee the outstanding pool from which they might choose. "Of the insiders, Ohrenberger by far made the most favorable impression with his plan and presentation," Hunt recalled two years later. However, he considered the outside candidates clearly superior by training and experience.[31]

Arthur Gartland announced he liked three of the outsiders. William O'Connor said he now understood that outsiders already solved problems Boston was facing. A Connecticut superintendent impressed Eisenstadt. Mrs. Hicks on September 18 accused the Citizens of pressure tactics, of trying to "cram its choice for a superintendent down the throats of the School Committee," and that this was pushing her toward an insider.

The September 24, 1963 School Committee primary election was an overwhelming victory for Mrs. Hicks, followed by Eisenstadt and Lee. The two Citizens candidates O'Connor and Gartland trailed far behind, raising questions as to whether their enthusiasm for outsider candidates diminished their support. Two days before the election, blacks demonstrated against the inadequacies of a ninety-one-year-old school in Roxbury. The major election issue seemed to be whether the Boston School Committee would hold firm in denying any form of segregation, and most of all, not appear to bend to angry black complaints.

On September 30, the final workday for retiring Fred Gillis, Mrs. Hicks called a special Committee meeting at 12 noon to select Boston's superintendent. O'Connor was busy teaching a Suffolk University class a few blocks away, but said, "Go on with the meeting." Gartland objected to voting without O'Connor, but Mrs. Hicks nominated as superintendent one who "worked his way up through the ranks, William H. Ohrenberger." Eisenstadt seconded the motion, praising his comprehensive blueprint for Boston's schools. Gartland nominated an outsider. Lee voted for Ohrenberger, who became elected superintendent with the necessary three votes.[32]

Mrs. Hicks in her final meeting as committee chair, on December 19, summarized a year of progress, including selecting Superintendent Ohrenberger "whose vigorous proposals, including the 'Boston Plan' have won deserved acclaim." Ohrenberger later explained, "An inside candidate needs to show a plan describing what he would do if selected, in order to compete with outside candidates." Dr. Hunt tossed his Boston search file in the wastebasket, upset that he let himself be used by the Boston School Committee.[33]

Ohrenberger's Boston Plan actually acknowledged black parent complaints, that their children's schools needed more resources, extra staff, better teachers, and innovative approaches to teaching. Many of his ideas for low-income students, borrowed from other cities, within eighteen months became eligible for President Johnson's War on Poverty programs and funding through the Elementary and Secondary Education Act. Ohrenberger, however, was allowed no leeway to admit that Boston willfully assigned black students into segregated schools. Although he favored many educational innovations, Mrs. Hicks and the School Committee majority rejected his suggestion to transport black students from an overcrowded school to an underutilized white school. Boston was not ready for race reforms. Boston was not alone. In the mid-1960s a public opinion poll showed that "65 percent of all Americans felt the pace of civil rights was too fast."[34]

During his nine years as superintendent, Ohrenberger nominated and won approval for the first black principals and the first black assistant superintendent of Boston schools. As his deputy superintendent, he recommended Marguerite Sullivan, the first woman deputy, his advisor on compensatory education in elementary schools.[35]

Black parents decided to prepare a new strategy. They welcomed a coalition of new supporters, Boston Jews, Unitarians, and a few Catholic priests who supported the NAACP strategies, supporting either new state laws or litigation. This option became evident during 1963, more than a decade before federal judge W. Arthur Garrity heard the decisive Boston school desegregation case, *Morgan v. Hennigan*.

During the summer of 1963 attorneys from the American Jewish Congress Edward Barshak, Herbert Hershfang, and Gerald Berlin, met with two of Boston's black lawyers, Richard Banks and David Nelson, to discuss litigation strategies. Barshak's August 1 cover letter to the NAACP cautioned that a lawsuit was only "one weapon in a balanced arsenal." The five attorneys recommended a strategy focused mostly on desegregation, with compensatory education as an appendage but not a substitute. They urged preparation of a workable plan for desegregation, such as the one in Princeton, New Jersey, achieved through pairing mostly white with mostly black schools. They suggested preparation of a suit by an individual parent of a child who was refused a transfer from a racially imbalanced school to another (mostly white) school. The petition would go not to the federal court but to the Massachusetts Supreme Judicial Court and could request appointment of a special master, an expert (perhaps a Harvard Law School professor) to review charges that less money was spent on Negro schools and that segregation was detrimental to Negro students. The expert would then propose specific remedies.[36]

The lawyers recommended public-awareness tactics, including picketing, media briefings on racial imbalance, support of candidates running against desegregation, and voter registration drives (a full array of "voice" options). They suggested asking the State Board of Education, the attorney general, the governor, Massachusetts Council of Churches, and the Harvard Graduate School of Education, either to bring pressure or help design a desegregation program. The legal team urged tapping the "reservoir of power, expertise and energy" of civil rights groups including the American Jewish Congress, CORE, the Americans for Democratic Action, the Catholic Interracial Council, and labor groups to "accent the basic moral and democratic problem" and avert the criticism that this was only a local Roxbury problem.

They warned that a litigation strategy was full of risks, including the choice of judge, the inevitable legal defense by the city, and the discretion a judge might exercise. They acknowledged the dire effect of losing the case. However, even the press coverage of a lawsuit might be useful and, given the "point zero" response of the School Committee, the five urged filing a case.

The Reverend Robert J. Drinan, a Jesuit priest, was an energetic law professor totally committed to racial justice. Associate dean of the Boston College Law School, he was both an academic and moral activist who later served five terms in the U.S. Congress representing Boston's western suburbs. His religious order, the highly educated Society of Jesus, taught moral philosophy at universities. Occasionally Jesuits were known to upset Boston's cardinals with their unfettered quest for truth and justice. In the summer of 1963 Mrs. Batson was advised to bring a Catholic clergyman with her to the School Committee hearing; she brought Father Drinan. Later a friend told her, "He was the wrong person. He's a Jesuit," presumably too intellectual and too progressive. Father Drinan served on the NAACP Education Committee and on the Massachusetts State Advisory Committee to the U.S. Commission on Civil Rights established under the 1957 federal law.

The State Board of Education on August 20, 1963 urged Boston to take action to eliminate "racial imbalance" in the schools. This was a term defined by New York State Commissioner James Allen to describe schools that enrolled a majority of black students.[37] Massachusetts Education Commissioner Owen Kiernan announced that the state would provide $250,000 in special program money to help Boston equalize educational opportunities. Farther Drinan wrote Paul Parks, chair of the State Advisory Committee education subcommittee, that he thought the state dollars were inadequate. He thought Massachusetts needed to pass a school "de facto" desegregation law such as the Illinois Armstrong Act, and that the Board should spell out how plans to offset racially imbalanced schools would be developed.[38]

This was the summer of the peaceful march on Washington D.C. capped by the eloquent "I Have a Dream Speech" by Martin Luther King, Jr. on August 28. The next day the national Black Elks (IBPOEW), meeting in Boston, marched on Boston Common to protest school segregation and honor the one hundredth anniversary of the Emancipation Proclamation.[39] Support for racial equality grew that summer.

The Boston School Committee on September 4 announced a new pupil transfer option listing vacant seats, but with transfers approved only by the principal, and parents responsible for transportation costs. Parents must assume the full burden. On September 5 and 6, the NAACP staged an unannounced sit-in at School Committee headquarters, led by Ruth Batson, Attorney Richard Banks, and Melnea Cass, "First Lady of Roxbury." Mrs. Cass was a pillar of the community so revered that police would not arrest her. Committeeman Joseph Lee was unsympathetic, declaring that "the Negro can make their schools the best in the city if they attend schools more often, on time, and apply themselves," the acerbic voice of a Beacon Hill patrician.[40]

Dr. Charles Pinderhughes, a black psychiatrist on the Veterans Administration Hospital staff, wrote Mayor John Collins a letter on the ill effects of segregating Negro children, on the cultural deprivation visited upon former slaves, and the need for the mayor to form a committee to take positive action.[41]

On October 9 the 93-year-old Sherwin School (identified as obsolete in the 1944, 1953, and 1962 school surveys) was destroyed by fire, 19 days after 10,000 marchers demonstrated against the school's inadequacies. Roxbury Republican Representative Alfred Brothers declared, "Thank God it was burned down." But it was less an act of God than an act of arson, perhaps by teenagers inspired by popular protest against the ancient classroom building.[42]

On October 23 the Ford Foundation announced an $874,000 educational grant to the city antipoverty agency, the ABCD. The School Department launched Operation Counterpoise in the overcrowded Henry L Higginson School, in response to parent protests.[43] Ohrenberger and Deputy Rita Sullivan coined the unusual phrase "Counterpoise" to describe their new remedial education and enrichment programs.

In the November election, Mrs. Hicks topped the School Committee ballot with 128,000 votes, Eisenstadt, Lee, and O'Connor following. Gartland barely won reelection (56,000 votes), with Mel King only 4,000 votes behind. The message was clear, that denying the existence of de facto segregation was twice as popular as acknowledging it. Mrs. Hicks had heeded this message from Superintendent Gillis and from white constituents all around the city. The election results communicated this strong public sentiment against admitting to any form of segregation.

That November a sniper killed President John F. Kennedy outside the Dallas school textbook warehouse, propelling Vice President Lyndon B. Johnson (LBJ) to the presidency. LBJ emerged as a vigorous champion of civil rights and federal support for urban education. In December 1963 three black legislators, Royal Bolling, Lincoln Pope, and Alfred Brothers, filed legislation denying state funds to any Massachusetts school system that permitted racial imbalance to exist in the public schools.[44]

When the School Committee in January 1964 elected William O'Connor chairman, he announced, "We have no inferior education in our schools. What we have been getting is an inferior type of student"—this perhaps stating the low point in the dialogue about what urban schools should do for black students. O'Connor had been a Boston teacher; he was listening to former colleagues in the Boston public schools urging him to fight black parent criticism. Eight days later the Boston Teachers Union and the Boston Teachers Alliance formally objected to listening to mandatory lectures on how to aid culturally deprived children, but Ohrenberger stood firm.[45]

Another student boycott was proposed, scheduled for February 26. Citizens in twenty-two suburbs signed newspaper ads endorsing a Boston school boycott. So did the Massachusetts Council of Churches, the Young Democrats of Harvard and Radcliffe, and the Brandeis and Simmons faculties.[46] This time a few universities and suburban liberals joined the ministerial voices in Boston.

Mrs. Hicks in a radio discussion February 4, 1964 suggested that "an independent study commission might determine whether local Negro youngsters were deprived educationally by attending predominately Negro schools."[47] On February 10 State Senator Beryl Cohen (D Brookline) filed a bill to establish a commission to study racial imbalance, to include eight elected officials and two appointed by the governor.[48]

The School Committee agreed to meet again with the NAACP on educational matters. This time Education Committee Chair Paul Parks brought expert witnesses, two of them Harvard Psychology professors, Thomas Pettigrew and Gerald Lesser, and Boston College Law Professor William Keneally, S.J. (another Jesuit lawyer). Parks proposed a desegregation planning commission, three members chosen by the Boston School Committee and three by the NAACP, with the Harvard Graduate School of Education advising on what to do for the thirty-four schools presumably racially imbalanced. From the School Committee only Gartland voted "yes," Mrs. Hicks insisting that it was only a hearing and not a regular meeting. She had been urged by supporters not to yield, not to give black parents an inch.[49]

That winter, on February 26, 1964, a black Episcopal minister Canon James Breeden, Mel King, and others ran the second one-day school boycott with 8,000 students assigned to 24 Freedom Schools at churches and community centers.[50] This was one more vocal expression of discontent designed to push the Boston School Committee toward action on parent and NAACP complaints. The *Herald*, the Boston *Pilot* (the Catholic cardinal's paper) and Commissioner Owen Kiernan each warned parents that school truancy was illegal.

Because Boston was so Catholic, the Catholic Church was potentially influential on the school desegregation question. Cardinal Cushing explained his opposition to school boycotts after black comedian Dick Gregory denounced his caution. He recognized that inner-city black children needed more than schools provided. The cardinal offered church space for after-school study halls, staffed by college and parent volunteers, use of church recreational facilities, and "perhaps a good hot supper."[51]

Several Boston parochial schools already accepted black students, whether Catholic or not. Earlier in the century Cardinal O'Connell recruited the Sisters of the Blessed Sacrament to serve what were then called Colored Catholics, mostly from the West Indies. Three Roxbury parishes enrolled 882 black students as of 1965, St. Joseph's, St. Leo's, and St. John's (with St. Hugh's, a consolidated parish). These formerly Irish neighborhoods and parishes turned mostly black in the late 1950s.[52] To make this program work, the cardinal archbishop and the Catholic pastor had to agree and an Association of Urban Nuns made teaching black children a priority. This use of parish schools happened in Chicago and New York as well.[53]

On March 1 State Education Commissioner Owen B. Kiernan announced that the State Board of Education authorized him to convene a "blue ribbon" panel of community leaders to consider a program of action on racial imbalance.[54] This was three weeks after Mrs. Hicks and Senator Cohen had called for studies. On March 6 he named twenty-two leaders to an advisory committee on racial imbalance, which he would chair, assisted by two task forces of academics and state staff preparing research and statistics. Kiernan, a graduate of Bridgewater State with a doctorate from the Harvard Graduate School of Education, made the recruitment calls himself. His panel included the presidents of Boston University, Tufts University, Boston College (Michael Walsh, S.J.), Radcliffe and Northeastern, and the president of the state League of Women Voters. A black attorney Herbert Tucker and a white Springfield woman, Mrs. Roger Putnam, contributor of Negro Scholarships, agreed to serve. Religious leaders included Bishop Burgess (black) of the Episcopal Church, Rabbi Ehrmann of the Massachusetts Board of Rabbis, Cardinal Richard J. Cushing, and Erwin Canham, editor of the *Christian Science Monitor*. Other luminaries included Ralph Lowell, member of an old Boston Brahmin family serving on dozens of civic boards, Gillette Razor CEO Carl Gilbert, former Attorney General Edward McCormack, and another senior attorney Oscar W. Hauserman of the Council of Christians and Jews. It was an outstanding, presumably unassailable, panel of Massachusetts higher education, corporate, church, and civic leaders.

The liberal Democratic Governor Endicott Peabody was highly supportive, his brother chairing the advisory committee for the Massachusetts Commission against Discrimination. Police arrested his activist mother, upset by racial injustice, several weeks later on April 1 while she helped a black-white group integrate the segregated restaurant at a Florida motor lodge.

Black parents at the severely crowded Garrison school learned in June that 250 students would be assigned to the old Boardman School next fall, right in the middle of the Washington Park urban renewal construction project. The parents met, sought an injunction on safety grounds, and when refused, resolved to avoid Boardman and send their children to the Peter Faneuil School on Beacon Hill. The Boardman Parents Group raised private contributions to pay for bus transportation to a safer location. The Faneuil School was actually overwhelmed, but Chairman Hicks had directed that Beacon Hill leaders such as Gleason in effect be punished for their openness.

On July 1 the Kiernan Commission released a preliminary finding that only 3.8 percent of the state students were nonwhite but that 7,500 were concentrated in 20 Boston schools. The Commission defined a racially imbalanced school as "one in which the composition of the school population is sharply out of balance with the racial composition of the society in which Negro children study, serve and work."[55] Critics of this definition later pointed out that this exonerated all-white schools, including the suburbs, and placed an undue burden on blacks.

The Catholic Church's reaction to this report, given Boston's Catholic majority, was important. The Archdiocesan newspaper, the Boston *Pilot*, editorialized about "a good beginning," a reliance on facts, and an end to confusion about the troubling phrase "de facto segregation." Of course, the *Pilot's* publisher, Cardinal Cushing, served on the Commission but the editor was just as committed. Two weeks later the Boston Area Seminary Faculties, forty ordained faculty from the BU and Harvard Divinity Schools and the Catholic St. John's, Oblate and Jesuit seminaries, signed a statement united "in the demand for the rectification of this injustice" and calling for specific recommendations.[56]

That fall Boston opened with 96,000 students attending 196 public school buildings. Boardman parents "sat in" at the Garrison school protesting pupil assignments to a dangerous school in a neighborhood under construction. The School Committee approved the purchase of a recently vacated Beth El, a forty-year-old Dorchester synagogue, to relieve overcrowding. Black parents opposed this action as did Joseph Barresi, the Municipal Research Bureau director who suggested that busing students to vacant seats elsewhere would be less expensive than refurbishing a structure that might be obsolete in ten years. He cited a school census revealing almost 2,000 vacant seats in other Boston schools. Meanwhile, 500 pupils from the Columbia Point Housing Project in Dorchester were bused into mostly white South Boston elementary schools to reduce overcrowding without a word of protest.[57]

The national mood that year supported justice for blacks. Shocked by Southern violence against blacks, the Congress strongly backed Lyndon Johnson's efforts to pass a new Civil Rights Act outlawing racial barriers to employment and public accommodations. Elected overwhelmingly in November 1964, Johnson promoted an aggressive legislative agenda including the Headstart program and the Elementary and Secondary Education Act. Reverend King, meanwhile, won the Nobel Peace Prize on

December 10, 1964. The police brutality at Selma, Alabama, over voter registration prompted enactment of the Voting Rights Act of 1965.

The School Committee in January 1965 elected Mrs. Hicks chair on the eighth round of balloting, only Thomas Eisenstadt and Arthur Gartland withholding their support. This ended the usual rotation of the committee chairmanship, but Lee and O'Connor felt that, in a time of heavy pressure, Mrs. Hicks could best articulate white majority opposition to persistent black demands. She was staunch in support of "neighborhood schools" and opposed changing any of Roxbury school attendance patterns.

Commissioner Owen B. Kiernan on January 10 released a preliminary state report declaring that Boston's sixteen racially imbalanced schools were educationally inferior. The next day Federal Judge George Sweeney ordered the Springfield, Massachusetts School Committee to file a plan ending racial concentration in six elementary and two junior high schools. When questioned by reporters, Mrs. Hicks denied any relevance of this ruling to Boston. Although the Sweeney ruling was later overturned on appeal, Martin Luther King visited Massachusetts and spoke at Harvard that week on the need to eliminate the "hard core of de facto segregation" in Northern schools.[58]

Endicott School parents on January 18 requested transportation of one hundred students to other schools with available seats. On January 19 the Boston School Committee instead voted to expand Counterpoise enrichment programs, and on January 26 voted to buy Beth El Temple to relieve Endicott overcrowding, keeping black students in their neighborhoods. When Superintendent Ohrenberger on June 12 submitted a staff plan to transport 560 willing black students to 10 schools with vacant seats, Eisenstadt countered with a proposal to purchase portable classrooms, another device to keep black students in their zone.[59] Eisenstadt's office notified parents at one white school that he would fight the superintendent's busing plan, which stirred up those parents, much to Ohrenberger's surprise. Eisenstadt was listening closely to white parents. An Eisenstadt motion to forbid any expansion of transportation was passed 3–2, Lee and Gartland voting "no." A federal judge later reviewed these decisions and found they violated the Constitution.

Business leaders recognized the severity of the impasse. On February 25 the Boston Finance Commission proposed locating a new English High School in Roxbury, the facility recommended three years earlier by Cyril Sargent. In March Greater Boston Chamber of Commerce President Gilbert Hood issued a public statement calling for positive steps to correct racial imbalance in the public schools.

Kiernan's state panel on April 2 released the final report entitled "Because It Is Right, Educationally."[60] It was dubbed the "Kiernan Report" for the commissioner who had recruited members, personally chaired the meetings, and announced the findings. His report concluded that racial imbalance existed in three Massachusetts cities, Boston, Springfield, and New Bedford, and "represents a serious conflict with the American policy of equal opportunity. It is detrimental to a sound education." The state recommended building larger schools to house the several races, closing eleven ancient Boston schools, transferring pupils, and expanding summer and remedial programs as remedies. It placed no blame and stopped short of recommending busing or transfers, except while awaiting construction of newer larger schools. Mayor Collins urged the School Committee to meet with the state, with educators and the Negro community to work out solutions.[61]

Mrs. Batson and the NAACP requested another meeting to discuss the report recommendations, but the School Committee refused. The School Committee referred the Kiernan Report to the Board of Superintendents for review and refutation, as it had on so many prior occasions. Meanwhile, the Reverend Vernon Carter, a black Lutheran clergyman, announced an around-the-clock Freedom Vigil outside the Boston School Committee headquarters until the racial imbalance bill was signed into law. Beginning on April 26 and for the next 114 days this black minister, often accompanied by sympathetic marchers of other faiths, patrolled outside the 14 Beacon street headquarters of the Boston Public Schools. At one point hospitalized for exhaustion, the determined Reverend Carter picketed for up to twenty-one hours each day, more than his slender and aging physique permitted.[62]

Roy Wilkins of the NAACP criticized Mrs. Hicks, denouncing her recalcitrance as "humiliating." Attorney Robert Carter of the NAACP Legal staff threatened a Boston lawsuit for violations of the Fourteenth Amendment. On April 22, 1965 Martin Luther King Jr. returned to Boston to address a joint session of the Massachusetts House and Senate on de facto segregation and the damage it causes. "I come not to condemn but to encourage.... Now is the time to end segregation in the public schools. Segregation debilitates the segregator as well as the segregated." He met with a willing Mayor Collins, while Mrs. Hicks declined a meeting. The Southern Christian Leadership Conference organized a march of thousands to support the racial imbalance bill, marching from Dorchester to Boston Common.[63]

Mrs. Hicks proposed a presumably neutral site in Franklin Park for the new English High School. When Park commissioners protective of parkland rejected the location, she commented, "We'll just have to forget about it."[64] Earlier sites such as Columbia Point, South Boston, were rejected in favor of a new shopping center. City and state legislators opposed

Columbus Park, as its location would attract black students too close to South Boston.[65]

Two more Boston schools were torched on April 26, the Everett (built in 1860) and the Hyde (1884), an illegal expression of hostility by students or young adults but part of the collective frustration about construction delays. (Mayor Collins two years earlier authorized $29 million for new schools in a 1963 bond issue.) By June, another blaze at the Norcross School (1867) was the fifth school fire that year. Mrs. Hicks said, "The clergy is largely responsible for inciting these people." It bothered her that so many seminarians and ministers supported the black cause.[66]

Boston Redevelopment Authority's Ed Logue on April 30 proposed busing 4,000 students to suburbs to relieve both overcrowding and racial imbalance; the idea seemed incredulous then but within a decade 3,000 black students were transported. Brookline and Newton leaders accepted his proposal. The Brookline School Committee had already begun discussions of making school spaces available.[67]

Boston that June (1965) dismissed Jonathan Kozol, a substitute teacher at the Gibson School, ostensibly for teaching "Ballad of the Landlord" by Langston Hughes. The thirteenth teacher of his fourth grade class that year, he was told that the official curriculum did not authorize works by Hughes, a black writer.[68] Kozol later wrote *Death at an Early Age,* a searing indictment of deplorable conditions confronting both teachers and students in Boston's black schools.[69]

The Racial Imbalance Law

Royal Bolling's short racial imbalance bill required major revisions to accommodate the Kiernan Commission recommendations. Republican Governor John Volpe in June sent a special message to the legislature recommending action. The NAACP legal team of Barshak, Banks, Hershfang, Father Drinan, and Senator Beryl Cohen redrafted the bill that passed the House on June 22, the State Senate on July 27. Thirty urban Democrats opposed the measure, proposing restrictive changes including an anti-busing rider. Governor John Volpe signed the bill into law on August 18, 1965. Approximately fifty Massachusetts schools were labeled "imbalanced," more than forty of them in Boston. In final form, the new Racial Imbalance statute offered a 25 percent increase in school construction aid for newly "balanced" buildings, authorized suburban participation in imbalance plans, and provided for either court review or court enforcement. Boston legislators made sure the law did not require compulsory busing, although Boston transported thousands of students each day for other reasons.[70]

U.S. Senator Edward Kennedy asked for $50 million in new federal funds to overcome racial imbalance. At the 1965 Northeastern University commencement, Kennedy declared that "racial imbalance was wrong" and a community that continued to practice it should lose state aid. Kennedy remained a strong voice for racial integration.

Still, the Boston School Committee by a 3–2 vote denied the existence of any problem and declined to prepare any plan to reduce racial imbalance. In fact, the majority voted to schedule double sessions at overcrowded schools and rejected the NAACP request to discuss possible alternatives.[71]

The Boston Redevelopment Authority staff recommended an alternative site for the new English High School, one in the Madison Park section of Roxbury. The School Committee decided by a 3–2 vote that the new English High should go elsewhere, eventually in very small site across the street from the Boys Latin School. The English High School had always been a white high school, and the Committee feared that a Roxbury location would discourage all but black students.

Mrs. Hicks was very upset with the Kiernan Report, describing it as the work of "outside agitators, undemocratic and un-American." Yet these "agitators" included her own Roman Catholic cardinal from South Boston, along with the president of Boston College, another eminent Boston Irish-Catholic American. After she reported threats on her life, a large police dog guarded her South Boston home that spring.

If new schools were to help rebalance the schools, the city had to build new schools rapidly. Anthony Adinolfi, a New York City consultant to Boston, recommended that a Public Facilities Commission replace the School Building Commission that failed to live up to its name. The superintendent of schools and mayor's staff would share responsibilities, a constructive proposal implemented after 1967.

The Reverend Virgil Wood interrupted the June graduation at the Patrick Campbell Junior High School, humiliating Mrs. Hicks, the speaker that day, calling her the "Hitler of Boston." The voices were becoming shrill. Black parents arranged for a makeup graduation a few weeks later at St. Hugh's Catholic Church in Roxbury, with black Boston Celtics basketball star Bill Russell as speaker and a conciliatory letter from Cardinal Cushing read to all.[72]

It became abundantly clear that the Racial Imbalance Law was not self-implementing and that the Boston School Committee would thwart efforts of black parents seeking equal education for their children. The fall 1965 Boston city election turned into a referendum on racial imbalance. The Citizens for Boston Schools hired a campaign coordinator and screened School Committee candidates beginning in June of 1965. O'Connor was not endorsed because he opposed teacher bargaining, and had denigrated "inferior" pupils.[73] Arthur Gartland was unanimously endorsed, and then Mel King 20–3. Other endorsements went to George Parker, a suburban teacher committed to civil rights, to John F.X. Gaquin, attorney and father of seven, and Velia DeCesare of Hyde Park, a state employment supervisor. None except Gartland and King were well known in Boston political circles.

Unquestionably, Mrs. Hicks commanded the most attention as she reiterated her support of "neighborhood schools" and her strong opposition to busing. Mrs. Hicks won two-thirds of those Bostonians (28 percent) who voted in the September primary while Gartland won one-fifth, slightly more than Mel King. In the November final election, candidate John McDonough who was placed ninth in the September primary election unseated Arthur Gartland from the fifth committee slot, removing the strongest School Committee voice for desegregation. McDonough was from a well-known Boston family, brother both to a former city councilor (Patrick) and to an assistant principal (Joseph) in the Boston Public Schools (BPS).

Boston school custodians endorsed all the incumbents except Gartland. A photograph of Mrs. Hicks, Lee, Eisenstadt, and McDonough posing with custodians appeared in neighborhood weeklies. The Hyde Park Neighborhood Association, a property-owner group, endorsed the same four. The Citizens candidates, it was said, supported "forced busing" and were backed by outsiders, a charge repeated by *The Boston Herald*, a paper popular in working-class neighborhoods.[74]

An Opinion Research poll ten days before the election found that a narrow majority of Boston voters supported this statement: "Irish, Italians and Jewish immigrants overcame prejudice and worked their way up. Negroes should do the same." A full 60 percent agreed with the idea that "all children of grammar school age should attend school in their own neighborhood school districts, regardless of the condition of the school."[75]

A statistical analysis of voting patterns found that Citizens candidates did well in black areas, Jewish neighborhoods, and a few high-income areas but badly among Irish voters in working-class and middle-class neighborhoods. Forty-seven percent of the voters participated in the 1965 election and Mrs. Hicks won 64 percent of their votes. They understood perfectly her slogan, "You know where I stand." Her vote in predominately black precincts ranged from 1 to 4 percent, compared to Mel King's 93–95 percent share. Gartland clearly lost votes citywide because of the accurate perception that he favored transporting blacks to less crowded white schools.[76]

Lawrence O'Connell, a Syracuse University doctoral student, attended School Committee meetings that year and analyzed election results by ward.

He concluded that the Irish usually vote in all elections for their friends, for retaining their jobs, and in 1965 believed that "Negroes overstate their problems." O'Connell described a Boston College Citizen Seminar when "a Negro speaker (asserted) that the Boston schools had been bad for the Negroes for twenty years." The mostly white audience registered a visible shock. "The Irish know the schools are not bad. They know the teachers, they know the system, and they conclude that is the Negroes who are bad—not the schools."[77] Boston's 4,000 teachers and 3,000 other support staff each had a dozen Boston relatives and friends. They resented sharp criticism by blacks and suburban liberals, opposed the call for reform, and at the ballot box fought any plan to upset the status quo.

Two Exit Options for Black Parents

How might black children and their parents leave old and racially imbalanced schoolhouses? Could they leave Boston, or at least break out of overcrowded schools? During August of 1965 Roxbury parents rebelled against the proposed double sessions, the overcrowding, and inadequate facilities. They sought ways to move their children to underenrolled, better schools. Ellen Jackson, mother of five children, emerged as spokesperson. Her articulate presence on television intrigued Ruth Batson who had never met her. Beginning in September 1965, Jackson arranged transportation for 450 children to Hyde Park and Mattapan schools in a program with a name drawn from the Old Testament and redolent of exit, *Operation Exodus*. Mayor Collins offered to pay $1,500 a week for transportation, if the School Committee requested the money. The School Committee was unwilling. For the next two years the parents raised funds in the Roxbury community from bake sales, church collections, fashion shows, benefit nights, and theatrical performances.[78] The Episcopal Church Mission donated $1,500 for one week, and appeals went out to foundations, individuals, parents, and to other churches.[79] Jackson explained the motives as "relief of overcrowding, and improved educational opportunities, not racial integration."[80] In many ways, *Exodus* was both an exit strategy from an unacceptable school yet an expression of continued loyalty to Boston schools, parents assuming that a less crowded white school with available seats would provide better education. That was the hope. In fact, Citizens leader Herbert Gleason recalled that several Boston schools were overwhelmed with black student applications, quietly authorized by Chairman Louise Day Hicks.

The more radical exit option was called METCO, the Metropolitan Council for Educational Opportunity, and required students to leave the city of Boston for schooling. At first, elected school officials in three communities, Brookline, Newton, and Lexington provided the METCO leadership. Brookline School Committee Chair Leon Trilling, an MIT Professor of Aeronautics, in December 1965 proposed a voluntary plan whereby black students might attend suburban schools on the basis of the availability of seats. Newton Superintendent Charles Brown and Brookline Superintendent Robert Sperber wrote a federal grant proposal under Title Three of the Elementary and Secondary Education Act for $259,000 to support an innovative multi-community student exchange program. The Carnegie Corporation contributed another $126,700 for METCO staff. Arlington, Braintree, Brookline, Lexington, Lincoln, Newton, and Wellesley schools made seats available for Boston minority students—240 the first year, then 380, then 1,000, eventually 3,200 participants a year during the 1970s and beyond. Thousands of other black students waited patiently on standby lists. Joseph Killory, a state education administrator, became the first METCO director and Ruth Batson became associate director, succeeding Killory as METCO director from 1966 to 1969. While Killory worked with white suburban superintendents, Mrs. Batson took charge of selecting and counseling students, and arranging tutors for black METCO students.

One injustice Superintendent Ohrenberger corrected was the total lack of black principals. On July 1, 1966 he named Gladys Wood, Roxbury Memorial High School and Boston Teachers College graduate, to lead the Dearborn elementary district including four Roxbury school buildings.[81]

Black parents sought quality education in safe school buildings for their children. During 1966–67 the black community, unhappy about Boston School Committee resistance, created three new urban schools:

The New School for Children, in Roxbury, was led by an experienced Chicago educator Bernice Miller and four teachers for seventy-four students, with the Harvard Graduate School of Education contributing two board members and student teachers searching for an urban school laboratory.

The Roxbury Community School, with forty students, had five classrooms, kindergarten and grades one and two. An underutilized Catholic church housed the school.

In 1967 the Highland Park Free School opened with Luther Seabrook, a New York City educator as principal. The 117 pupils paid no tuition, the curriculum emphasized black culture, and neighborhood residents served as "community teachers" supplementing the paid staff.

Then, the state appropriated money for a Massachusetts Experimental school in Roxbury—the Community Corporation for Educational Development (CCED), with Ophie Franklin, another New York educator, as principal. By 1969 the three independent schools and CCED enrolled 670 children between the ages of 4 and 14. All of the principals were black, as were half of the teachers. Eighty percent of the students were poor, and 90 percent of them were black. Was this a separatist alternative? Yes, these schools were imbalanced, although open to all races.

The Roxbury community also organized a black Montessori school and the Hawthorne House Model Community School (with the Educational Development Center). The *Bridge* program brokered black private school enrollment and college preparation. The Urban School (at the Commonwealth School) in the Back Bay added an evening summer school to help dropouts reenter high school. The Volunteer Education Exchange helped adults return to school offering tutoring, baby-sitting, and other help. Afro House offered free courses in African languages. The Elma Lewis School, organized in the early 1950s, ran programs for black students in drama, dance, and the arts, including a summer Playhouse on the Park attracting crowds of up to 4,000. These were institutions that Boston's black community created while waiting for Boston school officials to take the requested actions.[82]

These new schools and programs were examples of what Mel King described as community "institution building." They started with voice (complaints) and overflowed into pursuit of "exit options," a determined effort to pursue alternatives to white-controlled schools and agencies. They exemplified "exit," the determination to leave an unsatisfactory governmental system and seek better educational options. Black parents expressed their discontent by leaving unsafe and underfunded schools.[83] This was the mechanism Hirschman thought would alert officials to the need to change school policies, theoretically.

Elsewhere, black leaders demanded more voice in governing local schools. In New York City, Detroit, and other cities leaders proposed "community control" of their schools. In Boston, two new school councils included the principal, teachers, and parents. Several Harvard University advisors guided the King and Timilty Middle School councils. When the School Committee assigned two new white principals, the Black United Front threatened to take over these schools. The two Boston principals resigned, requiring the superintendent to appoint two acting principals. The King School experienced considerable chaos that fall, and closed in December to allow time for the staff to regroup.

In September of 1968 the Gibson School, where Jonathan Kozol taught before being fired, also erupted over a new white principal appointed without parent consultation. On September 8, parents led by Sue and Bill Owens (a state legislator and black caucus leader) took over the school as "Liberators," an action denounced by School Committee members Eisenstadt and John Kerrigan as "lawless." Six teachers joined parents and students forming a Liberation School that held classes for two months.

The Boston teachers including Mary Ellen Smith were dismissed, and lost subsequent court appeals. The message from black parents was abundantly clear, "We want a stronger voice in our schools." The School Committee stoutly resisted.[84]

Jewish families, the strongest supporters of Boston schools and of rights for black students, had already begun leaving the city before 1940. Years later, a controversy broke out about whether this was a voluntary or involuntary exit. After World War II Boston was still home to almost 100,000 Jews. Middle-class Jews left for the western suburbs Brookline and Newton increasingly during the 1950s. Once 50,000 Jews could walk from their Roxbury homes to Mishkan Tefila, Boston's oldest (1895) conservative synagogue. The numbers dropped to 20,000 by 1960. Mainly the older, less mobile Jews stayed in Boston.[85]

The Washington Park urban renewal project replaced 2,500 slums on the edge of the South End and Roxbury with only 800 new units. The displaced black families moved south into North Dorchester, a classic case of what was called "Negro removal."[86] They took over housing vacated by Jewish families, including larger homes near Franklin Park. Pressure grew to expand black family access to home mortgage funds. During 1967 Kevin White became mayor and NAACP leader Tom Atkins won a seat on the Boston City Council. State Representative Royal Bolling filed a bill requiring that 40 percent of city mortgages become available for minorities. Boston's black population grew to 90,000 that year. President Lyndon B. Johnson signed a series of federal civil rights bills between 1965 and 1967 and named a black economist, Robert Weaver, as the first secretary of Housing and Urban Development (HUD). HUD guaranteed new mortgage loans to help low-income blacks become homeowners. In Boston, $29 million suddenly became available to build or rehabilitate homes.

Then the Student Non-Violent Coordinating Committee (SNCC) announced that black America's problems were "due to Jewish landlords... and Zionism." After the 1968 King assassination, the Black Panther organization ordered Jewish shops to be closed. In Boston Jewish stores were looted and windows were shattered. About this time Jewish leaders agreed to donate the Mishkan Tefila Temple to Elma Lewis for her school, rather than seek payment for a facility worth a million dollars.

Meanwhile, the Black United Front announced that it was the umbrella organization for all Boston black organizations and organized a rally of 5,000 in Franklin Park. Its fiery young leader, Chuck Turner, asked that white-controlled businesses be transferred to the black community. He demanded black principals and teachers for all of the mostly black schools, the naming of black schools after black leaders, and black control over private and municipal agencies. These strident demands upset

Boston merchants and school administrators, who thought the demands completely inappropriate.

Mayor White, however, urged the Boston Bankers Urban Renewal Group (BBURG) of mortgage bankers, mostly savings and cooperative banks, to expand the numbers of home loans for black families, primarily in neighborhoods still occupied by 40,000 Jews. The banks offered homeowners a good price. Real-estate agents went house-to-house urging a quick sale. Levine and Harmon described a concerted campaign to drive old and poor Jews out of the city using ruthless blockbusting techniques funded by bankers. Unscrupulous realtors told Jews that their neighbors had sold to blacks, that violence was likely, that housing values would fall, and that they should sell their homes before it was too late.[87]

Real-estate turnover affected Mattapan, especially around the Solomon Lewenberg Middle School on Dorchester's Wellington Hill, a 1,200-student school named after a local judge who supported Mayor Curley in the 1920s. This had long been a high-achieving Jewish school, students often transferring to the Latin School. The Lewenberg was also one of the few schools that made empty seats available to black students after 1965. In 1967 the school was perfectly balanced with 450 white Jews, 450 blacks. By 1968, the school housed 220 white and 530 blacks, sharply out of racial balance. Problems erupted. Student extortion rings were reported, food fights broke out, an angry black mother assaulted a white teacher, and the image of the school changed. The Lewenberg suddenly appeared on the state list of forty-five racially imbalanced schools in Boston. Local lumber dealer Arthur Bernstein formed the Mattapan Organization Education Committee to save the school and neighborhood. Lewenberg teacher Allan Cohen wrote grants to organize parents into a school council, mediate the threats, and help the beleaguered principal restore stability to the school. Too late, the Jewish community tried to fight back. Rabbi Meier Kahane, native of Queens, New York, brought in his militant Jewish Defense League with the "Never Again" motto. Forty JDL members showed up at a Boston SNCC meeting with bats and brass knuckles. Their retaliatory tactics horrified as many Jews as blacks.[88]

This was a major displacement of an ethnic group so loyal to Boston and to the Boston schools from the 1890s well into the 1960s. Now the last Jewish families exited, this time to secure their safety. Only the most stubborn families stayed in Dorchester into the 1970s. Were Boston's bankers and realtors the reason Jews left Boston? Peter Blampied, in the 1960s a young assistant to Robert Morgan, president of a large mortgage bank, recalled heavy pressure from federal and city officials to allocate new mortgage money to minorities very quickly. In other words, the White

House, HUD, and state and city leaders ordered a new focus on black family home purchases.[89]

Gerald Gamm offered another response to the question "Why the Jews Left Boston and the Irish Stayed?" He argued that Jews left because it was easy to move and purchase a single family house with a lawn in the suburbs. First of all, Jewish synagogues were never bound to one permanent location. He pointed out that synagogues could be sold, rabbis hired or fired by the local congregation, and a new temple or synagogue built in a more attractive community. In contrast, bishops controlled Catholic parishes, laid out parish boundaries, and assigned the pastors and assistants. In Boston, a series of cardinal archbishops approved clusters of churches, schools, and convents, building long-term loyalty to a Catholic neighborhood. When Catholic families left, they had to return to the old parish for certificates of baptism, confirmation, or marriage, documents the original parish retained.

So keeping a temple or church location was optional for Jews and more often obligatory for Catholics. Roots in a neighborhood were typically permanent for Catholics, but temporary for Jews who moved more easily. Jews, resenting discrimination against them in Europe over many centuries, were willing to sell their homes to black families. Gamm quoted the old and compelling sociological research that "Negroes have pushed forward in the wake of retreating Jews."[90]

By 1950 one-third of Brookline, 17,000 people, was already Jewish. Hebrew Teachers College moved to this tolerant residential town, surrounded on three sides by Boston, in 1951. Then the New England Hebrew Academy, and finally the Moses Maimonides School (Boston's only Jewish day school for decades) relocated to Brookline in 1962. A few miles west, Newton's Jewish population quadrupled by 1960, rising to 27,000, becoming the largest Jewish suburb in Greater Boston. Gamm estimates that Dorchester's Jewish population dropped to 70,000 in 1950, to 47,000 by 1960, and 16,000 by 1970, then to a few hundreds. He attributes the migration mostly to dreams of nicer homes and newer schools.[91]

The impact on the city was dramatic. Four major Hebrew Schools in Dorchester and Roxbury by the late 1940s became insolvent, and were forced to seek loans from the Associated Jewish Philanthropy to avoid closing. Meanwhile, sixteen Dorchester Catholic parishes added schoolrooms during the 1950s. In fact, the Cardinal created three new parishes, since a parish serving more than 10,000 Catholics often became unwieldy.[92]

Gamm believed that Catholics remained in North Dorchester and Upper Roxbury in large numbers, although their actual numbers declined by one-third, from 137,000 in 1950 to 105,000 in 1967. He noted that the BBURG map initially included Catholic neighborhoods and that arsonists burned down several Catholic churches, along with several synagogues. After each incident, the Catholic archdiocese rebuilt the church and stabilized the parish, a strong commitment to Boston neighborhoods.[93]

In fact, Catholic parishes in Roxbury could not hold most of their white Catholic parishioners. According to the official history of the Archdiocese of Boston: "The North, South and West Ends, Charlestown, South Boston, East Boston have seen a steady exodus of Catholic towards southern Dorchester, Jamaica Plain, West Roxbury, Brighton and the cities and towns beyond the Boston line."[94]

Roxbury was the second stop for many Boston Irish after leaving the overcrowded North and West ends of the city. Then they moved a third time to newer neighborhoods. The church historians explained, "To put the matter simply, the Jews have been moving in vast numbers, and the Catholics have been moving out." Also, they described how "that exodus produces a remarkable efflorescence of parishes in Jamaica Plain and West Roxbury," parishes with proud Catholic names such as Holy Name or Blessed Sacrament Parish. Irish Catholic families left an appropriately named Mission Church in Roxbury—its neighborhood turned Jewish, and later mostly black.

Whose explanations about why Jews moved are correct? Brandeis University scholar Leon Jick agreed with Gamm's assertions that "as Boston's Jews moved up economically, they moved to the suburbs."[95] Most Jewish suburbanites left Boston of their own free will. However, block busting accelerated the end of the Jewish exodus from Boston, most of that involuntary. Unquestionably voter support for Boston's public schools eroded, especially after the Solomon Lewenberg and Jeremiah Burke High School lost their predominately Jewish constituency in the mid-1960s.

Observations on Boston's Quest for Racial Solutions

Black Bostonians protesting inadequate schools first tried political remedies such as running for office, the strategy that worked so well for the Irish. Instead, the vocal techniques that attracted state attention eventually were those of the Southern Civil Rights movement: the marches, the boycotts, the push for new laws to outlaw discrimination and racial isolation. Mrs. Batson and Paul Parks were articulate, committed leaders facing a strong phalanx of city resistance from a two-thirds white conservative majority voting in every city election.

The citizens most supportive of the black family cause were suburbanites, Jews, Unitarians, Quakers, liberal Protestants and a few Catholic leaders including clergymen. State Education Commissioner Kiernan was accused of putting together the ultimate good government (derisively termed "goo goo") panel of university presidents and corporate leaders. The Catholic leaders on the study group included Father Michael Walsh of Boston College, Thomas Hennessy, CEO of the Edison, and two prominent Catholics born in South Boston, former Attorney General Edward McCormack and Cardinal Richard J. Cushing.

However, including the cardinal or U.S. House Speaker John McCormack's nephew Edward on a state commission did not persuade South Boston or Dorchester voters to welcome black students in public schools, except at a few underutilized buildings. For the most part Boston voters stoutly and viscerally resisted, reelecting only those school committee members who held the line against black demands.

Frustrated, black leaders raised money for a voluntary busing program within the city, and accepted federal and foundation dollars for a suburban solution. They organized their own community-controlled schools. Mel King described how blacks developed a capacity to build institutions to achieve power and educational opportunity. This happened in the late 1960s. Finally, the increased black population and federal home loans accelerated Jewish exit, punctuated by violence, threats, and unsavory blockbusting techniques. Gamm suggested that Catholic parishes were durable, but certain inner-city parishes could not survive the Jewish or black migrations. Roxbury parishes remained open for black students but with limited resources. Only diocesan support kept three parish schools open for blacks seeking Catholic schooling. During the 1950s and 1960s many Jews and Catholics increasingly sought a better life in suburbia, while the high-pressure blockbusting accelerated the exit of older Jews in a particularly rude fashion. For a city school system under fire, the notion of exit grew increasingly attractive for those families who could afford to move out.

Boston leaders in the 1960s responded to black concerns about schools and housing in several ways—denial of claims at the city level and moderately constructive responses at the state level. Suburban schools, Catholic schools, new community schools, foundations, and the federal government provided a few alternatives, but none of them addressed the fundamental criticism voiced about racially isolated and unequal public schools. These public policy questions remained unanswered into the mid-1970s.

CHAPTER 5
THE COURT ORDERS REFORMS
(1974–89)

Boston black leaders, exasperated with delays over compliance with the Racial Imbalance Act, filed a class action suit in federal court against the Boston School Committee in 1972. The Boston School Committee meanwhile tried to repeal the Racial Imbalance Law, opposing racial integration of schools in the loudest of voices.

More than one judge in state and federal courts found Boston schools out of compliance with applicable civil rights laws. Judge Garrity's federal court ruled that Boston schools violated the U.S. Constitution and ordered immediate remedies. In 1974 Boston's white majority lost, and black plaintiffs won. Suddenly the mid-1970s witnessed a dramatic reversal in roles, white voices seizing every tactic available to protest black parent victories.

By the 1980s, what were the effects of the court order on Boston? On the quality of the public schools? On Catholic schools? Parental voice? On the willingness to appoint black superintendents? On the Boston School Committee itself, its membership and decision-making?

For seven years Mrs. Hicks had stood in the doorway, in effect saying about desegregation "not in Boston." She convinced herself and followers that desegregation in any form would never happen in her city. In Boston the Suffolk Superior Court in September 1972 ordered the Boston School Committee to prepare a plan complying with the Racial Imbalance Act. The court assigned Harvard Law School Professor Louis Jaffe to hold hearings. He recommended a compliance plan for most of the city, but exempting South Boston the first year because that neighborhood was "intensely hostile to blacks."[1]

Each year the Boston School Committee had filed limited racial imbalance plans relying entirely on voluntary transfers (including *Operation Exodus*) and new school construction. The State Commissioner told Boston that the "imbalance" plans submitted fell short of compliance, and he would withhold state funds until Boston's plan was acceptable. Boston sued the

State Board of Education, but a state judge ruled that the imbalance law did apply to Boston and state money was withheld until Boston complied. At this point, the Boston School Committee decided that the correct solution was to repeal the Racial Imbalance Law. They instigated a march of 5,000 white parents on the State Department of Education on April 3, 1973. Public sentiment by that time, even in presumably progressive Massachusetts, had shifted away from civil rights. The legislature in 1972 and 1973 voted to repeal the Racial Imbalance Law; this action was vetoed by liberal Republican Governor Francis Sargent.[2]

The Boston School Committee in January 1974 elected as chairman attorney John Kerrigan, another staunch opponent of desegregation. His fellow members John McDonough and Paul Ellison announced that they personally were "ready to go to jail" rather than comply with a busing order. State Representative Raymond Flynn of South Boston helped Mrs. Hicks organize the "Massachusetts Citizens against Forced Busing," which recruited 200 block captains for each neighborhood. A meeting of 1,400 white citizens discussed resistance tactics including boycotting of public schools and creating alternative private schools, the mirror image of black tactics in the 1960s.[3]

Nationally, President Nixon in March agreed with Hicks and Kerrigan, saying, "Your children can only be educated by you in your home and by the teachers in 'neighborhood schools.'" The U.S. Congress then voted 293–117 to ban federal funds for any busing past the nearest school.[4] Neither the party of Lincoln nor that of Franklin Roosevelt and Truman could withstand mounting Northern white opposition to strong desegregation remedies.

On April 13, 15,000 antibusing demonstrators met on Boston Common to demonstrate against the imbalance law. That day the legislature's education committee held a tumultuous eight-hour hearing. The governor's political advisers told him that his veto would certainly be overridden, and he should propose a moderate substitute. On April 22 State Senate President Kevin Harrington (D) announced his support of repeal. Sargent, on May 10, proposed a new package: state-supported magnet schools, expanded suburban participation, voluntary busing, and extra funds for innovative Boston school partnerships with colleges and universities. The State Board of Education was shorn of all enforcement responsibilities. The governor warned, prophetically, that a court might render this new law moot. Hicks, Flynn, and Bulger on May 29 endorsed Sargent's package, and the watered-down measure passed.[5]

Hicks and Flynn persuaded Mayor White to hold a city voter referendum on whether students could be assigned to any school without consent of a parent or guardian. White agreed, but Governor Sargent vetoed a referendum bill in October 1973 and April 1974. The governor would only authorize a nonbinding advisory vote. On May 21, 1974, 30,789 Boston voters overwhelmingly voted to require parent consent for any student transportation. The strength of this opposition was confirmed in a *Globe* poll (May 1974) showing that blacks favored busing 2:1, Hispanics were opposed 49 percent to 37 percent, and whites 3:1 opposed involuntary busing.[6]

When the NAACP filed its case in federal court, a black student Tallulah Morgan was named lead plaintiff and James Hennigan was the Boston School Committee chairman. Thus, the case became "Morgan versus Hennigan," with hearings conducted during 1973, and decided in June 1974. The federal judge was Wendell Arthur Garrity, son of a white NAACP member who continued a family tradition of naming a son after Wendell Phillips, the great abolitionist leader. Garrity graduated from Holy Cross College and Harvard Law School. John F. Kennedy appointed him U.S. attorney for Massachusetts, in part rewarding his 1960 services as a "Kennedy for President" campaign organizer. Later President Lyndon Johnson made him a federal judge. Garrity was assigned the Morgan case as the result of a judicial lottery. As a judge, he was deliberate, thorough, meticulous, and hated being overturned on procedural or substantive errors. The judge refused public comment outside the courtroom and declined news interviews lest any side remarks prejudice the case. Judge Garrity supervised the Boston "race case" for fifteen years, issuing implementation orders when the School Committee refused to accept his decisions. A series of his appointed experts ("masters") visited schools, proposed remedies, and monitored compliance for the court, but the key decisions were his alone.

Judge Garrity's 1974 written ruling vividly described Boston's illegal actions. He found that the Boston School Committee had "knowingly carried out a systematic program of segregation affecting all of the city's students, teachers and school facilities and had intentionally brought about or maintained a dual school system; that the entire school system of Boston was unconstitutionally segregated."[7] He discovered that Boston had drawn school-building district lines and feeder patterns so that all black elementary schools would feed into mostly black middle- and high schools. The School Committee had acquired space (the Jewish temple) and authorized new buildings either just for white pupils, or only for blacks, in some cases transporting white students past underutilized black schools. Boston had employed less than 4 percent minority staff in a school system already 25 percent black, and relied on an antiquated, unreliable, unvalidated, and inequitable system of staff ratings and administrative promotions. Five education deans and the Harvard-MIT Study had previously documented the last two findings.

Garrity's decision and the entire desegregation movement were criticized for moving students around with insufficient attention to educational quality. However, dozens of his specific orders invited school and citizen leaders to help upgrade schools, select qualified minority staff, and let parents participate in educational decisions. He created opportunities that potentially might lead to better schools.

Legislative gutting of the state board enforcement role made little difference. On June 21, 1974, the last day of school, Judge Garrity announced his decision, citing other federal court precedents under the Fourteenth Amendment. He ruled that both the city and state must comply. Governor Sargent proposed 4 million dollars of state funds to support an orderly implementation.[8]

Judge Garrity decided that desegregation should start the new school year in September of 1974, only seventy days away. Lacking time to devise a new plan, he adopted one that the State Board staff prepared for Boston a year earlier. That would be Phase One. He would arrange for a more comprehensive plan, called Phase Two, for fall 1975. Phase One was the "Short Term Plan to Reduce Racial Imbalance in the Boston Public Schools," desegregating 80 of the 200 Boston schools. The plan required transporting 14,000 schoolchildren, the most drastic component being the pairing of Roxbury and South Boston High Schools. Garrity's adviser, Dr. John Finger of Rhode Island, had drawn up comparable plans for the Charlotte-Mecklenburg (1971) and Denver (1973) court-ordered desegregation. Garrity's order also closed ten of the oldest and least safe school buildings in the city.[9]

The ROAR of Disapproval

White ethnic leaders in Boston were profoundly unhappy with the Judge's decision. The Massachusetts Citizens against Forced Busing group, responding to the court order, changed its name to "Restore Our Alienated Rights" (ROAR), with a lion roaring in protest as the symbol. Mrs. Hicks was elected national president of the new group. ROAR called for a school boycott the first two weeks of school that September. Most South Boston, East Boston, and Hyde Park parents kept their children at home that month, partly in protest, partly fearing violence. South Boston citizens led the vocal opposition.[10]

School was to open September 12, a Thursday. On Saturday, September 7, a 250-vehicle motorcade drove around the city, beginning in South Boston, to build citywide support for a demonstration on Monday the ninth. Ten thousand protesters against the court order rallied on City Hall Plaza near the Federal Building to tell Senators Kennedy and Brooke how upset they were. Senator Kennedy, addressing the crowd and calling for reason, was pelted with fruit and forced to quickstep back to the building, the glass door shattering behind him.[11]

On Thursday, the opening day, South Boston citizens held signs such as "Kill Niggers," "Go Back to Africa," "KKK," and worse. A mob of mostly young men threw bottles and rocks at buses carrying black children to South Boston. Police tried to disperse the mob. In response 300 whites trashed benches and ripped out pay telephones in South Boston's Andrew Square. Police arrested thirty-four protesters.

Reporter Alan Lupo described how Mayor White and his staff that summer consulted with national experts and held meetings in neighborhood homes to prepare for an orderly opening of school. The mayor assigned additional police to protect the schools, including 125 members of the blue-helmeted Tactical Police Force. After stones were thrown at police from a tavern called The Rabbit Inn, reputedly the watering hole of South Boston's notorious Mullen Gang, police retaliated a day later and left thirty-five tavern patrons bloody.[12]

ROAR's "propaganda arm" was the South Boston Information Center, staffed by James "Jimmy" Kelly, an intensely energetic sheet metal worker, committed ally of Flynn and Hicks. Kelly led efforts to start the all-white private South Boston Heights Academy, which in the Deep South would be called a "Segregation Academy." South Boston busing opponents declared October 4 as the "National Boycott Day." All the techniques of "voice" white conservatives deplored in the 1960s were wheeled into action: signs, songs, slogans, marches, and protests, even violence. Hundreds of young white men volunteered for street duty as South Boston "Marshals," challenging the police and stoning school buses. After ROAR proposed boycotting downtown department stores, vandals in 1976 threw torches through store windows to mobilize merchant opposition. They trashed the U.S. Constitution gift shop in Charlestown in protest.[13]

One night 300 anti-busers drove to Wellesley to serenade Judge W. Arthur Garrity. A cordon of police kept protesters from his lawn and house. He received death threats against himself and his family. A Haitian man at a South Boston stoplight was dragged out of his vehicle and badly beaten. Hundreds of State police, Boston's Tactical Police Force, and finally the National Guard were mobilized to try to restore order. National media, especially television, portrayed the "Athens of America" as a strife-torn, violent city, torn to pieces over race.

The major target of the mob was the assignment of black students to South Boston High School. Angry parents and youth acted to make sure the school could not function. Fights broke out and racist graffiti appeared on school walls. White students staged walkouts, most of them fomented by adults. On December 7 a fight between black and white students resulted in the stabbing of Michael Faith, a white student hospitalized for lung and liver punctures. Enraged white students protested the incident in South Boston. At Hyde Park High School 250 students walked out in sympathy.[14]

Most of the noise came from two working-class neighborhoods, South Boston and Charlestown, 8 percent of the city, with a few incidents elsewhere. At 150 middle and elementary schools, the order was quietly, if begrudgingly, accepted by most whites and embraced by most black parents.[15]

Judge Garrity in May 1975, undeterred by protests and violence, ordered a Phase II integration plan for September, increasing the busing from 14,000 to 21,000 students. Most of the bus rides were short, averaging 1.5 miles and 15 minutes in length. He divided Boston into eight community school districts, each one 39 percent black and 61 percent white. Each district had a superintendent and a community district advisory council (CDAC) with twenty members including parents, teachers, police administrators, and others.[16]

Those favoring Boston school desegregation mobilized. On May 17, 12,000 supporters of "quality, integrated education" marched to Boston Common where they joined 20,000 others celebrating the *Brown v. Topeka* desegregation decision 21 years earlier. Planes and buses brought supporters to Boston from Texas, Chicago, and elsewhere. Speakers included Rabbi Gittelson of Temple Israel and Joseph Rauh of the Americans for Democratic Action, along with local and national NAACP leaders Thomas Atkins and Nathaniel Jones.[17] Each side voiced passionate emotions.

Judge Garrity named a twenty-two-member Citywide Coordinating Council to monitor implementation. Martin Walsh of the U.S. Department of Justice Community Relations Service helped recruit and staff this panel. Former School Committeeman Arthur Gartland served as interim chair, with university presidents John Silber (Boston University) and Robert Wood (UMass), Ruth Batson, Hubert Jones of BU, Robert Kiley of the MBTA (Transit Authority), three high school students, and others.[18]

Opponents mustered additional support. The Massachusetts legislature voted to endorse a constitutional amendment to prohibit forced busing. The Boston Patrolman's Association union opposed busing although, while on duty, they were directed to control unruly mobs surrounding beleaguered schools. The Boston Firefighters union, the local Teamsters, the Massachusetts Building Trades Councils all passed resolutions or spoke against busing. Eventually George Meany, president of the AFL/CIO, reminded the Massachusetts unions to abide by the national union policy that supported racial integration.[19]

The School Committee voted to appeal Garrity's decision to the U.S. Supreme Court. They told the judge that they would do only what he specifically directed them to do, openly inviting the hundreds of orders. While observers thought judicial intervention excessive, Garrity felt he had to counter School Committee defiance. School Committee members narrowly escaped contempt of court citations, disbarment of three attorney members, and possible jail sentences that might have made them popular martyrs in Boston.[20]

Journalists wrote vivid books on Boston's busing struggle, between 1974 and 1976, especially Alan Lupo's *Liberty's Chosen Home,* Pam Bullard and Judith Stoia's *The Hardest Lesson,* and the prize-winning story of three families disrupted by the order, *Common Ground by* J. Anthony Lukas.[21] These books, along with Hillson's *The Battle for Boston* told the terrible story of hatred and violence, intimidation and destruction against students, school buses, police vehicles, black and white individuals innocently passing through the wrong neighborhoods at the wrong time in the half decade 1974–79. Boston's Police Commissioner Bill Bratton, then a junior officer, confirmed, "It was anarchy. Racial animosity in Boston had spurred several horrendous beatings and murders." He described "racial tensions" in South Boston as "incredibly high."[22]

The Lukas best-seller graphically described three affected families, but slighted the prior ten-year black struggle to integrate the Boston schools. He painted a picture of a white liberal judge tangling with an intransigent School Committee, suggesting an economic "class" battle rather than a struggle for racial justice and equal opportunity. For Judge Garrity, Ruth Batson, and her neighbors, however, it was always a "race case."

The "battle for Boston schools" was not all black versus white, for courageous white parents supported the judge's desegregation order. James O'Sullivan, a South Boston High School graduate, thanked Cardinal Humberto Medeiros for endorsing the court decision. O'Sullivan, a Gillette Safety Razor employee, served on the Roxbury-South Boston High Council despite his neighbors' pressure to boycott the council. He deplored the "ugly spectacle" of white adults spitting, stoning, and hurling obscene words. "It made me ashamed to be from South Boston."[23] He required police protection to protect his home from white neighbors.

Tracy Amalfitano, also living in South Boston, found bottles broken against her wall and windows cracked when it became known that she favored orderly desegregation. Her family was ostracized, her van firebombed by neighbors.[24] Opponents splashed red paint on the home of Evelyn Morash, an East Boston school activist and Catholic Charities worker. Her family suffered hate calls and threats on their lives. Earlier, State Education Secretary Joseph Cronin nominated Morash to the State Board of Education after critics complained there were no white Bostonians on the board. Fearless, she served as well on the City Wide Coordinating Council.[25] Mary Ann Hardenburgh of Hyde Park, former Boston League of Women Voters president, also served on the State Board. Staunch supporter of Commissioner Greg Anrig's imbalance stands, she and her husband Dan fought for racial justice in city schools.

Thirty years later disagreements continue over why the court order was defied. Without a doubt the opposition to Boston desegregation was based on racial hatred, ethnic bigotry, and deep antipathy to minorities, traceable back to before the Civil War when blacks and Irish immigrants competed for scarce jobs. It was not about busing. Prior to the 1974 decision 30,000 Boston students (a full third of all) rode buses, trolleys, or taxis to school. Boston Technical High School attracted hundreds of white students to a Roxbury site. No one demonstrated against subsidized transportation then. As civil rights advocate Jesse Jackson later summarized the situation, "It is not the bus, it is us."

Globe Editor Thomas Winship, a staunch supporter of Northern desegregation, dismissed Lukas's conclusion that the controversy was all about social class, a punishment imposed by the middle class on white poor and black poor. Winship commented, "From where I sat for twenty-five years, if I wasn't looking at racism, I don't know what I was looking at, racism in the rawest sense." Judge Garrity's adviser Robert Dentler, an urban sociologist, in his review of *Common Ground* declared racism the most important cause of violence in Boston.[26]

Even Cardinal Cushing, life member of the NAACP, explained to State Education Commissioner Neil Sullivan that Boston Catholics "carried with them deep feelings of prejudice and distrust toward black people, and they trusted to too great an extent the leadership of bigoted and narrow-minded parish priests."[27]

South Boston leaders denounced the notion of racism and offered other explanations for their staunch resistance. In the 1970s arguments advanced against racial integration included community preservation for South Boston and the dangers of life in Roxbury. State Representative, later State Senator William Bulger, spoke repeatedly on the damage the court decision inflicted on his South Boston as a community, a section of the city with especially strong family loyalties. He railed against social scientists and planners who upset community traditions. These traditions included traditional football rivalries between South Boston High and East Boston High, St. Patrick's Day celebrations, and swimming at the L Street bathhouse.

The closed nature of South Boston was described in a unique neighborhood anthem that threatens outsiders in one stanza of the song "Southie Is My Home Town":

> We have Biff Mahoneys and Buff Maloneys,
> And clowns who know how to clown
> So, if you want to stay healthy, stay the hell out of Southie
> 'Cause Southie is my home town.[28]

This tune is sung by South Boston's elected officials at such events as the immensely popular March 17 breakfast before the annual St. Patrick's Day parade, celebrating the British evacuation from Boston Harbor early in the American Revolution.

Boston College historian Thomas O'Connor, a South Boston native, suggested an alternative explanation he termed "defensive pluralism" to describe how local groups reassert community ties. He described South Boston in 1974–75 as a sullen, angry Belfast. He thought South Bostonians saw busing as an out-of-town liberal conspiracy, a radical assault on their proud neighborhood.[29]

Another explanation voiced was "safety." Mrs. Hicks and Representatives Bulger and Flaherty characterized Roxbury as a dangerous place. They issued a Declaration of Clarification in 1974 explaining that "there are at least one hundred black people walking around in the black community who have killed white people during the last two years." Crime in Roxbury was such that "no responsibly clear-thinking person...would send his child there." They cited cabdrivers, repairmen, and even medical doctors refusing to go there while an insensitive judge assigned South Boston schoolchildren to Roxbury schools.[30]

Judge Garrity allowed historian Ronald Formisano to read hundreds of angry letters he received during the controversy, many from Boston's elderly who were beaten or witnessed beatings in Roxbury. "They made a hell-hole of Mission Hill (the once Irish immigrant enclave) so let them stay there," suggested one correspondent. White safety was an understandable concern. In 1973 six black males assaulted Renee Wagler, a white woman living in Roxbury, dragged her into a vacant lot, and doused her with the gasoline she brought to her stalled vehicle. Set on fire, she died four hours later. Larry DiCara, city councilor during the 1970s, felt Boston tensed up after that incident, a trauma that would not ease for many years.[31] Meanwhile, South Boston was hardly a community exempt from violence, drugs, and gangs as Michael MacDonald described in *All Souls,* the account of his large family victimized by drug traffickers in the 1970s and 1980s.[32]

Formisano described the hostile reactions of ROAR and other busing opponents as "reactionary populism," a revolt of working-class masses against forces changing their lives in disruptive unpleasant ways, comparable to the negative reaction voiced over urban renewal or plans for new expressways carved out of a neighborhood. Boston workers protested not only busing but also the liberal expansion of criminal's rights, gun control, the abolition of capital punishment and, in Puritan-Catholic Boston, any expansion of abortion and pornography rights. Busing was one more assault on neighborhood and family values, foisting liberal suburban solutions on the powerless city dweller. Mike Barnicle, then a *Globe* feature writer, wrote about one Hyde Park housewife upset with the court order who tried to see Mayor White: "Rita is not a hater. She isn't a bigot. She isn't a racist. She worries about the five kids she's got in this city's public schools and another one in college." She felt powerless and alienated, according to Barnicle, who wrote about working-class perspectives.[33]

More than one leader talked about the reaction to the court decision in terms of voicelessness; on March 26, 1975, Louise Day Hicks said, "We can no longer be lambs, but lions who come forward to have our voices heard."

On October 16, 1974 Representative Raymond Flynn explained to Judge Garrity, "The people of this city feel in their hearts that they have no effective voice or spokesmen before your court." Again, voicelessness is described as the problem.

On September 20, 1975, Reverend Robert J. Boyle, Charlestown pastor, said, "There is frustration on several levels...unemployment, the economic crunch, Vietnam, Watergate, poverty, a feeling that they have no voice in their own destiny."[34]

Robert Coles, Harvard professor quoted another white Boston parent,

> I am not against any individual child. I am *not* a racist, no matter what those high-and-mighty suburban liberals with their picket signs say. I just won't have my children bused to some god-awful slum school, and I don't want children from God knows where coming over here.... We want our children to grow up in a quiet, decent neighborhood...we want to see them off to school and not sit for the rest of the day wondering, are they safe? And will there be a big fight, and are they afraid even to walk home if they miss the bus....Anyway, no one asks us about anything, so I guess we're going to have to learn how to band together and take care of ourselves.[35]

Did Boston's "reactionary populists" accept help from national racist groups? They borrowed KKK slogans, but rejected help offered by Ku Klux Klan emissaries such as David Duke from Louisiana. Nor did the American Nazi Party suggesting "white supremacy" for Boston gain any support. This was Boston's own struggle, and the remedy was not a fascist alliance but greater voice for Bostonians. Of course, Alabama segregationist George Wallace, campaigning for president, ran quite well in Boston, winning 29 percent citywide and over 60 percent in two South Boston wards in the 1976 presidential primary. However, his citywide appeal as a third party candidate in November faded to below 10 percent in traditionally Democratic South Boston.[36]

Was racism confined to the city? Who else did not want black students living nearby or attending their schools? Boston's forty-five suburbs welcomed less than 1 percent minority homeowners during the 1960s and 1970s. The Massachusetts legislature enacted "affordable housing" targets mandating all cities and towns to accommodate their firemen, policemen, teachers, the elderly, and possibly a few low-income minorities. Most affluent towns balked at compliance, still failing to meet minimal 10 percent affordable housing goals thirty years later.

Several suburban towns rejected METCO, the voluntary one-way busing of black students. Winthrop voted not to join METCO. A few towns with crowded classrooms pleaded "no room." The prosperous professional communities of Wellesley and Winchester initially voted "no," only to be shamed into cooperation by ministerial sermons and the positive example of other suburbs. Racial antipathy, the avoidance of having their children learn with low-income people, and the denial of housing for blacks were not just urban phenomena. The college-educated middle-class in the white "suburban noose" around the Boston could be as intolerant as the urban working class.

The upper echelons of law firms, insurance companies, banks, and higher education institutions strongly reflected white only preferences. Until the 1980s few of Boston's law firms hired black associates or promoted more than one black attorney to partner status. The only black Boston bank president ran a small inner-city mortgage bank. After the King assassination the universities recruited more minority students who then encountered few black faculty, staff, and administrators. Ron Homer was the one black banker invited to join the all-white business coordinating committee called "The Vault."

The city slowly turned away from discredited School Committee leaders. Committee members lost credibility after the court order because they could not stop busing, which Hicks and Kerrigan promised could never happen. Chairman John Kerrigan's approval rating in April 1975 fell to 35 percent, his disapproval rating rising to 38 percent.[37] James Colbert, publisher of the *West Roxbury Transcript,* wrote that parents felt hard-line School Committee members "oversold to voters the idea that they would prevent compulsory busing.... That is exactly what happened." He concluded that the Committee "missed opportunities to make revisions in the plan advanced by the State Board of Education."[38]

Paul Ellison, another committeeman, falsified pay slips for a phantom staff assistant to enrich himself, was indicted in 1975, convicted, and removed from office in early 1976. Understandably, public confidence in the School Committee evaporated that year.[39] When the School Committee responded to student violence by hiring security aides, committee members used those positions for patronage, unashamedly hiring dozens of friends who had marched against busing. School Committee members seeking financial bribes from bus companies committed the most hypocritical offense; Committeeman Gerald O'Leary accepted $650,000 in illegal payments for which the FBI arrested him in 1980. Witnesses implicated two other School Committee members, Pixie Palladino and John McDonough, who were indicted but acquitted for insufficient evidence.[40]

The School Committee corruption cases built a case either for the abolition of the School Committee, or the mayor's appointment (if one trusted the mayor to do better), or the enlargement of the School Committee to let unrepresented neighborhoods expand their voice and reduce the baneful impact of citywide politics. ROAR shouted down the second option, and Mayor White's 1974 referendum for an appointed board lost by 20,000 votes.[41]

Brighton Representative William Galvin placed on the ballot the larger School Committee option in 1977. Despite *Globe* support, anti-busers also opposed this measure and delayed approval for four years. The city formally adopted the larger committee option, with citywide and neighborhood representatives, in 1981, to take effect in 1983.[42]

During the 1975 reelection campaign, Kevin White sought Mrs. Hicks's support against State Senator Joe Timilty, his challenger that year and again in 1979. White placed several ROAR lieutenants and Hick's son in minor patronage jobs to buy her election year neutrality. He also appointed her to the city public pension board. ROAR leaders split over whether to support George Wallace or Scoop Jackson for president; ROAR ousted Pixie Palladino from East Boston who attacked Mrs. Hicks for seeking federal funds to help Boston. Palladino, City Councilor Albert "Dapper" O'Neill and John Kerrigan formed "United ROAR" as an alternative to Hicks's "ROAR Incorporated." ROAR thereafter shrunk to a whisper, and the competing groups lost impact.[43]

What was the fate of School Committee desegregation opponents? John Kerrigan, elected to the City Council in 1975, unsuccessfully sought the district attorney's post and moved to Quincy. Mrs. Hicks lost to Kevin White for mayor in 1967 and 1971, served one term in Congress, and was defeated by popular South Boston State Senator Joe

Moakley running as an Independent for the U.S. House (where he served for two decades.) Both Kerrigan and Hicks lost City Council elections in 1977. Tom Eisenstadt was elected Sheriff of Suffolk County but the press reported him living well off proceeds from fees, and he resigned rather than face charges. A School Committee member who found the middle road was Kathleen Sullivan, daughter of Billy Sullivan, owner of the Boston Patriots football team. Sullivan, while disagreeing with the court order, felt the Committee must comply. She was the only moderate in 1975; now others fell in line.[44]

Judge Garrity believed parents should have a voice in helping to bring about peaceful integration of each and every school. He reviewed other federal desegregation decisions and read reports on the Boston public schools, consulting with masters and other experts. A Harvard- MIT report in 1970 had recommended that each school form a school council with five parents, two teachers, and the principal. The council would review school-budget requests, help select new principals, and expand voice for parents on student learning, with results displayed in an annual "school achievement profile."

Each council could send a delegate to an Area Council that would select Citywide Council of twelve parents and six educators. Several Boston schools already had councils, the King, the Timilty, and the Lewenberg middle schools.[45] Mayor Kevin White, advised by Robert Schwartz, endorsed a Parent Council bill filed by the legislative Black Caucus.[46]

Judge Garrity ordered the following three-tiered network of school councils:

1. A Racial and Ethnic Parent Council (REPC) for each school, elected by parents (Phase One);
2. A Citywide Parent Advisory Council (CPAC) to coordinate all of the school and district councils, with forty members, one white and one black per district, plus two Asians, and two Latinos elected citywide (also Phase One);
3. A Community District Advisor Council (CDAC), one for each of the nine districts within Boston, plus community spokespersons chosen by the judge himself (Phase Two).

He asked these councils to support students, teachers, and principals and to send him reports on progress in each part of the city. This network of many "voices" ultimately required 2,000 participating parents, chosen by elections at each school. The Judge consciously chose not to empower the Boston Home and School Association, accurately perceived as a loyal arm of the School Committee.

Donald Montgomery Neill's Harvard doctoral dissertation analyzed the performance of Boston's parent councils.[47] He also examined another vehicle coordinating the three levels of councils, a Citywide Coordinating Committee (CCC). Judge Garrity asked UMass President Robert C. Wood, political scientist and former secretary of HUD to chair the CCC. Ellen Jackson of Freedom House, organizer of Exodus, participated along with other black leaders. Canon Jim Breeden, the Episcopal minister who organized Freedom Schools in the 1960s, served as the CCC director from 1976 to 1978.

ROAR at first tried to intimidate parents from serving on school councils. Nevertheless, Dorchester parents who were opposed to the decision, like Rita Walsh-Tomasini, participated anyway, explaining, "I needed to know what was going on." It was often difficult for black parents to go to evening school meetings in white neighborhoods. The first year only 60 (of almost 200) public schools organized a council by January 1975, and council attendance was uneven.

The CPAC won a few victories, such as removing a Hyde Park High School headmaster who struggled ineffectively to meet the challenges. The judge needed voices supporting desegregation, both as an ideal to be realized and an opportunity for full community dialogue.[48] Hattie McKinnis, a black parent who became a citywide leader, made her two school councils effective instruments. She joined the John Marshall Elementary School Council, then the Grover Cleveland Middle School Council that she chaired. To elicit action, she leaked problems to Boston media when the school system, for example, did not hook up equipment. She discovered that faculty and parents easily could agree on proposals to improve the school library.[49]

In October 1975 only 3,000 (of 80,000) Boston school parents voted for local school councils, filling 1,326 of the 2,000 REPC seats. The main barriers black parents faced were overt racism, the insults, and discouragement voiced by white parents. All the council coordinators were teachers, most of them white including many opposed to the court order. All the CDAC coordinators were white; this racial "imbalance" Garrity corrected in a subsequent order.[50]

Both the independent City Wide Education Coalition (CWEC) and CPAC sought federal grants to help organize councils and train parents, most of them lacking prior experience with advising schools, let alone judges. CWEC, led by former Gibson School teacher Mary Ellen Smith, assisted councils in the white neighborhood. CPAC, meanwhile, helped other school councils. Parents often could not agree on affirmative action or other race questions. However, they found agreement, black and white, on proposals to lower class size and other educational issues.

Arguably, the latticework of councils was overly complex and the councils struggled with reforms promoted by the judge and masters. The judge disbanded the CCC (not the independent CWEC) in 1978 while Robert Wood was Superintendent. In 1981 the CPAC was a victim of internal squabbling over director positions, the staff members fighting among themselves, and councils arguing about class size and school closings (mostly in black neighborhoods). Roxbury, for example, lost its only High School. The schools that were closed were often the smallest buildings, which Mel King and educators such as James Fraser thought had been conducive to good education. The judge's adviser Robert Dentler regretted the CPAC becoming a force for the "status quo in protesting against transfers of principals, reductions in the teacher force, and school closings."[51]

By the end of the 1979 school year, 135 of 150 schools had local REP Councils. Tensions mounted between the districts, the CDACS, and the central office Councils. The District 7 Council became a problem after Charlestown whites ran and spoke up, putting to use the voice mechanisms they earlier shunned.[52]

The most difficult challenge was the court request that Councils monitor classroom instruction. Teachers wanted prior notice of any parent visits and insisted on scheduled appointments. Boston schools were not rigorous at systematically evaluating teacher performance. Neill found that only 3 of the 4,000 teachers were rated unsatisfactory. Principals rarely submitted to evaluation, and like teachers, after three years enjoyed permanent tenured status. What was worse, when vacancies occurred, a white educator would be named "acting principal" which, according to Boston's promotional system, added experience points to one's qualifications for a permanent post. Mel King had been optimistic about councils as a vehicle for parent and citizen involvement. He later criticized their failures, "They blew an incredible opportunity."[53]

Neill concludes that by 1982 councils, despite their potential, became almost irrelevant. However, progressive state legislators still felt the basic concept of parent involvement had potential. As the judge prepared to withdraw from the case, the State Legislature in one of its periodic reform moods mandated school councils for every school in the Commonwealth. Professor James Fraser helped State Senator Gerald D'Amico draft legislation for school councils. Except this time, the Teachers Union insisted that the number of teachers on a council should match parent numbers, learning from New York City where community control led to wholesale dismissal of teachers and principals.[54]

One of the major issues troubling black parents was continued use of old, unsafe, inferior schoolhouses. Would their voices be heard? Judge Garrity ordered more than thirty school buildings closed, including the oldest and the worst of Boston's schools, many in Roxbury where they first housed generations of Yankee children, then Irish, Jews, and finally blacks. Mayor Kevin White completed the major school construction plan that Mayor Collins and Boston Redevelopment Authority (BRA) Director Ed Logue authorized in the early 1960s. The ineffective School Building agency was ill equipped for planning and building new schools. The new Public Facilities Commission (PFC) included the School Superintendent and appointees of the mayor. Kevin White seized upon the new organization and appointed his deputy mayor who chose Malcolm Dudley, an unlikely suburbanite, to get the planning underway. Robert Kenney, a gifted planner who later directed the BRA, followed him. From 1967 to 1983 the PFC and Mayor Kevin White constructed 14 new public school buildings, 2 of them large 1,000-pupil elementary schools, called the Joseph Lee and the John Marshall schools, located to bring whites and blacks to a common site. The Racial Imbalance Law provided a 25 percent state financial bonus for new schools designed to reduce racial isolation; state reimbursement for the Lee and Marshall was, therefore, 65 percent of construction and debt service. Unfortunately, white parents refused to send their children to the attractive new schools, and the remedy of larger schools bridging white and black neighborhoods failed.

The Campus High School proposed by Cyril Sargent in 1962 became Madison Park High School. It might have been the new English High but the School Committee choked at locating this historic facility in black Roxbury. Instead, the Committee placed the new English High on Louis Pasteur Avenue facing Boston Latin School (a more appropriate site for Girls Latin). It was a high-rise disaster, later sold to Harvard as a medical research facility. Robert Peterkin, the first headmaster at the new English High School, said, "It was the worst facility I have ever worked in, totally unsuitable for high school males."[55]

William Pear, a young aide on Cyril Sargent's 1962 task force and later a Public Facilities Commission planner, worked on new Boston schools. He recalled how the new schools actually got built:

> We built a new Jamaica Plain High School because the Boston public school structural engineer Tony Galeota lived there. The new Charlestown High School was paired with Chinatown. West Roxbury High School was a response to heavy neighborhood political pressure on the Mayor. The Umana High School in East Boston was planned as a middle school, but opened as a senior high magnet school paired with MIT for technology, and later reverted to a middle school.

The new schools were not perfect, but replaced old and outmoded facilities. The new William Monroe Trotter, named after a Boston crusader for black opportunity, may have been the most successful, opening as an integrated magnet school.[56]

Too Many Voices?

One question was whether "a strong superintendent could implement court-ordered reform, or would other players thwart the initiatives needed?" Marion Fahey served a four-year term in the 1970s, following William Leary. The Committee allowed neither leader any freedom to comply. The School Committee after 1978 was finally open to outside leadership, hiring a new superintendent who might convince the judge to return school management to the School Committee and superintendent.

That ideal candidate was seen as Robert C. Wood, a Ph.D. urban planner specializing in public administration, an MIT professor who once chaired the MBTA metro system, and became undersecretary of HUD under Lyndon Johnson. Judge Garrity in 1974 asked him, as University of Massachusetts president, to chair the CCC. Wood, having left the state university, interviewed with the School Committee in the summer of 1978 and a few weeks later was elected unanimously, the first outsider superintendent since the Storrow-Stratton Brooks era. He seemed the most likely person to persuade Judge Garrity to leave the Boston public schools. Mayor White was supportive, since his education aide Bob Schwartz had suggested Wood. State Education Commissioner Greg Anrig, who earlier worked with Wood at UMass, waived the state superintendency certification requirements and provided him a $100,000 planning grant.[57]

A new state law, Chapter 633, gave the Boston Superintendent of Schools control over business as well as academic appointments, including the right to nominate only one candidate for each leadership position. Superintendent Wood brought in more than 100 persons to new posts, naming Bob Peterkin his deputy, Boston's first black headmaster who opened the new English High School.[58]

When Wood complied with the judge's 1979 mandate to create a Unified Facilities Plan, he discovered that his plan had to run a gauntlet of seven attorneys, one each from the black plaintiffs, the Boston Teachers Union, the Boston School Administrators, the Boston Home and School Association, the State Board of Education, the State Attorney General, the CWEC, and had to be analyzed by the two court experts, Robert Dentler and Marvin Scott. He recommended closing only thirteen schools, rather than the seventeen the judge's experts wanted closed. The judge declined to approve Wood's plan.[59]

Unfortunately for Superintendent Wood, his two strongest supporters left the School Committee. Kathleen Sullivan Alioto (marrying the former

San Francisco mayor) ran for U.S. Senate, and David Finnegan ran for mayor in 1979. The new committee was much less supportive, with Elvira "Pixie" Palladino strongly opposing both busing and any applications for federal aid, and Gerald O'Leary inordinately interested in bus transportation contracts.[60]

Wood's greatest challenge was opening the new centralized Occupational Resources Center, named after Hubert Humphrey, the great champion of workers and labor. Wood's search committee recommended Colonel Francis Nerone who managed the acclaimed U.S. Army vocational education programs prior to retirement. However, three committeemen (including Palladino) preferred an insider, Carmine Scarpa, headmaster of East Boston High School. On August 7 the Committee refused to accept his nomination, so Superintendent Wood and senior assistants walked out of the meeting. On August 22 the School Committee on trumped-up charges of budgetary mismanagement fired him. Of the Committee, only John O'Bryant and Jean Sullivan McKeigue wanted Wood to stay.

The Judge issued a fourteen-point draft plan for his disengagement from the Boston case in August 1982, but most of the attorneys opposed his plan. In September of 1982 the Federal Circuit Court upheld his facilities ruling but cautioned the judge about his oversight procedures. Until the State Board took over the monitoring chores, the multiple voices of plaintiffs and parties frustrated the most senior of public planners from carrying out leadership duties in a timely fashion. There were too many voices, or as Wood later put it "too many cooks" stirring the pot, leading to disruption and delay of reform initiatives. Everyone seemed to have "legal standing" in court, and nothing important was decided in timely fashion.[61]

Boston city neighborhoods changed dramatically from 1970 to 1980:

Charlestown, home of the Navy Yard, whose 15,400 citizens, mostly white and working class, declined to 13,400 in 1980 (losing mostly school parents). Only 26 blacks lived in Charlestown in 1980.[62]

East Boston was dominated by Logan Airport and two tunnels and its mostly Italian population declined from 39,000 to 32,000 by 1980, a loss of 7,000. Only 326 blacks lived in East Boston, a neighborhood excluded from the court order because of threats to bomb the connecting tunnels.

The Central City included the North and West Ends, Bay Village, and Chinatown, with 20,000 inhabitants. Desegregation here had little impact. Prior to the order the School Committee submitted a plan categorizing Chinese as white students.

Beacon Hill and the Back Bay, the pricey white Anglo-Saxon enclaves, were inhabited by well-to-do professionals, 30,000 people, of whom 90 percent were white, 1,284 black, and 937 Hispanic. Desegregation had little effect on the handful of children who attended public schools.

In South End 125,000 people (110,000 white) resided in the neighborhood by 1980; efforts began to gentrify and restore old townhouses. Superintendent Wood moved his family here from suburban Lincoln.

South Boston, with 38,500 people (8,000 left during the 1970s), by 1980, comprised only one-third Irish.

Dorchester, declining from 107,300 in 1970 to 83,000 in 1980, still remained with 20,000 of Irish ancestry; 39,000 whites had left, replaced by 20,000 blacks moving into the north and west neighborhoods. The increased numbers of black families, despite the court order, complicated the desegregation planning.

Roxbury consisted of 90,000 blacks, half arriving after 1962, after 15 Jewish congregations left. Their schools, many built in the nineteenth century, were those most often closed by court directive.

Hyde Park and West Roxbury totaled 56,000 people, each village gaining 3,000 families, mostly Catholic Irish American, and easily politicized. After 1940, these neighborhoods continued to grow as magnets for teachers, attorneys, and city workers.

In Jamaica Plain and Roslindale, the population of 148,136 declined to 111,712, a loss of 36,000, mostly whites including 18,000 under 19. Some 4800 Hispanics lived in Jamaica Plain, on the edge of Roxbury.[63]

The major white out-migrations occurred in Dorchester, South Boston, Roslindale, and Jamaica Plan, fewer families moving out of East Boston and Charlestown. Of course, many neighborhoods already experienced population decline, families moving to suburbia beginning in the 1920s.

How Much Did Desegregation Accelerate Exit?

Court monitor Robert Dentler rejected Boston's 1974 reported headcount of 95,000 students. He told the judge the 1974 numbers were vastly inflated. As a court-appointed expert, he and Marvin Scott discovered 5,000 names of students either dismissed, enrolled only for a few days, or in some cases enrolled at up to five addresses and counted each time as one. He felt it served Boston well, in seeking state aid for education, to count students more than once if possible.[64]

How substantial was the flight from Boston's schools? Dentler and Scott determined that 10,231 Boston students left the BPS between 1974 and 1978. More than half were white, but another 3,000 were black, and 1,730 were classified as "other." Of this number 1,200 black students enrolled in private schools. Some 3,400 Boston students actually left Massachusetts, 1,200 of them black. Students over 16 who could legally leave high school "dropped out," including 346 black and 390 white. Dentler conceded that, "heavy white flight took place and it damaged not only school desegregation but also the income mix of students and the tax base of Boston."[65] This loss of 12–15 percent students (down to 65,000 by 1980) was substantial, but paled in comparison with earlier massive declines in white school population from 1935 to 1965.

Dr. Christine Rossell, a Boston University researcher, in December of 1975 analyzed white flight in eighty-six northern school districts. She found desegregation only one of many factors, "that in Boston the white school age population declined from 75% of the city in 1964 to 64% in 1970, then to 57% in 1973 (still before the court order) and to 47.8% in 1975."[66] She thought the media and politicians portray as "massive" what might have been minimal, that the court order might be the least of the factors. White families, she thought, sought the larger homes and house lots and social amenities of the suburbs.

Anthony Lukas and others criticized the Roman Catholic Church for allowing parochial schools to serve as refuges for those who opposed segregation. How much of an exit option did Catholic schools provide? And exactly where did the Catholic Church stand?[67] Education Commissioner Owen Kiernan in selecting senior church leaders for his 1963 Racial Imbalance Ribbon Commission approached Catholic Bishop Lawrence Riley. When Kiernan sought Cardinal Richard J. Cushing's consent, he was told, "This is too important for a bishop. I will take this assignment myself." Cushing, his body racked by cancer and other afflictions, attended all but one commission meeting that year and was a staunch advocate for measures to end racial imbalance.[68]

Could a Catholic student move easily from a public school to a parish school? Parishes often saved scarce seats for parishioners using collection envelopes (contributing every week, which pastors could verify). Children of less affluent Catholic parents were often relegated to public schools.[69] In fact, some prosperous families previously using parish schools were moving out to suburbia in the 1960s and early 1970s. Except for a temporary surge of possibly 1,500–2,000 students served during the years 1974–76, the Catholic school population soon resumed a downward trend.

Cardinal Cushing's successor, Cardinal Humberto Medeiros, on April 4, 1970 testified in support of the Racial Imbalance Act.[70] He took advice on racial matters from two prominent black Catholic advisers, Patricia Goler (a Lowell State College dean) who chaired the Archdiocesan Commission on Human Rights and David Nelson, attorney who worked closely with the NAACP. The Diocesan Board of Education on January 25, 1974 (after the state decision, and before Garrity's ruling) voted not to allow Catholic schools to accept white students fleeing desegregation. The cardinal told pastors that only new first grade students could be admitted to Catholic schools. They might admit siblings and black students. Cardinals Cushing and his successor Humberto Madeiros supported desegregation and the court order, even while many pastors did not.[71]

Opponents of busing conceded that the church ban on student transfers worked fairly well, with a few exceptions. Virginia Sheehy, a ROAR lieutenant, complained bitterly of Catholic Church pressure

> which makes you feel immoral. It's the law, they say... I tell them I never read a commandment saying "Thou Shall Bus Thy Child."... Some people have moved already. Some have their kids in parochial school. Someone has a friend or knows a sister (a Roman Catholic nun, perhaps a school principal). You know, there's politics in the church too.[72]

In December of 1972 teaching nuns, members of two large orders, withdrew from dozens of schools, citing fewer vocations and tightening finances. Their Boston departure decision preceded Judge Garrity's decision by two years.

The Catholic press itself was divided. Maurice Ford of the Harvard Law School argued in *Commonweal* that court-ordered busing was constitutional and "symbolically necessary." The Jesuit *America* took a similar position. Michael Novak, defender of Catholic ethnics, in *The National Catholic Reporter* in 1975 called busing "an immoral policy" and "unfair to working people," and an action "against family, neighborhood, class, ethnic and even educational realities."[73]

Bostonians, accustomed to 120 years of Irish Catholic archbishops, were not comfortable with the new Portuguese cardinal, nor was he personally ready for rough and tumble racial politics. School Committee Chairman John Kerrigan, his most abusive critic, wondered aloud whether the soft-spoken cardinal understood English.[74]

Diocesan authority reduced the flight to Catholic schools, even as distraught pastors reported phone calls and numerous petitions for exceptions. The increase in Catholic school enrollments 1974–76 within Boston was 1,500, of whom 210 were black. Another 1,500 Boston students migrated to suburban parish schools, of whom 423 were black, almost a third. Some of the exits represented family moves already planned. Others sent Boston children away to relatives for the duration of racial conflict. By 1977 Catholic school enrollment fell again. Ten Catholic schools accounted for 25 percent of the 1,300 whites accepted by Boston's Catholic schools, and

20 Catholic Schools in the suburbs accepted another 1,000. The cardinal chastised those pastors and principals.[75]

Therefore, Catholic schools enrolled a total of 600 new black students during those 2 years. Mel King was one of the few who thought this trend should be encouraged. St. Gregory's parish school in Dorchester, then all white, had empty seats and enrolled black students. Boston's Catholic schools by 1976 enrolled 4,000 minority students. No one complained vocally about this "black flight."[76]

Glinski concluded that the cardinal and the church did not promote racial understanding very effectively during the desegregation years, though Lukas oversimplified a complicated situation. Total Catholic school enrollments in the Archdiocese of Boston dropped from a high of 153,344 in 1965 to 81,540 in 1974 and to 71,000 by 1980. Desegregation certainly did not rescue for more than three Septembers a Catholic school system in steady decline.[77]

The Larger School Committee

Boston voters in 1981 approved a larger School Committee, expanded to thirteen members, four elected at large, nine by distinct districts within the city as of fall 1984. The new School Committee configuration mirrored exactly the restructured Boston City Council. The Harvard-MIT study team in 1970 assumed that minorities would not gain any seats on the School Committee until Boston chose a larger Committee with district representation. In fact, Boston chose two black candidates, John O'Bryant in 1977, and Jean McGuire in 1981. O'Bryant as a teacher had earlier organized the Mass Negro Educators Association, later renamed the Black Educators Association of Massachusetts (BEAM), directed a Roxbury health clinic, and later became Northeastern University vice president of student affairs. Jean McGuire became the fourth executive director of METCO, the black suburban busing and counseling program.

O'Bryant and McGuire, articulate and vigorous, enjoyed strong support in the black communities. Each had a name that sounded somewhat Irish. Many Irish Americans recognize instantly Irish names with prefixes "Mc" and "O'" and, given five votes, will choose several individuals they recognize and may cast another vote or two for an Irish name. The "Irish name" may be only a partial explanation, but O'Bryant and McGuire actually won 4,000 votes from South Boston precincts. They won even more in West Roxbury, a white enclave where votes for black activists were not automatic.[78]

In 1983 both O'Bryant and McGuire ran for "at large" citywide School Committee seats and won, partly because they were then well-known incumbents, and partly because minorities felt they could elect another minority member from their district as well. Two of the nine districts elected minority women, Shirley Owens-Hicks and Grace Romero, the first Hispanic on the Committee. So the 1984 School Committee became 44 percent minority, four minorities of the nine members.

Two other at-large members served on the prior committee, Kevin McCluskey (a South Boston Harvard graduate employed by the Greater Boston Chamber of Commerce) and Rita Walsh-Tomasini, Home and School Association leader who cared deeply about public schools, visiting one school each week. The larger Committee potentially might discuss education issues.

The new superintendent, Robert "Bud" Spillane, came to Boston in 1981 with substantial experience, several New York State superintendencies (including New Rochelle) and former deputy commissioner of education in New York State. Superintendent in Boston until 1985, he was an outspoken critic of Judge Garrity's intervention in Boston schools. He was also a vocal advocate of improved performance measured by student achievement examinations. When the Committee expanded from five to thirteen members, he felt the momentum for constructive change eroded. At one meeting, after a caustic exchange over guns in school with South Boston Committeeman Joe Casper, the two almost came to blows. After four years, Spillane, unhappy with the larger School committee, accepted the Fairfax County, Virginia, superintendency in February, leaving Boston in August 1985.[79]

The new School Committee chairman, thirty-year-old John Nucci of East Boston, was willing to shake up the system. He won quick acceptance from the Committee for a national superintendency search. Joe McDonough, a solid, quiet insider who took several turns as "acting superintendent" enjoyed some support, but most members wanted to consider other names. Nucci designated Roxbury School Committee Member Shirley Owens-Hicks to head the search; she chaired the personnel subcommittee of the full board. Nucci swiftly assembled a blue-ribbon recruitment panel including State Education Commissioner Jack Lawson, UMass Boston Chancellor Robert Corrigan (Hick's nominee), CWEC Director Ellen Guiney, Mayor Ray Flynn, Boston Teacher President Ed Doherty, an Hispanic leader, two business representatives, three parent leaders (one with a special needs child), and a student leader. Of the nineteen (including the three School Committee officers), seven were black or Hispanic. Five School Committee members served on the search committee.[80]

An Illinois executive search firm winnowed the fifty-four nominees to three deemed highly qualified. One was Hispanic, Peter Negroni, a bilingual education expert from New York City. Another was Larry

Cuban, white, who had left the Arlington Virginia superintendency for the Stanford University faculty. Laval Wilson, black, had been superintendent at Berkeley, California and then at Rochester, New York. School Committee members visited each of their cities.

Laval Wilson was described as a "stern, no nonsense educator" who felt that students lagging behind should attend school extra hours each day and on Saturday to make up the difference.[81] Committeeman Joe Casper, South Boston undertaker, quickly perceived that Wilson was the most conservative educator. O'Bryant was thought to favor Negroni, whom he supported in 1981. A *Bay State Banner* editorial supported Wilson, asserting that Boston needed a black superintendent, an opinion echoed by NAACP President Jack Robinson. Blacks favoring Negroni accused the *Banner* and the NAACP of bullying the Committee and favoring "skin pigmentation."[82]

What a difference from the 1963 search, only twenty-two years earlier, where Harvard's Herold Hunt thought only white Catholic candidates would be seriously considered! The three finalists were Hispanic, black, and Jewish. O'Bryant concealed his own preference until the very end. Mayor Flynn remained neutral. The business community played a minor role. The committee members essentially expressed their own personal convictions. On July 31, 1985 the School Committee voted 9 to 4 to appoint Laval Wilson, with Negroni winning 4 votes. Edwards concluded that race (the Morgan case) and collective guilt were factors, but that Wilson's focus on basic education skills was decisive in his winning over the white majority. He credits Nucci's aggressive and progressive leadership for opening up the process, but, in the end, all of the white conservative Catholic members voted for Wilson. Ostensibly, Laval Wilson's appointment was a signal to the nation that Boston was no longer a city school system antagonistic to blacks. Second, the decision again alerted Judge Garrity that he might end his oversight of Boston's schools.[83]

Wilson's superintendency was as mainstream as supporters predicted. He was a "bulldog" on educational issues, a tireless worker developing a comprehensive plan with dozens of detailed recommendations aimed at strengthening the curriculum. Rejecting school-based management, Wilson was a centralist who believed that ultimate responsibility for delivering education was his, not that of some local school council.

City voters for a while appeared to accept the larger School Committee, with one exception. Grace Romero was indicted for falsifying signatures on her School Committee nominating papers. She was considered unpredictable by School Committee colleagues; an articulate black woman named Juanita Wade replaced her. The other School Committee incumbents were all reelected, none of them punished at the polls for their superintendency selection. This was the new Boston, after the court order, either more racially tolerant or accepting of the reality that black parents had won the right to share leadership.

Over time, three of Wilson's strongest supporters left the School Committee. Boston school test scores did not improve measurably. Edwards later summarized Wilson's contributions: "Early learning centers, appointments of minority directors of facilities and food services, and an Asian zone superintendent. Wilson's overall education plan won national acclaim, the Timilty middle school ('Project Promise' with a longer school day and Saturday classes) earned a President's Award for Excellence, and he replaced Phase II busing with the controlled choice student assignment plan."[84]

What Wilson did not do was implement a school health services plan advanced by Hubie Jones, leader of a city social services collaborative. Wilson cut $285,000 from Spillane's school-based management, favored by business. He did not cultivate support from black ministers or from Mel King, regarding himself not as a black educator but as an educator "who happened to be black." He worked incredibly hard, delegated few tasks, and assumed he would be respected for his contributions.[85] His demeanor expressed the old Boston Puritan values, a conservative Calvinist committed to extra effort and longer hours. However, the School Committee, frustrated by stagnant test scores, in 1989 ended his superintendency.

John O'Bryant moved very quickly to select another black superintendent, Lois Harrison-Jones, a school administrator from Texas, the first black woman superintendent for Boston. Her professional expertise was curriculum development. She stayed for four years, locked in by contract, much to the discomfort of a new appointed School Committee impatient to break the old school department mold.

The expanded School Committee provided added voice but not much else. Three of the nine voting districts accounted for fully half of the public school children in Boston (Roxbury, Mattapan, and Dorchester). In another three districts (Roslindale, West Roxbury, Charlestown) almost half of the school-age children went elsewhere to school. Those neighborhoods were presumably entitled to representatives, too. This may explain why two districts elected Catholic school educators, Dan Burke and John Grady, to the School Committee. Arguably this Committee represented all city parents, although not necessarily the public system.[86]

Unfortunately, in the late 1980s and early 1990s the School Committee got carried away with their status as a public board structured similarly as the city council. They wanted not only higher salaries for themselves but also additional staff, like the City Council. School Committee staff expenses rose to 1 million dollars a year. Committee staff members constantly barraged school department staff with questions, chores, and distractions, consuming valuable time and competing with the management of the schools. "Unwieldy" was a gentle description. Edwards, reviewing official minutes, found the Committee still made hundreds of detailed personnel decisions about faculty and custodial appointments, transfers and contracts. Few policy issues were discussed, let alone decided. Even acceptance of the new and more palatable desegregation "choice" plan was delayed many months.[87] The School Committee showed little appetite for discussions of school quality, the curriculum, or the program evaluation reports required by federal and state education officials. The Committee, little changed since the 1930s, remained primarily a school personnel board rather than a board of education. But, after Judge Garrity's rulings on race matters, the larger School Committee on two occasions selected out-of-state black educators to run Boston's schools.

The Suburban Exit Strategy: METCO

With minorities filling two seats, which made up 40 percent of the old five-member School Committee by 1981, rising to four members in the 1980s, and selecting two black superintendents in a row, why would black families still send their children to white suburban schools? One might envision a new surge of black loyalty to the Boston public schools? METCO instead, after the 1960s, grew from 300 to 1,000 students, and eventually to more than 3,000 a year, supported by state appropriations. How popular and effective was it? An early evaluator David Armor reported that 80 percent of the black METCO students went on to college, but he thought true racial integration had not been achieved. Black leaders denounced his "evaluation" as severely flawed. Two METCO directors, Ruth Batson and Robert Hayden, wrote a much more positive twenty-year history and concluded the opposite, that METCO achieved far more than founders hoped—the quest for a better education for thousands of inner-city children.[88]

To evaluate METCO required an independent scholarly assessment performed by Susan Eaton of Harvard University. Over the first 25 years, 1965–90, 4,300 black METCO students graduated from high schools in 32 suburbs in which they did not reside. As late as 1990 one-third of Boston residents were minority (24 percent black, 11 percent Hispanic) while only 1 percent of suburban residents were black. Meanwhile, by the year 2000, 77 percent of Boston school pupils were of color (50 percent black, 27 percent Hispanic). METCO provided an alternative, a way out for 1 in 10 of Boston's 30,000 black children each year.[89]

What did the students gain from METCO? Eaton's interviews with sixty-five METCO graduates revealed that suburban schools usually assigned more homework, and focused more on college preparation and

SAT test taking. Suburban schools not only taught academics but also how to "make it" in a majority-white setting, a microcosm of the real adult world. Many METCO students gained a network of suburban friends to help them conduct business in the white-dominated city, state, and region. The disadvantages included diminished teenage friendships with neighbors and cousins, exposure to vicious racism (the epithet "nigger"), excessive time on school buses (students rising as early as 5 a.m.), and the ambivalence of having to "talk white" at school, "black" at home. Some METCO alumni reported there were days when they hated the program. A percentage dropped out, pursued a General Education Diploma (GED), or transferred to a less demanding school. METCO did not work for all students.

However, 90 percent of METCO graduates applied, were accepted, and attended college, an impressive figure approaching that of the Latin Schools, which admitted a few hundred new students each year, only a third of them black. Did METCO students turn their back on Boston or on their black origins? Large numbers of METCO graduates, Eaton reported, returned to Boston or lived in multiracial neighborhoods, and gave back as urban volunteers or community workers what they gained from METCO. Almost all METCO graduates told Eaton they would enroll sons or daughters in METCO, despite the considerable sacrifices. Some would consider independent or charter schools, preferably in the city. Black parents wished that suburban schools enrolled more students of color.[90]

As the new century dawned, 300 new METCO students were selected each year while 13,000 Boston applicants languished on a waitlist. If enough suburban seats were available and all could go, almost 50 percent of Boston's 30,000 black children would select suburban schools. This is a devastating comment on the magnetism of Boston Public schools twenty-eight years after desegregation, and twenty-three years after the election of black School Committee members and superintendents. Winning more "voice" on desegregated school councils did not generate enough improvement nor expand parent loyalty to city schools. Black students wanted greater opportunities to be challenged academically, and did not feel satisfied with many Boston schools.

Critics accused METCO of draining support for city schools, eroding black self-esteem, competing with neighborhood causes or black causes. Eaton's interviews found the opposite, that METCO graduates subsequently cared about their city and their neighbors.[91] METCO's popularity and later success of most METCO students suggests that this exit was, for one-tenth of the black students, a highly effective by-product of the racial imbalance/civil rights movement. It required acceptance and receptivity from thirty Boston suburbs. METCO remained voluntary, the least controversial of desegregation remedies, and a dramatic example of student choice and parental exit from a once stagnant school system. The purpose of enrolling in METCO, black parents and children said, was to secure a better education. METCO alumni did not view it as suburban desegregation, although presumably the social and educational benefits included expanding the racial sensitivity of suburban youth.

METCO was not the only program exporting black students out of the city. The program called A Better Chance (ABC) enrolled several hundred minority children in New England prep schools, Andover, Groton, and Milton Academy among others, often residential. ABC prepared students for highly selective New England colleges that between 1980 and 2000 boosted their minority enrollments above 30 percent. Massachusetts in 2006 elected an ABC alumnus, Deval Patrick, graduate of Milton Academy and Harvard, governor.[92] ABC included many Asian high achievers. The children of the well to do attending private schools escaped court-ordered busing, but studied with other races.

Boston's BRIDGE program recruited black and Hispanic children to Catholic schools with vacant seats and the willingness to take minorities whose parents supported firm discipline, rigorous academics, and completion of homework. Cathedral High School in the South End reached out to Hispanic youth. The most selective Catholic high school, the Jesuit Boston College (BC) High School, by the late 1980s took aggressive steps to recruit black, Hispanic, and Asian boys, including scholarships, to what was the white Catholic equivalent of the Latin School. The BC High multiracial enrollment rose to 100, the total percentage to 10 percent by 2000 and to 13 percent by 2004.[93]

The Long-Term Effects of Desegregation

Most of the public attention was on court-ordered busing, and especially on the violent South Boston High-Roxbury High School exchange. Without question, this initial pairing was a social disaster, the mixing of youth from three Southie white housing projects and three Roxbury black housing projects. It did not work. A few years later Roxbury High School closed, the building converted to a middle school. South Boston High eventually emerged from receivership with a new headmaster and achieved stability. But as Professor Jaffe, former Attorney General Ed McCormack and others (including Mrs. Batson) feared, the court plan for pairing those two high schools was doomed from the start.

Was South Boston High School destroyed by the court receivership? Dentler reported that attendance at South Boston High School in 1980 rose from 60 percent to 78 percent, with 45 percent white, 46 percent black, and 8 percent Hispanic. Under Headmaster Jerome Winegar, South Boston became a viable high school. Winegar acknowledged that Mrs. Hicks, Senator Bulger, and Councilor Ray Flynn behaved well and did not interfere with efforts to restore South Boston High School as a multiracial high school. Jonathan Kozol described to federal educators a successful South Boston High School.[94]

One major effect of the court order was accelerated flight of more than 10,000 whites and a few thousand blacks from the Boston Public Schools. Off they went, to suburbia for the most part, just as many thousands had moved out of Boston before the court order. Some attended private schools. Some left the state, a few families transferred by the military or corporations such as IBM. So was desegregation a necessary intervention? What of any value resulted from the orders?

Robert Dentler and Marvin Scott listed as one major accomplishment increased teacher desegregation. While the total teaching force shrank from 5,443 to 5,064, the number of black teachers rose from 500 (10 percent) to 872 (18 percent) by 1979. The number of bilingual teachers, mostly Hispanic, increased from 211 in 1975 to 299 (6 percent) in 1979. Teachers of other races rose from 33 to 158, a multiethnic mix better than in comparable American cities.[95]

Also, Judge Garrity ordered the closing of many antiquated, substandard, even dangerous school buildings. The court closed forty buildings over five years, as well as thirty school annexes and portable units, all of them "unfit, outmoded, and antithetical to good teaching and learning." Eight new Boston public schools (eventually fourteen) were opened, financed by Massachusetts Racial Imbalance Act state aid, and fifty other schools were repaired.[96]

Dentler reported a dramatic decline in minority student suspensions, expulsions, and non-promotions due to a new, clear code of student discipline.[97] Also, the order ended discriminatory race assignments of teachers and students, the crux of the case. One bonus was the creation of magnet schools with attractive themes or special resources, such as the William Monroe Trotter or the two-way bilingual school, the Rafael Hernandez. Another boon was the greater participation of employers, universities, and cultural organizations, many of which avoided working with Boston schools until the judge invited their support.

The role of patronage in selecting teachers and principals markedly declined, dramatically after a 1973 decision by the Boston Teachers Union no longer to buy tickets to School Committee member parties and testimonial events, which helped break subservience to elected officials. Desegregation ended "whites only" favoritism. School Committee Members McKeigue and McCluskey turned down the traditional cash-filled envelopes offered by donors who thought all School Committee members accepted tribute money.[98]

Dentler reported great improvements in the transportation system, but a Northeastern University study of Boston schools in 1991 showed that even greater efficiencies could be achieved. Dentler also thought that communications had improved with Bob Wood's appointments of Elizabeth Cook and Mary Ellen Smith as Community Relations directors, but Smith resigned in frustration two years later. The Boston schools became more responsive to the media and eventually to parents as well.

Dentler bluntly complained that the quality of instruction in Boston remained the greatest continuing failure after desegregation. Staff development, the in-service training of teachers, he described as inadequate before the court order and remained poor afterward, with few exceptions. Student counseling and psychological services remained serious problem areas into the 1990s.[99]

As Judge Garrity once explained, this was mainly a "race case," one where laws and court precedents allowed him to sweep away racial barriers. He could not redesign education or make teachers better instructors. All he could do was offer black students the same access to instruction available to white students. It would take state legislation in the 1980s and 1990s to raise expectations and standards for all education programs.

Twenty years later, white parents challenged the court-ordered racial preferences for Boston Latin School and Academy, effectively eliminating Garrity's black 30 percent "set aside" access to exam schools. The city schools resegregated when fewer young white families stayed in the city. The black student numbers (28,000) remained remarkably constant over 30 years. Hispanic, Brazilian, and Cape Verdean students increased substantially between 1980 and 2000 to more than 20,000.

How Costly a Victory?

Additional school transportation costs were only the most visible expense. The City of Boston in 1975 paid $13 million in unbudgeted overtime for police officers. When police costs rose to $29 million a year, Mayor White warned that the court order would bankrupt the city.[100] During 1976 Mayor White announced that school funds had run out and schools would close early.

Judge Garrity directed Mayor White to find another $13 million to keep the schools open. White proposed a major property tax increase to the City Council, which their members rejected. Finally, the judge invoked a statute requiring state funds to cover compliance with a federal court order, and the schools remained open.[101]

In 1980 a commercial real-estate owner named Norman Tregor successfully argued before the State Appellate Tax Board that Boston commercial property owners were taxed at a higher rate than residents. He won, and the Tregor case decisions cost Boston more than $45 million in tax refunds. Mayor Flynn froze the Boston School budget at $195 million, denying to teachers recently negotiated raises.[102]

Also in 1980 the citizens of the Commonwealth voted to place a percentage cap on property tax increases, Proposition 2 ½, in the same spirit as Proposition 13 in California some years before. In 1980 Boston's property tax generated 67 percent of all city revenues. This ballot initiative required cutting the local tax levy by 15 percent per cent each year, $185 million over three years, severely squeezing the schools, fire, police, and other city services.[103] Tregor and Proposition 2 ½ dramatically reduced the capacity of Boston to pay for education. State aid including school funds increased in the 1990s, eventually making up much of the difference.

After the third year of desegregation, public safety costs declined. Transportation expenses added 10 percent to the costs of schooling. The new buildings, however, were larger, cleaner, and easier to heat and maintain. It had been costly to perpetuate so many small segregated schools in the 1970s.

If busing were viewed as a war, both sides took casualties. Innocent people, students, passers-by, and at least one policeman died during 1974–76. Hundreds were wounded, physically or psychologically. Thousands left the public schools, and thousands left Boston entirely. Mistakes were made. One of the strongest defenders of busing, Gary Orfield, calls the 1974 Boston plan "perhaps the least successful in recent years" and "explosive" in pairing South Boston High with Roxbury High.[104]

Ruth Batson, before she died in 2004, said that the desegregation struggle was worth the effort. Before 1975, "they gave us the old schools, the out of date textbooks, the least experienced teachers, and denied us access to the schools of our choice." It may not have been a perfect decision, but it was a strong blow for equal opportunity in Boston. Who lost credibility? After the state declared racial imbalance illegal in 1965, the Boston School Committee misspent nine years of precious time, refusing to let black students enroll in underutilized white schools. Eventually a disenchanted Boston electorate ended the political careers of those school officials who fought desegregation.

The Garrity plan, legally sound, contained several logistical flaws. In retrospect, he should have listened to his own appointed masters: Keppel,

Willie, Spiegel, and McCormack. They felt the pulse of the city, and their slightly less ambitious plan would have reduced the worst tensions, the violence, and the loss of faith in city school integration. The Boston schools never reached Cyril Sargent's buoyant projections of 100,000 students in the 1970s. They stabilized at between 58,000 and 63,000 for the rest of the twentieth century. Newcomers to Boston thought long and hard about enrolling children in a school system notorious for contentiousness and violence. Most immigrants who came to Boston and used Boston's public schools had little choice in the matter.

After the oldest, most dangerous buildings were either torched or demolished, the inner-city neighborhoods lost their access to convenient schools. So did affluent Beacon Hill and the Back Bay. Most blacks were bused a considerable distance from their homes, making parent involvement in school affairs more difficult. Not until 2000 did the mayor and superintendent propose building five new inner-city schools and expand provisions for students walking to school.

Boston had to overcome racial isolation, the New England equivalent of apartheid. Boston did grow more tolerant of racial differences, and the need to end racial separation in all public facilities. Raymond Flynn of South Boston ran for mayor in 1983 and defeated Mel King in the November election. Flynn took a Master's degree with Professor Charles Willie at Harvard University, the Garrity master, and sought his advice on the "controlled choice" student assignment plan, more acceptable than earlier state plans. Flynn became a statesman, a moderate on racial matters, implementing desegregation of city housing projects. Flynn's new appointed school board had a majority of citizens of color, chaired initially by former NAACP activist Paul Parks. This was for Boston immense progress.

After Cardinal Medeiros died, his successor Cardinal Bernard J. Law supported Flynn's efforts to implement racial integration of public housing, including formerly all-white projects in Charlestown and South Boston. Despite the unpopularity of this action, no one wanted a replay of the violent 1970s. The planning was solid; the implementation took hold. A few black advocates argued for separate cities, one Boston for whites and one for blacks (the proposal to make Roxbury and Mattapan "Mandela" lost). Housing apartheid in Boston was officially dismantled.

Boston, like other big cities, appeared unable to solve intractable problems without resort to litigation, a court order, and receivership. Reliance on parent "voice" neither solved the problems nor effectively implemented the court decision. Perhaps the issue of racial justice required stronger measures, judicial oversight to enforce the Constitution. Ending segregation in

Boston schools and housing were two racial issues finally addressed and resolved only through court intervention. Another insoluble issue, which neither executive agencies nor elected officials could handle, was the cleaning up of Boston Harbor even when continued wastewater pollution seriously threatened public health. Certain unpopular public policy solutions on occasion require judicial intervention and persistent court monitoring to ensure compliance.[105]

Boston's police and fire departments also implemented court orders to integrate racially the lower ranks as well as command positions. At the end of the century firefighters were still resisting, and a task force chaired by former State Secretary of Public Affairs Kathleen O'Toole recommended a civilian commissioner to "change the culture." Mayor Menino adopted several recommendations, and in 2004, invited O'Toole to become police commissioner.

Housing values plummeted in the years after Boston's desegregation court order. But during the 1980s they came back, and during the 1990s soared to heights unimaginable, not only in West Roxbury and Jamaica Plain, but also in South Boston which, like the South End, "gentrified." Desegregation initially reduced the desirability of Boston homes but mostly during the years of violent protest, ending a decade later when opposition subsided.

The City Council at the end of the century included an amazing melange of veterans of the civil rights battles: Chuck Turner, the organizer of the Black United Front, argued in meetings with Jimmy Kelly, council president, alongside another South Bostonian, Mayor Flynn's former Police Commissioner Mickey Roache. Collectively they represented the full spectrum of Bostonian public opinion.

Boston educators were seen as respected leaders after Judge Garrity's decisions. Before desegregation Boston public school educators ended their professional careers in Boston, with few exceptions. Other communities rarely considered hiring administrators from the old decadent and reportedly corrupt school system. After the court order, Boston's educators provided local superintendents for Brookline, Canton, Milton, Cambridge, Brockton, and Shrewsbury (Dr. John Doherty, former BTU president). Diana Lam, former Boston principal and deputy superintendent led the Chelsea, Dubuque, San Antonio, and Providence city schools. Bill Leary, leaving Boston, ran the schools of Gloucester, Rockville Center Long Island, and Florida's Broward County (Fort Lauderdale). Laval Wilson accepted New Jersey and New York superintendencies. Once the boil of school corruption was lanced, Boston school administrators became eligible to lead school systems elsewhere.

The city and its public schools were for a decade traumatized by the court decision, but eventually both came back. Chapter 8 examines the role that the business community took in raising educational standards and student achievement expectations for Boston schools. Chapter 6 reviews the city school reform initiatives of area universities.

CHAPTER 6

UNIVERSITIES SPEAK UP

Cambridge University graduates founded both the Boston Latin School and Harvard College in the 1630s. One might assume local universities kept up an intense commitment to Boston's public schools for the next 370 years. After all, colleges and universities admit their high school seniors and prepare teachers for city schools. In fact, all but two universities lost interest in Boston schools during the 1930s and, for a generation, the Boston system turned inward, ignoring all but Boston College and Boston State Teachers College.

Did university leaders realize they had lost touch with city schools? Harvard President James B. Conant in 1938 was upset that "American universities have avoided a wholehearted or systematic attention to public education at the school level...yet such an effort is imperatively needed."[1] He kept Harvard's tiny school of education alive during the lean years of War and Depression. But in the 1950s Harvard turned its attention to schools of the growing suburbs, such as Lexington, Concord, and Newton, ignoring the declining cities.

Boston, meanwhile, clung to old and presumably proven methods of instruction. The Boston State Teachers College trained most of the new elementary school teachers. The new high school teachers, once prepared mostly at Harvard, in the 1960s came increasingly from Boston College (of the 150 BC student teachers in 1968, Boston hired 109). Local Catholic women's colleges, Regis or Emmanuel, were also favored. Harvard and Tufts Universities prepared fewer than twenty new Boston teachers each year in the 1960s.[2]

Many universities awoke from their slumber during the 1960s when national foundations began to finance studies of urban education. Lyndon Johnson's administration invested substantial federal funds in city schools. University professors on short notice voiced "expert" recommendations. After the 1974 desegregation order, additional Boston area colleges and universities stepped up, offering assistance to Boston's schools.

Superintendent William Ohrenberger was both humble and astute enough to seek advice from universities. Even before his 1963 appointment it troubled him that a few outspoken Harvard professors thought so poorly of the Boston schools. An aggressive competitor, he used the leverage of foundation and federal funds to build constructive alliances with area universities. Theodore Sizer, Harvard's School of Education dean during 1964–72, recalled Ohrenberger phoning to propose lunch at the Faculty Club, ostensibly to discuss his own children's education, but actually to seek Harvard support for new federally funded projects.[3]

Ohrenberger's 1965–66 Annual Report (his third year as superintendent) listed Boston's new university collaborations including Northeastern University's linguistics program at Jamaica Plain High, and Boston University's (BU) advanced calculus course offered at two high schools. BU also consulted on a new music program for the Boardman Elementary School, and helped design a new Horace Mann School for the Deaf. Boston College agreed to partner with a multiservice center serving low-income families in Charlestown. Tufts conducted research on raising the skills of Boston's Special Class students. The Harvard Graduate School of Education developed junior high courses in modern grammar.

By 1968 the number of Boston area colleges collaborating with city schools grew from six to twenty-seven.[4] Of course, many professors and even university presidents were inexperienced in helping city school systems. Dean Sizer described an unusual 1966 confrontation when Harvard invited the Boston School Committee to dinner to try to break the Racial Imbalance impasse. Harvard president, Nathan Pusey, Dean Sizer, and others felt that "the stakes were too high" for Boston, the state, and Harvard not to seek areas of agreement. However, School Committee member John Kerrigan arrived at Harvard's Holyoke Center dining room dressed completely in green, socks, suit, tie, even to his shoes, a burly leprechaun visibly spoofing the Harvard crimson. Louise Day Hicks, by then an accomplished critic of assaults on "neighborhood schools," laid low Harvard's president as she did anyone who suggested that Boston accommodate either the state rules or black advocates for desegregation.[5]

Ohrenberger was the first strong inside voice for university collaboration. Then, early in 1967, new Boston School Committee chairman John J. McDonough asked the superintendent and staff for ideas for his inaugural remarks. His opening comments announced new possibilities: "Within recent years we have seen the awakening of the public to the problems of education. Prior to the 1960s *the public slumbered peacefully, secure in its faith that its school system was properly educating its children*" (emphasis added). He acknowledged that the news media, business, and others now questioned the system.

Chairman McDonough proposed six one-year graduate degree grants for administrator study at Stanford, Columbia, Harvard, Chicago, Michigan State, Oregon, and Northeastern, Boston University, and Boston College. Why Stanford? The superintendent told him two Boston administrators could study at Stanford on a federally funded Great Cities research project. Suggesting six national universities was an unusual stroke. Even more remarkable was McDonough's comments that this "may avoid the dangers of stagnation and inbreeding," an astonishing admission of reality.[6] In fact, one Boston principal studied at Stanford with Professor H. Thomas James, and beginning in 1968 Harvard awarded doctoral fellowships to two Boston staff members each year for the next seven years. One of them, William Leary, after doctoral studies at BU and Harvard, became Boston's superintendent during the desegregation years.

The urban challenges of the 1960s attracted the attention of universities to city problems. The Ford Foundation and the federal government provided major grants for university experimentation on urban issues including "de facto school segregation," low student achievement, and community schools. Harvard won many urban study grants on housing, city planning, and schooling. Harvard's Sizer assigned staff to work on Boston school projects in the late 1960s including the King-Timilty Council and the Boardman experimental subsystem, programs preparing parents to participate with teachers and principals in school decision-making, aimed at providing the "voice" once denied black parents.

The Danforth Foundation in 1968 financed studies of urban school decision-making in five cities: New York, Chicago, Los Angeles, Columbus, Ohio, and Boston. The central question was, "How do city school boards get the information they need to make decisions about urban schools?" especially in the face of militant teacher unions, aggressive civil rights advocates, and other contenders for power and influence.[7]

The Massachusetts Advisory Council on Education (MACE), a new state watchdog agency, also decided to study Boston schools. MACE Director William Gaige asked that Boston put up at least a token amount ($12,000 to match $70,000 from the state) to make the city a stakeholder. Richard Hailer, Boston Latin and Tufts University graduate, returning from a Peace Corps assignment, offered to work with the Danforth Boston school study. Negotiating the state and city contributions, he led the arm of the Harvard-MIT study addressing Boston school management problems. His older brother Fred Hailer served as a city councilor a decade earlier; Dick Hailer knew how Boston worked and those who knew his family trusted him.

Previous surveys of city schools from 1910 to 1945 assumed what was good for students and schools. The 1968–70 Boston study began by asking a sample of Boston parents what they wanted and what should change. This time a university study tried to discern the voices of school parents prior to making recommendations. During 1968 Jeffrey Raffel, MIT doctoral student, polled 400 parents from 10 different elementary schools to see what issues they thought important. His sample included 200 Catholics, 100 Protestant, and 100 of "other" or no religion. While 39 percent were Irish or Italian, 24 percent were black and 15 percent Asian (parents at the Chinese school); the remaining 20 percent were "other" including 2 percent Jewish parents.[8]

The survey asked what parents liked or disliked about their children's schools and about curriculum preferences. They were asked how the School Committee should be selected, by election or appointment. Black parents were angry with the School Committee in 1968. Yet the majority of Boston voters in 1965, 1967, and 1969 returned to power those committee members pledged to preserve "neighborhood schools." Was there a parent preference for neighborhood schools, as Mrs. Hicks believed?

Of the 400 Boston school parents polled, 57 percent rated their own elementary schools "good or very good," 27 percent "fair," and only 9 percent "poor." However, if parents could choose a school, only 52 percent would stay in their current public school. These were the facts on parent loyalty: 19 percent preferred a private school, 13 percent a parochial school, and 16 percent would send their child to another public school. Only half were loyal to the nearest neighborhood school. A full third of Boston parents in 1968 would exit the public schools entirely if they could.

Was the Boston school system properly organized? Many parents said "no." Thirty-two percent preferred a metropolitan school district (a much larger multi-community unit), and 22 percent wanted a smaller community district within the total city. In total, 54 percent favored either a much larger or smaller base for school operations. Fifteen percent did not know. Less than one-third of parents (30 percent) endorsed the current structure.

Polled about likes and dislikes, 33 percent parents said they liked their children's teachers. Only 10 percent liked the location of their school, while 27 percent actively disliked the school plant and facilities. When asked which special academic topics or problems should be taught, parents listed their instructional priorities. The greatest support was for teaching the dangers of drugs (71 percent), proper behavior (44 percent), and loyalty to the country (39 percent). One-third (33 percent) cited race relations and "preparation for a job." One-quarter wanted schools to teach "good grooming," or about "pollution" or "black history." One in four (22 percent) mentioned "creative writing" and 20 percent teaching the dangers of Communism. Only 14 percent wanted sex education taught and 13 percent favored music appreciation.

Most Boston parents wanted their children growing up loyal, well behaved, drug-free, and job-ready. During the liberal 1960s, they remained solidly conservative, at the opposite end of the spectrum from well-publicized progressive or counterculture values. Blacks and a few Chinese parents worried about race relations, but two-thirds of all parents failed to rank racial harmony among their top concerns. Teaching law and order and loyalty were Boston parents' highest priorities.

The Harvard-MIT study team solicited parent opinions about community control of the schools. What was the proper role of parents in schools and school decisions? Respondents could endorse one or more roles. More than half checked "helping with a child's homework," discipline methods, and a general say about the schools. Only one-third listed participation in budget, curriculum decisions, and teaching methods. Only one-quarter wanted a voice in selecting the principal or hiring teachers.[9] They may not have felt qualified. Fewer than 10 percent of the parents had college or professional degrees. Many of the parents surveyed (53 percent) were clerks, laborers, or workmen, and one-third had not completed high school.

The study also focused on the recruitment of black teachers and principals for Boston schools. Black leaders bitterly criticized Boston's failure to find more than a half dozen black principals or assistants for 200 public schools. Also, Boston recruiters traveled ineffectively to Southern states to recruit newly graduated teachers, many already "indentured" to teach in their home state or else pay back their state scholarships. Hailer designed a teacher recruitment workshop for Boston administrators. Participants proposed a more productive recruitment approach visiting Northern and Midwestern cities such as New York, Detroit, and Chicago whose black graduates were willing to consider another city, and whose black candidate pools had not been tapped by Boston recruiters.[10]

Meanwhile, five School of Education deans, Boston College, Boston University, Harvard, the University of Massachusetts, and Northeastern University reviewed Boston's teacher recruiting, evaluation, promotion, and administrator selection systems. *A Study of Promotional Policies and Procedures in the Boston Public Schools* in April 1970 recommended elimination of the local Boston Teachers Examination and reliance on the National Teachers Exam. Also, principals should interview teachers for their school rather than accept choices made by an assistant superintendent.[11]

The deans also recommended eliminating the "biennial service mark," the old and very subjective numerical rating relied on for promotions. They proposed scrapping the Associate Superintendents Personal Qualities Interview as an administrator screening device, for the same reasons.[12] Judge Garrity read about this study, and mandated an end to the old service mark system.

The deans recommended a six-year renewable contract for principals, headmasters, and assistant superintendents (replacing administrator tenure) so that no administrator was guaranteed a lifetime assignment, a reform that took another thirty years to implement.[13] The deans couched their recommendations in diplomatic language rather than suffer the inevitable "reply from the Board of Superintendents." Boston decided to use the National Teachers Exam in the 1970s, one of Strayer's recommendations that Ohrenberger and his associates finally accepted twenty-five years later, and Boston recruited new teachers from other cities.

What might be done to modernize the way decisions were made? University experts understood that few changes were likely under the current decision-making structures. Two major structural barriers to reform, the Board of Superintendents and the School Committee itself, were given special attention. The Harvard-MIT report described the Board of Superintendents as a "graveyard for innovations." Instead, the report team recommended a new Superintendent's Cabinet to advise the superintendent on planning issues. The absence of professional planning for new schools, for accommodating population changes, needed to be corrected.[14]

The all-Caucasian School Committee in 1970 was totally unrepresentative of, and out of touch with, a racially diverse city. So the team recommended a nine-member board, three at large (elected or appointed by mayor, confirmed by the Council) and six by districts within the city. The following would be the new electoral districts:

- Jamaica Plain, Roslindale, West Roxbury;
- Allston, Brighton, Back Bay, Beacon Hill;
- South End–Roxbury (mostly minority);
- Charlestown, East Boston, Downtown, South Boston;
- Dorchester; and
- Hyde Park–Mattapan (increasingly minority).

The larger Committee would then include two minorities, perhaps a black and a Hispanic, and probably an Italian American (of whom only three had served in seventy years). The rationale was egalitarian and populist, to spread the base of decision-making, recognizing the emerging diversity of the city not represented on the old School Committee. The recommendation aimed at extending voice to alienated minorities who could not, it seemed then, ever penetrate the at-large elective system.

Jeffrey Raffel's had asked parents, "What type of school committee would you prefer?" The parents split almost evenly on their choices, one-quarter supporting the present five-member elected committee, one-quarter for an appointed five-man committee, and one-quarter for a larger committee with community representatives. One-quarter said they did not know. There was as of 1970 no clear Boston parent consensus. A bare majority of 51 percent wanted change, either to an appointed or a larger elected committee. The final report recommended a larger, nine-person committee. After a decade of intense debate, city voters approved a larger City Council and School Committee with both citywide and community or district representation in 1981 to take effect in 1983. The larger School Committee in 1970 seemed an appropriate recommendation, but it was not, for two reasons. First, a second black School Committee candidate won in the 1981 citywide election, under the existing electoral rules. Also, the larger School Committee behaved erratically and gave the school superintendent considerable trouble as members jockeyed with him and with each other for power and influence.

Furthermore, the real problem was the continuing School Committee preoccupation with jobs rather than educational policy. The city later decided, after prodding by three consecutive mayors and business leaders, that only an appointed board would make decisions based on educational priorities rather than political and personal advantage. The 1970 poll revealed only 25 percent support for an appointed board (but another undecided 25 percent who might be persuaded to support other options). A determined mayor could, with enough allies and funds to promote reform, convert undecided voters to approve appointment by the mayor. Hindsight is 20:20. The failure of the "appointed board" recommendations in 1905 and 1944 seemed to say that Bostonians strongly preferred democracy, elections over appointment. Not until the 1990s could that equation be changed.

The report also raised the question of whether Boston's cultural organizations might work more closely with city schools. Boston public school students regularly took field trips to the zoo, Freedom Trail, and Children's Museum. The Museum of Fine Arts and the Museum of Science welcomed visits by Boston schoolchildren. Otherwise, Boston schools were only superficially connected to the rich treasures of Boston's cultural world. "The fine arts in Boston have traditionally been a privately supported elitist preserve," a researcher on the Boston art scene reported. The task was "to reach out to the next generation."[15]

The Harvard-MIT team recommended creating a council of artistic and cultural organizations, for example, Metropolitan Education Cultural Coalition (MECCA), to advise schools in establishing new programs. The Mayor's Office of Cultural Affairs should identify expanded opportunities for arts and educational programs.[16] In 1973 Mayor White appointed a Secondary School Commission to involve leaders from the arts, universities, business and city departments to produce a detailed master plan for helping Boston schools.[17]

Dick Hailer's contributions to Boston Public School solutions were shaped by his two Peace Corps assignments, the most recent as a country administrator in West Africa. Hailer led organizational development workshops, inviting Boston school administrators to diagnose the problem and brainstorm possible solutions. Rather than treat Boston insiders as defendants, as had Strayer, he enlisted them as partners to invent the reform strategy. This mingling of university and school system talent in the search for solutions was novel and provoked new trust among Boston administrators. What made it work was strong inside support from Ohrenberger and two key assistants, Paul Kennedy and Herbert Hambleton, who shared his desire to improve Boston schools.

The Strengthening of University Partnerships

Boston school administrators despised professors who publicly criticized Boston schools as racist or ineffective without ever coming near one. Their strident "voices" exacerbated Boston's traditional defensiveness. What would a constructive program or school-university dialogue look like? Hailer's January 7, 1970 workshop on university relations produced several ideas for helping city schools. Universities should recruit experienced urban educators to train new teachers, beginning with sophomore- and junior-year service in schools as aides and volunteers, rather than waiting until senior year student teaching assignments. Universities might assist with program research, evaluation, curriculum development, special education, reading projects, and other issues. One radical idea was that academics and inner-city administrators might exchange places for a semester or year. The group decided it was time for a new era of mutual criticism and collaborative problem solving.

Workshop participants proposed creating a school system-university forum, which might include university medical and business schools, not just schools of education. This idea caught the attention of Superintendent Ohrenberger, Mayor White, Governor Frank Sargent, and Judge Garrity. One of the first university collaborations was the "open campus" program, during 1971–74, a national movement liberating adolescents from the "joyless school" culture (described by Charles Silberman) and introducing them to the adult world. Conservative Bostonians called the local version the "flexible campus" approach; Professor John Gibson of the Lincoln Filene Center at Tufts University and Gregory Coffin, former Evanston Township superintendent, then working at Northeastern University, helped launch this for all but one Boston high school (Girls Latin School declined to participate). Boston agreed to place high school juniors and seniors in business or collegiate settings for part of the day, an effort to assist students in the transition to grownup roles.[18]

Mayor White and his education advisor Robert Schwartz in 1973 invited each college or university to "adopt" a district high school and its feeder schools. Existing efforts they deemed "sporadic and piecemeal." White especially solicited a partnership from the University of Massachusetts Boston, recently opened at seaside Columbia Point, but asked all the tax-exempt colleges to help city schools.[19] This idea later appealed to Judge Garrity and his university expert, Robert Dentler, who implemented White's proposal.

After the Garrity court order, a new state-funded Boston Higher Education Partnership supported extensive college and university pairings with Boston's high schools and with a few middle schools such as the M.L. King, Jr. and the Timilty. Robert Sperber of Boston University (the former Brookline superintendent who helped METCO get started) provided a central forum for more than twenty colleges to assist Boston's schools. He recruited the BU School of Management to help with prospective school administrator training in a management academy.

The Harvard- MIT study opened up to public scrutiny the inadequate programs for low-income students, dropouts, children with special needs, and those in vocational and bilingual education programs. Again, the question was how effective were the Boston Public Schools in the decade after the Racial Imbalance Law was enacted but before the court ordered many changes? The 1970 MACE report diagnosed Boston's educational strengths and the numerous shortcomings.

Serving the Special Needs of Children

Boston in the 1800s had pioneered special learning opportunities for blind and deaf children, and later expanded classes for those students called "emotionally disturbed," and physically handicapped children.[20] By 1968 serious problems emerged. Harvard doctoral student Brooklyn Derr conducted an organizational study of Boston's Special Education structure. He proposed to analyze the difficulties encountered by parents seeking special services for their handicapped children. Committeeman Joseph Lee in 1968 tried to ban the "Harvard Study," fearing intrusion, such as researchers "reading his mail" (as he complained to Superintendent Ohrenberger). Since Derr took a management research course at the Sloan School of Management, he called his review "The MIT study" to gain access to Boston schools. The worst problems Derr identified were the assignment of special education services to three different associate superintendents, creating barriers to sharing diagnostic information. He found work rules stipulating that Pupil Adjustment Counselors need not work after 2:15 p.m., ruling out afternoon visits to homes or after- school conferences with teachers or other professionals. Also, he reported that black students were assigned to residential schools in disproportionately high numbers.

Within four years both the Massachusetts Legislature (Chapter 766) and the U.S. Congress (PL94-142) mandated sweeping changes in the way children with special needs were "delabeled" and assured more appropriate and less "restrictive" services. Boston ultimately agreed to designate one associate superintendent for Special Education and began to cope with the revolutionary changes that would follow.[21]

Boston's Vocational Educational Programs

What was the state of the vocational curriculum? Boston's trade and vocational programs in the 1970s carried on essentially as they had prior to World War II. Four directors of vocational education supervised the old traditional specialties, secretarial and clerical, merchandising, buying and selling, trades and manufacturing, home economics and nutrition.

> "Existing departments reflect the philosophy and labels of the first third of the century," the team reported. One million dollars a year in new federal funds earmarked for the vocational education of disadvantaged children was left on the state table each year, for lack of a Boston grant proposal. With 7% of the state's low-income students, Boston sought and received only 1% of available federal vocational funds allocated to Massachusetts.[22]

Boston's old trade and commerce high schools had closed. Vocational programs consisted of one or two shops in each district high school, sheet metal at South Boston High, agriculture at Jamaica Plain High, and carpentry classes elsewhere. There was little recognition of emerging career opportunities. Plans to build a central Occupational Resource Center (ORC) had been postponed. The Harvard-MIT team recommended hiring a new headmaster for the ORC with "demonstrated capacities for developing new, exciting vocational education programs." Boston's critical occupational shortages were in the health and medical field. Boston prepared licensed practical nurses, but other health and hospital specialties had emerged. A Northeastern University study reported a shortage of 5,000 health workers in the Greater Boston area.[23]

On June 28, 1970 Hailer organized a working session with health and hospital representatives meeting with Boston public school staff. They recommended putting new courses in health careers and skills in the ninth grade, using Boston-based New England Hospital and Lemuel Shattuck Hospital training centers. Boston should appoint a highly qualified health career coordinator to brief guidance counselors about career opportunities. Health was used to exemplify a growing field, in contrast to declining demand for machine tools and traditional agriculture (taught at Jamaica Plain High School into the 1970s). Another recommendation suggested, "What applies to training for careers in health also applies to careers in data-processing. Educators must (also) master data-processing information for their own purposes and for counseling children."[24]

Bilingual Education

Spanish-speaking students and parents struggled with an unfamiliar language in school. The report described how the 25,000 Puerto Rican children in Boston in 1960 grew to 40,000 Spanish-speaking children by 1970. Only half of the Hispanic children actually attended school. Fewer than ten Hispanics graduated from Boston's senior high schools in June 1970. As many as 1,000 Spanish speakers each year dropped out, usually alienated by the end of eighth grade, destined for the lowest-wage jobs in the city, cleaning hotel rooms or offices after hours or serving as aides in hospitals. Community advocates, including an outspoken Roman Catholic nun, Sister Francis Georgia, herself bilingual, pursued the School Committee in 1969 until members agreed to establish bilingual classes with teachers fluent in both Spanish and English. At one School Committee meeting she badgered a skeptical School Committeeman Paul Tierney into voting for it by promising him "I will pray for you, Mr. Tierney!" She was, in her flowing black habit, an eloquent voice for bilingual services.

Bilingual problems began with a lack of census information about the Hispanic population and a staff unable to converse with parents who spoke only Spanish. The university report recommended printing report cards, notices, and instructional materials in Spanish as well as English, starting a university teacher certification program for bilingual teachers, and staff development for all school workers to help them understanding the needs of newcomers to Boston.[25]

At about the same time, a Brandeis University team documented the tragedy of out-of-school youth, accusing the Boston Schools of deliberately excluding categories of students such as pregnant students, the Spanish-speaking, and disruptive minority youth in numbers disproportionate because of race. This report *The Way We Go to School* was prepared by Larry Brown of Brandeis for a task force chaired by Hubie Jones, professor and later dean of the Boston University School of Social Work. This report, in strident language, called for ending the excessive use of expulsions and long-term suspensions of minority youth in Boston schools. The state should require bilingual education classes for children whose first language was other than English. Also, the state should mandate programs allowing pregnant teenagers and young mothers to continue studies toward a diploma.[26]

Neither the Brandeis nor Harvard university team knew the other was working on bilingual education issues. Brown and Jones, the social workers, sharply attacked Boston's deficiencies, visibly irritating Superintendent Ohrenberger who denied that Boston policies excluded any student. Cronin and Hailer were moderate advocates of hiring bilingual staff and preparing faculties to serve what would be called Limited English Proficiency students a few decades later.

The Brown-Jones report generated support for the Massachusetts Bilingual Education Act in 1971 and establishment of the Massachusetts Advocacy Center, a group that closely monitored and reported student exclusions and suspensions by race. How effective was this? Thirty years later Boston had one of the lowest percentages of minority student exclusions and suspensions among the dozen major urban centers of the nation. Brandeis mainly prepared sociologists, scientists, and social workers, not elementary and secondary educators. But their 1969–70 report made waves and paved the way for increased sensitivity toward minority children who were encountering difficulties in a white, Anglo school system.

Meanwhile, the team reviewed nonteaching staff policies because changing the "employment system" was in Boston a very special challenge. Boston once pioneered the system where school doctors and nurses responded to the health needs of children. The idea of bringing medical doctors into schools was, in the twentieth century, a progressive reform. What happened to it, and what concerns might a university team voice? By the end of the 1960s medical visits were a joke in many schools. Fifty-four medical doctors conducted physical examinations, each visiting three or four schools a day, generally in the morning. The doctor's arrival was announced by the ringing of a special bell. An anonymous teacher quipped "But if you had a foot or leg injury, heaven help you, because you couldn't get to the office in time. In five minutes the doctor would have gone 'on to the next school.'" Most of the doctors were well along in age. The oldest was seventy-eight. Only one was a pediatrician. Each worked on contract for $5,500 ten hours a week, spending the rest of their day with private patients.

The seventy-five school nurses were assigned one to each Boston high school, others with two to five school buildings. School nurses legally could not administer medicines nor treat patients, less they be liable for malpractice. They tested the vision, hearing, and checked the height and weight of every student every year, "light lifting" some might say. Fifty percent of their time was spent maintaining health records, with five dozen official health forms recording every contingency. They worked the same hours as teachers, enjoyed the same Christmas, spring, and summer vacations, and in general could boast of a very good deal. School nurses were paid $5,000 more than their counterparts at the city hospital that provided full emergency and surgical services. The Harvard-MIT report noted "turnover is low and the waiting list is long."[27]

The Cronin-Hailer team tallied school health expenditures of $2 million a year, 3 percent of a $68 million budget. Meanwhile, local community clinics offered serology (blood) and urine tests to identify problems never discovered in the old-fashioned eyes, ear, and throat, and heart examinations. The modern neighborhood health clinic model (Harvard Medical School in Charlestown and Tufts New England Medical at Columbia Point) was potentially much more effective. The team recommended phasing out the obsolete School Physician role and contracting with neighborhood health clinics. "The daily school call could be eliminated."[28]

Another set of concerns was the truant officer. Many cities employed truant officers, the old "hooky cops" to ferret out and chase after students, mostly males, who "skipped school" violating the compulsory attendance laws. Boston upgraded the role by labeling them "attendance supervisors" with two functions, protecting the right of children to attend school (e.g., if others were bullying or harassing them) and enforcing the law requiring school attendance until age sixteen.[29]

Boston employed forty-one attendance supervisors, most of them former Boston police officers, and paid them the equivalent salaries of police lieutenants. They too enjoyed Christmas, spring, and summer vacations and rarely worked during the latter half of the afternoon unless on a "case." They were in 1968 supervised by a coordinator and two Department of Attendance heads (a promotional rating exam resulted in a tie score, so both were chosen). Only 1 percent of truancy cases actually went to court. None of the attendance supervisors spoke Spanish, although Spanish lessons had recently been offered. Sometimes truants lacked winter clothing, or adequate emotional support to continue schooling in a new land. The team recommended a new "child advocate" role, working year round with social welfare and health agencies.[30]

New Boston school custodians were paid as much as teachers and grew better paid with seniority. Eighteen schools had already converted from coal to oil and gas furnaces, requiring advanced technical training and fewer men shoveling coal or tending furnaces.

The report recommended that the Chief Schoolhouse Custodian position be retitled Director of Plant Maintenance, reporting to the business manager and superintendent rather than directly to the Committee. But it was an academic mistake to underestimate "blue collar power." The custodians union knew how valuable their members were during election campaigns. They planted candidate signs on their house or yard, on their brother in law's storefront, and contacted cousins recommending votes for "a good candidate." Placing signs high in a tree could prevent teardown vandalism by an opponent's supporters. Custodians had a high comfort level with ladders and their signs held up well.

Although half of Boston's teachers lived in suburbs, most custodians lived in the city and voted regularly as though their jobs depended on 100 percent turnout. When Boston's custodians endorsed a candidate, neither the *Globe* nor the *Herald* carried this news. However, photos of custodian leaders with their endorsed candidates appeared in the West Roxbury, Dorchester, and South Boston neighborhood weeklies. Firemen, policemen, trash men, and other city and county employees knew which candidates were loyal to them.[31]

Committeeman Joseph Lee was especially grateful to custodians for their steadfast loyalty. He acknowledged this whenever they needed a raise or delay of a school closing, since closing an old school meant the loss of custodial jobs. Lee's own Beacon Hill Brahmin constituents were dwindling; his main support was wherever custodians and their neighbors lived, Dorchester, South Boston, or Charlestown. Throughout the controversies about busing and school closings, custodians supported Joe Lee, and Lee supported the status quo. Lee certainly did not want universities messing around, especially Harvard where he studied before finishing his studies at a Texas college.

One issue was how parents might voice their concerns and get serious problems resolved without having to call a School Committee member and have their request treated as a political favor. Cronin was impressed by the Swedish approach to cope with unresponsive bureaucracies, the use of an ombudsman or special agent assigned to listen to grievances and resolve consumer or constituent problems. The report recommended an "impartial officer appointed to receive, investigate, and expedite solutions to complaints received from individuals." Such a role might allow parents to voice concerns about unfair treatment, and develop procedures for handling problems. Hirschman commented favorably on how ombudsmen effectively responded to citizen grievances about malpractice.[32]

University reports often sound like an authoritative voice, but are strictly advisory. What impact did the Harvard-MIT report have on Boston Schools? Was the reception any better than the icy rebuttal of the Board of Superintendents to the 1944 Strayer Report? The study was released in October of 1970, a few weeks after school opened. On racial matters, Superintendent Ohrenberger used the report to recommend immediately the Boston School Committee appointment of Boston's first black assistant superintendent, Rollins Griffith, former principal at two middle schools. Griffith was a mild-mannered music teacher but he broke the invisible color barrier after the 1970 report recommended minority recruitment at all levels.

There were several ways to measure the impact of a university report. During 1970–71 a Harvard Graduate School of Education seminar on urban education used the Boston School report as a "case study" for analysis. The focus was on the issues surrounding the implementation of urban education reform. Of the fifteen students, one was William Leary, a recently admitted doctoral student and curriculum developer from the Boston Public Schools. Within eighteen months he would succeed William Ohrenberger as Boston's Superintendent of Schools. He spent 1970–71 studying urban education issues, one semester reviewing a highly specific plan for reforming Boston's schools. He recruited to Boston a black Harvard classmate, Charles Leftwich, a former Philadelphia principal who helped Leary try to implement the 1974 desegregation court order.

Another seminar member was Shirley Owens-Hicks, sister of State Representative (later senator) William Owens from Roxbury. Within the decade she won election to the Boston School Committee, then to the State Legislature where she served until 2006. No School Committee member knew Boston school reform proposals as well as Shirley Owens-Hicks in 1971. Still another student was Jeanette Hargrove, Federal Reserve Bank of Boston research analyst, who for more than a decade tabulated annual statistical reports on the specific college and career plans of Boston high school graduates.

None of these effects could be anticipated in 1970. The State Department of Education asked for a nominee to work on urban school issues for the Bureau of School Building Assistance. The author nominated a doctoral student, Charles Glenn, a white Protestant minister living in Boston, member of the Harvard-MIT team, and a strong advocate of racial deseg-regation. Glenn soon became the key state administrator on racial equality and later approved the Controlled Choice student assignment plan that replaced the initial busing plan.

The seminar class itemized the specific recommendations Boston imple-mented. The superintendent mandated school councils of which seventy had been formed, but the students found that council members still needed training on how to function. The number of Spanish-speaking teachers increased from six in 1970 to seventy-five in 1971, including two new junior high guidance counselors. The new black Assistant Superintendent Rollins Griffith recruited seventy-five new black teachers in one year. The Chamber of Commerce invited 150 companies to help with the "flexible campus" idea, of which 65 responded favorably. School Committeeman James Hennigan and City Councilor Gerald O'Leary proposed the larger School Committee for the November 1971 ballot, winning six city councilors' and the mayor's approval (although legal issues on wording the question delayed the vote).[33]

The Home Rule Commission in Boston, conducting its own study, recommended abolishing all citywide boards, the mayor to name an education commissioner, with school boards for each area of the city. This proposal died for lack of support. That year the Harvard Center for Law and Education recommended improvements for the racial imbalance law.[34] The Center suggested a metropolitan plan involving the suburbs, and loosening the rigid fifty-fifty pupil standard (one Boston school was one-third black, one-third white, one-third Asian American, demographically balanced but legally imbalanced).

William Boyan, president of the John Hancock Insurance Company, invited the author twenty years (1991) later to address a management seminar on Boston schools. The central question was whether Boston schools had changed since the 1970s. This was another opportunity to evaluate the university impact after two decades. What happened to proposals for Hispanic services, occupational education, a larger School Committee, and university involvement?

Massachusetts enacted a Bilingual Education Act in 1972 after testimony from Spanish-speaking advocates, Hubie Jones, Larry Brown, State Education Secretary Cronin and Dick Hailer, Cronin's Assistant Secretary of education, returning from service as director of Peace Corps Training Programs for Latin America. The law lasted thirty years, repealed in 2002 by an electorate angry at delays in immersing immigrants in English. The Hernandez School survived as a two-way bilingual magnet school, teaching both English and Spanish.

Federal funds helped Boston establish an Occupational Resource Center (ORC). A key deputy coordinated occupation vocational and technical education. The old trade programs were removed from district high schools. The business community formed a Trilateral Council to try to make desegregation work. The Boston Compact and Boston Plan for Excellence won national acclaim for efforts by corporate leaders to invigorate the public schools, about which more is discussed in chapter 8.

The larger School Committee was tried and failed, replaced by an appointive board. (In 2003 Boyan was appointed a School Committee member.) Boston schools employed an ombudsman for a while until a budget crisis eliminated the post. The legislature mandated school councils for all schools in the Commonwealth.

Reports never implement themselves. Superintendent Ohrenberger adopted several reforms before stepping down in 1973, the year William Leary was appointed. Judge Garrity read every report or proposal he could find on Boston schools, built school councils into his plan, and asked universities and arts groups to work closely with city schools. The Massachusetts State Legislature and U.S. Congress separately enacted sweeping reforms for the education of special needs children during the 1970s.[35]

The university that stepped forward time and time again for Boston schools over the next thirty years was Boston University. Three times, whenever a superintendent of schools stepped down, BU President John Silber offered to take over the management of the Boston Public Schools; the School Committee declined this offer. Silber hired Brookline Superintendent Dr. Robert Sperber (former personnel director for Pittsburgh Public Schools) as his special assistant and director of the Boston Higher Education Partnership, coordinating university interventions for Boston Public Schools for more than twenty years beginning in the mid-1970s. Silber awarded full four-year BU scholarships to the four top-scoring Boston high school students from all seventeen public high schools. Subsequently he added scholarships for Boston's Catholic high school graduates as well. The fifty-one full scholarships for Boston public graduates carried a cash value that soared from more than $5 million in the mid-1970s to $15 million in the late 1990s, an extraordinary commitment to city schools. President Silber took over management of a city's public schools, that of nearby Chelsea in 1985, an agreement still in place in 2007. Governor William Weld named Silber chair of the state Board of Education to raise the standards of performance for all Massachusetts schools in the 1990s.

Northeastern University, whose mission included the phrase "Friend of the City," also ranked high in support. Northeastern pledged, "I Have a Dream" scholarships to students at a Mission Hill elementary school if they persisted through high school, and later to all Boston Housing Authority children. Northeastern (NEU) abolished its school of education but in 2000 reinvented it as part of the College of Arts and Sciences. Northeastern hosted both the Teacher Union Reform Network (TURN) and the Critical Friends study group, keeping pressure on city school superintendents through the 1990s. NEU became the university partner to the Boston Technical High School, later renamed after John O'Bryant, a Northeastern University vice president.

Northeastern University in 1990–91 conducted a major management study of Boston schools, with strong personal support from President John Curry who asked his CFO Robert Culver (former Price Waterhouse Coopers partner) to supervise the project.

The study proposed more than 20 million dollars of cost savings.[36] Northeastern also revived the Harvard-MIT suggestion of an ombudsman to take the complaint resolution function away from the newly appointed

School Committee. In 1996 new superintendent Tom Payzant chose an ombudsperson, Maureen Lumley, who responded to parent and other inquiries within twenty-four hours. A "manager of voice," she handled 4,000 calls each year on matters concerning discipline, special education, and transportation. She referred most matters back to the school level. If a policy change or clarification was needed, she informed the superintendent or deputy.[37]

Harvard's partnership with Roxbury High School ended when that school closed, a failed desegregation initiative. Instead, Harvard invited Boston administrators to join the popular Harvard Principal's Center. Boston's first black headmaster and deputy superintendent, Bob Peterkin, led Harvard's Urban Superintendent Program training city school leaders, most of them of color and 60 percent of them women. Peterkin chaired the 1993 transition team welcoming new Superintendent Thomas Payzant to Boston and a similar team in 2007 for Carol Johnson. Several of Peterkin's doctoral graduates served as Boston deputy superintendents for Teaching and Learning under Payzant. Harvard professors worked on policy strategies, on English High School, and economist Richard Murnane spent a sabbatical year in Boston developing ways for schools and the central office to use pupil achievement data to improve classroom instruction.[38]

The University of Massachusetts at Boston paired with nearby Dorchester High School and several other schools. MIT sponsored the Mario Umana science and technical high school in East Boston but it closed, became a middle school, and MIT withdrew from Boston for two decades, until the 1990s when it formed a partnership with the O'Bryant (Technical) High School.

Both Harvard and MIT in the 1980s complained about finding the bureaucratic styles of Boston incompatible with their intentions, and subsequently deferred partnerships with other high schools into the 1990s. The Harvard Business School (HBS) faculty later partnered with a nearby Brighton school and HBS alumni funded a study of management practices in large school systems including Boston. Hundreds of Harvard undergraduates volunteered as tutors in Boston schools and, in the late 1990s, Harvard allowed undergraduates to take courses to become urban teachers. It helped to have a Harvard-educated school superintendent, Thomas Payzant, and a mayor and School Committee who were conscientious about improving education in Boston. Harvard hired former School Committeeman Kevin McCluskey to help coordinate relationships with Boston.

Boston College accepted responsibility for working mostly in Brighton schools including Brighton High School, not far from the Chestnut hill campus. By the year 2000 half the School of Education faculty worked on one or more Boston school interventions. President J. Donald Monan, S.J., for more than a decade took seriously his responsibilities in urging other university presidents to stay involved, all the more so because BC, during the dark decades, enjoyed a near monopoly of Boston's administrative promotions. BC, after the court order, readily shared school reform obligations with other universities.

By 1995 Superintendent Tom Payzant acknowledged the help of universities, which the Boston University staff documented in an encyclopedic annual report. However, Payzant complained about too many fragmented initiatives, and urged universities to focus on a few high-productivity initiatives under the banner of "whole school change." Also, too few universities recruited enough teachers of color to help Boston exceed the minimum 25 percent minority hires.[39]

Evaluating the Role of Universities

The university accomplishments fall short in several respects. Most area universities avoided contact with Boston schools during the 1930s, 1940s, and 1950s, for a full generation. The racial turmoil of the 1960s, intervention of judges, state stipends supporting city school university coordinators, the federal and foundation grants, and a rediscovered moral commitment to cities enticed universities back into the urban school arena.

No university found the magic wand needed to reinvent urban teacher education. In fact, in the mid-1990s the number of teachers failing a Commonwealth of Massachusetts teacher exam embarrassed most local colleges. At a dozen colleges, state and independent, the initial teacher exam failure rate exceeded 50 percent, raising fundamental questions about teacher preparedness.[40] (The high scoring exceptions were Wellesley College and Harvard test takers, but the numbers were very small.)

University faculty members are well equipped to criticize public schools, to articulate a loud "voice" about what should be done, complete with scholarly documentation including footnotes. However, none of the university "management" studies or advisory policy reports by themselves brought about structural changes. More accurately they were an academic product, "expert voice," issued from the professional schools of education, or law or social work. They attracted public attention, often commanded media attention, and focused on new strategies and remedies. They provided ideas to senior school administrators, mayors, and judges, and to legislators and governors committed to educational improvements including the expansion of access to services.

The university reports proposed ways of extending voice to underrepresented populations. They suggested new ways to serve children who were ill, pregnant, disruptive, or subliterate in English. They told a traditional public school bureaucracy how to respond to new ethnic and career challenges. They made suburban voters and business leaders more conscious of what needed to be done for Boston's schools. The most effective work might have been the consultative workshops led by Richard Hailer, inventing new ways to recruit teachers of color, and new ways to win support from higher education representatives.

It is fair to ask whether universities themselves changed to serve better Boston's school needs. Universities can be even more difficult to reform than urban public schools. Several of the great universities felt stymied by Boston, especially Harvard and MIT from 1980 into the 1990s. University faculties often felt more comfortable working with docile suburban schools rather than turbulent city schools, and vice versa. Boston University, offering thrice to manage Boston's public schools, won instead the schools of a smaller city, Chelsea. Boston University and the state established early childhood programs and, with state help, replaced seven ancient Chelsea buildings with all new school facilities.

Larry Cuban of Stanford University, a former superintendent of schools in Virginia, in 1970 expressed pessimism about university responsiveness to city school requirements. "Conspicuously missing from the analysis is the university role in producing effective teachers and changing the conventional arrangements in these schools." He thought only a handful of universities (Hunter College in New York City and Temple in Philadelphia) made the commitment; the others "failed miserably." He urged schools of education to immerse their faculty and prospective teachers in inner-city schools, to develop a new teacher preparation curriculum, and to prepare relevant reading lists in urban culture and minority studies. As of 2011 the foundations, led by Carnegie and Gates, are still working on this daunting agenda.[41]

Universities found it difficult to make lasting improvements in Boston schools. Part of it was the fragmented nature of a university wherein faculty members pursue their own research interests. Rarely do universities coalesce around a dynamic revitalization strategy to lift an urban school system from decay to new heights of productivity. Universities can articulate issues and propose recommendations but are poorly positioned to drive them home. The net results of university help during 1974–94 included stagnant test scores and too many isolated university projects, what Superintendent Payzant called "projectitis."

After 1995, prompted by the Massachusetts Educational Reform Bill and a reorganized Boston Plan for Excellence, universities regrouped and decided to support a coherent school improvement strategy. The Boston College education faculty committed themselves to Boston school improvement projects. Harvard professors studied city teacher unions, student test data analysis, and more effective professional development strategies. Lesley University prepared a dozen urban teachers each year in a Boston school, one of five committed teacher education schools. MIT launched at least twenty projects, several around a technology theme. Boston's metropolitan area universities recommitted to systematic urban school improvement in Boston by the end of the twentieth century. However, the Boston public schools with a philanthropic grant launched a Teacher Residency program to recruit and train hundreds of new teachers from the best colleges, more than half of color, with immersion in Boston schools right away after a summer program cosponsored with UMass Boston. This was the twenty-first century version of the old normal school, except for the exceptional outreach to liberal arts colleges.

Edward Doherty, former president of Boston Teachers Union. Courtesy of *The Boston Globe*.

Federal Judge W. Arthur Garrity, who in 1974 declared Boston Public Schools in violation of the U.S. Constitution. Courtesy of *The Boston Globe.*

Boston Mayoral Candidates Mel King and Ray Flynn, advocates of higher expectations for the schools. Courtesy of *The Boston Globe*.

Ruth Batson, Boston NAACP education chair, and Massachusetts Attorney General Edward Brooke, who disagreed over school boycotts. Courtesy of *The Boston Globe.*

Louise Day Hicks, with State Representative William Bulger, protesting the Racial Imbalance Law. Courtesy of *The Boston Globe*.

Boston Mayor Thomas Menino, Massachusetts education commissioner, and Boston School Superintendent Thomas Payzant announcing improvements in state test scores. Courtesy of *The Boston Globe*.

Joseph M. Cronin, author, with former Massachusetts commissioner and author of the Kiernan Report on Racial Imbalance in 1977, Owen B. Kiernan.

CHAPTER 7
THE ORGANIZED TEACHER VOICE
(1965 TO THE PRESENT)

The Massachusetts Public Sector Collective Bargaining Law was designed as a progressive reform allowing public school teachers a voice for improved salaries and working conditions. The goal was to bring civil discourse to public sector employee discussions and to prevent strikes in schools. Potentially it might revive teacher participation in school decision-making, as was done briefly in the 1920s. What was the impact of giving Boston teachers a formal voice in school decisions?

Teacher turbulence accelerated after World War II when school-age population began to grow again and the legislature authorized state funds to build new school facilities, especially in suburbs. Teacher salaries fell behind wages for manufacturing and other services, especially accountants and engineers. The GI Bill helped more men become teachers; their numbers rose by 93 percent. Women traditionally led teacher organizations, but male teachers fresh from battle were very aggressive and more willing to strike for better salaries.[1]

AFL-CIO subsidies for organizing public employees stimulated teacher unionism in the 1960's. Walter Reuther's Industrial Union Department provided $1.2 million for the American Federation of Teachers to expand. Those organizing efforts boosted AFT membership from 60,000 teachers in 1960 to 200,000 in 1970 and 444,000 in 1974.[2]

Teacher strikes attracted considerable national attention, beginning with the 1947 Norwalk, Connecticut, strike followed by Buffalo and Minneapolis walkouts. The United Federation of Teachers (UFT) New York in 1960 struck and won an important election over the National Education Association. There were five teacher strikes in 1963, twelve in 1964, eighteen in 1965, and sixty-four in 1966.[3]

The civil rights movement influenced teachers in both New York City and Boston in the 1960s. Teachers watched black parents and civil rights leaders boycott public schools, closing them down to voice concerns about equality and opportunity. Parent and teacher rights collided in 1968 when Ford Foundation President McGeorge Bundy recommended black community control for three New York City districts. The new Ocean Hill-Brownsville (Brooklyn) board and administrator Rhody McCoy terminated six white administrators and thirteen teachers, referring them to New York City School headquarters for reassignment. The UFT complained about the involuntary transfers from one school to another, and the loss of jobs for white teachers and administrators, and the absence of any due process. How did teachers fight back?

> Three times that fall the unions went out on strike, teachers and administrators and usually the custodians with them. Regents, Mayor (John V. Lindsay, the reform mayor) and mediators—none could bridge the gap for many weeks. Thirty-six out of the first forty-eight days of school were lost to all but a few thousand children attending the demonstration schools, which remained open.[4]

New York teachers later negotiated an especially generous teacher contract with the city and Mayor John V. Lindsay. Urban teachers elsewhere, including Boston, were again impressed at victories won by militant New York City schoolteachers—the good contract, stunning salary increases, and protection against arbitrary removal of white teachers in minority schools. They voted to emulate the New York City model.[5]

As late as 1960 neither the American Federation of Teachers (AFT) nor the National Education Association believed teachers should strike under any circumstances. In fact, the AFT constitution for many decades prohibited teacher strikes. The 1965 Public Employment Relations Acts passed in industrial states, mostly the Northeast and Middle West (none in the South), set up mediation procedures to resolve public employee conflicts before they came to impasse, and authorized strict penalties for work stoppages.

Unions differed in purpose and style. Boston teachers in theory could choose among three alternative union models. The first would be a traditional bread and butter industrial union, bargaining for salaries, terms, and conditions of employment (such as benefits and seniority rights). Nationally, mineworkers and steelworkers exemplified this option. Or Boston teachers might behave as a "professional association" committed to a service ideal, joining with parents to negotiate reduced class sizes and better services for children with special needs. This was the traditional stance of the National Education Association. Nurses and librarians generally reflected community and client service values. The third choice was to become an "ideological force," helping schools transform society and fight for justice for the underclass and oppressed minorities. This was the vision of philosopher and teacher union advocate John Dewey, and of David Selden, a 1960s leader of the New York United Teachers Federation. Nationally, the United Auto Workers and the black Railroad Porters and Farm Workers (Chicano) adopted progressive positions, even while seeking better wages and working conditions.[6] The AFT in the 1950s strongly supported the civil rights movement, as did the Auto Workers and many other industrial unions. Union teachers in general strongly supported school desegregation, and the AFT expelled 8,000 members in the south for refusing to merge separate black and white teacher unions.[7]

Teacher unions in Boston and elsewhere typically fought for educational initiatives such as smaller class sizes, student disciplinary procedures, and teacher participation in new educational program decisions. In private industry bargaining, these issues would be dismissed as "management prerogatives." For teachers, having some voice on educational matters was considered a proper professional opportunity, or at least a responsibility to be shared between teachers and administrators. Teachers prized their professional status, and aspired to control their work environment, as did other professionals, especially medical doctors and lawyers.[8]

Massachusetts school committees in the 1950s told teachers that existing state law did not permit them to bargain with teachers for contracts. The Massachusetts legislature in 1960 responded by allowing local governments, including school committees, the power to make collective bargaining agreements with public employees, including teachers. This law still only permitted, but did not require, teacher bargaining.

The Boston Teachers Union (BTU) in 1962 was a tiny organization with fewer than 200 members. The AFL-CIO sent Lucille Swain, a professional union organizer, to Boston. She had experience helping Autoworkers, Meatcutters, and the UFT. She told Boston teachers to rally around a concrete benefit, such as "sick leave," a good starter issue. Boston teachers packed a School Committee meeting, held signs urging "Sick Leave Now," marched, spoke up, and perfected the tactics of voice in pursuit of a bread-and-butter objective.[9]

The successful campaign for teacher sick leave stimulated a doubling of the BTU membership to 400 members, 12 percent of all teachers, and upstaged the larger Boston Teacher's Alliance. In June 1963 BTU members voted to request collective bargaining rights. Although many teachers considered formal union bargaining too aggressive, several thousand teachers signed petitions to the Boston School Committee requesting an election in early 1964. Louise Day Hicks expressed her reservations and voted against an election, hers the swing vote denying approval. Only two members, one of them Arthur Gartland, the most liberal school committeeman, supported teacher bargaining rights.[10]

When in 1965 it became clear that the state would require public employee bargaining, Mrs. Hicks finally voted to authorize an election. On November 9 teachers voted at the Boston Arena, a hockey auditorium. This was the night of a massive regional electrical power outage and far more men than women ventured out to vote. The BTU won by a 3:2 margin over the Alliance. If the lights stayed on, the Alliance might have prevailed.[11]

Teachers tested their new bargaining rights by demanding a $7,500 minimum salary, which would make them then the highest-paid teachers in New England. The first Boston contract included not only a salary increase but also language defining the scope of bargaining to embrace almost any issue or working condition. The School Committee, preoccupied with hiring and promotion decisions, worried little about educational issues and granted many of the teacher demands. Committee members relied on teacher and staff campaign contributions; they were not very concerned about policy matters. The initial 1968 Boston teacher contract provided a $1,000 increase in teacher pay, a gain whose value eroded rapidly during two years of high inflation.[12]

The contract at first did not change the way the School Committee looked at teachers or personnel matters at all. Traditionally, members devoted most of their meeting time, at least 80 percent of their recorded votes, to school personnel matters, appointments, transfers, leaves of absence, upgrades in salary classifications, and most of all promotions. The culture supported a school board that mainly made decisions about employees, their jobs, and careers.[13] The Committee focused on employment matters because that is where the money was. Frank Power, popular Charlestown High School headmaster, explained to Bill Spring (then president of the Boston Trilateral Council for Quality Education) how the system worked. School Committee members expected ambitious teachers to attend their political fund-raisers, usually billed as "receptions," birthday parties, or testimonials. Teachers selling tickets to such events improved their chances to compete for assistant principalships or higher posts. Every school employee was invited. No one was forced to attend. Those not paying tribute were less likely to be rewarded with promotions, or transfers to a school closer to one's home, which perquisites secretaries and custodians often sought.[14]

School Committee members often delayed starting the public meeting for forty-five minutes or more in order to debate privately the superintendent's personnel recommendations. On occasion they recessed to determine which candidates could muster the required three votes. This incident describes one process. In 1968 Tom Johnson, an able English High School teacher, wrote a grant proposal on Crisis Management, new ways to handle racial conflicts erupting in high schools. When the grant was approved, Johnson, an Army Reserve officer, was the best-qualified nominee. An anonymous phone call suggested the position was his if he placed $5,000 in an envelope in a certain desk drawer on the fifth floor of 15 Beacon Street (where the School Committee and their assistants worked). Johnson responded negatively to the bribe-seeker, and three weeks later a less plausible candidate won this new position. His attitude toward the old way of determining appointments remains less than complimentary forty years later.[15]

The historical reliance of School Committee members on employee donations must not be underestimated. Members by teacher solicitations could raise 10–20,000 dollars a year or more for campaigns or private use. George Higgins, close observer of Boston politics, described School Committee candidates as "discontented dreamers bored with drafting wills and divorce libels," spending time and money seeking offices with no compensation. "What this office did confer was the hiring power, the ability to make or break the career plans of young people whose backgrounds and upbringing had convinced them that to 'get on the city (payroll)' was the sole feasible route...to a lifetime of contentment and financial security."[16]

Two Major Boston Teacher Strikes

How might the victorious BTU display and consolidate its new strength? The first teacher contract expired in 1970. New BTU President John Reilly aspired to higher AFT office. He talked openly of striking, even warning Mayor Kevin White about a possible strike as early as August of 1969. Committeeman John Kerrigan later admitted that the School Committee listened but did not negotiate, making no serious salary offer until March when teachers threatened a one-day walkout. The Committee ignored union educational demands, which included hiring art, music, science, speech, and physical education teachers who might relieve regular grade school teachers allowing time for planning. Nor did the Committee take seriously union requests for remedial reading teachers for secondary schools, or authorizing faculty senates to express voice in school policy.[17]

The BTU on March 25, 1970 announced teachers would stay out of work for a "Professional Day." Some 3,000 teachers rallied in support of union requests at the Hotel Bradford and marched to School Committee headquarters. Thirty schools closed.[18] Superintendent Ohrenberger was extremely upset, calling the work stoppage an "Unprofessional Day." Associate superintendents, accustomed to rating prospective administrators on their cooperation and decorum, murmured that this was "no way to get ahead in the system." The School Department persuaded the Superior Court to invoke the state law banning strikes by public employees.[19]

The one-day walkout, however, generated an improved School Committee salary offer on April 26. On April 29 the union membership met, rejected the offer, and voted 1,132 to 704 to strike. The issue became "teacher power" and "the ability to effect change in the system."[20] The first Boston teachers strike ever lasted nineteen days in May 1970. Most schools remained open, the few children showing up met by principals and by those teachers reporting for work. School Committee statistics showed that 80 percent of junior high teachers went out on strike, perhaps 65 percent of high school teachers, and only 35 percent of the elementary teachers.

Two-thirds of the elementary school teachers agonized over the conflict between their loyalty to schoolchildren versus their loyalty to the teacher union. Many worried about breaking the law, possible dismissal from jobs, and being banned forever from teaching. On May 5 the Elementary Teachers' Club collected signatures in favor of accepting the School Committee offer. State Commissioner of Education Neil Sullivan offered to mediate, and sent thirty-five state staff to monitor the teacher referendum. By a vote of 1,389 to 259 teachers voted to continue the strike. Half of Boston's teachers had abstained from voting.[21]

On May 14, 200 Boston members of the Massachusetts Negro Educators Association asked the BTU to endorse proposals to hire more minority teachers and administrators. Supported vocally by union officials, these priorities passed by a large margin.[22] The BTU never pressed these initiatives because it was late in the bargaining process and teachers of color amounted to only 5 percent of the 4,200 teachers. The court sent BTU President John Reilly to jail for disobeying an injunction against the strike. He remained behind bars for the duration of the strike. The School Committee sought contempt citations for another thirty-seven teachers. Commissioner Sullivan and his state staff tried to get the two parties talking, but the strike lasted two more weeks.[23]

How did other unions and parents react? Reactions varied. The Greater Boston Labor Council vowed never again to support John Kerrigan and Paul Tierney of the School Committee because of their uncooperative stance. Boston custodians on the other hand declined to take part in "an illegal strike."[24] This was not their fight. Mayor White stayed aloof until May 7, when he assigned an observer. The national AFT sent two organizers, lent money to strikers, paid the $13,000 in fines, and replenished the empty BTU treasury with $2,000 after the strike. Parents were angry but quiet, except for 600 Boston Latin School parents who held a strike protest meeting. The Home and School Association said little except for a fiery East Boston parent named Elvira "Pixie" Palladino, who picketed with the teachers and addressed a teacher rally; later she was elected as a militant anti-busing School Committee member.[25]

Committee Members John Craven and James Hennigan proposed use of binding arbitration to resolve the crisis, but three members demurred. On May 15 Paul Tierney finally agreed to send unresolved issues for outside review. Teachers voted 965 to 296 to return to school before knowing details on how the arbitrator ruled. The long strike was over, voices stilled for a while, but the point was made—that most teachers would stick together. The arbitrator subsequently awarded higher pay, additional reading teachers, and a faculty senate for secondary schools. He approved an "agency fee" provision requiring nonunion members to pay dues to the BTU, since the union negotiated their wages as their agent. The Committee asked the mayor for new funds for more reading teachers.

The 1970 strike was an experiment in raising teacher voice, and a testing of wills. It destroyed old formats wherein teachers showed deference for School Committee members, rarely confronting them with collective demands. The union provided a unified voice for higher wages, for better working conditions, and remedial help for students falling behind their classmates. The strike changed how decisions were made about teachers and clearly altered their feelings toward the superintendent and School Committee. Mayor White in September 1970 accepted most of the teacher pay package. However, the independent School Committee angered him by approving a teacher contract unilaterally and then trying to pass costs to him and the City Council. In October, White promoted a Home Rule Commission report urging the legislature to allow Boston to vote on abolishing the elected School Committee and to let the mayor run schools as a city agency. It was a signal of his frustration over his minor role in approving teacher contracts and pay. Teachers in December voted to accept the new contract, including collecting dues from nonunion members.

During 1972 teachers opposed extending William Ohrenberger a new six-year term as superintendent, mostly because he publicly criticized the teachers for striking. The Committee members instead chose as Superintendent William Leary, Boston's curriculum director, whom they thought they could control. During 1973 Superintendent Leary proposed cutting 100 teaching positions to balance the School Department budget. The teacher union responded with a counterproposal for a four-day workweek. In October 1973, both sides agreed on a new teacher contract with a 5.5 percent salary increase.

On May 4, 1972, the School Committee removed several teachers from Boston High School, the work-study school. Teachers denounced this "firing" as retribution for their unwillingness to buy tickets to School

Committee member fund-raising events. On May 14, the BTU voted no longer to attend School Committee testimonials, the receptions during which School Committee members "shook down" employees for $25 and $50 contributions. In June both the *Globe* and *Herald* ran stories of how the School Committee sold tickets in exchange for patronage, describing a blatant abuse of political power.[26] The union action broke the mold of individual or personal bargaining for employee raises, taking another step toward achieving professional self-respect and unity.

The second Boston teacher strike came in the wake of the 1974 and 1975 desegregation orders. Judge Garrity scheduled Phase II of the desegregation of Boston schools for September 1975. The 1975 teacher strike threat context differed dramatically from 1970. School Committee members were now quite willing to see teachers disrupt the schools and thereby thwart the judge; they declined an early contract settlement. The year 1975 was bad for teachers even to consider a strike. Teachers were ambivalent on racial matters. The BTU in 1972 and 1973 opposed state racial imbalance solutions, even while affirming teacher support for "quality integrated education."[27] Perhaps 10 percent of the teachers were militant critics of all imbalance remedies, but BTU President John Doherty reminded teachers that on racial issues they "must be a positive, constructive voice at this time.... We cannot in any way contribute to the voices of disruption and despair."[28]

Bargaining over the 1975 contract began in the fall of 1974. Chairman John Kerrigan suggested that the School Committee again just listen but not negotiate. The BTU proposed binding arbitration to avoid a September 1974 strike. The Committee members agreed. Arbitrator Mark Santer awarded teachers a 5 percent increase in January 1975. The mayor tried to enjoin this decision, with Deputy Mayor Edward Sullivan (a Boston assistant principal on leave) proposing another two weeks of contract negotiations. However, the School Committee would not agree, and the contract expired on August 31. Santer's arbitration award authorized salary increases and additional reading specialists with a total price tag approaching $7 million.[29]

The Mayor refused, arguing that Santer exceeded his authority, especially in deciding educational matters. On September 2, 1975 new BTU President Henry Robinson convened his union, and 3,000 teachers voted to strike on September 22. Union leaders shrewdly proposed this date because school would open for two weeks under the court order. The strike would occur the day before city primary elections, potentially embarrassing School Committee incumbents. Teachers would also receive their first two paychecks before the strike took effect.[30]

On September 18, four days before the strike, the Massachusetts Labor Relations Commission directed the School Committee to bargain seriously. The federal court order was only one reason for School Committee disinterest in settlement. *Globe* Education reporter James Worsham suspected Committee member retaliation over the teacher ban on buying tickets.[31] Black plaintiffs asked Judge Garrity to enjoin teachers from striking, which would deprive their children of educational services. He ordered the School Committee to bargain in good faith and sent an attorney to monitor the talks. The BTU was ready to defy a Garrity order, whose intervention Kerrigan had mischievously requested.[32]

More than 90 percent of Boston's teachers went out on strike in 1975. Why this expanded loyalty to the union cause over 1970? Former elementary teacher Kathy Kelley was the BTU field representative visiting elementary schools to build union solidarity. She suggested that Boston's elementary teachers could gain planning time during the day only if teachers insisted on hiring music, art, math, and other specialists who could take over their classes. Kelley was a cheerful, gregarious, and highly effective organizer, and tireless in pointing out what the union could do for grade school teachers. She won hundreds of Kindergarten-grade five teachers over to the union tactics.

Racial issues became divisive, largely because of Judge Garrity's order. The 500 black teachers split over the strike, many worried about undermining desegregation and upset about student safety issues. Black union leaders urged a compromise to allow teachers to cross picket lines so they could teach black children. A new Black Caucus within the union strongly supported the strike and urged black parents to keep their children at home. Loyalty was thus divided, some favoring the union, others favoring the NAACP pursuit of better opportunities for black students.[33]

The BTU spent $30,000 for newspaper ads to explain their cause. Teachers addressed multiethnic school councils and lobbied voters outside the polls on primary election day.[34] The union tried to punish politically the uncooperative School Committee members. Despite teacher criticism, three School Committee incumbents were reelected, only Paul Ellison losing, and John Kerrigan was elected to the City Council.

The key controversy was not over the salary increase (other city workers won 6 percent increases) but the provisions guaranteeing teacher in-school planning time and assuring job security for teachers who might be laid off when enrollment declined. Judge Garrity ordered additional minority teacher hiring, increasing the black teaching staff from 19 percent to 25 percent of all teachers, which provoked resentment among white teachers. Blacks objected to union suggestions that courts should prohibit "reverse discrimination" against white teachers.[35]

The weeklong strike was expensive for the BTU. Superior Court Judge Sam Adams raised teacher fines to $25,000 a day, and announced that he would also dock teachers' pay. The new contract was accepted by a 2:1 vote just in time, on September 29, 1975.[36] In the end, Mayor White accepted the salary settlement but, blaming school cost overruns, refused to fund additional reading specialists or smaller class sizes. Only tenured teachers enjoyed job security. Provisional teachers were deemed expendable. Any sense of BTU accomplishment was canceled out by frustrations concerning the great effort expended for marginal gains. The one by-product was increased union solidarity. Once again, Al Shanker, now president of the AFT, paid the $100,000 court fines and reimbursed the Boston newspaper ads. Other Boston unions supported the 1975 teacher strike, even the Teamsters who refused to deliver milk to schools during the strike.[37]

The Union quietly debated ideological matters as well as professional priorities. Fifteen BTU members in 1971 had organized a Reform Caucus, committed to civil rights, better libraries, smaller classes, and to making faculty senates work. Two caucus members, the Doherty brothers, John and Edward, became BTU presidents who paid attention to "bread and butter" priorities but always included several reforms designed to improve education.[38] The union support for educational improvement potentially yielded multiple benefits. If music or remedial teachers were hired, this might help children and would also provide planning time for teachers. The emergence of job security as a factor as important as wage increases suggests a classical bread-and-butter union protecting their positions. In fact, job protection did become the major BTU priority during 1975–2000.

After the new 1975 contract, a few high schools installed a faculty senate, often underutilized except in crisis situations. BTU relations with the School Committee members as a body deteriorated after 1970. Teacher grievances once expedited now went through all the steps to arbitration, a time-consuming and (for both sides) costly process. Previously, most School Committee members cheerfully accepted teacher grievances, but that was before teachers voted to boycott their fund-raisers. The School Committee members viewed this defection from past political support as an act of disloyalty. So members delayed acting on teacher grievances.[39]

Welcoming teacher aides into the BTU in the 1970s generated controversy. Aides were paraprofessionals with little or no college training. Some studied to become teachers, but they were not yet certified professionals. Including them as union members, President John Doherty's recommendation, was designed as a principled act reaching out to lower wage workers who supported the teachers. It exemplified middle-class professionals embracing the working class. Kathy Kelley recalled intense arguments pro and con; the matter was resolved by a one-vote margin.[40] John Doherty tried to build coalitions with other municipal unions but that potentially progressive initiative failed. Hogness, a Harvard scholar, concluded this was fatal to building the "working class" or proletarian coalition that old Left liberals hoped might evolve.[41]

Union struggles over racial employment issues varied dramatically by city. In New York, the UFT bitterly fought community control of schools as fomenting revolution and Black Nationalism. The UFT denounced the displacement of Jewish teachers as a form of anti-Semitism. In Boston, the teachers initially supported minority teacher recruitment. Judge Garrity directed that for every new white teacher a black teacher also be hired, a much less provocative remedy than the New York City forced transfers that Al Shanker called a "pogrom in the making" since so many white teachers were Jewish. The Boston Teacher leadership, while opposing busing, accepted most of the desegregation court orders, largely due to the moderate union leadership. Motions to repeal the BTU 1972 vote supporting "integration" failed. Other Boston unions vocally opposed the court orders, but many rank-and-file Boston teachers supported desegregation at least until 1981.[42]

Hogness attributed increased teacher militancy to the declining age of Boston's teacher workforce, the median age dropping from fifty-six to thirty-eight years.[43] Older teachers hired in the 1920s and 1930s retired. New teachers hardly remembered the Depression, or the insecurity over keeping jobs in those dark days. However, Hogness also concluded that the "new Left" movement, inspired by civil rights protests of the 1960s, did not move teachers toward progressive alliances with parents or community groups, nor toward radical ideas of social democracy and economic reconstruction of the cities. The BTU during the 1970s acted more as a bread-and-butter union promoting better working conditions for teachers. They broadened their base by including teacher aides, many of them black parents, but even this innovation divided teachers.[44]

The first three union contracts dramatically constrained the way administrators were able to make decisions about the staff. Robert C. Wood in 1978 came into the superintendency hoping to provide modern management techniques. Wood hired additional women and black administrators.[45] But Wood found that "inexperienced school committees had given away crucial management rights. No principal (they were organized in their own union!) may be transferred involuntarily, new school programs must be negotiated, and new teacher classifications must be adjudicated."[46] Wood was surprised at the unusually generous sick leave, personal leave, or bereavement provisions in the teacher contract. A teacher could take up to five days of leave for death of a family member, and a day or two to mourn for a distant relative or friend. For the ordination of a priest, one could seek a one-day leave. These contract rights were won while teachers contributed financially to School Committee campaigns.

Superintendent Wood discovered that three powerful forces constrained his leadership: the court, the union, and consumer constituencies, including parent councils and parent advocacy groups for bilingual and special education. Unions could

> prescribe and restrain professional behavior, sharply limiting if not replacing management direction. Grievances...challenge managers' decisions at every level, the performance of an individual teacher, the use of sick or vacation leave, the assignment of specialists, the development of curricula. The arbitration procedures that are provided for in such contracts stand alongside the courts in limiting and diffusing managerial choice and accountability.[47]

The union challenged Wood's plans to close old schools. Enrollments in the 1970s had decreased from 85,000 to 65,000 students leaving underutilized spaces, crumbling buildings, and too many teachers. Union President Kathleen Kelley told the judge that counts of 8,500 excess elementary seats were inflated.[48] Although both the union and the Citywide Parents Advisory council opposed Wood's December plan to eliminate only 5,300 seats, court experts countered that this number was too small. Wood needed swift approval to reduce a $10 million budget deficit, notify redundant teachers and principals, and prepare for an orderly September opening of schools. Garrity, listening to all eleven attorneys representing parties to the case (including the union), rejected Wood's plan.

The 1980 round of bargaining began with an even broader coalition of school employees. The BTU in January proposed a 15 percent salary increase for the next contract. A new organization Substitutes United in Boston Schools (SUBS) asked the BTU to bargain for 600 of their members, too. The 160 teacher aides threatened with layoffs also requested BTU support.[49] These were additional votes of confidence in the capacity of the BTU to speak for all educational workers.

Judge Garrity in May 1980 ordered thirteen schools closed. The black plaintiffs asked to postpone closings. Judge Garrity reconsidered, delaying the plan for one year. The unintended result was that Wood lost all of his projected budget savings and any remaining School Committee credibility either as a budget-balancer or "friend of the judge." Teachers in May began preparations for a fall strike.[50] However, neither side really wanted the pain of a work stoppage, and soon reached an agreement for a three-year 1980–83 contract. The talk of a strike spurred School Committee negotiators to meet with teachers frequently that spring. Both sides agreed on a

7 percent raise, costing $15 million, only to learn that the mayor had no new funds for schools that year.

State and City Taxpayer Revolts
Threaten the School Year

During the summer of 1980 the Committee abruptly dismissed Superintendent Wood, citing management and budgetary weaknesses. The Committee appointed as acting superintendent Paul Kennedy, a veteran insider, son of a former Boston Teachers College president. Kennedy rose to the top as an aide to William Ohrenberger in 1963 because of his intelligence, discretion, and talent for handling complex personnel matters. He was an intense, tightly wound administrator, trusted by all sides and able to talk School Committee members out of their worst personnel recommendations.

Massachusetts public employee unions that year strongly opposed Proposition Two and One Half, the citizen ballot "initiative," which limited annual property tax increases to 2 ½ percent unless overridden by a public referendum. Massachusetts's voters ignored public employee protests and approved new local tax limits in November 1980. Many communities including Boston had to terminate teachers, policemen, and firemen, reducing public expenditures to a level 20 percent below current levels. All during the 1980s public schools felt the negative impact. Communities laid off the youngest, most recently trained, teachers—effectively banished from careers in teaching.[51]

The School Committee had to respond to this financial crisis. In January of 1981 John O'Bryant assumed the presidency of the Boston School Committee, the first black chair. Despite the signal honor, his first challenge was addressing the severe budget shortfall. Boston's finances allowed schools to run only through March. When the committee asked Kennedy for a plan, he proposed closing 28 Boston public schools, nearly one-fifth of Boston's 146 public schools; this action required public hearings.

Shocked, the 6,800-member BTU appealed for public support to save schools, and the jobs of teachers, aides, and permanent substitutes. "Parents and teachers must unite," BTU President Kathleen Kelly insisted at an English High School rally in February 1981.[52]

Boston schools needed $241 million to remain open through June but the mayor provided only $195 million, a drastic 20 percent reduction. The city also lost revenue due to a court decision rolling back commercial property tax rates (a case with a plaintiff named Tregor). Mayor White disapproved $15 million in teacher raises, but the state Supreme Court upheld both the contract and the pay raises. O'Bryant and White met to resolve the impasse. They compromised by authorizing $20 million in additional city funds accompanied by a $30 million reduction in school spending, allowing schools to continue into May.

The School Committee voted to lay off 400 full-time employees, most of the 9 area or district office staffs, and 120 special education teachers. The Committee abolished two central office departments and canceled spring sports.[53] The next day, despite teacher protests, jeers at meetings, and threats of ballot box retaliation, the Committee voted unanimously to close twenty-four elementary schools, two middle schools, and one senior high school.

The BTU angrily responded that the city must find additional funds for the schools. Surely $40 million in uncollected parking fines could be allocated to schools, along with property tax abatement funds and a supplemental tax levy. In March 1981 other municipal unions joined teachers threatening a mass walkout if members were laid off while Mayor White's own patronage employees remained on the city payroll.

Traditionally, reductions in force required that those teachers longest in service remain employed while newer employees are let go. This is the seniority principle, long established in industrial settings. Judge Garrity had accelerated minority teacher recruitment, and most of the black and Hispanic teachers enjoyed less than six years of seniority. At a meeting on March 11, 1981, 3,500 Boston teachers voted more than 2:1 to reaffirm the seniority standard in making layoffs.[54]

Two weeks later, the stoic Superintendent Paul Kennedy, died suddenly at age fifty-three, victim of a massive heart attack. Mayor Kevin White praised him for carrying "an enormous burden in silence and with dignity."[55] His Quincy funeral was attended by 1,200 mourners. Deputy Superintendent Joseph McDonough became interim superintendent. His great challenge was to keep Boston schools open, and students educated for a full year. His strongest ally was State Education Commissioner Gregory Anrig who voiced his conviction that state law required a minimum of 180 school days. The State Board of Education requested the Massachusetts Superior Court to assure that Boston schools remain open the full year.[56] Judge Thomas R. Morse, Jr. appointed Harvard Law Professor Charles Haar of Cambridge, an expert on municipal finance, to examine Boston's resources. The State Board of Education asked, as BTU suggested, that $10 million of property tax rebate money be transferred to keep schools open. Judge Morse threatened to issue his own court order if the mayor and Council could not resolve the fiscal crisis.

Boston's school budget crisis was an exceptional challenge caused by a totally new set of voter-imposed fiscal constraints. The Boston School administrators issued 2,000 termination notices to Boston school employees, a full 25 percent of the staff. After years of postponement, twenty-seven school buildings closed in one year. The School Department total staff roster dropped from 7,842 to 5,826 employees, the reduction implemented under Acting Superintendent McDonough. Only these economies allowed the schools to live within the $210 million budget.

Judge Morse ruled that despite a "no layoff" clause in the teacher contract, the BTU could not force the Boston School Committee to fail to provide children an adequate education. The BTU asked Judge Morse to stop teacher dismissal hearings. The state found an additional $40 million for the Boston schools, and Judge Morse allowed one week for the BTU to challenge dismissals.[57] Judge Garrity in a separate federal court decision concurred with the school closings. However, he ruled that South Boston high school senior teachers, then under court receivership, could not "bump" new teachers of color. He said Headmaster Jerome Winegar must approve teacher transfers in or out of that high school, which in effect canceled seniority rights. The BTU appealed Garrity's exception to the U.S. Court of Appeals. The AFL-CIO Public Employees Division voiced support for Boston teachers. When the appeal was denied in 1982, the union asked the U.S. Supreme Court to rule that laying off 1,100 tenured white teachers was an unconstitutional deprivation of their employment rights.[58] But Garrity's ruling remained in force. Two years later, May 1983, the School Committee and the BTU said the crisis was over and upon their joint request Garrity ended Winegar's veto over teacher transfers.

Garrity also ordered that the proportion of black principals or headmasters could not drop below 20 percent, rejecting the School Committee plan to demote administrators in reverse order of seniority.[59] The union had appealed Garrity's order protecting minority teachers but the U.S. Court of Appeals in February 1982 decided his order was "necessary to safeguard the progress towards desegregation."[60] Twice the BTU appealed to the U.S. Supreme Court, which twice declined to consider charges of "reverse discrimination" against Caucasian teachers.

Judge Morse was much less visible than Judge Garrity but just as involved with Boston school issues. State Education Commissioner Anrig, bilingual education advocates, and the BTU at various times sought his intervention. His steady hand pressured the city into providing a full 180 days of education despite the financial shortfall. The State Supreme Judicial Court valued Judge Morse so highly that he was named Chief Justice of the Massachusetts Superior Court (supervising fifty-nine state judges) for a five-year term beginning in 1983.[61] The priorities several state and federal courts insisted on were those of a full school year for the children and keeping in place the additional black educators deemed necessary to provide an equal education. Court decisions overruled a series of teacher union contract provisions including seniority and employee "bumping" rights. This eroded teacher support for desegregation and raised the specter that teacher seniority was a lesser, even a disposable employment doctrine.

Boston in the summer of 1981 selected another outsider superintendent, Robert Spillane, deputy state commissioner of New York State, a veteran of local teacher strikes and racial conflict. The new superintendent entered Boston in August of 1981 just in time for the dramatic reduction of schools and staff. At his first School Committee meeting he faced 600 angry teachers wearing black armbands. That was the week that 1,043 Boston teachers actually received their dismissal or demotion letters citing "declining enrollment, Proposition 2 ½, and insufficient funds" as reasons.[62] By September 710 tenured teachers and 250 probationary or provisional teachers were gone, a decision ratified by a 4:1 School Committee vote. Boston school bus monitors were also terminated, replaced by parent volunteers.

Would Boston teachers once again strike? The BTU strongly considered a strike, which the BTU Executive Committee recommended in August. Spillane warned that strikers would be fired and replaced by recently laid-off teachers, a potent threat. The School Committee asked the State Labor Relations Commission to declare any strike illegal. On September 7 the BTU meeting at the Hynes Convention Center voted to defer a strike for two weeks (September 21), allowing school to open. At a September 20 follow-up meeting at the Commonwealth Pier exhibition hall, teachers voted 836 "yes" to strike, and 1,404 "no." More than 1,000 members were absent, demoralized by the layoffs and scarcity of dollars. The "no" voters included older teachers and black teachers, protected either by seniority or court orders unless they went out on strike.[63]

Boston voters in November returned John O'Bryant to the School Committee with the highest vote of all candidates, acknowledging his success at keeping schools open, successfully negotiating with the mayor for more money for the schools. Voters also elected a second black advocate, Jean McGuire, along with Rita Walsh-Tomasini, a longtime Home and School leader and parent council member.

The year 1981 was a terrible one, arguably the worst ever, for Boston teachers and their union leadership. Teachers in their bargaining efforts tried every known tactic of voice: meetings, protests, litigation, strike threats, political action, alliances with other unions, and alliances with parents. Voice was not enough. Previously agreed-upon salary increases had to be deferred. Fifteen percent of Boston teachers were terminated from service in draconian fashion. More than two dozen Boston public schools were closed. Larger forces were in play, especially Massachusetts voters revolting against inexorable increases in the property taxes, and judges putting the rights of long neglected minority children ahead of teacher rights. Finally, the venerable tradition of teacher seniority was overridden by affirmative action, the remediation of past racial injustices so that more members of their race could teach black children.[64] Most teachers could support affirmative action while the numbers of teachers were increasing. Tensions escalated when Caucasian teachers were terminated and teachers of color kept in place.

One lesson learned by the teacher union was that the signing of a new contract was never the end of the process. A union still had to persuade the mayor and Council to honor and fund the agreement. Next, teachers often required support from courts, sometimes two of them, to try to win contract implementation battles. Even then, court orders could override provisions such as "no layoffs" or seniority clauses. This was not the textbook labor bargaining model taught in university classes. The constant turmoil and travail persuaded Kathy Kelly to conclude that four years as BTU president was quite long enough.[65]

There were issues of teacher personal security as well. The Civil Rights movement preached nonviolence, but Boston teachers suffered physical casualties on all sides, minorities as well as Caucasians. A Lewenberg teacher was assaulted in the 1970s. The BTU asked that security guards be deployed in the schools to protect teachers and students. During 1982 Superintendent Spillane ordered swifter hearings for students possessing dangerous weapons or accused of violent acts against other students or teachers.[66] He proposed a tougher school discipline code including expulsion of students who assaulted others or brought weapons to school.

Although the state approved additional bonding authority for Boston, the city was still financially constrained. The State Supreme Court ruled that the 1980 teacher contract was binding and that Boston must appropriate money for salary increases. Boston's City Treasurer predicted that financing teacher raises would require additional layoffs. The Boston Municipal Research Bureau issued an advisory report saying that, given additional enrollment declines, the Committee should close eleven more schools. Another Bureau report, in May, found Boston schools overstaffed compared to other city schools. The School Committee notified another 700 of the 3,700 Boston teachers of possible further reductions in staff. Again, the BTU filed suit to enjoin the School Committee from taking this action; this time Superior Court Judge Andrew Linscott ruled against the union's requested preliminary injunctions. The school department on June 10, 1982 sent 595 Boston schoolteachers termination notices.

Superintendent "Bud" Spillane in 1982 urged the School Committee to take back management rights that earlier School Committees conceded.

Spillane disliked the contract language allowing older teachers to bump younger teachers and take their teaching positions. He proposed instead that principals select all of the teachers in their building. When teachers demanded a 20 percent increase, he urged the School Committee to propose a 20 percent decrease in salaries with fewer steps on the salary scale. This was hardball bargaining. Kathy Kelley called the Committee proposal "an insult" and "far beyond the bounds." School Committee President Kevin McCluskey, responding to the howl of teacher protest, modified the School Committee negotiating position to a "freeze" at current salary levels.[67]

Spillane was far tougher on teachers than any of his predecessors. He notified six tenured teachers of their unsatisfactory performance as grounds for dismissal. He warned 500 teachers of possible layoffs and told 126 assistant principals that they might revert to teacher status if new funds could not be found. [68]

When Kathy Kelley stepped down as BTU president, two candidates competed for the BTU presidency. The finalists were Edward Doherty, BTU executive vice president (whose brother Jack was BTU president during 1971–78) and James (Timo) Philip, a black teacher of history at Brighton High School.[69] Doherty was elected in June of 1983 by a 1,439 to 597 vote, less than half of the teachers voting. The election was especially important because Doherty would be reelected for the next twenty years. Doherty was a hardworking, dour union leader and Boston school parent, whose often grim demeanor concealed an enthusiasm for progressive ideas, other than yielding any ground on teacher seniority issues.

As of Labor Day, the two sides remained far apart on issues of management rights, seniority rights, benefits, pay, class size, and teacher security. The BTU rejected the School Committee's "final offer," but teachers returned to school, and continued to negotiate into the fall. Negotiations continued through December when Kevin White stepped down after sixteen years as mayor. The new Mayor Raymond Flynn asked for more time to review the contract, but the BTU, stung by delays in getting the last raises, threatened a one-day strike. Spillane again promised to fire striking teachers. Eventually, both sides agreed on 5 percent increases, which Mayor Flynn used that year as the standard for other city unions. The BTU, burned badly by wholesale teacher layoffs, refused any concessions on teacher transfer seniority policy. This was bread-and-butter unionism, basic job protection for members. The new mayor offered his sympathy, promising to try to prevent any future layoffs.[70]

Superintendent Spillane brought to the table high expectations of the Boston school professionals. He was convinced that principals and students could work harder. He believed parents wanted not just advisory councils but "school based management," local school panels actually shaping the school budget, expenditures, course offerings, and hiring decisions. School councils would hold school principals accountable for the success of their school. He proposed school-based management for eight schools the first year, then sixteen, and then expanding to all schools once principals, faculty, and parents were properly trained.[71]

Spillane spoke out for higher academic standards, deploring the fact that 30 percent of Boston students ranked in the bottom 20 percent on national reading tests. He warned high school seniors that they must pass examinations in reading, writing, and math to qualify for a diploma.[72] Later he advocated tougher grade promotion requirements and middle school academic standards as well.[73] Superintendent Spillane unquestionably raised the bar for students, teachers, and principals. But in the summer of 1985 he accepted an offer to assume the Fairfax County, Virginia superintendency.[74] His successor Laval Wilson came to Boston that September.

During 1986 the School Committee again bargained aggressively, asking for more teacher workdays (188), greater flexibility in laying off teachers, and that teachers help with school bus duty. The BTU proposed a 15 percent raise, smaller classes, and a $100 allowance for instructional supplies so teachers would not have to spend their own funds. The BTU complained that Boston ranked eighteenth out of twenty-one comparable American cities in classroom supplies.[75]

Superintendent Laval Wilson that year recommended closing four more schools. Mayor Flynn pointed out that his budget approval required accepting Wilson's plan. Wilson also proposed reducing ninety-one teaching and administrative positions, a move the BTU sharply criticized.[76] The BTU also objected to Wilson's suggestion that some teachers work longer hours including Saturdays in a "Project Promise" middle school, raising minority student achievement by providing more instructional time (after-school and Saturday mornings) on math and reading. The BTU opposed assigning teachers to schools with longer hours unless teachers volunteered and received extra pay. Wilson proposed expanding a Timilty Middle School "extra hours" pilot program for 105 students to all Timilty students and then to the Grover Cleveland and Thompson Middle Schools.[77] Responding to skeptics, Wilson the following June announced significant math and reading test score gains in Project Promise schools.[78]

The Union opposed extending the Boston Latin School day by 5 minutes unless the 120 teachers earned extra compensation. An arbitrator, reviewing this grievance, awarded $60,000 in overtime pay to the Latin School teachers.[79] The teacher voice was clear that extra time in classrooms should bring extra pay. The 2000 contract continued additional compensation for Project Promise late afternoon and Saturday work.[80]

In early September 1986, the BTU rejected the School Committee offer of 4.5 percent raises in each of three years, warning of a possible strike.[81] The BTU rejected a 5 percent offer after Labor Day, holding out for 8 percent. On September 12 teachers agreed to a 6.5 percent increase for each of three years. The Municipal Research Bureau priced the new agreement at $76 million, predicted a serious city budget deficit, and deplored the bad example set for other municipal unions.[82]

Public confidence about schools in the mid-1980s was eroded by the outraged national response to *A Nation at Risk* and other reports highly critical of public schools. No one in 1986–87 seemed satisfied with the performance of Boston schools, not the mayor, not the superintendent, not parents, and not even the teachers.[83] During 1987 Mayor Flynn, listening to the Boston Municipal Research Bureau, proposed further Home Rule legislative reforms that would strengthen the superintendent's role, relieving the School Committee of having to approve every personnel decision. Each school would set specific goals for which the principal and teachers would be held accountable. The School Committee could then focus on strategies for educational improvement. The BTU objected, saying teachers had not been consulted, and sought stronger protections against arbitrary employee termination. The City Council watered down the Flynn proposal.[84] The lesson learned that year was that school-based management would be undermined by not listening to teacher voices.

Racial hiring goals remained an issue. The BTU protested Judge Garrity's 1987 draft final orders, especially those making racial hiring targets permanent. Earlier the union objected to employment protection for Asian and Hispanic teachers on the grounds that racial discrimination was proven only against black teachers. White union members argued against assuring teachers of other races continuous employment. A U.S. Court of Appeals overturned Garrity's guidelines as unnecessary, since the committee now included minorities committed to eliminate racial discrimination.[85]

BTU leaders recognized that the 1988 teacher contract discussions required some new approaches. The BTU polled members on their attitudes toward the national school reform proposals. Leaders found 97 percent of Boston teachers wanted to help shape the more rigorous curriculum, and 93 percent wanted influence over student grouping in classrooms. However, Laval Wilson's agenda included neither school-based management nor teacher participation in decision-making. The School Based Management initiatives of Bud Spillane had stalled, despite support from business leaders and Mayor Flynn.[86] Superintendent Wilson, the press reported, was losing the confidence of school groups. School Committee

President John Nucci tried to bring parents and unions together, at least in support of the school budget.

The AFT and BTU endorsed national reforms that would raise student achievement, responding to growing dissatisfaction with city schools. In October 1988 the BTU, while suggesting salary increases of 14 percent, proposed a greater role for teachers in deciding on school improvement. The BTU sponsored workshops for first grade parents, advising them on ways to support their child's schooling. In November AFT President Al Shanker addressed the Boston Private Industry Council annual meeting on the radical changes needed in American schools—higher standards, tougher tests, and a total commitment to high-achieving schools.[87] All of this was a backdrop to seeking closer teacher and administrator collaboration in remaking each school. In many respects Shanker's beliefs grew closer to what American business leaders and President Ronald Reagan felt schools should accomplish. During the 1990s Shanker emerged as a major spokesman on higher expectations for public schools. He served on national commissions prescribing better America's schools. This public statesmanship seemed a far cry from his financing teacher strikes or stridently denouncing community control twenty years earlier, but Shanker warned teacher leaders that the alternative to higher standards might be school "vouchers" and the dismantling of public schools.

Wilson's own contract as superintendent came up for renewal while his School Committee support dwindled. A reporter asked Edward Doherty of the BTU whether Wilson would be able to turn around the schools. "If his contract is going to be renewed and he's going to strive to be a leader, there are many changes he's going to have to make."[88] The media criticized Wilson for Florida trips staying at a hotel owned by textbook providers. He was blamed for delays in submitting expenses on a city credit card, hardly a major offense. Wilson bought time, proposing a shorter-term superintendent's contract, with no raise. The Committee decided to keep him on, pending a six-month review, while Wilson looked for other assignments.[89]

In May of 1989 the superintendent and BTU agreed on a contract offering teachers 7 percent raises for three years. However, a deepening regional recession reduced both state and city tax revenues. Mayor Flynn announced, "Right now, the city cannot afford any salary adjustments." However, the contract also called for more parent and teacher involvement in teacher hiring, in curriculum decisions, and in budget allocations at the school level. The plan built on progressive school-based reforms tried out in Pittsburgh, Miami-Dade County, Rochester New York, and other cities, placing more accountability at the school level.[90] The BTU, conferring with teacher union leaders in other cities, embraced these reforms.

Wilson proposed school budgetary reductions, shaking the central bureaucracy by eliminating forty-eight more central office positions and moving eighty staff to neighborhood zone offices.[91] Other economies included halving the school police force, curtailing school sports, eliminating pre-kindergarten classes and dropout prevention programs.[92]

Meanwhile, the mayor asked the City Council to approve a city referendum abolishing the School Committee so he could appoint a smaller board. The Committee proposed closing five more schools, but neglected to schedule the required local hearings. Teachers and parents took the School Committee into Suffolk County Superior Court, which declared the closings invalid, an injunction later lifted by the State Appeals Court. However, the Committee and superintendent, by failing to schedule public hearings, lost the short-term savings needed to pay for teacher raises.

City and state revenues fell during the serious 1990 recession that severely hurt banks, insurance companies, and real-estate sales. The mayor searched for innovative ways, including new local taxes, to finance the teacher contract. Meanwhile, Flynn in December asked the BTU to renegotiate their salaries, possibly deferring raises for only one year. While City Hospital staff announced a work slowdown, the BTU scheduled a one-day strike on December 14 to force the mayor and civic leaders to consider teachers' needs, scheduling the first teacher walkout in fourteen years. Some 4,000 protesting teachers rallied in City Hall Plaza. The union executive board just before Christmas announced a two-day strike for January 25 and 26, leading possibly to a longer strike. Mayor Flynn on January 18 and 22 met with the BTU to search for a compromise. On January 26 the BTU voted to accept an 8.75 percent raise for 1989–90, a 4.5 percent raise for 1990–91, a third raise to be determined later, a total wage package costing $65 million rather than $89 million.[93]

Ferdinand Colleredo-Mansfield, a business leader, urged City Council approval of the $13.6 million supplemental budget, but also endorsed the sweeping changes in school governance desired by city employers. He chaired the Municipal Research Bureau board and was active in the Private Industry Council.[94]

In February 1990 the School Committee dismissed Superintendent Laval Wilson. On March 15 the City Council released funds needed to implement the first year of the teacher contract. The school budget remained out of balance. Acting Superintendent McDonough, responding to Mayor Flynn's budget limits, issued 785 staff layoff warning notices. Meanwhile, a twenty-nine-member search panel searched for a new superintendent. The School Committee, upset with Flynn, reduced layoff notices to 125, continuing a $42 million deficit.[95] A Suffolk Superior

County judge later found serious technical and legal flaws in the Boston layoff warning notices.[96]

Judge Garrity in June issued his final orders specifying that teacher layoffs could not be based on seniority alone but on racial mix.[97] More than half of the BTU members voted one more time to appeal his staffing guidelines. However, the U.S. Supreme Court 5–4 still supported the affirmative action remedies previously authorized by Congress. Meanwhile, John O'Bryant and the School Committee on May 13, 1991 selected Lois Harrison-Jones of Dallas, Texas, from a pool of ten finalists, seven of them minorities, as the first black woman superintendent of Boston schools.[98]

Mayor Flynn spent a full two years getting the City Council, legislature, and voters to approve his plans to appoint the Boston School Committee. The BTU sharply criticized his school council proposals that denied any voice to classroom teachers. Meanwhile, Flynn denounced the level of School Committee expenditures, and asked Northeastern University to audit school expenditures and recommend possible savings. Ed Doherty of the BTU grew so angry at the mayor's criticism of schools and teachers that he gathered enough voter signatures to run against him for mayor. But Doherty could not stop Flynn, who won a record 75 percent of the vote for a third term as mayor.[99] The mayor won state legislative approval for an appointed School Committee and in January 1992 named a new School Committee with Paul Parks, the former NAACP education leader serving as chair. Another member was Northeastern University CFO Robert Culver, whose July 1991 task force report proposed $20 million in Boston school savings. Culver's appointment led to the first balanced city school budget in years.

The BTU in March of 1992 asked for a new three-year contract with a 27 percent raise. School nurses were still paid on a teacher work year. One initiative, which Superintendent Wilson did not accept, was a proposal to establish comprehensive health clinics in each senior high school. The mayor suggested relocating the eighty-six school nurse positions to the City Department of Health and Hospitals. The city would then pay school nurses the lower wages provided city nurses, saving Boston 1 million dollars. The BTU sought a court injunction to block this transfer.[100]

As happened in previous teacher bargaining rounds, an agreement was not ready in September 1992. Teachers returned to school classes without a contract. The BTU supported an innovative proposal that a number of school buildings would be labeled "pilot schools," free both of central office rules and most union requirements. Unlike autonomous charter schools, pilot schools would remain part of the Boston Public Schools and teachers remained union members. After a full twelve months of discussion, on September 1993, both sides agreed.

Around this time, Mayor Flynn, who had campaigned for President Bill Clinton, resigned to become U.S. ambassador to the Vatican. City Council President Thomas Menino became acting mayor. Menino thought the teacher settlement too costly, but facing eight primary election challengers, asked for additional time. The BTU sued the mayor and School Committee for reneging on an agreement.[101] The union also announced a one-day strike for October 27, the week prior to primary elections, a demonstration designed to win City Council member approval. After the November election the BTU and Mayor Menino worked all weekend, agreeing on a $11 million increase, a one-year contract with a 3 percent raise, the first actual raise teachers received in three years. Menino pledged additional money once the new appointed School Committee was in place.[102]

The years 1992–93 was also the period for a major state education reform law authorizing independent charter schools, liberating those schools from state regulations and from union contract provisions perceived to impede school reform. One reason Boston agreed to "pilot schools" was the growing public enthusiasm for charter schools, twenty-five initially authorized in the 1993 state reform statute. Pilot schools, a milder version of charters, remained within the Boston public school employment system, allowing teachers to transfer to a pilot school without losing tenure, pension, and other benefits.

During 1992 state business leaders proposed aggressive teacher and principal accountability measures that threatened teacher organizations. Boston teachers fought specific reform proposals advanced by the governor, the Business Alliance, and legislators that would limit seniority, abolish tenure, and expedite teacher dismissal procedures. The organized teachers fought proposals extending the school day by an hour, or the school year by forty days. The Massachusetts Federation of Teachers and Massachusetts Teachers Association reluctantly accepted higher state educational standards, and modest revisions in teacher dismissal procedures. Democratic legislators, listening to 12,000 teachers protesting outside the State House, agreed to test only new teachers but deleted language to expedite the release of ineffective incumbent teachers.[103]

The Massachusetts Education Reform law authorized additional state funds to most Massachusetts cities including Boston. The new resources helped Boston Teachers win a new three-year contract priced at $75 million in June, the first time since 1972 that teachers returned to school with a timely agreement.[104] Teacher morale improved. In August the BTU hosted a meeting of one hundred teachers and administrators to develop programs for six new pilot schools authorized under the contract.[105]

For many reasons Boston educators could hardly protest benign parental or student exit options such as pilot and charter schools. Half the public school teachers living in Boston sent their children to private or parochial schools, a much higher percentage than other Boston parents. In other words, 50 percent of Boston's teachers exercised the exit option for their own children. This was in addition to the 50 percent of teachers, and 66 percent of Boston school principals, who lived in Boston's suburbs.[106] Perhaps three-quarters of public school workers were loyal to schools other than the Boston Public.

The new School Committee chair in January 1996 was Robert Gittens, a black attorney and Suffolk County prosecutor. The new Superintendent Thomas Payzant, hired in 1995, brought a strong, steady commitment to educational improvement without the fireworks of a Bud Spillane. Payzant's demeanor was quiet but persistent. He looked like a Clark Kent but was committed to Superman feats of raising Boston literacy and mathematics competence school by school.

What were the issues in the 1997 teacher bargaining round? The School Committee sought more thorough teacher performance evaluations, and more flexibility for principals to select teachers. The Committee also proposed selecting new teachers much earlier, so often slowed by contract provisions allowing existing teachers to transfer during the spring. The BTU demanded extra pay for the fifteen additional minutes in the longer instructional day required under the new state Educational Reform Act. The bargaining for the most part went smoothly. In September 1997 union members ratified a three-year contract providing generous salary increases and 3 percent increases in benefits, costing $65 million.[107]

Of course, increased pay might be measured against school performance. Should the city blame teachers for low student test scores? Boston's tenth grade test scores in 1998 had shown little improvement. The consulting firm Bain & Company analyzed school achievement results and concluded that as many as one-third of Boston teachers were ineffective in raising student reading or math scores. Their report questioned whether actually "restructuring" schools would work well unless teachers were better qualified.[108]

Teachers responded by blaming increased student misbehavior. Of 1,500 teachers polled, 54 percent said student behavior was worse than the previous year, and 56 percent believed the student discipline code was not consistently enforced. Certainly Dorchester High School, the mayor acknowledged, took in too many previously incarcerated youth. The superintendent and Union decided to "intervene," sending in a joint management-labor union team to restructure the troubled school.[109] Both sides recognized that low achievement scores meant students were not learning enough either to succeed in college or at entry-level jobs.[110]

Did anyone ever acknowledge the commitment, the ideas, the effective teaching by the best Boston teachers? The Bank of Boston in 1984, celebrating the 200th anniversary of the bank, created the Boston Plan for Excellence, in which teachers and principals each year could apply for private funds to try out new ideas in the classroom, grade, or school.[111] The Bank of New England announced a fund offering seven effective teachers a $9,000 scholarship or graduate fellowship. Superintendent Spillane thought this a superb way to recognize high-performing teachers. But when the BTU found out that this would reward only teachers rated as outstanding teachers, and thus resembled "merit pay," they denounced the plan. The bank later revised the nomination process to satisfy Boston's teachers.[112]

The City Wide Education Coalition (CWEC) in 1986 issued a report card on Boston schools, handing out some failing grades. This action upset the union. However, in 1987 Ellen Guiney of CWEC scheduled an annual Golden Apple awards ceremony acknowledging the stellar contributions of fifteen individual teachers and other school workers each year. Corporations supported the awards and Boston's newspapers profiled award recipients. Parents, students, administrators, and BTU members each year nominated more than 500 teachers for recognition.[113] Most media coverage of teachers was bad news: strikes, scandals, or low student scores. Boston between 1987 and 2001 recognized a few teacher accomplishments.

The biggest controversy remained the protection of teacher seniority. During 1999 and into 2000 the Union defended the rules that allowed veteran teachers priority in transferring to other schools ahead of newly appointed teachers, or over provisional teachers still completing three years on probationary status. The Union pointed out that in-system teacher transfers were all completed by March 23. The administration complained that veteran teachers could "bump" younger white teachers more qualified by degrees, or replace valued members of a cohesive departmental or grade team. Principals had no say about accepting veteran teachers contractually "entitled" to a transfer to their school. In effect, transfer to a new school was a teacher's entitlement or property right.

Mayor Menino in his January 2000 State of the City address pledged Boston principals more flexibility in hiring teachers. He knew he could count on support from business leaders, the Black Ministerial Alliance, and the Boston Plan for Excellence board.[114] Ten weeks later, the Boston Plan for Excellence (the Bank of Boston 1984 program) released a policy paper "Towards an Open Teacher Hiring Process," documenting how 417 first-year teachers could lose their jobs to veteran teachers with greater seniority. Boston's Chief Operating Officer Michael Contompasis recommended abolishing seniority rules, hiring only the best-qualified teacher for each job.[115]

The BTU, representing senior teachers and remembering the 1980s layoffs, took the Boston Plan paper as a declaration of war. The BTU accused principals of persuading ineffective teachers to transfer out rather than give substandard evaluations, a practice described as the "lemon exchange." President Doherty asserted "veteran teachers deserve more privileges than younger teachers in a school system."[116] The BTU, upset about criticism of older teachers, voted that teachers "work to rule" rather than participate in after-school meetings or literacy workshops. The *Globe* reported this as union retaliation for the public airing of contract talks.[117]

Thirty community groups including many churches and the Greater Boston Chamber of Commerce joined in opposing teacher seniority transfer rights. BTU President Doherty sharply criticized their reform coalition, "Boston United For Children." Seniority became the central issue in the 2000 bargaining round. Boston teachers purchased ten days of August television ads to present their side of the case. Doherty warned that "my membership will not ratify a contract that takes away its assignment and seniority rights" and denounced "teacher-bashing."[118] Business leaders released a poll of 400 Boston voters, 70 percent favoring principals being able to select the best candidate available for a teaching position. Teachers once again resumed teaching in September without a new contract, voting against a September strike but continuing to "work to rule" within the six-and-a-half hour day. Observers predicted an October strike, prompting the School Committee to seek a State Labor Relations Commission "cease and desist" order. Thousands of teachers rallied on City Hall Plaza, demanding both a contract and more "respect." Finally, on October 11, the BTU ratified a three-year contract with 12 percent pay increases (costing $100 million), very modest changes in seniority rules, transfer rights, and other measures approved in especially tense contract discussions moderated by Mayor Menino. Mainly first- and second-year provisional teachers would be protected from position "bumping," a modest victory.[119]

This time the BTU won, using rallies, ads, strike threats, and loud voices to assert the employment rights of senior teachers over the less potent forces of advocates for letting principals staff the classrooms. A century was about to end. Boston teachers emerged unified, powerful, and effective in advancing the fundamental rights of teachers as workers. They pulled a popular mayor deep into the settlement talks; for once, they did not need to litigate to gain further "respect" and implementation.

Were teacher unions open to new ideas? During the 1980s and 1990s BTU leaders regularly met with progressive union counterparts in Rochester (NY), Milwaukee, and other cities exploring educational reform issues. Together they discussed ways that schools might promote academic success, even those requiring changes in work rules. The U.S. Department of Education and the Annenberg Foundation convened teacher union leaders from key cities, seeking more effective ways to improve low-performing schools. The BTU and other unions established the national Teacher Union Reform Network (TURN) which was housed at Northeastern University.[120]

The Boston Teachers 2000 contract reflected progressive ideas. It began with a preamble acknowledging the importance of parent involvement, and the desirability of a plan for each school and school-based decision-making. The contract provided for school intervention teams to assist, and if needed, "restructure" schools in trouble (with three union designees and three administrators on a team). The contract recognized the need for collecting performance data on individual school achievement, retention and dropout rates, parent and staff satisfaction surveys. Teachers were expected to complete eighteen hours of teacher professional development courses each year, and could consider exchange programs with business, industry, and government. Teachers would take part in seminars on multiculturalism and the changing needs of the population. The contract also provided career ladders identifying "lead teachers" and mentor teachers earning extra pay helping neophytes. The National Board for Professional Teaching Standards certified excellent teachers who might then qualify for higher salaries. These provisions departed dramatically, in attitude and process, from the old antipathy to "merit pay." By 2006 some but not all of these constructive commitments were implemented.[121]

Progressive ideas came from several sources after 1985, including the national education reform movement, from the TURN city unions, and the "Getting to Yes" strategies developed by Roger Fisher of the Harvard Law School whose staff helped the Boston school bargaining at least once. They advanced the potential for new modes of teacher responsiveness to emerging urban educational priorities. Another influence was the Boston Plan for Excellence that in 2002 supported aspiring Boston Principal Fellows and in 2003 accepted a $2.2 million private grant to train Boston Teacher Residents in and for the Boston public schools, many minorities, and new mathematics or science teachers.[122] Another foundation provided funds for Boston teachers for summer travel to other countries and special studies, as many as ninety teachers at a time.[123]

Collective bargaining was supposed to work according to this format: teachers would elect one organization to represent them. Majority rule would resolve internal disputes, since periodic elections would assure union democracy. Teacher leaders would negotiate salaries, hours, and working conditions with a school board, which would ask a mayor and council to provide funds. If there was an impasse during negotiations, a mediator mutually agreed upon would help resolve the issue. No public workers would ever strike, since schools were a service monopoly, and strikers by law would be imprisoned, the union fined, and possibly decertified.

The serious national recession from 2008 to 2010 diminished state and local budgets for all public services, including education. Democrats (and a few Republicans) in Congress approved a Stimulus Package of almost $900 billion, of which $100 billion was prioritized for states to save as many teaching positions as possible, some at public universities but most for public school teaching positions. Boston over two years received $21 million dollars, helping Boston schools avoid layoffs in fiscal years ending in June of 2010 and 2011.

Additional funds were allocated for federal Title One, Special Education, Teacher Quality, and a new $4.35 billion initiative called Race to the Top. These RTTT grants would go only to those states that committed to an academically challenging Common Core of English and mathematics skills, engage in rigorous school evaluations, use data for key decisions about teachers and principals, and would close, transform, or turn around the lowest performing schools.[124]

Massachusetts Governor Deval Patrick proposed a new education reform bill aimed at closing the "Achievement Gap" and encouraging the creation of "Innovation Schools" with the freedom to try out new ideas enjoyed by Charter Schools and Boston's Pilot Schools. The bill also selectively raised the cap on charter schools in cities, and gave city superintendents extraordinary power to replace teachers and principals at twelve underperforming schools. A coalition of business groups, minority leaders, Mayor Menino, and The Boston Foundation lobbied for the bill, which passed.

The 2010 Act to Reduce the Achievement Gap strengthened the hand of Superintendent Johnson, doubled the charter school spending cap in cities, and increased the chances for a RTTT grant of $250 million. State Education Commissioner Mitchell Chester released a list of thirty-five underperforming schools, twelve of them in Boston. The new law required that half of the teachers and certain principals be replaced using a school "turnaround" strategy suggested in the Race to the Top guidelines. Another "Fresh Start" option replaced all teachers.

BTU President Stutman denounced the federal requirement that if a state has more than nine low-performing schools, you must consider such a drastic strategy, "I don't think you have a fair chance of improving a school by brooming out more than half the people and starting over." He told the Boston GLOBE "I find it insulting and counterproductive".[125]

Earlier that year, the national press took notice of a major event in Central Falls, Rhode Island, just over the Massachusetts border, where the superintendent fired all the teachers for their reported reluctance to agree to a longer school day and provide more tutoring assistance. Rhode Island Education Commissioner Deborah Gist, U.S. Education Secretary

Duncan, and President Obama strongly supported the Central Falls superintendent's action, much to the chagrin of unionized teachers around the nation. Within weeks, the Central Falls teachers returned to discussions and a "turnaround" agreement was reached. For the Massachusetts Federation of Teachers (MFT), the heavy reliance on student test scores for teacher evaluations was a form of "teacher bashing," and the thought of tenured teachers being fired was repugnant. The MFT refused to endorse the second Massachusetts RTTT proposal, unlike the NEA affiliate, the Mass Teachers Association, which indicated support.

As the Boston Teacher contract was about to expire in August of 2010, two groups announced their support of a shorter, streamlined contract that would allow principals a freer hand in selecting and assigning teachers and determining the length of the school day. One group called itself the "Put Students First" coalition and complained that Boston's 250-page contract overly prescribed teacher work hours, transfer rights and protection for less effective teachers. Paul Grogan, president of The Boston Foundation, convened twenty-one civic, businesses, and foundations to advocate a "thin" contract.

Another group of thirty-five grassroots organizations was named "Boston United for Students" and also called for an extended school day, more flexible hiring, rigorous teacher evaluations, and a stronger voice for parents and students in local school decisions about budgets and personnel. John Mudd of Massachusetts Advocates for Children said "too few schools had functioning school councils, and that principals and school councils needed more training if parents, students, teachers, and high school students were to have a voice in local school matters".[126] Several Boston area foundations asked the Boston Municipal Research Bureau to play a leading role in this campaign. City Councilor John Connolly held a seven-hour public hearing in late October to listen to parents and others complain about the overly prescriptive teacher contract that protected ineffective teachers.

Richard Stutman, BTU president, said that his union might accept longer school days with appropriate extra compensation. He felt they could support "objective" teacher evaluations and giving students and parents more of a say. Contract discussions began during the summer of 2010 but, as in previous bargaining rounds, school began after Labor Day without a new agreement.

Superintendent Johnson proposed that the contract include a longer school day, and allocated new federal education funds for an additional half hour of instruction and tutoring. She proposed extra pay for teachers at improving schools, those that increased student scores and came off the underperforming lists. She said that new money could be used for either merit bonuses or for additional school equipment.[127]

Would teachers commit to excellence? The BTU in 2009 opened its own Pilot School in the Jamaica Plain neighborhood of Boston, with a full program including Spanish classes and a partnership with Simmons College. Previously the BTU had blocked several new pilot schools and insisted on two-thirds of a faculty voting "yes" on new pilot school proposals, several of which included a longer work day. The union felt that the new BTU school would be "an opportunity to develop a new culture of collegiality and accomplishment," while showing that organized teachers could run their own effective school.[128] In 2010 the BTU school enjoyed a waiting list of applicants as it added classes to a kindergarten-grade eight school. In effect, Boston teachers, like counterparts in Minnesota and New York City, were saying "Give us a chance to show how professional teachers can find the keys to academic achievement on our own terms."

What had Collective Bargaining Accomplished?

For Boston teachers from 1965 to 1999 the ideal model broke down almost every time the contract was close to expiration. Contract negotiations often spilled over into the next school year, teachers working without a contract. Teachers either had to strike or threaten to strike to get the attention of elected officials. Once a contract was approved, the mayor rarely came up with enough money in a timely fashion until 1992. After the contract was signed, the union usually had to file one or more lawsuits to enforce the provisions.

The BTU from 1965 to 2004 united over which Irish American teacher would lead them: two Reillys (unrelated), Henry Robinson, Kathy Kelley, and two Dohertys (brothers). The union increasingly represented more dues-paying black, Hispanic, and Asian teachers, even when that meant layoffs for hundreds of young Caucasian teachers, mainly in 1981–82 but with recurrent warnings of layoffs for another decade. The AFL-CIO supported teacher desegregation (in the South) but the BTU, especially after 1981, repeatedly challenged local racial protection orders for Boston teachers. The BTU never accepted defeat of the seniority principle, taking it all the way to the U.S. Supreme Court in the hopes that judges might overturn "reverse discrimination" against white teachers. The court orders prevailed for more than thirty years.

Collective bargaining for teachers was the final straw that drove Boston mayors crazy. They were asked to find new funds for teacher contracts without any say over what appeared to be inefficient, ineffective education, for which they were invariably blamed. Mayors White and Flynn separately concluded that the solution was appointing a School Committee whose spending they could then constrain. Eventually, by 1991, the governor and legislature recognized the failure of grassroots democracy to manage Boston schools and authorized greater mayoral control and accountability.

The 1965 state statutes governing public employee bargaining laws were initially designed as a reform, a device to outlaw debilitating teacher strikes and establish clear state policies and mechanisms to avoid them. The public sector bargaining laws helped teachers find their voice, to request new salary levels every three years, and to assert their rights. But teacher unions were at important moments bowled over by major taxpayer revolts and overridden in the battle to save white teacher jobs when pitted against judges enforcing the Fourteenth Amendment of the U.S. Constitution.

On the whole, collective bargaining in Boston and other cities has raised pay for teachers, perhaps by as much as 10 percent more than before, almost always recognizing years in service. Health and pension benefits have become embedded. Class sizes have been lowered, and exceptions subject to grievances enforced by contract provisions. So the cost of schooling has been increased because of bargaining. Individual teachers have been better protected against incompetent administrators or arbitrary dismissal. But a series of Harvard conferences on bargaining in 1998 and 2005 revealed a paucity of research and an abundance of diverse opinions on the positive effects, including on school effectiveness and student learning.[129]

Was unionism compatible with educational reforms? Teacher unions supported certain reforms with a broad constituency, such as parents supporting lower class size, or expanding authority at the school level. But the basic purpose of unions was basically to seek wage increases and protect teacher jobs; other professional priorities might be pursued only after basic needs were met. Other reforms would be stoutly resisted unless teachers were allowed a strong voice, a seat at the table, and compensated for any extension of the workday or year.

How might teachers become full partners in educational reforms proposed by others? The potential contribution of teacher unions depended on their right to be consulted, to be involved in professional decisions such as teaching methods, textbook selection, testing and graduation policies. Cora Bigelow proposed a strong teacher voice in Boston in the 1920s, winning it but only for a decade. Myron Lieberman defined such a proactive role for teachers as professionals in the 1950s.[130] If teachers were treated with the respect accorded doctors and accountants, the necessity for teacher unions might have vanished. Chapter 2 described how Boston teachers 1900–65 were isolated, marginalized, and treated as low-level workers despite their central role in educating children. If the city and state properly supported teachers, then teachers presumably could support more of the larger battles to reform and reinvent quality education.

Boston teachers on school councils won a voice in choosing their coworkers and colleagues. By the year 2000 no Boston superintendent could assign a new principal or hire teachers without other teachers interviewing the candidates. Teachers could also apply to teach in a deregulated pilot school. Teachers could assist in recruiting or coaching new teachers. These were the tasks of a professional guild, more than just another public employee union. Teachers might yearn for a still greater voice, but they had made great strides over the previous generations of Boston schoolteachers. They may not have transformed the social order, but they certainly gained a voice in shaping a new one.

David Tyack decades ago recognized the importance of classroom teachers; they were

> "the group with the greatest power to veto or sabotage proposals for reform. No realistic estimate of strategies for change in American education could afford to ignore teachers or fail to enlist their support. No meaningful improvement of life in classrooms could take place without the skill, empathy, strength and commitment of teachers."[131]

Boston teachers through their union supported a few significant reforms, but held fast on protecting veteran teachers, competent or not. In the end, the enforcement of seniority rights conflicted with the emerging education reform of student proficiency and greater school productivity. "Work to rule" behavior reduced teacher availability for any special training or assigned project outside the workday. Union attitudes toward change stimulated parent interest in charter schools that provide students with more flexible hours and learning opportunities. If teacher unions were to survive, union leaders would need to accelerate a commitment to their own professional improvement, the mentoring of new teachers, the upgrading or easing out of ineffective teachers by peer reviews, the use of student achievement data to improve instruction, and the embrace of effective new technologies and instructional formats. Otherwise, collective bargaining for teachers must confront the harsh assessment that teacher negotiations generally retard the pace of urban school reform.

CHAPTER 8

BUSINESS CALLS FOR
EDUCATIONAL IMPROVEMENTS

Boston business leaders early in the twentieth century won substantial control over the Boston schools for the decade 1906 until 1915. Businessman James Jackson Storrow and Superintendent Stratton Brooks managed the Boston school system like a corporation.[1] But business dominance over Boston ward politics did not survive the decade. For the next sixty years, politicians ran the schools as a public employment "jobs" system. Was it possible for Boston's business leaders in the 1970s to reverse the tide and make schools respond to the needs of children, parents, and employers? Was the desegregation suit a detriment, or stimulus to corporate participation and voice?

The Boston business community in the 1980s included four strong economic clusters: finance, insurance, medical services, and higher education. The burgeoning mutual funds industry (Fidelity, Putnam, Vance) complemented the financial prowess of major commercial banks such as the Bank of New England, Bank Boston, Shawmut, and State Street Bank. Insurance companies then included the John Hancock, Liberty Mutual and New England Life. Seven teaching hospitals were affiliated with Harvard Medical School, while Tufts University and Boston University each had their own teaching hospitals. More than 60 higher education institutions brought 200,000 students a year to Boston, Cambridge, Newton, and Medford, spawning auxiliary enterprises from bookstores to coffeehouses.[2]

Press coverage of Boston school desegregation raised national concerns about whether Boston itself had ceased to be a civilized city. After the network television clips on school busing, during 1974–76, recruiters encountered great skepticism from young minority professionals invited to Boston. They considered Boston a racist, unfriendly, violent city.

Most business leaders lived in quiet suburbs where their children attended private schools or the excellent public schools of Weston, Wellesley, Lincoln, or Lexington. Few business leaders voiced anything but disdain for elected officials, including the Boston School Committee members. Kenneth Rossano, a Boston bank executive who for more than a decade was secretary to the Coordinating Committee (nicknamed "The Vault"), recalled "the suggestion that business leaders meet occasionally with members of the City Council was received with genuine dismay."[3] Business executives thought most City Council and School Committee members were self-serving schemers, grafters, and publicity hounds. Periodic indictments of school committeemen and other city officials did not surprise corporate leaders, many of whom already suspected the worst.

The basic instinct of business leaders was mainly to restrain city property tax increases and municipal expenditures, as had their predecessors in previous decades. Boston's leaders prior to 1974 essentially gave up on public schools, recruiting their new employees from the business schools, managers from Harvard and Dartmouth, accountants from Bentley, Northeastern, and Suffolk, salesmen from Tufts and Babson. By 1980 the ban on Irish employment had long ended at most firms. Graduates of Holy Cross, Boston College, Villanova, and Georgetown began to fill the top echelons at Shawmut Bank, the Bank of New England, the utilities (Boston Gas, Edison, and New England Telephone), and even a few investment firms.[4] Access to the best jobs remained more difficult for Italo-Americans and Poles, and well into the 1980s for blacks.

In the late 1960s some Boston businessmen paid special attention to one public school, Boston High School, a work-study high school, designed to keep a few hundred probable dropouts in school at least half time. (President John F. Kennedy had announced that a 35 percent high school dropout rate was a national problem.) Boston companies agreed to divide jobs to employ two high school students, each for half a day, especially while the economy grew (until the oil price shocks of 1973.)

The leader who invited corporate leaders into new relationships with Boston Schools was a federal judge, W. Arthur Garrity. The judge read reports urging corporate involvement in urban schools and accepted the suggestion of Edward McCormack, one of his masters, to seek business help. He met with corporate executives before issuing his desegregation decision. The leaders agreed to finance a Trilateral Council for Quality Education involving business, universities, and the Boston schools. They warned the judge about adverse stockholder reaction if he ordered them to participate. However, the big banks and insurance companies, Gillette and the utilities agreed to partner or "pair" with a Boston senior high school, offering corporate support to headmasters, teachers, and students.[5] Cronin and Hailer earlier reported how three companies, New England Life, The Bank of New England, and New England Telephone already worked in the schools. Other companies agreed to assign staff to work with a school to determine what resources might be provided, for example, the First National Bank of Boston with Hyde Park High, Gillette with nearby South Boston High School, and New England Life with Jeremiah Burke High.

It was often hard to tell who spoke for Boston's business leaders. One business association spoke for greater Boston, and another for state manufacturers. One group represented Massachusetts taxpayers, and another Boston's municipal taxpayers. On school issues other groups spoke up, the Boston Compact and the Private Industry Council. An umbrella group, the Greater Boston Chamber of Commerce, included more than 1,000 businesses, from stores and shops to utilities, banks, and manufacturers. Even a few universities belonged, although the Chamber had no standing committee on education until 1985. Occasionally corporate leaders spoke out on education issues, but not very often.

Many Bostonians suspected that the real corporate power resided in a secretive group called The Coordinating Committee, or "The Vault," so called from their meeting room near the vault of the Boston Safe Deposit and Trust Company. Boston's business leaders huddled in 1959 when the city faced bankruptcy. City property taxes were high, the city bond rating had plummeted, new construction was stalled, and City Hall was larded with unproductive employees, legacies from the Curley years. State Senator John E. Powers was the likely next mayor, but Registrar John Collins impressed Vault members with his ideas on how to restore solvency and rebuild the city. Once elected, Collins with strong business support cut city expenditures and lowered the tax rates.

Mayor Kevin White, Collins's successor, ignored the Vault until he needed funds to avert a racial crisis (the night of the King assassination), or summer jobs for youth in the turbulent years of the late 1960s. He had to meet with the Vault in 1976, when Moody's dropped the city bond rating to "Baa" and the banks refused to purchase city bonds or notes. Mayor White then agreed to cut the city workforce by 10 percent.[6]

The Vault tried to coordinate Boston's corporate philanthropy but never actually ran any programs or partnerships. The members were impressed by the new Superintendent Robert Spillane's 1981 proposal that schools should meet higher standards of student attendance and achievement. He helped negotiate the first Boston Compact (350 years earlier Pilgrims signed the Mayflower Compact) spelling out expectations for greater school performance in return for increased employer commitments. Spillane also proposed to decentralize certain administrative decisions to the school level under the banner of School Based Management, an idea the corporate leaders preferred over the stifling central school management.[7]

The Private Industry Council (PIC) funded by the U.S. Department of Labor worked closely with Boston schools on workforce issues. Congress had authorized mayors to appoint local councils where 51 percent of members represented employers. The Boston PIC staff worked with schools, universities, companies, and other employers on both youth and adult employment programs. The PIC took on the task of monitoring Boston high schools and their graduates for the next twenty-five years, 1982–2006, assisted by a senior staff coordinator in the superintendent's office and for many years by the Boston Federal Reserve Bank research department.

The most important business watchdog was the Boston Municipal Research Bureau (MRB), a private association of major taxpayers monitoring city budgets, tax rates, agency expenditures, and efficiency. Republican City Councilor Henry Lee Shattuck in 1932 founded the "Bureau" when Governor Curley's appointments eviscerated the state-controlled Boston Finance Commission. The banks and major law firms paid for excellent MRB financial analysts, Joseph Slavet in the 1950s, Joseph Barresi in the 1960s, Jack Delaney during 1975–79, Harry Durning until 1983, and Samuel Tyler for more than twenty years. Although an independent entity, MRB reports helped mayors and alert city councilors pursue management efficiencies, and after 1965 to review union contract proposals.

The Boston Herald in 1976 summarized the persistent concerns of business leaders whose dues supported the MRB:

> While most executives said they are not certain as to just how serious Boston's financial problem is, all cited inefficient management, lack of cost controls, too many people on the payroll, insensitivity to the responsibility that goes with handling the people's tax payments, and an adversary relationship between local, state, and federal governments that bars cooperative use of public money.[8]

Boston's schools were only part of the larger problem.

One solution the Bureau favored was a stronger superintendency that could control hiring and school expenditures. Boston School Committees, as Strayer complained, required multiple executives to report directly to them, the business manager, the school house custodian, the structural engineer, and the secretary to the School Committee. This enabled committee members to dabble in staffing decisions. The managerial meddling troubled Sam Tyler of the Bureau who sought to strengthen the role of the superintendent and to tighten school budgeting practices. Beginning in 1972 the Bureau proposed placing the superintendent in charge of all personnel and day-to-day operations. In 1978 the Bureau helped School Committee Chairman David Finnegan win passage of Chapter 633 of the General Laws of Massachusetts, making the superintendent the source of all appointments. The mayor, the Vault, and the School Committee agreed to that change. However, the School Committee members ignored the structural reforms. If the elected School Committee continued to undermine strong executive leadership, then the MRB preferred an appointed school board along the lines of New York, Chicago, Philadelphia, and Pittsburgh. An appointed board would end the illusion that the School Committee decided budgets, or could approve an expensive teacher contract, when the mayor actually controlled revenues, appropriation levels, and tax rates.[9]

The Boston Compact

Mayor White in 1981 announced a $38 million school financial shortfall, the year the State Appellate Tax Board ordered substantial property tax abatements, the refund of back taxes due to the complaints of a taxpayer named Tregor, along with other commercial property owners. This forced the mayor to close fire and police stations, and announce that schools would close forty days early. He proposed as an alternative a city payroll tax on all workers in Boston, plausible because suburban workers would then support the city where they worked.

Business leaders decided instead to support an emergency state loan of $30 million to the city, in part to keep the children in school into June. They also wanted a change in City Council and School Committee electoral structures, choosing most members by district, rather than at large, to empower neighborhoods rarely represented. That year they supported a campaign to elect "fresh faces" to the Council and School Committee. Finally, they endorsed the school site management reforms proposed by superintendent Robert Spillane.

Their next move was to negotiate with Spillane and the mayor a new "social contract" pledging business support for sustained efforts to upgrade the schools. The need was urgent. *The Boston Globe* dissected Boston Public Schools shortcomings in devastating detail; most of Boston's high schools, other than the three exam schools, suffered a 50 percent dropout rate. One-quarter of the students were absent on any given day, "the worst overall attendance rate of any of the big city schools nationally." More than one-third of vocational students failed their courses, and 39 percent of all students (except at the exam schools) failed math, and 42 percent failed science. Hispanic student scores were in the lowest quartile. Boston teachers were often ill prepared to teach classes assigned to them, and the teacher absentee rate exceeded that of ten other major cities.[10]

Teacher salaries had risen during the 1970s, while school repairs and renovations were deferred. These and other deficiencies prompted business leaders to get involved. But they demanded school improvements in exchange for their support. The Boston Compact, as the accord was named, committed each side to specific goals. Business leaders, through the Private Industry Council, would ask 200 companies to provide 800 summer jobs and offer more than 1,000 jobs (more in subsequent years) to high school graduates. In return the Boston Public Schools would increase the number of high school students graduating by 5 percent each year, supply annual reports on improved student attendance, on reading and math achievement, and evaluate headmasters on progress toward agreed-upon goals.

The Compact was initially directed by Bob Schwartz, education aide to Mayor White, with help from Bill Spring, president of the Trilateral Council whose passion was linking youth to jobs through education.[11] Initially, black School Committee members John O'Bryant and Jean McGuire opposed the Compact, an agreement forged without involving any black leaders. They objected to white corporate executives negotiating with Spillane and Mayor White, who for the first time in a decade appeared at the School Committee offices to sign the Compact. Black leaders insisted that this top-down initiative must be amended to include explicit minority youth hiring targets.[12]

Corporate leaders through the Compact opened job access at 273 Boston firms, hiring 415 Boston high school graduates in 1983, and 600 in 1984. Employers accepted 1,200 students in 1983 for summer jobs, then 1,500 in 1984, and 2,000 in 1985. Half the companies had never before employed Boston school graduates. Twenty-five colleges and universities signed a parallel Boston Higher Education Partnership, promising financial aid, advice, and tutoring in exchange for higher student achievement and attendance.[13] The school dropout rate began to decline, a direct response to the lure of jobs. Jim Darr, a Private Industry Council designer of the Boston Compact, explained, "The one thing that companies have which kids want, that the kid's parents want, and that the companies already have, as a normal part of their business, is jobs."[14]

The BTU refused to support the Compact until the Private Industry Council agreed to hire some of the 1,100 teachers laid off in 1981 to staff city high school-to-jobs programs. The BTU then saw value in the business partnership.[15]

The Boston Plan for Excellence in the Public Schools

The First National Bank of Boston prepared for its 200th birthday in 1984. Kenneth Rossano, the bank's senior vice president for community and governmental relations, was a passionate believer in education. He sought advice from Harvard President Derek Bok. When Rossano suggested a Boston scholarship program, Bok replied, "Well, that might get you into heaven, but it is not what Boston schools need." He advised Rossano to meet with Education Dean Patricia Graham and two senior faculty members, both of them former U.S. Commissioners of Education Francis Keppel, dean in the 1960s, and Harold "Doc" Howe, once a Ford Foundation vice president. Howe volunteered to draft plans on how Boston teachers and principals might apply for innovation funds, "a small grants program for the schools." Such grants might develop school site leadership and break the stifling effects of a centralized system. This became the basis for the bank's anniversary gift to Boston schools.[16]

Bank leaders announced the Boston Plan for Excellence for the Public Schools in April of 1984 at a dramatic ceremony at the Old State House, the political epicenter in 1784. The Bank offered $1.4 million to endow grants for which any Boston school might apply.[17]

The John Hancock Mutual Life Insurance Company later that year announced a 1 million dollar fund for Boston's middle schools, grants for academic and intramural athletic programs. A Boston law firm, Goodwin, Procter, and Hoar, contributed 1 million dollars to support Boston's early childhood programs, a cash gift unheard of from a major law firm. Each firm had identified a "weak link" that might be strengthened.[18]

When Rossano became chairman of the Greater Boston Chamber of Commerce in 1984, he asked Cronin to organize an Education Committee. The Committee decided to work on improving Boston student access to college. Rossano and Cronin consulted with Robert Sperber of Boston University (director of the Higher Education Partnership) and Robert Schwartz, COMPACT director. Together they developed a college counseling and scholarship program called ACCESS, which the New England (Life Insurance Company) CEO Edward "Ted" Phillips thought deserved a 1 million dollar endowment. Despite what Bok said about scholarship programs, city students often decided in June to attend college the next September. They needed expert advice on how to file financial aid applications in the winter of senior year, early enough to qualify for state, federal, and other aid programs. ACCESS replicated the Cleveland Foundation "last dollar" scholarship program wherein students were counseled how and when to apply for federal and state dollars as well as private scholarships, then given funds to help close any remaining financial aid gap. Schwartz was the first director of the Boston Plan, followed by Mario Pena, the first ACCESS coordinator.[19]

The Boston Plan within a few years accumulated $3.5 million in corporate donor pledges. Also, Boston Foundation executives Geno Balotti and Anna Faith Jones provided another million dollars for expenses until the bank's gift of Continental Cablevision stock soared in value. Technically, only 5 percent of the principal could be spent each year, with proceeds reinvested so that the total fund might grow faster than inflation and be available "in perpetuity." Potentially $175,000 of investment proceeds could be expended each year. Boston school faculties could request several hundred dollars for a small project or as much as 10,000 dollars if teachers of several grades collaborated.[20]

Kenneth Rossano described these as "venture capital investments" a full decade before young philanthropists popularized the concept of Venture Philanthropy. He aspired to make grants that "contributed to significant improvements in student attendance and reading and math scores." The Plan became a way for companies and a law firm to put money behind their voice, a powerful expression of support.[21]

During the 1980s the bold concepts of the Boston Compact and the Boston Plan for Excellence attracted substantial national attention. Previously, only colleges benefited from private endowments, in contrast to public schools funded by taxes. Other cities and suburbs imitated Boston's innovative models of corporate support, creating local educational foundations to augment public expenditures. For teachers and principals, this was "free money" with few strings attached. For students, the Compact held out the promise of real jobs, summer and permanent, an additional reason to complete high school.[22]

Was the Compact effective? The national acclaim surrounding the Compact exceeded actual school performance gains. Although business leaders delivered jobs, Boston school results rose and fell. Spillane left for Fairfax County, Virginia, unhappy with the larger School Committee that corporate Boston helped install. While Spillane was in charge, high school attendance rose from 75 to 80 percent. Metropolitan Achievement Test scores appeared to rise (skeptics said teachers coached students for this test) and the percentage of students attending college increased in 1985 by 10 percent. Black and Hispanic students found jobs in record numbers, partly due to the Compact and due to the robust economy of the mid-1980s dubbed the Massachusetts Miracle.

Superintendent Laval Wilson was much less committed to Spillane's corporate priorities or to school-based management (favored by business leaders). He spent two years designing his own elaborate educational improvement strategy. On his watch the cumulative high school dropout rate actually rose from 36 percent for the Class of 1982 to 40 percent for the Class of 1986. The new Hubert Humphrey vocational center lost state and federal aid because of low-performing programs and low retention rates.[23]

Only the school attendance rate improved, from 80 percent to 85 percent in 1987. This alone did not assure the business community that Compact goals were taken seriously. The Compact Steering Committee faced angry corporate leaders who said schools had not delivered. They discussed not renewing the Compact. They called for expanded school-based management so that individual schools handled budget allocations and staff hiring, to be included in the 1990–91 collective bargaining contract. They expected more parent involvement in school programs. They wanted high school graduates monitored for an additional four years, to see whether they attended, completed, or dropped out of college. They expected dropout rates to decline by 10 percent each year through alternative education and vocational education programs. Finally, they insisted on increased academic performance on standardized tests, requiring every high school to offer a precollege curriculum.

Business leaders, troubled by vague commitments, sought quantifiable, measurable goals. They listened to policy veterans of the Carter administration who knew schools did not improve by themselves, not without stronger parent support, alternative high schools, and a curriculum tailored to each school.[24]

Mayor Raymond Flynn watched all of this from 1984 to 1989 and, like Kevin White before him, grew frustrated and angry with the schools. While a state representative and city councilor, he took a master's degree at the Harvard Graduate School of Education. Long an advocate for the white working class, he transformed himself into a moderator between the races. Too many people of all colors told him they were unhappy with the schools. His predecessor Kevin White built fourteen new schools. The universities had voiced their recommendations, the judges ordered an end to racial isolation, and teachers for fifteen years had won most of their contract demands. Elementary schools now employed specialists providing teachers with planning time. Were Boston schools any better? The annual school budget ballooned from $236 million in Flynn's first year as mayor (1984) to $356 million in 1989, and yet schools showed few signs of improved academic outcomes.

Furthermore, the business community had offered Boston youth thousands of jobs in exchange for school pledges of better attendance and graduation rates. Although the Boston Compact won national acclaim, Boston employers threatened exit because schools had not kept their promises. What specifically troubled business leaders was that the student dropout rate (the percentage of the ninth grade cohort not graduating) was increasing, not decreasing, rising from 33 percent in 1983 to 39 percent in 1985 and 40 percent in 1986 and 1987. Eight high schools lost more than 15 percent of their students each year, and four lost more than 25 percent. Boston's reading scores on the Metropolitan Test dropped in five grades and rose in only one. Math scores dropped in six grades. The achievement gap between whites, black, and Hispanic students increased between 1984 and 1988. The State Basic Skills Tests categorized 44 percent of Boston's elementary schools as "at-risk," as were 80 percent of the middle schools, and all but four of the fifteen senior high schools. As many as 14 percent of the students were either absent or their answer sheets marked "incomplete" the day of the tests. These performance (or nonperformance) indicators reflected retrogression rather than the promised academic improvements. They confirmed the "rising tide of mediocrity" judgment deplored in *A Nation at Risk*, the critique of American education issued five years earlier.[25]

Mayor Flynn in October 1988 sought advice on what to do about substandard education performance and what changes were needed. He asked Hubie Jones, Boston University dean of the School of Social Welfare, to chair an advisory committee on school reform. Jones previously chaired the Out of School Youth Commission in 1970, founded the Massachusetts Advocacy Council that monitored suspensions and expulsions, and organized a Health Services collaborative to work with the schools.

Flynn also appointed to the advisory committee Bruce Bolling, black city councilor, whose father Royal Bolling twenty-five years earlier filed the first racial imbalance bill. He invited Juanita Wade, black School Committee member, and Franklyn Jennifer, state chancellor of Higher Education to become members. Also serving were Latino, black, and white parents and Ed Doherty, president of the Boston Teachers Union. Corporate leaders included William Edgerly, president of the State Street Bank, a Vault leader, and a chair of the Private Industry Council, and Ferdinand "Moose" Colleredo-Mansfield, senior executive of Cabot Partners. Together with the articulate black leaders and Boston's teacher union president, this panel, once they agreed, presented an impressive front. Chairman Jones asked the mayor to attend every committee meeting, which he did right up to the May Day report in 1989. The Municipal Research Bureau provided background data on school governance models in other cities.[26]

One challenge was deciding what to do with the School Committee. The larger Boston School Committee, four elected at large and nine by districts, had failed. After the 1983 elections, the 1985 and 1987 elections suffered from a shortage of credible candidates and low voter turnout. Committee meetings grew contentious, even raucous at times. The committee worried more about hiring their own personal staff, first one then a second staff aide (because the City Council, with their thirteen members chosen similarly had two paid assistants). One business executive said the School Committee turned into a "gong show" of bizarre and unpredictable behavior. When Laval Wilson's support oozed away, it was clear that the populist solution of additional neighborhood representation had not produced good school policy.[27]

The most serious problems were committee members getting "involved in daily operations and tying the superintendent's staff down with work that had nothing to do with establishing policy guidelines."[28] Also, black plaintiffs by 1987 sought a more flexible program of student choice among schools. As the judge receded from the case, the committee was encouraged to approve a better student integration plan with more choice and less transportation. The committee failed to seize this opportunity.

The NAACP, the Urban League, and the BTU sent a strongly worded joint memo to the School Committee on expanding student school "choice," but the committee only promised to hold hearings, not act. Parent and community leaders turned instead to Mayor Flynn.

Flynn decided to take on the schools. He hired Charles Willie (formerly a Garrity master and Flynn's own Harvard advisor) and Michael Alves as consultants to develop a new student assignment plan offering more parent choice of schools, while maintaining racial balance. Then he asked the Mayor's Special Advisory Committee on School Reform in October 1988 to advise him on five school issues: school-based management, school (committee) governance, school facilities, student assignments (choice), and values in the school curriculum.

James Jackson Storrow and Harvard professors in 1905 had recommended an appointed School Committee, and failed. Strayer's similar recommendation in 1944 was ignored. Kevin White's initiative to appoint the School Committee in the 1970s died because ROAR activists thought it a trick to lock in racial busing. Mayor Ray Flynn decided that he must appoint the School Committee or else the city would spend more and more money, getting less and less results from the schools.

The mayor's Committee decided early on to recommend strongly the "controlled choice" Willie-Alves student assignment plan, providing parent selections that would not resegregate the schools. They urged School Committee approval in a December 23 letter, recommending that 9,000 students entering grades kindergarten, grades one and six be assigned under a new system in 1989, where parents might actually visit schools before making choices. Next, the mayor's Committee endorsed school-based management. After visiting six schools, they concluded schools should manage themselves with a lump sum budget, reviewed by a council (of parents, with a majority of teachers) headed by the principal, with school-improvement strategies submitted by an Instructional Cabinet. The teacher contract should be amended to provide more operational flexibility. The school would mail parents each July an easy-to-read summary of school performance data.[29]

The mayor's Committee sharply criticized the elected School Committee, which got "bogged down in the details of day-to-day operations" and held meetings "dominated by details about personnel—who would be hired, for what job and at what salary—and the larger policy issues were deferred or ignored." The Jones Committee concluded that the system was fractured with responsibility hopelessly divided. The largest city school board in the nation each year voted themselves 1 million dollars worth of staff, while failing to balance the school budget.[30]

The Committee suggested that, if the mayor appointed the board, he must choose among nominees recommended by an independent citizen nominating panel reflecting all ethnic, racial, and socioeconomic groups, parents, a teacher, a school administrator, a college president, a business leader, and representatives of the state commissioner of education, and the mayor. After reviewing Research Bureau analyses of other cities, they agreed on a new format, a seven-member school board serving four-year terms, with staff limited to one secretary for the entire school board and a single assistant to the chair.

The City Council immediately appointed its own Special Commission on Public Education, which included City Council President Michael McCormack, Councilor Bruce Bolling (his second panel on the topic), two other black leaders, one Asian, one Latino, and a white special needs parent advisory council member.[31] Black elected officials, including the Black Political Caucus, opposed the appointed board recommendation on the grounds that it would eliminate black voter participation now that the student majority was black and a black superintendent in charge. From 1989 into 1990 the City Council debated many alternatives including a hybrid School Committee, half-elected and half-appointed, or possibly placing multiple choices before the electorate. Mayor Flynn formed a Better Education Committee to mobilize school activists behind an all-appointed board. *The Boston Globe* initially opposed the change. A 1989 public referendum found the city divided almost evenly 28,719 "yes" and 28,049 "no" (the opposition coming from Roxbury, South Boston, East Boston, and Charlestown). The mayor recognized that the margin of support was too thin to proceed.[32]

The mayor a year later pressed again for the all-appointed option, and won. The Council in 1991 sent the state legislature a home rule petition seeking an appointed School Committee, a proposal again opposed by black legislators but this time supported by the black Ministerial Alliance, 20 clergy representing 20,000 church members, and by the *Bay State Banner*, the black newspaper. The *Globe* endorsed this version. Meanwhile the School Committee let Laval Wilson go, rushed the search for a successor, but failed to balance the budget (leaving a $20 million deficit). The legislature, despite objections from the Black Caucus, passed an appointed board bill, which Governor Weld signed into law in July of 1991. Included was a five-year "sunset" provision, requiring a voter referendum in 1996 on whether the appointed board worked.[33]

Mayor Flynn fulfilled his pledge to appoint a majority of minority school committeemen, appointing two blacks, a Chinese leader, and a Latino advocate. Paul Parks, the former NAACP Education chair and state secretary of educational affairs became the first chair. Bill Spring, then a vice president of the Federal Reserve Bank and Robert Culver, CFO of Northeastern University, who coordinated the 1991 Northeastern University report on school economies, were the business nominees. The Research Bureau informally staffed the search for new School Committee members the first few years.

Elsewhere in Massachusetts, other business leaders took on the issues of school reform far beyond Boston's issues. Their ideas on school accountability transformed all Massachusetts schools in the 1990s, including Boston, going beyond the Boston Compact objectives. Massachusetts earlier responded to the highly critical national report *A Nation at Risk* by passing an educational reform law in 1985. The state at that time authorized innovative "Carnegie Schools" and Horace Mann grants, and strengthened school councils. The new law represented an earnest, well-intentioned start but, full of compromises and patches, it did not survive a state financial shortfall beginning in 1989.

Corporate leaders in Massachusetts, as in other states, formed Business Roundtables to strategize on how to resolve the education "crisis." Business sentiment shifted from industrial education (strongly supported from 1905 to 1950) toward academic proficiency. The reasons included increased trade competition from other nations (especially Japan in the 1980s). New technologies required a higher level of literacy, critical thinking, and problem-solving skills well beyond general mathematics. The Massachusetts Business Roundtable members rallied around higher education standards. Banker Rod MacDougall outlined a possible deal. "If new (school) programs eliminate excesses, bring in new efficiencies, and guarantee improved curriculum, an increased pace of academic learning, and enforce standards among students and teachers, then some new tax dollars might be possible." His was the clear, unequivocal voice of business leaders.[34]

During 1988 a state group calling itself the Massachusetts Business Alliance for Education wrote the next prescription for state education reform. The leader was Jack Rennie, CEO of Pacer Systems, a West Point trained engineer. Half the MBAE, Inc. board members came from high-technology firms, including Digital Equipment, Bull Honeywell information systems, and Lotus Development. Paul Reville, executive director of the Worcester Alliance for Education assisted Rennie and recruited Bill Densmore, retired Vice President of the Norton Company, a former member of the State Board of Education. This was not a Boston reform group (mostly Route 128, Worcester, Springfield, and Cambridge firms) but worked with the Boston-based AIM (the Manufacturers) and the Boston Private Industry Council. They sponsored policy research from university experts on teaching, curriculum, and school finance. The MBAE report, entitled "Every Child a Winner," proposed a comprehensive reform package beginning with high stakes, actually "world class," education standards, answering such questions as "What should students know" and "What can they do?" Both state and local student performance indicators would measure achievement. Schools would be rewarded for achievement or penalized by the privatization of failing schools, an "educational bankruptcy" option.[35]

Students, the report argued, must be given more time to learn. Preschool education should be offered to three-and four-year-olds so that all elementary schoolchildren would be ready to learn. The school day and year should be lengthened by 20 percent, at least by thirty days. Certain management changes were needed. Principals would be banned from unions, teachers dismissed for nonperformance, and School Committees would allow the superintendent to make all personnel decisions. School-based management councils with teacher and parent involvement would make decisions at each site.

The Alliance hired economist Ed Moscovitch, former Governor Sargent's state budget director, to devise a school aid formula ensuring equity for city school, predictability, and requiring greater local tax effort from those communities underfunding local schools. MBAE's report also recommended greater minority teacher recruitment, teacher peer evaluation (a reform favored by Harvard Professor Susan Moore Johnson), excluding School Committee relatives from key positions, and closer integration of schools with other community services. The report recommended greater use of technology, additional school choice, and upgrading regional vocational schools.

Consultation with school superintendents and principals led to a legislative victory. Peter Finn, executive secretary of the Mass. Association of School Superintendents recalled the question, "Will you and the superintendents accept more accountability in exchange for more resources for education?" He replied, "Yes," since much more would be gained than lost from taking principals out of unions, School Committees out of teacher hiring decisions, and accepting high stakes testing based on rigorous academic standards. This was the price for an infusion of up to a billion new dollars over the next seven years for quality education.[36]

The Massachusetts Federation of Teachers and the Massachusetts Teachers Association (NEA) fought "expedited" teacher dismissals, and complete principal discretion over seniority transfers, and scuttled those provisions of the proposed law. Also, unions felt longer school days and a longer school year deserved major salary increases; perhaps more instructional time could be wrung from the existing school day by shortening recess time or eliminating study halls? Many individual School Committee members resented losing control over teacher hiring, including their neighbors and relatives, but they reluctantly agreed. By the time the legislature reported a school reform bill, easing teachers' worst fears, the new governor, patrician William Weld (R), an independent school graduate, was ready to sign a bold education bill into law. He appointed his gubernatorial opponent, John Silber, president of Boston University, advocate of much higher academic standards, to chair the State Board of Education and preside over implementation.

Boston schools benefited financially from the reform. More than 200 millions of new dollars flowed into Boston schools from 1995 to 2000 because of the revised school aid formula. Principals left their union and earned one- to three-year employment contracts depending on their effectiveness in raising student achievement scores and working effectively with parents and teachers. By the school year 2000 Superintendent Payzant appointed some 85 of the 134 principals, 60 percent of them retired or replaced. Finally, intense publicity followed the annual publication of school test scores, following a format advocated by Boston business leaders. What was new in 1995 was publication of explicit state curriculum standards and frameworks, and the substitution of rigorous grade four, eight, and ten state tests for the old Metropolitan Achievement Tests.[37]

Thus, major corporate employers defined the new rules of engagement for schools, throwing overboard antiquated notions of School Committees voting on every teacher hire or transfer, or of principals filing union grievances against the superintendent, their fellow manager. The focus of state and local education henceforth would shift to student achievement, and on upgrading underperforming schools.

Mayor Ray Flynn resigned in 1992 to become ambassador to the Vatican. City Council President Thomas Menino automatically became acting mayor for the balance of the term. This was one reason the new Compact signing was delayed three years. Another reason was a severe economic recession hurting employment in Boston (regulators closing the Bank of New England). Also, federal priorities for the PIC shifted away from youth and toward adult job training.

Compact III eventually included more than school and business leaders. President Edward Doherty of the BTU also signed this Compact, along with Robert Sperber for the Boston Higher Education Partnership. The new Compact featured principal leadership training, which Boston University (Schools of Management and of Education) provided. In the late 1990s, a revised Compact IV incorporated the new state accountability measures, SATs, and other indicators of academic achievement, along with data on success in college.[38]

All four Compacts included student attendance, graduation rates, and achievement measures but dropped or added other criteria every five to seven years. As Massachusetts grew more high tech, academic preparation for at least two years in a community college moved up in importance.

The last elected School Committee appointed Lois Harrison-Jones to a four-year term. Her public critics included Robert Consalvo, the former Flynn chief of staff who became executive secretary of the new appointed Committee. Consalvo in the 1960s taught in a Boston school and later earned a Ph.D. in educational measurement and evaluation at Boston College. Boston's "intolerable" test scores and the lack of activity to improve Boston schools infuriated Consalvo. He lashed out at Superintendent Harrison-Jones, suggesting that offering school vouchers to families might lead to better performance. The ensuing controversy required Committee chair Paul Parks to request Consalvo's resignation.[39] Mayor Menino and the new appointed School Committee asked Federal Reserve Bank President Cathy Minehan in 1994 to chair the search for a new superintendent to replace Harrison-Jones.

The educator chosen in 1994, Thomas Payzant, was President Clinton's assistant U.S. secretary for elementary education. Payzant, a Williams College and Harvard graduate, had five superintendencies behind him, including San Diego, California, for eleven years in the 1980s. He once chaired the mainstream Council on Basic Education (emphasizing academic fundamentals) and advocated "whole school change" whereby all teachers and administrators planned how to raise school achievement levels. This strategy required teachers to commit more time to basic literacy, engage in collaborative planning, upgrade their teaching skills, and "look at" student work analytically along with achievement test analyses. Ellen Guiney, who had directed the CWEC and was Mayor Flynn's education advisor, more recently worked for Senator Edward Kennedy on the reauthorization of the Elementary and Secondary Education Act with Payzant. She thought Payzant would be an excellent leader for Boston.

Although Mayor Menino appointed the search committee, the selection technically was made by the School Committee, which he had appointed as well. Never had a mayor been so involved in the superintendency selection. The three finalists included Harry Spence, court receiver for both Boston and Chelsea housing authorities, and for the City of Chelsea. Another was Anthony Alvarado, the New York educator famous for improving Manhattan District Two schools. Guiney and others strongly urged Tom Payzant's selection in 1995. Guiney returned to Boston as executive director of the Boston Plan for Excellence in the Public Schools, working with Payzant on literacy strategies and other reforms.

Together, Payzant and Guiney evaluated the Boston area university contributions and the grants previously made by the Boston Plan for Excellence. State desegregation assistance grants signed into law by Governor Frank Sargent in 1974 funded other university projects. However, Guiney and Payzant found too little evidence of increased student and school achievement. They urged universities to focus on "whole school change" and staff development, intensive coaching to upgrade teaching effectiveness in each school. In 1996, with another $1.8 million raised from the Hyams and Boston Foundations, they designated twenty schools committed to improving classroom instruction as "Twenty First Century Schools." The Boston Plan initially assisted only those schools selecting a "whole school improvement" strategy.[40]

Elsewhere, the Annenberg Foundation (the Philadelphia publishing fortune) placed large bets ($20 to $50 million) on urban school reform initiatives in New York, Chicago, and Los Angeles. Boston was not one of the original cities, but Annenberg in November 1996 agreed to support Boston, if local corporations and foundations matched Annenberg's 10 million dollars with 10 million from Boston area philanthropies and 10 million from city and state sources. Bill Boyan of the John Hancock contacted local companies and foundations, raising the 10 million dollar match within a few months. Fleet Bank CEO Terry Murray (whose bank acquired Bank Boston) gave 1 million to Harvard to assist Boston schools, a pledge counted for two fund-raising drives. (Harvard that year was raising 2 billion dollars in a separate campaign.)

Payzant decided the Annenberg funds should entice all Boston schools into comprehensive reform work. The Boston Plan staff added two more cohorts of twenty Whole Change Schools, helped by a second Annenberg grant of $10 million in August 2001. The Carnegie Corporation in 2001 granted $8 million to tackle low literacy in the twelve comprehensive high schools, and then Gates Foundation in 2003 gave $13.6 million to create small academies of 300–400 students within those large high schools to combat student alienation. In all Payzant, with help from Ellen Guiney and William Boyan, former Hancock president, attracted $100 million in private grants to the Boston public school literacy and mathematics achievement initiatives.[41]

Other businessmen gave money to individual Boston schools, especially to the Latin School. Until the 1990s rarely would a businessman donate money to any public school. Investor Harry Keefe, Latin School graduate, was an exception. His mother had been adamant, "You *will* go to the Boston Latin School" and Harry did. Early on he showed entrepreneurial talent, purchasing sticks of candy for four cents to sell to Latin School classmates for a nickel.[42]

After Latin School, Keefe won degrees at Amherst College and his MBA at Boston University, entering the field of investments and founding a successful brokerage firm, Keefe, Bruyette, and Wood. Remembering the Latin School, he donated more than 4 million dollars for the Keefe Library, a dramatic act of public school loyalty. Other loyal Latin School alumni contributed another $20 million toward a $50 million goal. Grateful graduates included Joseph P. Kennedy, Vincent Learson of IBM, and others. The old Girls Latin School and English High School raised scholarship funds as well, but not millions.[43]

Where were the alumni of other Boston high schools? Did these donations simply not reinforce the academic and social class advantage of the Latin School? Pam Treffler, wife of a successful software entrepreneur, donated 1 million dollars to Dorchester High, a troubled school that needed all the help available. Dr. Penny Noyce used her family fortune (Intel) to support mathematics and science education programs at other schools.

Even so, urban school philanthropy can be uneven in scope and coverage. Individuals and companies provided gifts to a few schools, such as the Mather Elementary School in Dorchester, the oldest public elementary school in Massachusetts, led from 1987 to 2002 by Kim Marshall, an exceptional education entrepreneur. A grateful parent of a special needs child donated 1 million to the Mary Lyon Public School in Brighton. Who would help younger schools with no alumni and short histories?[44]

It is important to assess the business impact on schools. Boston's business voice between 1916 and 1975 was muted, refuting the old Marxist assertion that those who control the "means of production" dominate cultural institutions such as education. Boston's business leaders, and most of their preferred candidates, were regularly defeated at the voting booth. The "workers" representatives captured the schools and school jobs into the 1970s. Business efforts to appoint the School Committee failed in 1905, 1944, the 1970s, and into the 1980s. So much for a monolithic capitalist power structure dominating Boston schools for most of the twentieth century.

Corporate Boston tried to keep school expenditures in line by financing the MRB, which proposed teacher contract language to improve school management. Then, the Massachusetts High Tech Council members funded the campaign to pass Proposition 2 ½. Tregor and other commercial property tax payers won the rollback of excessive tax assessments. These were highly effective local tax reduction programs, so damaging that business leaders agreed with state officials a few years later that schools should receive more state dollars but only in exchange for greater accountability. In the end, the business voice strongly influenced state school reform policy.

Boston business leaders advanced other priorities allowing a strong superintendent to control all staffing and personnel decisions, with the School Committee making broad policy decisions. They advocated school-based management, wherein a school principal made site staff and budget decisions, although in consultation with selected teachers and parents. These reforms kept sliding away. What impeded a better-managed Boston school system was the triumph of "democracy," the election of a School Committee viewing itself as constituency-oriented or a job-disbursing council rather than an educational policy board. One route to greater efficiency was to make the school a city department with senior managers accountable to the mayor. Second best might be to have the mayor appoint the school board. The trade-off engineered by business leaders was "efficiency" for democracy. "One is struck," Edwards and Willie commented, "by the strength of their (business) consensus for an appointed school committee; they were unwavering and totally uncompromising on the issue. In addition, of course, they had the resources to achieve their goal."[45] In fact, business supported the larger School Committee until it was clear that the elected school board was dysfunctional.

The other serious barrier to efficiency was the ambivalence within the black community. Their highest priority was better schools. The other concern was the legitimate right of black persons to choose public decision-makers. During the 1980s two, then four blacks were elected to the School Committee, leading to the selection of two black superintendents. Edwards commented, "From the outset, Mayor Flynn tapped into and exploited this dilemma." His strategy with the black community, as Edwards saw it, was "divide and conquer." He successfully pitted black academic and ministerial leaders against the Black Political Task Force, their elected state, and local officials.[46]

It was clear that the mayor could not have won the right to appoint the superintendent on his own. He needed the business community and their money to pay for ads and brochures and to muster editorial support from the *Globe, Bay State Banner*, and other media. Together, the mayor and Sam Tyler blocked compromises proposed by black leaders such as a hybrid School Committee, with several members appointed, others elected. Business leaders convinced Republican legislators and Governor Weld to support the purely appointed School Committee when the proposal was in legislative jeopardy.

Three years later Bostonians remained divided on the appointed School Committee. A 1994 poll showed as many as 60 percent favored a return to an elected committee.[47] In 1996 corporations contributed $300,000 for a referendum campaign to continue the appointed board, rather than return to the old regime.[48] Black elected officials worked hard, forming a Right to Vote group to restore the elected committee. They raised only a few thousand dollars, not enough to beat the business community. Alliances with state Republicans or with other racial groups could not be sustained. Edwards explained that too many followers were "co-opted" by the lure of better schools, a promise exchanged for the loss of ballot choices for School Committee.

What was the impact of business partnerships on individual Boston's schools? Business leaders assumed that corporate help would be welcomed by school officials deprived of equipment, textbook funds, staff positions, and presumably desperate for volunteers. Roderick MacDougall, Bank of New England CEO, was one of the few business leaders who talked openly about working with schools:

> For years it was a one-way partnership at many schools, with teachers and principals fighting the business involvement. Attempts to sit down with school officials and try to work out ways in which business could be helpful to a school often resulted in demands simply for money and complete rejection of any input from the business as to how that money might be spent. In some cases headmasters wouldn't even come to the table to talk, until they had been ordered by the superintendent.

This was true in suburban schools where teachers remained angry at the High Tech Councils' advocacy for Proposition 2 ½ local tax limits.[49]

Stephen Coan interviewed Boston public school staff and their corporate partners identifying other troubling cleavages in the partnerships. He found companies designated from two to eight employees to communicate with schools, leaving hundreds of other employees uninvolved in the school partnership. School employees rarely set foot in the company offices. The companies donated equipment and furniture, but it was usually surplus and often obsolete, such as old computers. Moreover, the school schedule, usually 7 AM–3 PM was not compatible with the nine-to-five corporate workday. Teachers were reluctant to meet with corporate representatives after school and lacked phones and fax machines to communicate with business counterparts. Finally, few teachers believed they were really involved in partnership planning; only two companies helped one school set goals in a school-based management council.[50]

Hardly any teachers Coan interviewed knew that their business partnership was linked to the Boston Compact, even at two schools with very committed corporate partners. One company invited teachers to tour the corporate headquarters, and take courses in quality management technology courses at the firm. Senior officers at one company agreed to "adopt a class," which required visiting the school several times each year, but this was uncommon.[51] Patricia Graham of Harvard commented that this partnering was "noblesse oblige," a gesture from the well-heeled corporate lords to the peasant workers in the schools.[52]

Also, periodic corporate downsizing had an adverse effect on the partnerships. The corporate budget for one Boston school partnership remained static for ten years, the after-inflation support declining by 3–5 percent each year. The worst outcome was the fate of the Jeremiah Burke High School whose partner was one of the most education-oriented corporations, The New England (Life Insurance Company). In 1995 the New England Association of Schools and Colleges withdrew the Burke's accreditation. One vice president raised concerns with city officials about the inadequate school facility and staffing budget but to no avail. The New England community relations staff suggested canceling the partnership in protest. Another option would have been for the CEO to lead the charge for greater resources, threatening a public cancellation of the partnership.[53] The "Burke" in 1990 was hailed as one of the nation's outstanding high schools but during the serious state economic recession in 1991, the Burke school budget was cut, losing 12 staff positions while adding 200 students. By 1995 test scores at the Burke hit rock bottom and, after a highly critical external review, the high school lost regional (NEASC) accreditation. It was the loss of accreditation, not corporate advocacy, which rang the alarm bell.

In 1995–96 Mayor Menino pledged $35 million in high school repairs. Steven Leonard, a school turnaround expert, was named headmaster, with a five-year commitment of extra resources including staff. Leonard established small "learning communities" in math and English, and in 1998 regained accreditation well ahead of schedule.[54] He required all Burke high school seniors to apply for admission to a college. However, after Leonard left, during another serious state recession in 2002, the Burke budget was reduced by $816,000 and 14 staff positions lost. Parents protested at hearings, but bemoaned the lack of elected school officials to respond.[55]

Coan raised ethical questions about business partnerships with schools. Should a business take public credit for a school partnership when the city is reducing per pupil expenditures? Should not the company vocally support adequate funding? Should not more than a handful of employees know about the daily challenges faced by Boston schoolteachers? Boston teachers expressed gratitude for the computers, the equipment, the training, and the financing of graduation ceremonies that companies provided.

But Coan concluded that both sides needed training in collaboration, and more technical assistance really to help each other.

What was really accomplished through the Compact, the Boston Plan, the appointed School Committee, the foundation gifts, and the new state academic standards? First of all, the comprehensive annual evaluations Horace Mann argued for in the 1840s were finally required of all schools. Students were tested at three checkpoints: grades four, eight, and ten until a new federal law passed in 2002 required testing in each grade three through eight and once more before graduation.[56]

Second, Boston ceased to offer "social promotions." Several thousand low-performing students were told either to attend summer school or repeat ninth grade, both of which happened. Third, achievement test scores in tenth grade math and English/Language Arts began to move upward at the district high schools, with 80 percent of seniors graduating in 2003.[57] Black and Hispanic student test scores also rose, but still lagged as much as 30 percent behind Caucasian scores. Also, more teachers began to accept content training or coaching, adopting new methods to raise student achievement. This help was less welcome at senior high schools where many teachers criticized the Boston Plan and the "hired gun" coaches brought in to help them. Not all Boston teachers felt they needed coaching. More than a few teachers despised the MCAS exam, along with the mandate of higher state academic standards. However, the 1998 state MCAS scores revealed that 57 percent of Boston's tenth graders failed the Literacy test and 75 percent failed Mathematics, and, therefore, would not graduate. These dire statistics triggered increased coaching of teachers and tutoring of students so that by 2000, 85 percent of Boston's seniors passed the retests and earned diplomas.

Finally, corporate initiatives closed the troublesome gap between the School Committee and mayors, ensuring that mayors took responsibility for school budgets and buildings and that seasoned superintendents from other cities could stay in Boston long enough to provide leadership.[58]

In 1983 candidates Ray Flynn and Mel King had each called for raising the school's expectations for all children, white or black or Latino. Flynn had won, finally appointing a new School Committee of which more than half the members were of color. Test scores moved up slowly in 1998, 1999, and 2000. However, in October 2001 test scores surged at most of the Twenty-First Century schools and moved up at other Boston high schools. The movement toward improved Boston student academic achievement began to succeed.

The Massachusetts State Board of Education was not always consistent in defining the standards. After five years, the state board changed the science (and the history) standards. Also, the intense focus on basic skills crowded out time for art, music, foreign languages, and other subjects including citizenship and character building.

Distant owners acquired many Boston corporations. From the 1960s, three companies most committed and loyal to Boston public schools included New England in their name. This would not last. Federal bank regulators closed the Bank of New England in the late 1980s for insolvency; former CEO Rod MacDougall had left to serve as treasurer of Harvard University. Metropolitan Life in New York City acquired New England Life. The New England Telephone Company became NYNEX and merging with Bell Atlantic, became Verizon, a New York based telecommunications company. The New England was swallowed by John Hancock, which became part of a Canadian insurance company. Shawmut and Bank Boston merged into Fleet Bank, a Rhode Island acquirer, later purchased by the Bank of America. Mellon Bank of Pittsburgh acquired the Boston Company, once the Boston Safe Deposit Company. The Mellon Foundation and Bank of America happily took an interest in Boston matters.

The Boston Globe, providing fifty Taylor Scholarships to University of Massachusetts Boston students (a campus visible from *Globe* windows), was bought by the *New York Times*. Gillette in 2005 became a division of Procter and Gamble. The State Street Bank remained independent but increasingly international in focus. The Coordinating Committee (Vault) disbanded. The leadership on school issues devolved to the Federal Reserve Bank of Boston, which under Presidents Frank Morris and Cathy Minehan strongly supported educational accountability and maintained a strong high school partnership.

So the number of major Boston-based businesses continued to shrink, down to only 11 of the Fortune 500 firms. Corporate signals would be called from New York City, Providence, Pittsburgh, or Toronto. Proud Boston did not enjoy relegation to regional office status. Major hospitals and health providers were distracted by public health funding issues and their senior officers were less available to solve public school problems. The surviving law firms were helpful on litigation or in providing tutors and mentors. CPA firms (once the Big Eight) contracted in number. Individual executives might remain loyal to the Boston schools but the parent corporations became national or global, as had State Street and Gillette. The major drivers for school reform were as likely to be IBM and a few multinational corporations, or private entrepreneurs such as Chris Gabrielli who championed after-school programs. For Boston to rely on the same big companies decade after decade was a policy fraught with uncertainty. Companies come and go; they too exit the city or state, not exactly the continuous support needed by schools.

Patricia Graham, Harvard dean, and later Spencer Foundation president, put business involvement in programs such as the Compact and Boston Plan in perspective. She acknowledged that employers provided entry-level jobs and school-improvement funds. "These programs did no harm, but neither did they solve the problems of the Boston Public Schools." She was more impressed by Philadelphia where businesses provided extra funds for curriculum development, administrator training, and lobbied hard for state education funds. She warned about relying on corporations where "daily responsibilities can be delegated to the human resources or community liaison office." "Palliatives" and public relations will not suffice, resembling Coan's conclusion a few years later.[59]

What business really provided through partnerships, she concluded, is "a new and powerful advocate both for (children) and for the schooling they need. This is particularly vital for children in the cities, where until business began to take an interest there were woefully few effective advocates either for children or for education. The school custodians have fared much better than the city children."[60]

The business voices from the 1980's led major drives for explicit academic standards, greater school effectiveness, higher student achievement, stronger school management, and a focus on critical thinking and other skills needed in the new economy. Corporate executives provided new energy, becoming loyal supporters of achieving schools and a school system more responsive to international competitiveness. Their support came with costs, a diminished enthusiasm for art and music and for civic engagement, including community service. But without that renewed corporate support, schools were in danger of being marginalized or broken up by the voucher movement and other measures to repeal the common schools. Corporate voices rekindled the focus on basic literacy and numeracy in Boston and elsewhere. They raised expectations for city students, their teachers and principals. Their voices supported more efficient, effective, productive schools and the restoration of Boston's reputation as a center of civilization.

CHAPTER 9
FUTURE CHOICES, DISPARATE VOICES

Boston at the end of the twentieth century was a substantially different city from the working-class city that elected James Michael Curley four times, or even when moderate voters chose John Hynes and John Collins as mayors in the 1950s. Boston in 2000 became a smaller, less densely populated city, dropping by 200,000 inhabitants over a 50-year span. Who remained in Boston, and who used the public schools? Both the 2000 U.S. Census and the several university surveys provide a comparison and contrast as far back as with 1930, the highpoint of Boston Public School enrolments.

Boston population in the 1930s totaled 800,000 persons, but only 589,141 in 2000. Boston in 1930 included 32 percent immigrants, mostly European, and as of 2000, 25 percent now mostly Hispanic or Asian. The percentage of married adults was 50.5 percent in 1930, but in 2000 dropped sharply to 28.7 percent, halving the parental support base for schools. Divorced adults increased from 1 percent in 1930 to 7 percent in 2000. The number of little children under five in 1930 was 62,374 (1 in 12 persons) but in 2000 declined to half that number, 32,046 (1 in 20). While adult seniors over 75 in 1930 numbered only 10,915 (less than 2 percent), in 2000 seniors grew to 30,182 (5 percent), Boston suddenly hosting as many grandparents as toddlers.[1]

In certain neighborhoods, families with children vanished. For example, in 1930 some sixty adults and forty-two children (mostly Italian Americans) lived on North Street in the North End. In 2000, North Street hosted no children but fifty-seven adults, mostly young college-educated couples loving the Italian restaurants, markets, and proximity to downtown offices. Where longshoremen, fisherman, and dockworkers once lived, upscale condo apartments overlooked the ocean, housing "dinks" (dual income, no kids). Loyalty to public schools dropped to the waterline.[2]

Among the staunch new loyalists for Boston's public schools, and high achievers, were Asian families living in the South End and Dorchester. They brought the thirst for achievement that grandmothers and mothers instilled in them in Hong Kong, or the Chinese mainland, or Vietnam,

South Korea, and elsewhere in Asia. Asian student tests scores in Boston and the nation often surpassed those of Caucasian students. Ninety percent of Boston's Asian Americans were college-bound, compared to 69 percent of all Boston high school graduates.[3]

Most of all, Boston's Chinese parents took education very seriously, organizing English and civics classes for immigrants and urging children to study hard, as had Jewish parents in an earlier time. As the twentieth century ended, public school principal Bak Fun Wong asked the School Committee to authorize a high school just for the Chinese community. Meanwhile, Asian students attended the Latin schools in record numbers, scored high on exams, and won highest honors at many of the high schools. Boston's tiny Chinatown offered little space for other Asians. Several thousand Vietnamese immigrants settled in Dorchester, establishing markets and shops. They, too, were entrepreneurs and, like Chinese parents, took their children's school and studies very seriously.[4]

Asians are quick to point out that not all Asians are "model minorities," especially oppressed Cambodians or Hmong refugees. The immigrant children of educated shopkeepers or professionals tend to do well in school. However, semiliterate rural populations also included Asian parents and children deprived of schooling during times of civil war or famine.

The City of Boston published "Indicators of Progress, Change and Sustainability in 2000." This urban report card, formally called *The Wisdom of Our Choices,* told who lived in Boston, who attended public schools, and how well they achieved on tests.[5]

Boston in 2000 included 142,000 children under age 17, up from 110,000 in 1990 and still growing. In 1970 there had been 182,000 children. Only 23 percent of Boston's households in 2000 contained children, and only half of Boston's children lived in two-parent families. Forty-three percent came from single-parent homes, up from 25 percent in 1970. Another 7 percent lived in foster homes, group homes, and homeless shelters, or somehow on their own.

Boston adults in 1990 had been 41 percent minority and 59 percent white. A few months into 2001 the U.S. Census Bureau reported an even split, 50 percent of color, 50 percent white. Sixty percent of school-age children were black. White and Latino public school percentages exchanged places, from 26 percent white and 16 percent Latino in 1990 to 26 percent Latino and 16 percent white in 2000. Asians in 2000 accounted for 9 percent of public school student, Native Americans and others about 5 percent.

In 2000, 84,000 children were of school age, 75 percent of them enrolled in Boston Public Schools. Of the rest, 19 percent attended private and parochial schools, 5 percent attended out-of-district schools (mostly METCO), and 1,700 (2.5 percent) attended charter schools (public, but independent of BPS). Another 700 (less than 1 percent) enrolled in special education schools including private residential facilities. The total percentage of youth attending Boston Public Schools gradually increased from 70 percent to 75 percent as parish schools closed.

Half of Boston's public school students lived in only two neighborhoods, Dorchester (one-quarter of the city) and Roxbury. Of all Boston public school children, 36 percent resided in Limited English Proficiency homes where English was the second language. Another 22 percent had disabilities or physical handicaps requiring special services. More than 70 percent were eligible for free or reduced cost lunches, indicators of serious family poverty. The annual school dropout rates decreased for all races from 1,999 to 995, but remained above 8 percent for Black and Hispanic children.[6]

The achievement test scores of Boston students began to show progress. The new Massachusetts Comprehensive Assessment System (MCAS) tested academic proficiency, the higher state standards. In 1999, 55 percent of Boston's public school tenth graders failed the state MCAS tenth grade English Language Arts test; and 73 percent failed the Math test. Failure rates were highest among black and Hispanic schoolchildren. However, the 2001 MCAS scores for Boston tenth graders showed improvement, 60 percent passing the tenth grade English and 50 percent passing Math (low compared to statewide passing scores of 80 percent ELA and 75 percent Math). At the exam schools, especially Latin School and Latin Academy, 97 percent passed the MCAS and applied to four-year colleges as they had for centuries. Dorchester High and Hyde Park High School struggled to raise passing scores to a 25 percent level in 2001, which meant hundreds of students needed summer school and extra tutoring. Boston School officials decided 25 percent of ninth graders with low scores should repeat grade nine, rather than plunge unready into tenth grade. By 2003, after considerable tutoring and summer work, 85 percent of Boston's twelfth graders passed MCAS and won diplomas, a major accomplishment.[7] Eleventh and twelfth graders were given five more chances to retake and pass the MCAS, which hundreds did. Others passed the GED exam later.

The combined verbal and quantitative SAT scores for Boston public school students averaged 831 in 1995, rising to 859 in 1997, then 895 in 2004, strong gains but still 100 points below state and national averages, which were more than 1,000.[8] Boston School Superintendent Tom Payzant was well aware of SAT score trends. From 1997 to 1999 he chaired the College Board that administered the SATs.

The level of "public confidence" or citizen satisfaction is an indicator of parent loyalty to the schools of Boston. The 1997 Boston citizen survey rated public confidence in schools as six on a ten-point scale, ten being perfection. Dorchester, Mattapan, and East Boston citizens rated the schools at or near seven, good but not great. South Boston and West Roxbury where parish schools remained popular registered lower scores, closer to five, the mid-point of public confidence.[9]

College attendance requires student persistence and loyalty through twelfth grade graduation. The highest percentage of college-bound students in 1997 graduated from the three examination high schools, 95.2 percent of Boston Latin School graduates actually attending college, with Boston Latin Academy and John O'Bryant (Technical) High School both above 85 percent. High Schools that sent more than 60 percent of seniors to college included English High, Brighton, Dorchester, Charlestown, Jeremiah Burke, and Snowden (International). East Boston, South Boston, and West Roxbury High Schools graduated between 50 and 60 percent to college, a dramatic surge upward from the days when hardly any seniors applied. Hyde Park High and Madison Park (Roxbury) sent less than half of their graduating students to college, including community colleges and for-profit private career schools. However, perhaps half of them completed a degree within six years.[10]

Creating Capacity for Urban School Reform

Had Boston schools and outside groups done enough to increase the holding power and effectiveness of the public schools? A research team led by John Portz looked at the school reform initiatives of Boston, Pittsburgh, and Saint Louis to find out what was required to revitalize urban schools. They concluded that reform-minded cities needed to build expanded "civic capacity," expressing higher expectations for student achievement coupled with a common vision of what schools might accomplish, packaged in a unified strategy agreed upon by a network of community supporters. They concluded that in the 1980s Pittsburgh built a superior school reform capacity when the business community (through the Alleghany Conference), the University of Pittsburgh, and the Casey, Heinz, Mellon, and Pittsburgh Foundations strongly supported Superintendent Richard Wallace's efforts to raise student achievement.[11]

Boston, in contrast, relied more on a vigorous mayor, Tom Menino, who said "I want to be judged as your mayor by what happens now in the Boston public schools." The Portz research team felt Vault business leaders avoided visible involvement in raising school achievement for too long after desegregation, and allowed the larger School Committee too much time to squander resources. Not until the appointed board, a more responsive union, and Tom Payzant's arrival in the mid-1990s did schools improve. But by then the city schools were almost 90 percent of color, the families remaining mostly low income, and opportunities had been lost.[12] Unlike in Pittsburgh, which had a university federal Research and Development center focused on learning, the Boston area universities for the most part took on isolated projects or helped high schools without collaborating on a coherent achievement agenda. In Boston school administrators tightly controlled the old, stale curriculum, and turned down the three offers by John Silber of Boston University to manage the schools.

Portz concluded that a city actually needed two strategies, the first of which was internal and designed to change the curriculum, the role of principals and teachers, and their work with children. The internal strategy excited Tom Payzant and it was the process of moving each school faculty to focus on raising student achievement that commanded most of his attention. The other strategy was external, and here Ellen Guiney helped Payzant win support from financial leaders, higher education, and the foundations. They often spoke together at local conferences as professional partners. The Boston Plan board brought together bankers, insurance executives, donors, and university leaders who endorsed strategies to improve clusters of twenty schools at a time, to coach teachers to achieve better results, and to tutor students intensively until they could pass a graduation examination. By the end of the 1990s this academic tag team spelled each other and communicated hope about progress to the media, the civic leaders, and the skeptics. Beginning in 2002, Guiney and Fleet Bank President Chad Gifford each year invited fifty or more civic leaders to shadow a Boston school principal for a day, to observe the progress and comprehend the challenge of reaching low-income children in a highly mobile city. By the end of 2010, more than 300 CEOs and other leaders visited Boston schools and reported positive impressions.[13]

Contrary to Portz, Boston's corporate leaders tried to intervene much earlier, through the Trilateral Commission, the four Compacts, and the Boston Plan for Excellence. Business paid for Roger Fisher's team to help negotiate more enlightened teacher union contracts. The universities joined Compacts II and III, but it was the raising of major new foundation funds that lubricated the intensive teacher-to-teacher coaching and productive analysis of achievement test data by school and by classroom. Also, the appointed School Committee and willingness of the mayor to provide political protection allowed Superintendent Payzant to transfer or retire principals of the least effective schools with minimal turbulence. Most of all, city school reform requires the replacement of individual teaching styles with collective goal setting and total school collaboration.[14]

The Brookings Institution in a separate study of six major city reform initiatives, including Boston, reported generally discouraging results. In four of the cities the initial reforms had been watered down and courageous superintendents forced out of their leadership roles.[15] They grimly concluded, "The normal politics of school systems cannot support fundamental reform." They recommended strong remedies such as a permanent community-wide reform oversight mechanism, an independent data-gathering organization, an incubator for new schools, a real-estate trust to maintain and lease schools, and a British-style inspectorate to judge whether low-performing schools can improve.[16] They saw a need for new private funds and philanthropy, as much as $3–5 million a year per city to enable school reform to succeed. The Brookings researchers thought Boston acquired considerable assets in Payzant's reputation and focus, but as of 1999 needed greater capacity for improvement at the school level.[17]

Boston in fact benefited from several such independent organizations, including the Boston Plan as a public private "reform oversight" partnership. The Private Industry Council, with the Federal Reserve Bank and later Northeastern University, issued the annual scorecard "gathering data" on high school placements in college or jobs. As Hill recommended, those boards included senior influential leaders recognized by other civic influentials. The state education agency, although understaffed, released each year public data on test scores by school and conducted educational audits. Boston, like other cities, lacked an outside inspectorate other than ten-year high school accreditation visiting teams, which mainly pointed out the worst educational disasters. Boston never considered a "new school incubator" or real-estate trust for buildings other than charter schools, despite the need for attractive new facilities. Under Payzant, and with the help of Guiney, Boyan, and foundations, Boston attracted as much as $10 million each year in private contributions to support innovative teaching, coaching, tutoring, and other strategies such as stronger emphasis on student writing and math work in the schools. Without the new state funds and the private dollars, progress would have been much slower. The ultimate test, Hill concluded, would be "making sure reform strategies survive superintendent succession," a challenge Boston failed after Spillane and Wilson left. Another requirement is "helping to build a parent constituency for reform," the ultimate test of loyalty to public schools.[18]

Was the mayor's involvement that important for Boston schools? For three centuries Boston mayors set the tax rate, built schools, and determined school expenditure levels but were kept away from any personnel and program decisions. Education remained a sacred function, presumably protected from municipal politics. Collective bargaining, parent protests, and a series of costly court decisions ended this myth. Mayor Menino was intensely interested in raising student achievement, in selecting the superintendent in 1995, and determining who would be acceptable to him again in 2006. The same held true in Chicago where Mayor Richard J. Daley, the father, wanted little to do with segregated schools but his son Richard M. Daley assumed heavy responsibility for school reform. Another case study of city schools including Boston described the new consensus between business, the mayor's office, the unions, and schools, essential if urban education would be improved.[19] One holding this belief must assume that honest, pro-school mayors will be elected in each decade.

What other lessons can be learned from reviewing decades of efforts to reform Boston schools? Examination of the past seventy to hundred years reveals the following patterns:

School reforms are often delayed by major wars, depressions, and recessions. Economic disruptions drained the energies and reduced the resources needed to effect educational improvements. Good ideas were inevitably placed on hold, as in Boston's sluggish response to the 1944 Strayer Report recommendations.

One common theme is the persistent animosity among old settlers and newcomers, the tensions between ethnic and racial groups. Others earlier predicted serious difficulties. Henry Adams once described Boston politics as the "systematic organization of hatreds."[20] This judgment seemed harsh, until one recalls the Puritan treatment of Quakers and Native Americans, the Know Nothing persecution of the Irish, the Irish mistreatment of Jews and Italian youth, and the violent white working-class resistance to equality for blacks. No firewalls protected recent Hispanic migrants from the powerful political preferences of established inhabitants. Bigotry often obstructs school reform, constraining access to effective, tolerant education.

Each dominant ethnic group (Yankees, then white Catholics) wanted new immigrants to adhere to their own previously stated notions of the good life, and the way educational business had been and would be conducted. Those in power expected newcomer "assimilation" to traditional values and curriculum. Irish teachers loyally preserved academic priorities and disciplinary practices inherited from Yankee predecessors. The majority group usually registered surprise when newcomers rebelled, and those in power tried to hold the line against challengers (upstarts) rejecting the prevailing norms.

Governance reform of school boards and "merit hiring" rules rarely achieved the great expectations of reform proponents. Changing the educational structure provided no guarantee of better performance. In every decade reformers tried to alter forms of governance to protect their values from the aspirations of newcomers. New governmental structures too often proved to be sand castles, overwhelmed by the fresh tide of new Bostonians. Structural change cannot substitute for constant surveillance and attention to voice.

Battles over public schools were fought as much over employment rights as they are about ideology. The upper class disdained the pursuit of jobs as unworthy, or as "patronage." As Boston journalist Alan Lupo observed, the best citizens are invited to go to Washington or abroad in "appointments" while the rest of us fight to get "jobs."[21] But to the working class job opportunities in public schools were always important, especially when denied positions in the private sector.

Religious factors were tremendously important in educational decisions made by families and their children even in a secular society. The early Protestant dissenters fought to keep the King James Bible at the center of the curriculum. Catholic immigrants hoped public schools would treat their religion with respect; however, their cardinals concluded that Catholics needed parochial schools to "keep the faith." Jewish families, rather than establish separate schools, added ten hours a week of Hebrew School. Church and state were legally separated in Massachusetts after 1820, but the spiritual education of children remained a serious issue for families of all religions. Religious solidarity certainly influenced the school exit strategies of more than 100,000 Boston families of all persuasions in the twentieth century. Even so, by 2005 seven Jewish day schools serve Boston's suburbs, most often to protect orthodox values.

City and City School Exit Strategies

Few observers or critics discovered "white flight" from Boston's schools until 1975, the second phase of court-ordered desegregation. Yet, white family flight began even before the nineteenth century as the early waves of English Protestants outgrew Boston town and sought less congested neighborhoods. By 1965, 50,000 fewer white students attended Boston public schools than in 1935. This was twice the number of white students who left Boston schools during 1975–85, the decade immediately following desegregation. By the year 2000, Boston schools again served 50,000 fewer white students, the same size decline as thirty years before the racial imbalance law. This resembled the white exodus from other big cities, including those that did not desegregate under court orders during the 1970s and 1980s, such as New York City and Philadelphia.

Although thousands of Boston students left public schools during 1974–77 for parochial or diocesan high schools, these transfers only slowed the parallel departure of Catholic school students from the city for several years. Catholic city school enrollments during 1950–2000 also shrank sharply. The archdiocese closed seventy elementary parish schools and thirty-five high schools, city and suburban.[22]

Critics of desegregation blamed busing as the major source of white flight from cities. But the substantial drop in white children attending urban schools during 1935–65 had other explanations including the severe restriction in new immigration to the United States and Boston during the 1920s and the federal housing policies stimulating suburban home construction after the 1940s. Urban school populations declined because of urban renewal and family removal policies during the 1950s as well as highway subsidies for building roads out of cities to the suburbs.

The 1974 U.S. Supreme Court Detroit desegregation case (Milliken) exempted suburbs from busing because plaintiffs had not documented how state policies perpetuated segregation and racial concentration. But clearly federal and state policies had done just that, in Boston and other metropolitan areas. Governmental subsidies helped whites flee the city and confined blacks to ghetto housing, low-income projects, and aging schools. Surely federal and state decision-makers conspired to maintain residential and school segregation. The Milliken decision may turn out to be as misguided as *Plessy v. Ferguson,* "separate but equal" in 1896.

Black parents in the early 1960s fought for better, newer schools and teachers of equal quality. The NAACP demands for good teachers, books, and buildings reflected a strong belief in the potential benefits of public schools. When denied "equality" and confined to old ghetto schools, only then did thousands of parents choose METCO or community schools or, in some cases, private and parochial schools. Would black loyalty continue into the twenty-first century? The common belief is that black students took over Boston schools. In fact the number of black students in 1974, the first year of busing and in 2001 remained almost the same, 28,000 out of 65,000 students, or less than half. The numbers of black students never rose above 33,000 and stabilized over three decades. Recent enrollments reflect increased numbers of Hispanic, Asian, Cape Verdean, and "other" students, new immigrants from strife-torn nations searching for freedom in a new country.

Black families eventually benefited from fair housing laws and chose to move to Boston suburbs, such as Milton, Randolph, and Brockton further south. The latter two communities now reflect adult populations "of color" of 20 percent or more, and school populations more than 50 percent black. However, only seven of more than thirty metropolitan communities appeared to accept blacks and Hispanics, a suburban reluctance that perpetuates racial separatism.[23]

Thomas Pettigrew, Harvard social psychologist, was among the first to describe "black flight." In 2000 almost 40 percent of those students attending nonpublic schools in Boston were black, Hispanic, or Asian. Another 3,000 attend suburban METCO schools. Black parents sought for their children a more challenging and a more disciplined school, just as Yankees, Irish, Jews, and others did a generation or three earlier.[24]

The U.S. Census 2000 and *The Boston Globe* periodically report that new immigrants, Brazilians and Indians and Chinese, now find housing opportunities in suburbs. This was not possible in the 1950s and 1960s. It reflects the expanded openness of certain suburbs allowing minorities into their communities and public schools. It suggests a more mature America. But dozens of exclusive suburbs still remain under fire for "snob zoning" and resistance to "affordable housing," failing to reach even a legislated minimal goal of 10 percent of all housing stock.

By the end of the twentieth century it became common to dismiss busing as a failed social experiment, a great distraction from the pursuit of quality education. In several dozen American cities and counties, federal judges allowed school desegregation court orders to lapse.[25]

Editor Thomas Winship, who died in 2002 at age eighty-one, supervised the Pulitzer prize-winning *Globe* team covering Boston school desegregation. Toward the end of his life he told associates that he wished that in 1974 he had taken a "broader view" of Boston school desegregation:

> To this day I would come down on the same side—integration is my greatest gut belief. But having said that, I think...we should have stood back a little more editorially and urged phasing it in over a three-year period, starting with the lower grades. We should have fought much harder against the cruel pairing of Roxbury and South Boston (high schools). Also, we should have fought much harder for a metropolitan solution, bringing in the suburbs, making them share in the painful transition.

In the end he agreed with Harvard's Professor Jaffe, with Ed Logue, and several Boston School Committee chairs that the entire metropolitan area must participate in the solution.[26]

The courts expected Boston schools to overcome persistent racial isolation in housing tracts. Anthony Downs, a housing economist, argued in the 1970s for strong governmental policies that would require suburbs to accept racial minorities. His book *Opening Up the Suburbs* called for generous incentives creating suburban housing for low- and moderate-income workers who then could live near job openings, and allowing low-income children to attend predominately middle-class schools. He urged dissolving town boundaries, and allowing state or metropolitan authorities to combine student assignment patterns (as was done around Louisville, Kentucky, and St. Louis County, Missouri). He recommended higher governmental housing subsidies and extra school aid payments. He understood the likely sources of opposition. He quoted the Kerner Commission Report on the dangers of "two increasingly separate Americas" and the James Coleman research on the salutary effects of middle-income education on low-income black students. He knew that suburbanites did not realize that exclusion of the poor perpetuated the central-city problems. He thought labor unions, homebuilders, and employers would respond positively to the housing and employment strategy.[27]

Was this an idealist's pipe dream? The Gautreaux case against the Chicago housing authority (Gautreaux, a South Side activist tenant) resulted in HUD policies enabling low-income minorities to receive housing subsidies (under Section 8 of the Housing Act) to pursue lodging in suburbs. During the 1990s Boston was one of several cities (Baltimore, New York, Chicago, Los Angeles) that helped 600 low-income tenants move from city housing projects to suburban neighborhoods. So far, research on hundreds of these families revealed an increase in educational performance and attendance for young children. In Baltimore suburbs, school test scores for urban youth rose by 18 percentage points. Arrests of older youth declined by half. Downs's recommendations in modest form were implemented, never too late to reverse a half-century of American apartheid policies.[28]

Few believe that opening up the suburbs to low-income families, including racial minorities, will be easy. Massachusetts law (Chapter 40B, the "anti snob zoning" law) allowed housing developers to override local restrictions when the percentage of affordable housing was less than 10 percent. Boston, Cambridge, Chelsea, and Lawrence have affordable housing stocks of between 15 and 20 percent. Outside the cities, many communities provide far less than the required 10 percent affordable units. As Michael Blanding noted, "Affordable housing is still something built in someone else's backyard." Neighbors often protest the impact of "starter homes" on schools, traffic, pollution runoff, anything to preserve their restricted enclave. Each year a few suburban communities instruct legislators to dilute or delay the impact of such measures.[29]

Finding ways for low-income and minority families to live and be educated in suburbs remains an American ideal. Citizens living in suburbs and blaming the city for school problems might look in the mirror to look for conspirators perpetuating a racially separate status quo. Suburbs remain a major part of the solution to racial isolation and integration. Churches have not done enough. Sociologist Orlando Patterson criticized mainstream churches for reinforcing racial separatism.[30] The 1997 Gallup poll found that "the Christian churches remain the one 'highly segregated' major institution of American public life." He concluded that "segregation is outright un-Christian, and both African-American and Euro-Americans are guilty of it."[31]

Desegregation suffered in part because state laws and the Milliken (Detroit) federal court solution were limited to the Boston city limits.

The surrounding metropolitan area of 2 million people (and 400,000 students) could have absorbed Boston's 36,000 African American children. Suburbs with 1 percent black populations might have accepted 5 percent in mixed income housing. This was a missed opportunity for post-apartheid Massachusetts to live up to its progressive reputation, and an alternative to mixing low-income South Boston and Roxbury children in hostile territory.[32]

Certainly Brookline, Newton, and Lexington deserved commendation for their 1960s leadership in sponsoring METCO. So also another 25 suburbs responded positively and accepted 3,000 city children each year. But the pent-up demand was for 16,000, not 3,000, METCO seats, just about half of Boston black student population. The once liberal legislature, reflecting an ambivalent electorate, never acknowledged or funded this demand. The city instead emptied itself of white school-age children except at the exam schools, the pilot schools, charter, magnet schools, and parochial schools.

Critics labeled the Downs proposals as "social engineering." However, the real social engineering failures were the low-income, mostly minority, housing projects on Mission Hill and Columbia Point built fifty years earlier. They perpetuated a pernicious form of class discrimination and racial isolation. Eventually, a court order made Boston open the all-white housing projects of Charlestown, South Boston, and Allston-Brighton to a mix of white, black, Hispanic, and other families. This change was almost as painful as school desegregation but necessary under the Fourteenth amendment and civil rights laws. Why not involve the suburbs? Why have certain towns through the 1990s and into the twenty-first century resisted opening the suburbs to a mix of low and moderate housing? Is it residual racism? Is it high-income isolationism or social snobbery? For whatever reason, does it not continue placing the class and ethnic burden on Boston and the Boston public schools? This was the argument of Anthony Downs and Ed Logue in the 1970s and of Monsignor Geno Baroni of the National Ethnic Center.

What have black families gained from urban school reform? Black families made substantial gains after the Civil Rights acts of the 1960s and the desegregation court orders of the 1970s. Orlando Patterson cites the national increase in black college graduates from 1.5 percent of black adults in 1940 to 13 percent in 1990, and moving toward 20 percent in the twenty-first century. He declared as well that, "a mere 13 percent of the population...dominates the nation's popular culture, its music, its dance, its sports, its youth fashion...popular and elite literature. Meanwhile, now only 12 percent of white Americans tell pollsters that they dislike the Afro-American minority, a dramatic reduction in racial prejudice."[33] Not until 2000 could business journalists write about three black CEOS of major corporations including

Fannie Mae and AOL Time Warner. The prospects for racial equality, while not complete, have improved substantially over four decades. For black teachers, police, and firefighters, this required court mandates and for students of color, substantial new state support for city schools.

The Fate of Voice in Schools

The 1993 Massachusetts Reform Act kept strong school councils in place so parents and teachers might monitor school-improvement strategies. The federal No Child Left Behind Act in 2002 called for annual progress reports by school, parent notification of test results, and public disclosure about uncertified teachers.[34] Parents gained voice into key decisions, if not total control of Boston schools. The "community control" debates of the 1960s convinced teachers that they too must serve on school councils to provide educator voices on new hires, equipment, and other services. Not all the judicial mechanisms for parent voice would survive. Judge Garrity ordered resources for district councils, but they became adversarial and combative over time. During 1999 Superintendent Payzant accepted a task force report on family (and parent) involvement. The report recommended consolidating councils and parent support services into a Unified Student and Family Services unit, providing information about how to choose a school. One suggestion was for a part-time parent liaison in each school to help parents get to school conferences and school workers to homes.[35]

Superintendent Payzant, facing a state budget shortfall and cutbacks in 2001, canceled staff subsidies for the CityWide Parents Council. He eliminated resources for separate federal Title 1, bilingual, and special needs councils. Advisory council members howled in protest, but the School Committee voted to assign those functions to Parent Information Centers serving different quadrants of the city.[36]

Can parents be counted on to support school closings, staff layoffs, and other unpleasant changes? As the MACE Raffel survey described in chapter 7, parents often expressed conservative expectations about the schools. When it is time to redraw boundaries or close a school, the local parent-school council often opposed the action. On occasion, the city must override the local school council or else subsidize half-empty facilities. "Voices" are likely to be raised in protest over difficult school changes and closings.

During the 1990s parental impatience with public schools grew. Boston's parents sought new options for their children, more than the traditional private or parochial schools, including the following choices:

1. Charter schools, freed from city school board regulations yet eligible for public funds, authorized by state legislatures and supervised by

state educational officials. State tests would be required but local school officials and parents could decide whether schools closed at 2:30 PM or 6 PM, whether students would focus on technology, or the study of Chinese and the Pacific Rim, and whether students might bring portable computers home to help with homework.[37] Ten Boston charter schools served 2,800 students in 2001, the numbers increasing to above 4,000 by 2006.

2. Pilot schools, the innovative response of the Boston School Committee and Boston Teachers Union, freeing schools from many regulations but with teachers paid union salaries. The School Committee and BTU in 2001 agreed on 11 pilot schools that served another 4,000 students.

3. Home schooling, a quiet revolution that nationally (as of 2000) attracted more than 1 million students taught by parents, enabled by Internet curriculum materials, and with children sometimes eligible to take part in school sports or activities although taught at home. This total exit option served at least 1 percent of all school-age students, attracting parents with firm religious convictions or advanced degrees.

Was this really a new idea or the original Puritan home instruction during 1630–42 before public schools?

Parents in the 1990s sought more than racial integration. Through "choice," the right school they selected might treat their children with respect and love and help them learn. But choice required getting to know the schools. Single parents, especially, were often pressed for time to visit schools. One Boston principal confessed that getting parents to visit school was a genuine challenge, unless their children sang, performed in a play, or exhibited art. Then, those parents came to school events. The John Marshall school in Dorchester embraced Howard Gardner's notion of "multiple intelligences," that learning included not only academics but other forms of creativity and physical movement which society valued.[38]

Another issue for Boston or any city is whether public schools can meet all the expectations of parents, employers, and universities. The historian Lawrence Cremin warned parents not to expect so much of schools, that schools cannot solve each and every problem. Hannah Arendt said our great nineteenth-century faith that schools would overcome racism, poverty, drug abuse, obesity, careless driving, delinquency and violence was "political utopianism." Illusions can be dangerous if they cannot be fulfilled. Cremin explained how education actually begins with the family, includes day care and television (adult TV as well as children's), neighborhood agencies and recreation centers, libraries, the church, and other institutions. Parents in the future might expect "collaboration among many types of public and private agencies run by many different types of professionals."[39] Must schools teach every social and leadership skill in school? Certain educational tasks can be learned as well or better out of school "if America is to work, and to build a good society."

Acceptance of State Standards and Exams

The most amazing change in Boston was city school officials allowing the State Board of Education to define high school graduation requirements, part of the 1993 Massachusetts education reform law. The state approved total curriculum frameworks, the explicit standards of what shall be learned and what concepts and skills should be taught. The state in 1993 also abolished local teacher exams, substituting a rigorous state test that more than half of new teacher candidates failed at the first sitting. Massachusetts mandated rigorous achievement tests for students at the third, eighth, and tenth grade. The subjects tested included English/Language Arts, Mathematics, and eventually History and Science. Superintendent Payzant welcomed the high standards and the rigorous testing, feeling—as did other Massachusetts city superintendents—that higher expectations would bring stronger state financial support for city schools. But in effect the state voices, mobilized by high-tech employers, out-shouted the traditional preferences for "local control" over teacher selection and school curriculum.

Superintendent Payzant's immediate response was to require teachers and principals to schedule ninety minutes each day for literacy education, and even more time for those students scoring more than a grade or two behind. He mandated more time for math when the 2000 math scores lagged behind literacy. He visited each school each year and personally supervised a cadre of deputies and principals enforcing compliance. In 2001 he identified 25 schools as "effective practice" schools, recognizing successful school-improvement strategies. Five Boston elementary schools reported that from 90–100 percent of the students passed the fourth grade MCAS exam. Several district high schools reported major increases in passing scores, albeit from a low base.

The Boston Public Schools, once so defiant about racial imbalance, so sluggish in implementing state special education and bilingual reforms, quietly accepted the mandate of state curriculum standards and testing.[40]

The support for rigorous state testing within Boston, however, was less than unanimous. Principal Deborah Meier, recruited from New York

City to Boston's Mission Hill pilot school, felt such tests were oppressive and a danger to teaching and learning. The BTU and the Massachusetts Federation as well as the Massachusetts Teachers Association believed tests should be used for diagnostic purposes but not as the single determinant of fitness for graduation. The opinion of experts, including the Educational Testing Service, confirmed that no one test should determine a high-stake decision such as awarding a high school diploma. The state Education Reform Act had called for multiple assessments of learning, more than one measure, not just the taking of a test five times until passing.[41]

The Loyal Support of Foundations

By the time Thomas Payzant retired in 2006, national and Massachusetts foundations invested $100 million in efforts to improve Boston's public schools.

In 2001 the Carnegie Foundation allocated $8 million to break Boston's district high schools into 39 small academies, after a study concluded that large, impersonal high schools of 1,000–1,200 contributed to student alienation and withdrawal. The Boston Foundation, Harvard University, the mayor, and a dozen other groups pledged more than $20 million for after-school programs in Boston.

After the first Annenberg Foundation grant ended in 2002, Annenberg contributed another $10 million during 2002–07 to continue the work in Boston, one of the few cities to attract a second round of educational assistance. Warren Simmons of the Annenberg Center at Brown University explained that Payzant's "whole school change" model was applicable to all of urban education. Once again companies and local foundations matched the second $10 million.[42]

The National Science Foundation provided 2 million dollars in funds for increasing science and math performance in Boston's schools. The Nellie Mae Education Foundation provided another $1.5 million to strengthen the teaching and coaching of middle school mathematics. The Boston Plan for Excellence served as administrative agent for many of these gifts. The total endowment of the Plan rose in the late 1990s to $37 million before the stock market dip in 2001. It became the largest "public education fund" in America, a commentary on the substantial corporate and philanthropic loyalty to Boston schools. These expressions of loyal support from corporations and foundations were unthinkable before 1974. During the 1990s they escalated, along with alumni contributions for the Boston Latin School. These were messages of confidence, of faith, and investments in a future "golden age" of educational attainment.

What is remarkable is the relative lack of loyalty from parents over several generations. In Boston there is enduring alumni loyalty mainly to the Boston Latin School. But thousands of families have transferred their loyalties to the leafy suburbs, or to private schools. Even the Boston teachers and administrators are mostly loyal to their jobs, but a huge majority educate their own children elsewhere. Hirschman's opinion that many citizens will fight from within describes only a small number of constituents, but also a few powerful foundations and corporations.

Exit has not done much for urban school reform. It is essentially flight, and even the waiting list for METCO shows that thousands, perhaps half of black parents, also prefer a suburban education for their children. Those exiting may come back for their golden years to enjoy city amenities; too rarely are they ready to pursue school reform. The exception was a Bill Boyan, John Hancock president, moving from Nahant (where he was a School Committee member) to Beacon Hill (where Mayor Menino appointed him to the Boston School Committee). Exit from Boston more typically is a plus for a smaller community.

The Evolution of Voice and Choice

During the twentieth century every mode of voice was employed to shape up, save, and reform the Boston Public Schools. In a democracy, one often supported political candidates who believed in improving the schools and or the conditions for teaching. Elections were not sufficient. The most aggressive reform tactics were those of litigation, asking judges to address an inequity or failure to enforce a civil right or a teacher contract, and adjudicate remedies. What has been lost is a total count of all the costly lawsuits filed and all the court judgments made during 1930–2000 over the policies and practices of the Boston schools. When citizens were unhappy with their schools, they also sought new laws to make the system respond, or pursued litigation, or both.

The most popular tactics of voice included public meetings, the formation of citizens' protest groups, marches, picketing, and efforts to attract media coverage of concerns. The least savory, and usually illegal, tactics include the burning of buildings, schools, and other sites in protests, the stoning of buses, the employment of death threats, the riots and mob action that terrorized neighborhoods and shamed the city. Tager suggested that less-educated citizens periodically boiled over with resentment and resorted to street tactics because they know no other way to articulate their unhappiness. These tactics contradict the idea of a civilized city, but they remain the underside of "voice" and a commentary on the limits of a republic to handle emotional interethnic protest.[43]

Hirschman's insights on voice emphasized the potential support for corrective changes. The Boston schools traditionally received at least strong vocal support for keeping the old ways of doing business, usually downright opposition to reform.[44] Boston's school councils remained a vehicle for articulating both progress and negative reaction. Voice was both a source of energy for change, and a vehicle for expressing resistance. On issues of race the majority whites frequently won the voice count, but not the court verdicts. The Ombudsman office, a concept Hirschman reviewed favorably, provided a safety valve for a myriad of lesser parent complaints. Voice may not guarantee local school reform. The larger issues often required state legislative action, federal and philanthropic support, and judicial intervention to revive an unresponsive city school system.

The phenomenon of voice in the twenty-first century has evolved into advocacy for "choice." Education reformers in the Year 2000 fell into the following three warring camps:

1. *Advocates for High Standards.* Proponents argue that city public schools still need to improve substantially. All students must achieve at the "Proficient" level, well above the initial 2003 state testing standards. Students should complete additional homework. Students who do not achieve at grade level, should pass summer courses before progressing to the next grade or repeat the grade. Students falling behind should get after school tutoring and extra work on skills. Advocates convinced governors and the president of the United States in the early 1990s to strive to make the United States the number one nation in literacy, science, and math, a goal still years away. Lawmakers concluded that the way to put pressure on schools was to test every student in every grade from three to eight, with another rigorous achievement test for high school student graduation. Most states accepted these requirements, embedded in the federal law No Child Left Behind as of 2002. Most leaders of business and industry, the American Federation of Teachers, and many state educators support higher standards. In Boston, the advocates included the Massachusetts Business Alliance for Education, the Boston Plan for Excellence, and the Federal Reserve Bank.

2. *Vouchers and Charter School Advocates.* The libertarian wing proposes breaking up the public school system monopoly in order to achieve top standing in international comparisons. Chicago economist Milton Friedman introduced the voucher idea more than fifty years earlier. Students would take a "voucher" to the private, parochial, or public school of their choice as in Milwaukee since 1990, Cleveland, and Washington, DC (21,000 students in these cities).

Charter schools for conservatives and moderates are a popular compromise alternative, offering freedom from most city rules and union contract provisions. The most radical libertarian "exit" alternative, the ultimate boycott, would be educating one's child at home, with parents or friend assuming schooling responsibilities. Several Boston think tanks (The Pioneer Institute), support vouchers and charter schools.[45] The BTU supported a milder form of charters called "pilot schools," freed of certain regulations but still operating as a unionized public school. Boston's pilots boast a higher rate of students passing the state 2005 MCAS English and Mathematics tests.

3. *The Humanist Approach.* Humanists feel each student is unique and special and no one standardized test fits all children. Children are endowed with multiple intelligences, some excelling at cognitive skills such as the new state standards require. Other children excel at sports, music, or art. The world rewards high talent. Some students will be stymied by advanced literature, but speedily repair an automobile or a heating system, using manuals and computers to diagnose problems. Surely educators might employ a variety of student assessment techniques to evaluate progress. For many students, a portfolio of essays, scientific lab work, poetry, and writings, would confirm their learning as well or better than a standardized exam. For some students offering their paintings or poems, entering a science fair or other exhibition, might be as appropriate as a demonstration of learning. A combination of evaluations makes more sense than a "one size fits all" examination under great stress, where some students achieve while others freeze.

Coalition of Essential Schools founder Theodore Sizer and Deborah Meier (whose Harlem schools succeeded before she came to Boston to run the Mission Hill Charter School) recommend multiple assessments of student learning. They view uniform state standards for all students as draconian, a retreat to the factory model of schooling, and a denial to parents and local officials the right to tailor education and assessment to local clientele. They favor rigorous standards but not by using the same measuring stick for all children.[46]

Jacob Ludes, executive director of the New England Association of Schools and College, the regional accreditor of Boston schools, also deplored the narrow reliance on testing: "Youngsters will spend more time in school taking tests and practicing taking tests. They will become test smart. Teachers will increasingly teach to the test and there will be, as the Rand corporation research suggests, an initial and temporary increase in test scores.... In the meantime, our focus in schools will narrow towards a national curriculum...." He argued for a wider focus, and that little children need music and languages early in their life in school.[47] His accrediting commission in the past cited Boston's severe high school deficiencies. But his voice and those of humanists portends the educational pendulum swinging back toward citizenship and character education, art, music, and physical education.

For decades Bostonians overreacted first to the academic performances of Russians or Japanese, to whomever threatened to outscore or outwit Americans. When the Russians launched Sputnik in 1957, it was a tribute to Russian education. When the U.S. rocket ship landed on the moon, it was announced as the triumph of American technology, not education. When the Japanese dominated U.S. electronics and automotive industries, we concluded that their superior schools—and longer school year—resulted in our shame. During the 1990s, however, the Japanese endured a decade-long business recession and were reported to be thinking of humanizing the strict curriculum. These national "mood swings" often drive educational reform, noted Larry Cuban.[48]

The mood of Boston, Massachusetts and the nation in 2000 was this: "First, we must bring reading and writing and math up to a higher level; then, and only then, can we reinstate geography and civics, art and music, and possibly physical education. Schools tried to do too much in mid-century and the focus must be on basic skills first."[49]

Boston after Ten Years of Whole School Improvement

In 2005 Thomas Payzant announced that he would retire in 2006, allowing ample time for a search for a successor. Many had praised his tenure. He was named state and national superintendent of schools of the year. *Governing* magazine listed him as one of five top public officials. Harvard University asked him to join the faculty as senior lecturer in Education. Then, after four years winning second place, Eli Broad's national Foundation named Boston as the most improved urban school system in America in 2006, with a $500,000 prize in the form of scholarships for graduates.

The Annenberg Institute for School Reform, with Payzant's consent, wrote a case study on the leadership transition challenge for the Boston Public Schools, intended as a resource for the mayor and School Committee. What had worked well and should be continued? What were the challenges for the new superintendent? The Annenberg Institute at Brown University met with ninety-eight informed observers and voiced almost unanimous consent on both the achievements and the problems yet to be solved.

Boston was a dynamic, successful city with declining rates of crime and office vacancies and rising levels of educational attainment. The Commonwealth of Massachusetts was one of five states with the most rigorous statewide assessment of education. FORBES magazine in 2004 announced that " Boston offered the best public education of any big city in the United States." Another collection of recommendations was entitled *A Decade of Urban School Reform: Persistence and Progress in the Boston Public Schools*, published for the Rennie Center by the Harvard Education Press in 2007.[50]

The Aspen/Annenberg report observed that race remained an issue, that the schools were more racially isolated than when the desegregation lawsuit was filed in the 1970s and that 61 percent of the teachers were white while 86 percent of the students were either black, Hispanic, Asian, or Native American. Payzant had increased the number of school administrators of color to 62 percent, including three deputy school superintendents. The heaviest concentrations of white students were in two exam schools, Boston Latin School 53 percent and Boston Latin Academy 39 percent.

The study found that Boston dedicated 35 percent of the city budget to Boston's schools, compared to 23 percent of the New York City budget. The state had been generous until the 2003 and 2004 austerity budgets when staff cuts were required, schools closed, and support services reduced. The report praised Boston's After School and Beyond initiative serving the low-income children.

The report concluded that few American cities supported aggressive and effective school reform for as long as a decade. The authors praised Payzant's vision, his raising expectations for students, parents, and teachers, his appointment of ninety principals committed to school improvement, his support of teacher coaching and professional development, and the increasing reliance on data on school achievement to improve instruction. Boston had been unique in raising both elementary, middle, and high school achievement in most years, both in English and in mathematics. The percentage of African Americans passing the tenth grade state mathematics test soared from 15 percent to 62 percent, while the Hispanic scores rose from 13 percent to 65 percent during 1998–2005. White and Asian scores moved from 50 percent passing to 85 and 95 percent. The number of graduates attending college rose from below 62 percent in 1993 to 74 percent for the Class of 2003.

Boston had begun recruiting Teacher Residents from the best colleges of the Northeast to learn to teach in Boston schools, and created a School Leadership Institute to grow its own principals. Each school had an Instructional Leadership Team including teacher leaders. They often reviewed classroom and student achievement data from MyBPS (My Boston

Public Schools), developed by Boston's data experts with the help of Harvard Professor Richard Murnane and his staff.[51] Best of all the Boston School Committee appointed by Mayor Menino supported all of the instructional improvements rather than fight among themselves and contend for higher office.

However, serious issues remained for the next leadership team. One was the matter of only 25 percent of the students attaining Proficiency, twenty points above the passing scores on the state test, and considered vital to success in college or the workplace. Coupled with a 24 percent dropout rate, higher for African Americans and Hispanics, half of Boston's high school students were not ready for higher education or challenging work Another issue was equity, in that instruction in many Exam and Pilot schools seemed so much more effective than in other Boston schools. So also the lack of equipment and level of teacher absenteeism were issues in too many regular schools. Too many students with disabilities and English-language deficiencies needed more effective instruction. The interviewers recorded concerns about insufficient curriculum alignment with state standards, and some schools reported that they faced a confusing array of subject matter coaches.

The final concerns were about parental and community involvement. Boston school partnerships seemed strongest with the corporate elites, the Boston Plan, the PIC, and Federal Reserve Bank but less robust with neighborhood agencies and social centers. The old walls between schools and communities remained high, and this had not been a high priority for Superintendent Payzant who focused on improving each school and each teacher.

The report wondered whether the Boston community was ready to reach a higher plateau of school reform and student proficiency. Had the tests scores peaked? Former State Senate President Thomas Birmingham told the Pioneer Institute in early 2007 that the state support for science and mathematics and money for tutoring was wavering. The organized teachers were less than excited about No Child Left Behind and adding a science test and then history and civic knowledge. The report ended with a call to respect the history of the last decade and the longer history of education in Boston.

This report and other local memoranda guided the Boston Superintendent Search Committee in 2005 as it began soliciting candidates. Community leaders and Boston Teachers union President Richard Stutman joined School Committee members in looking for a worthy successor to Thomas Payzant. Ed Hamilton was the same search consultant who helped Cathy Minehan and Tom Menino bring Payzant to Boston in 1995. However, when the names of aspirants were published in the *Globe* and *Herald*, one by one the five finalists dropped out. A schedule of promised community screening interviews was abandoned. The most likely, Manuel Rivera, who enjoyed success as Rochester New York superintendent, was quietly persuaded to reconsider, and then his appointment, approved by mayor and School Committee, was announced. This dismayed the community groups once guaranteed the chance to interrogate finalists, a loss of the promised voice. The process riled the editorial writers of the *Globe* committed to an open vetting of all superintendent finalists. Formal contract deliberations began, but in November 2005 Rivera stunned the city by saying he was not coming to Boston but would instead lead a New York State commission of public education, recruited by newly elected Governor Eliot Spitzer. Bostonians could not believe this turn of events and City Councilors demanded that longtime School Committee chair Dr. Elizabeth Reilinger Ph.D. step down, as an unfounded rumor circulated that she opposed Rivera's senior management changes.

Interim Superintendent Michael Contompassis, for years the Latin School headmaster and then Payzant's chief operating officer, agreed to remain as long as needed. The Teachers Union, months overdue on a new contract, threatened a one-day strike in February 2007 over the issues of paying pilot teachers extra for additional hours, class size enforcement, a better salary raise than 2 percent, and proposed reductions in health care payments by the city. It seemed the momentum for further school improvement had been stalled for the moment. On February 27, 2007 the city agreed to raises in the 13–14 percent range over four years and more flexible hours and hiring for twenty underperforming schools.

Carol Johnson's Agenda for Boston Schools

Dr. Carol Johnson, Boston's superintendent in 2007, previously led the city schools of Minneapolis and then Memphis. What were her ideas on bringing Boston schools to a higher level? She used her first 100 days to tour Boston's neighborhood and schools, listening carefully to parents, students, school staff, and community leaders. East Boston parents asked for a Montessori program and Chinese parents at the Quincy School wanted the rigor of the International Baccalaureate program.

She reviewed the lengthy appraisals of Boston school reform as of Payzant's departure in 2006, beginning with the Aspen/Annenberg Institute assessment of Boston schools, and the Rennie Center review of *A Decade of Urban School Reform*, edited by Paul Reville and Cecille Coggins. Senior black and Hispanic leaders led by Hubie Jones appointed their own Citizens Commission on Academic Success in Boston Schools, staffed by the Massachusetts Advocates for Children. The Commission recommended major changes in mathematics and language instruction, especially for immigrants, better induction and retention of teachers, improved special education, and much more. Dr. Johnson quickly concluded that the critiques of Boston schools were accurate, that too few students achieved proficiency, far too many dropped out of high school, and the large minority achievement gap for Hispanic and black students was unacceptable. These data would drive her plan.

She informed the Boston School Committee that Boston in 2008 enrolled 56,000 students, for the first time more Hispanic students (39 percent) than black (37 percent) and that there were 13 percent white student and 9 percent Asian. Three out of four Boston students qualified for free or reduced-price meals, indicators of poverty. For 24,000 students, English was not their first language and at least half had limited English fluency. She reported 11,320 students with disabilities (21 percent), half with moderate to severe conditions. She mentioned that 18,850 Boston students attended other schools, 6,400 in parochial and 3,770 in private schools. Suburban schools attracted 3,150 students through METCO and 4,820 attended state authorized public charter schools. Another 250 were reportedly home schooled.[52]

Superintendent Johnson proposed to the Boston School Committee three overarching goals in a five-year Acceleration Agenda, a strategic plan for city schools 2009–2014.

This would be the sequel to Payzant's two five-year plans entitled "Focus on Children."

Her new plan would do the following:

1. Ensure all students achieve MCAS proficiency, specifically in reading and mathematics, by 2014,
2. Close the "access gap" (access to academics, arts, and athletics) and close the several achievement gaps, by race, gender, disabilities and language, and
3. Graduate all students from high school prepared for college or career success.

The specific, quantifiable targets remained ambitious but were more pragmatic, aiming at significant improvements for most, if not all, Boston students and public schools.

- While 77 percent of grade three students in 2009 scored "Passing" on the MCAS English exam, the new 2010–2011 target would be 94 percent passing and 100 percent by 2012

- While 31 percent of grade three students scored as Proficient in 2009, the annual targets would be raised to 59 percent, then 72 percent, then 85 percent by 2012
- While the MCAS achievement gaps between racial groups were as high as 30 points in 2009, the target would be to reduce this by 5 percent each year to "Fewer than 5 percent" by 2014.
- While only 4 percent of eighth grade students took Algebra 1 in non-exam schools (exam schools were The Latin School, Latin Academy, and O'Bryant High) in 2009, those numbers would rise by about 10 percent each year reaching above 40 percent by 2014.
- While 75 percent of tenth graders passed MCAS in grade ten, the percentages would rise to 90 percent by 2011, making more students eligible for a diploma.
- The four-year graduation rates for all students would rise from 60 percent to 80 percent by 2012, to 85 percent by the fifth year, never reaching 100 percent but increasing the graduation rate by 25 percent.
- The annual student dropout rate would drop from 7.2 percent in 2009 to 3 percent or lower by 2012 and thereafter, a projected 60 percent reduction.
- The Scholastic Aptitude Test I scores (combined) would rise each year from 1321 to 1650 by 2012.
- The number of students taking at least one advanced Placement or Honors course, or the International Baccalaureate, or dual enrol-ment (taking college courses while in high school) would rise from 71 percent to 100 percent by 2012.

The graduation goals for special education and ELL students were set at 10 percent lower than the rest of the school population, partly because new immigrants came to Boson schools as late as their sixteenth or eighteenth year. Some special needs students are profoundly disabled or disturbed and might not pass MCAS or common core courses despite extensive help and alternative exam formats. Passing rates at Boston's Horace Mann School for the Deaf, for example, reached only 40 percent in 2009, evidence both of major accomplishments and a serious challenge. Given the high mobility of Boston families in and out of neighborhoods and schools, these still looked like "stretch goals" but clearly measurable each year.

The superintendent provided additional detail on her implementation strategies, which included holding low-performing schools accountable for dramatic improvements and replacing ineffective teachers and principals. She called for stronger community partnerships, extended learning time, multiple paths to graduation, and the improvement of district services while reducing administrative costs.

One page of the plan elaborated on the urgency of outstanding classroom teaching. She pledged that all teachers and staff would become "culturally competent," code words suggesting that the mostly white staff would need to know more about racial and ethnic customs, and develop positive beliefs about "diversity" when 87 percent of students were of color.

Would teachers be more closely evaluated? A National Council on Teacher Quality report announced that few Boston teachers were ever rated "unsatisfactory" and that in one quarter of the schools, no teachers were evaluated. Johnson's Agenda said: "Evaluations must be tied to student achievement; excellent teachers and leaders should be rewarded for their transformative work in our schools." Other teachers would need "guidance to go from good to great." She proposed a constructive partnership with the Boston Teachers Union to work on "flexible staffing, better use of professional development time, and on school autonomy and accountability." She called for "data driven decisions that put the needs of children before adults," which would require appropriate interventions.

She added tactics on "replacing ineffective teachers and leaders" using terms like "Termination" and "Expedited Dispute Resolution," alternatives to year-long court or arbitration proceedings. "Teachers who cannot improve students' academic growth must be properly evaluated and dismissed".[53] She added two staff specialists to the Human Resources office to help principals document better their faculty and staff evaluations.

Many new teachers would come from nontraditional sources. "We will continue to use Boston Teacher Residency (BTR), Teach for America, and other innovative teacher quality research and development programs, as well as institutions of higher education."

Political Allies for Education Reform

Boston schools were locally funded but relied on state and federal support, accepting the mandates and regulations that came with the money. Boston fared well in good economic times but in the recession that began in December 2007, strong political advocacy was important.

Massachusetts in 2006 elected a new Democratic Governor, Deval Patrick, a former Assistant Attorney General under President Bill Clinton. His own education took him from the South Side of Chicago to Milton Academy through A Better Chance program for students of color. Later attending Harvard College and Law School, he felt strongly about schools effectively educating for success in life. He quickly formed a giant (250 citizen) Task Force on Readiness for College and Careers.

Tom Payzant, former Boston superintendent, served as one of three cochairs.

Dana Mohler-Faria, president of Bridgewater State College, was the first education advisor to Governor Patrick, followed by Paul Reville who became Secretary of Education in the governor's cabinet. Reville had helped draft the 1993 state Education Reform Act, taught at Harvard, founded the Rennie Center (an education think tank in Cambridge), had chaired the State Board of Education, and edited a book on school reform in Boston. Both Patrick and Reville supported Innovation Schools within urban districts but resisted any blanket state-wide expansion of charter schools.

The national election of President Barack Obama coincided with the most serious national recession in seventy years. Massachusetts' tax revenues declined by several billion dollars. States and cities turned to the Congress for some form of revenue-sharing, which in 2009–2010 became the American Recovery and Reinvestment Act (ARRA) or federal stimulus package. Of the $100 billion allocated for education, most went to states according to Title One and IDEA (special education) formulae. But $4.35 billion was reserved for a Race to the Top competition, which required states to commit to a Common Core curriculum, use more achievement data to make personnel decisions, prepare "great teachers and leaders" especially for low-performing schools, and select among "turn-around" strategies to address the underperforming schools, most in low-income neighborhoods.

Massachusetts leaders felt confident about competing for RTTT funds because the state ranked number one in the last two biennial National Assessments of Educational Progress. The international math tests (TIMMS) showed that Massachusetts students scored equal to the top five nations of the world. Half the points were awarded for past accomplishments, with the rest allocated for future plans. Massachusetts standards and tests were more rigorous than those adopted by other states. The Secretary and State Board debated whether they could commit to common core courses developed by other governors and chief state school officers (education commissioners). The Governor, Commissioner of Education Mitchell Chester, and Board Chair Maura Banta submitted a full RTTT proposal in January 2010.

The Governor proposed a new education reform bill in 2009 to authorize Innovation Schools, to close the Achievement Gap, and selectively lift the spending cap on charter schools in Massachusetts cities. The bill allowed superintendents to override teacher contract provisions and transfer teachers out of low-performing schools without regard to their seniority. A Race to the Top coalition led by the Boston Foundation supported the bill, while state teacher unions fought for appeals and due process in the teacher transfer provisions. The bill passed, strengthening the second round of RTTT commitments from Massachusetts. U.S. Education Secretary Arne Duncan in Round One approved RTTT grants for only two states, Delaware and Tennessee. He urged other states to revise their proposals in response to federal reviewer comments, and thirty-seven states resubmitted proposals in June 2010.

The Massachusetts Board in June 2010 voted to accept the Common Core standards. The national team called on state staff for advice on how to make the standards as rigorous as Massachusetts. The state RTTT proposal further committed to stronger teacher and principal training and evaluations. Massachusetts RRTT score moved from #13 to #1 in the summer review and qualified for $250 million over four years. One-half of the money would go to low-income communities and at least $8 million to Boston schools each year.

Reducing the Dropout Rate

Which of Boston's targets could be pursued first? There was one group ready and eager to help reduce the dropout rate and increase the high school graduation rate. That was the Boston Private Industry Council, the city's workforce investment board that sponsored One Stop Career Centers. The PIC previously negotiated a series of Boston Compacts (the last one in 2000) and each year conducted a survey of college and career decisions made by Boston's high school graduates. Neil Sullivan, PIC executive, was a Boston school parent passionate about the need to make all adolescents employable with good career prospects.

Critics of the 1993 Massachusetts Education Reform Act had predicted that the required graduation test (MCAS) would cause the student dropout rate to increase, especially in cities and for African American and Latino youth. Neil Sullivan observed that in fact it did not increase, but neither did it decline. The Boston cumulative (grade nine–twelve) dropout rate remained as high as 40 percent. This meant that 1,500 eighteen-year olds left school each year without a diploma.[54]

At Sullivan's urging, Mayor Thomas Menino in October 2004 invited leaders of eighteen social service and community groups to get involved in school dropout prevention and recovery strategies. The Carnegie, Gates, and Mott Foundations supported Boston's planning efforts, with the help of Northeastern University Center for Labor Market Studies. In 2006 Boston's Youth Transition Task Force included thirty organizations recruited by the PIC and released a report called "*Too Big To Be Seen*: The Invisible Dropout Crisis in Boston and America".[55] The report warned that the severe consequences especially for male dropouts included high unemployment, low-wage jobs, crime, and imprisonment.

Despite the existing alternative high school programs and two dozen adult education programs, the PIC discovered that as many as 8,000 Boston youth age sixteen–twenty-four still lacked a high school diploma. Furthermore, there was hardly any systematic outreach to bring dropouts back into school, other than a few phone calls to absent students. The Task Force created greater visibility for the dropout program, closer collaboration among state and city agencies, and a new strategy for reengaging students who left school before graduating. Leaders proposed state laws mandating better disclosure of graduation data, earlier identification of potential dropouts, and an increase in the age of compulsory education from sixteen to eighteen. Suggestions for new state grants for dropout prevention programs hit the harsh reality of decreased state revenues after 2008.[56]

Superintendent Johnson quickly agreed to cosponsor a dropout Reengagement Center at Madison Park High School in the heart of Roxbury, staffed by six professionals, three funded by the PIC and three by the city schools. One of the strategies was called Credit Recovery designed for students who mastered some but not all the skills or content to complete a course. Tutoring, summer courses, and online lessons were combined to help returning students earn the credits needed for a diploma.

In the first year, 400 dropouts agreed to return to school. The annual dropout rate declined and the graduation rate improved by 10 percent, a promising start.[57] Still there were more than a thousand dropouts. The Massachusetts Advocacy Center thought that not enough attention was paid to the early indicators that pointed out a student was likely to drop out, such as poor attendance and failing to meet grade standards.[58]

Boston's Circle of Promise

What could be done to improve educational, social, and family services for the children from the very poorest Boston neighborhoods? Of the twelve lowest performing schools, ten were in a five-mile square zone that included parts of Roxbury, North Dorchester, and the South End, sections of the city that traditionally served the lowest income immigrants. More recently, new families came from Haiti, the Sudan, Somalia, Brazil, and beleaguered nations in Africa or Latin America.

Mayor Menino and Superintendent Johnson in February 2010 announced a "Circle of Promise" plan to foster closer collaboration between 140 government agencies, community, and nonprofit organizations that usually worked in isolation. Loosely modeled on the acclaimed

Harlem Children's Zone, the Circle would begin very early to help young parents gain access to "wraparound" family services from infancy on through high school. In June 2010 the Boston Foundation, Combined Jewish Philanthropies, and the United Way announced a $27 million Opportunity Agenda over the next two years, integrating early childhood, after school and summer school programs. Michael Durkin, President of the United Way, said "We may have funded a few things together in the past coincidentally, but never with this thoughtfulness and planning".[59] One goal was to boost the high school graduation rate to 80 percent by 2014 (two years later than what Johnson projected.

The Barr, Nellie Mae, and Boston Foundations and The Beal Companies agreed to finance Circle projects. The Obama administration provided $500,000 to help two high schools in Boston's Circle. Boston was in effect declaring a new war on poverty. The EOS Foundation launched a new initiative in the Grove Hall neighborhood (within the Circle of Promise) called "Boston Rising". Dozens of agencies, foundations, and groups, including churches and business firms, pledged to provide more help to young mothers, many unmarried and needing advice and support. A new Parent University offered workshops on how effectively parents could work with the schools. Boston youth in summer could either go to school or camp or get a job, arranged through the mayor and PIC. Dropouts would be contacted, counseled, and reinstated in a high school program.

Obama stimulus funds provided tens of millions for extending the school day, and for paying teachers extra for teaching in turnaround schools. Most of the Circle of Promise money was either federal or private, but the Mayor provided visible leadership with the Superintendent at his side. Harvard's Kennedy School of Government provided three interns to monitor Circle of Promise collaboration, and the Mayor appointed Marie St. Fleur, a Haitian-born former state representative, to advise him on Circle of Promise progress.

Boston received other private sector gifts for urban education. Peter Lynch's family foundation donated $22 million to Boston College to support public school, charter school, and parochial school leaders. Lynch and his wife Carolyn previously made Catholic schools their top philanthropic priority, especially inner city parish schools and Boston College where he was an alumnus trustee. John Fish of Suffolk Construction pledged $1 million to revive high school athletic programs and promised to raise more. EdVestors launched a $2.5 million fundraising campaign to support more art in the public schools, another Carol Johnson academic access priority that also promoted student enthusiasm for attending school. The Boston Symphony Orchestra agreed to provide music lessons at the Edison school in the Brighton neighborhood.

Thomas Menino in 2009 ran for an unprecedented fifth term as Mayor. Challenged by two City Councilors, Michael Flaherty and Sam Yoon, he won 51 percent of the votes in the September primary and 57 percent in the November election. He enjoyed strong support from neighborhoods of color for delivering services for young and old, for the schools and social agencies. He asked universities in Boston to help low-performing schools and to make Success Boston a viable strategy to increase the 50 percent rate of degree completion for Boston students.

Searching for Highly Effective Teachers

Judge Garrity in the 1970's directed Boston to hire at least 25 percent teachers of color as part of his desegregation order. Over time it proved difficult to improve on that percentage, even as Boston's total population turned 50 percent "minority" and students of color reached 87 percent. Thomas Payzant increased the percentage of principals and headmasters of color to 65 percent, but not the teachers. Boston was totally dependent on the supply from public and private colleges whose schools of education enrolled mostly Caucasian students.

The Boston Public Schools launched its own teacher preparation program, modeled in part on the medical school "residency" requirements for future MDs working in hospitals under close supervision from experienced doctors. The Boston Teacher Residency (BTR) began in 2002 when Superintendent Payzant asked Ellen Guiney at the Boston Plan for Excellence to house and oversee the program led by a former teacher Jesse Solomon. After several years the program recruited and placed 60–85 new teachers a year for Boston: 75 percent of them remained in Boston schools, 236 of them by 2010. What was remarkable was that 48 percent described themselves as "teachers of color" and more than half taught mathematics, science, or special education, fields where Boston suffered from chronic shortages. By 2008 60 percent of all BPS mathematics and science teachers were BTR graduates. BTR aspired to prepare 30 percent of all Boston teachers, with Boston hiring 250–300 new teachers each year.[60]

The initial funds for BTR came from Strategic Grant Partners (several family foundations), later augmented by major national and local foundations. In 2010 U.S. Secretary of Education Duncan, who in Chicago worked with a similar Academy for Urban School Leadership, funded the expansion of Teacher Residencies in twenty communities, mostly cities. Boston qualified for two multimillion federal grants, funds to be shared with UMass Boston and Wheelock College who would provide the Master's degree after several years of BTR coursework.

Another potential source of strong teacher candidates was Teach for America, an idea initially frowned on by the Boston Teachers Union. However, Boston hired nineteen TFAs in 2009 and twenty in 2010. One strength of TFA was the great selectivity, with more than 30,000 applicants for 4,000 placements nationally, many chosen from very selective universities such as Boston University that offered them Master's degrees. Ellen Guiney pointed out that TFA asks teachers to make only a two-year commitment, while BTR pushed for teachers staying three or more years after the residency year.[61]

Boston sought to hire additional teachers with dual certifications, the second certificate in either special education or English as a Second Language, better to serve the almost 50 percent of students who brought limited English proficiency or severe learning or emotional disabilities to school. Boston was directed by the federal Justice and Education Departments to train all teachers in English Language Learners (ELL) techniques and discourage parents from "opting out" of English acquisition programs.

Another school improvement strategy was to assign teams of experienced and effective teachers to three of the lowest performing schools, asking them to lead other teachers in each grade and to provide extra help to students and parents. Turnaround Teach Teams (T3) would be paid an additional $4,000 for service in those schools and another $6,000 for twenty-five extra days, including two weeks planning in the summer. Most of the first thirty-six T3 teachers chosen were veteran teachers with eight or more years of experience, many were bilingual, and seven came from charter schools. Cecile Coggins designed what was called Teacher Plus while working with Paul Reville at the Rennie Center. Incubated with help from the Gates Foundation, other cities asked Teach Plus for help in their school systems.[62]

Adding bilingual teachers and extending the school day were constructive solutions, but possibly implemented too late for many inner city children were suffering the disadvantage of limited English vocabularies. Boston expanded the full-day pre-kindergarten programs for 2,500 four-year olds. Older immigrants age fourteen–eighteen who spoke little English were sent to a Newcomers Academy which provided testing and advice to families on appropriate educational program choices.

Controversies and Barriers to Reform

Who should make the decisions about Boston schools, the local School Committee, the state, the federal government, the foundations, or local parents? It was not clear. Who would determine the right balance for the curriculum? Were charter schools helpful or a drain on the system? Where would new money come from for the schools?

In Massachusetts the Educational Reform Act of 1993 mandated high state standards and assessments (mainly tests) of English and mathematics in three grades, and ten years later in science as well. Prior to that, the only state requirement was for physical education and a year of U.S. history. A few years later the second Bush administration and Congress insisted on state standards with tests in grades three–eight and in grade ten (seven of the twelve grades). The local school committee powers were sharply reduced; in Boston the Mayor had a big say in choosing the superintendent, approving the school budget, and achieving final settlements with unions. By 2010 the U.S. Department of Education emerged as the major player calling for higher standards. This troubled the Pioneer Institute and former Senate President Tom Birmingham who opposed any dilution of the Massachusetts high standards and rigorous assessments.[63]

Most of the ideas for the federal Race to the Top had come from critical reports on U.S. education standards and practices funded by the Gates and General Electric Foundations. The Gates Foundation investment in education reform was huge, far larger than the next three national foundations combined. Several former Gates Foundation staff members agreed to serve in key innovation staff roles in the Obama and Arne Duncan Department of Education. Gates earlier financed the Mass Insight study of school turnaround models. Bill Gates Jr. had strongly criticized American high schools and spent $2 billion dollars on smaller high schools designed to change the impersonal climate that presumably drove out urban high school students. Gates in 2009 made a major commitment to looking at teacher effectiveness and evaluations in city and charter schools. Gates also provided planning grants to states preparing Race to the Top proposals in 2010. Wherever new reforms were proposed and funded, Gates money and staffers seemed very much involved. Was this good for American education and urban schools?

Diane Ravitch, historian of school reform battles, thought that the heavy emphasis on student testing, and charter schools jeopardized American education. This was a dramatic reversal of her views as an Assistant Secretary of Education under Republican presidents. Her book, *The Death and Life of the Great American School System*, in 2010, delighted traditional educators and surprised former associates who previously fought at her side to expand testing and school choice.

She denounced several national foundations for their advocacy of unproven school reform theories. The Gates investment in small high schools, for example, had failed to make a difference. She criticized the way they imposed their educational policy preferences by awarding big grants. As a result, American education had sharply narrowed the curriculum so that history, science art, music, and other core subjects were marginalized and neglected.[64]

In Boston, Ellen Guiney at the Boston Plan agreed that most of the Gates-financed small schools had not moved beyond "structural change." Gates himself conceded that and cancelled the small school investments. Neil Sullivan at the PIC thought that several small (pre-Gates) Boston high schools with a magnetic theme had done well, such as Fenway High School and the Arts Academy. On the other hand, President Barack Obama on March 8, 2011, visited Boston Tech Academy, a high achievement school financed with help from Gates in 2002.

Guiney disagreed with those who thought that the billions spent by the Annenberg Foundation on urban school reform had been ineffective. She felt that in New York City, Chattanooga, and Boston those funds played a major role in raising citywide achievement overall. Foundation funds made possible adding teacher coaches and closer attention to "inquiry," as more teachers learned how to analyze gaps in achievement score results and student work.

In Boston, Paul Grogan at The Boston Foundation provided major leadership in school reform. Grogan had worked for the city, then on national low-income housing initiatives, and wrote *Comeback Cities*, "a blueprint for urban neighborhood revival".[65] Grogan grew enthusiastic about new models such as community development corporations and charter school providers. He concluded that "the obsolescent, bureaucracy-choked system of American education is done for, and with it will fall the last great barrier to livable, competitive inner city neighborhoods." The alternative to reengineering the schools, he thought, would be "a parent revolution".[66]

Grogan served briefly as the Harvard University vice president for community and government relations, but as president of The Boston Foundation (TBF) took on the urban school challenge. The Foundation published detailed studies of educational strengths and weaknesses in the schools of each neighborhood. He offered planning grants to twenty Boston principals and teachers who would consider more innovative Pilot School status (of which only three schools voted yes). He convened a coalition of community organizations to promote passage of the state 2010 Educational Reform package. He sponsored another coalition to take on the teacher union contract and strip it of many pages for elaborate protection for veteran teachers, In *Comeback Cities* he said it was wrong "to cast teachers and their unions solely as the demons of this story" although they had put up the fiercest defense against school choice in cities. He became frustrated by the power of the Boston Teachers

Union to either veto or slow down the pilot school movement and other innovations.

Grogan and The Boston Foundation strongly advocated the expansion of charter schools. Grogan financed a Harvard research study showing that Boston charter school students scored much better than comparable students at regular schools, their achievement levels rising to the levels of suburban school children. Others were critical of charters for not admitting enough special education children or more English language learners, who were then left for other public schools to teach. Ravitch complained that charters took out of the system the most highly motivated students and parents.[67] Critics felt that charter schools forced out low performing and spotty attendance students, sometimes removing them from school rolls just before the state MCAS exams. State MCAS scores revealed 100 percent passing scores at several Boston charters, while others displayed scores no better than noncharters. The debate continued, but more than forty charter school expansion requests were presented to the State Board of Elementary and Secondary Education. The 2010 reform act would allow the number of Boston charter school students to rise from 5,000 to 10,000 by 2016. In 2011 the state approved ten new or expanded charter schools for Boston.

Why had external grants become so much more important? Boston schools each year needed an additional $40–50 million to expand important initiatives (such as early childhood programs or subject matter coaches) and pay for salary increments for teachers and other school employees. Fiscal year 2008 was the last year that more than 5 percent budget increases were available, up to $795 million. After 2008, new city dollars were in short supply and Carol Johnson confronted tight budgets, probable staff layoffs, school closings, and program cutbacks:

Fiscal Year	Available Funds
2009	$810 million, reduction of $30 million from initial budget forecasts
2010	$817 million, requiring $20 million be cut from the budget
2011	$821 million, with $50 million to be cut.[68]

Accordingly, the federal stimulus dollars made a huge difference, reducing the number of staff layoffs, and funding new state and federal turnaround interventions. The value of these reforms would require two to four years to validate. Until the economy improved, as it had in the 1990s and early years of the twenty-first century, there would be limited resources for Boston school purposes.

In 2010 a Northeastern University study described Springfield and Boston metropolitan areas as including the most racially segregated city schools.[69] Aside from accepting 3,000 METCO students and affordable housing in a handful of the thirty suburbs, most metropolitan areas schools remained overwhelmingly white, while city schools were almost 90 percent of color. The racial desegregation solutions of the 1960s and 1970s had not held. Black advocates had become committed to improving city schools as an alternative to racial integration, a strategy endorsed by the Boston GLOBE. On the other hand, University of California Professor David Kirp wrote that school desegregation elsewhere raised the education and life chances of black males by more than 25 percent.[70]

Boston schools benefitted from energetic and experienced leadership, Mayor Tom Menino in his fifth term, Carol Johnson in her fourth superintendency, one strengthened dramatically by state reform laws. The schools were closely monitored and supported by the Private Industry Council, the Boston Plan for Excellence, the Boston Municipal Research Bureau (corporations and law firms), and the Barr, Boston, and other foundations. Massachusetts Advocates for Children staff attended every school committee meeting, arguing for parent and student rights, and pointing out any lapses in services for handicapped or immigrant children, or those bullied or traumatized by violence. The Boston schools suffered from slowly declining enrolment, divided loyalties (METCO, parochial, private, and charter schools), a persistent achievement gap, and constant criticism of the high cost of school transportation.

But on the whole, Boston had begun to raise student achievement and was strongly committed to additional, aggressive reforms in cooperation with the state, a level of collaboration never thought possible before 1993. Would students themselves commit to working longer and harder to meet expectations? Would parents acquire the skills to work closely with teachers and after school providers? Would Boston teachers and schools respond positively to the external pressures? Were federal and foundation dollars enough to close the achievement and graduation gaps? Could moderately performing schools get enough help to improve? These were major questions for the second decade of the twenty-first century.

The Future Prospects for Boston Schools

What were the prospects for further reform and productivity for Boston schools? The seventeenth- and the nineteenth centuries so far were the innovative centuries; why not expect excellence and high achievement in another odd-numbered century, the twenty-first? First of all, what are the demographic prospects? The Metropolitan Area Planning Council relies on census and other data to calculate likely births and age cohorts.

Planners feel that the most dramatic gains will be the growth in Bostonian adults aged 45 to 60, growing from 75,000 in 1980 and 90 to 110,000 in 2000 and 150,000 in 2010. The supply of apartment dwellings has increased dramatically including at the high end for professional athletes and prosperous retirees, units priced from 1–4 million dollars. Although the numbers of schoolchildren aged 5–19 dropped from 120,000 in 1970 to 96,000 in 1990, they could increase to 105,000 by the year 2010. If Boston schools maintain a 75 percent share, perhaps 71,000 students might again attend Boston public schools. "Market share" has increased slightly; three Catholic schools closed in 2002, and more are projected to close.[71]

The wild card once again is new immigration, tens of thousands of young families pouring into Boston from Brazil, Bosnia, Cape Verde, El Salvador, and other nations. Boston has long been a city of immigrants, and census figures reflect the past, rather than forecast the future. Boston Public School planners expect a growth in high school students from 18,500 to 20,000 by 2006, more if students continue to be retained in grade nine for not meeting standards for promotion into grade ten.[72]

In 2000 the mayor promised five new Boston public schools, three opening up in 2003 constructed at a cost of $30 million. If the class sizes in elementary were lowered from twenty-five to twenty-two (as provided for in the 2001 contract), school officials pointed out that more classrooms and school buildings would be needed. Another senior high school was planned for Mattapan. More new schools could be constructed.

An important question is the future of increased choice. The most popular option in Boston and nationwide became that of charter and pilot schools. Parents in Boston, and elsewhere, want a school that cares for their child, that employs teachers who do not "work to rule," that commits to a program of studies that adds value to the academic potential of a child. The Massachusetts legislature listened to dozens of proposals to expand the number of charter schools, despite opposition from superintendents and both the Massachusetts Teachers Association and Federation of Teachers. In the end, voters and constituents seeking choice and voice include more parents than teachers.

New charters face serious problems. Money has been scarce for facilities. And organizers of new charters usually have only a year to plan and organize the program. Seymour Sarason of Yale believes that charter schools will multiply as parents realize how little reassurance conventional tests provide in recognizing "critical thinking, independent thinking, doing experiments . . . amassing a portfolio of their work which others will critique." He also worries about whether charter school founders will be given enough resources to invent substantially better schools.[73]

Technology offers another solution. Boston Public Schools embrace technology; companies including IBM contributed hardware and software to Boston's public schools, including toward a new magnet school called *Match*. Nationally, the number of instructional computers in American schools soared from 2.7 million to 8 million in 1999, or one for every six students.[74] The issue is access to enough quality courses and program materials.[75]

The other dramatic impact of technology could be the further expansion of home instruction when parents can download entire courses to guide their children studying at home. Hypothetically, 5 million American children and 10,000 Boston youth might by 2010 take most of their lessons and examinations at home. Virtual Schools with a full academic curriculum are available online, instruction often self-paced so that students learn at their own speed.

On the other hand, public education has an impressive record in resisting any new technology other than the printing press. Radio education, the 16 mm film projector, public television, programmed instruction (teaching machines), the overhead projector, almost any new device can be marginalized, victim of excess loyalty to the traditional "jawbone and chalkboard." However, the Internet transforms the world of business, government, and academe at incredible speed. If schools remained in the nineteenth-century factory mode, leaders will invent new modes of education for the emerging technological environment. That story might well be a sequel to this book.

Several predictions flow from this review, including what follows.

In every decade, public education in Boston will confront new and often surprising challenges, economic, demographic, political, and pedagogical. Neither historians nor social scientists can predict with any precision the developments of the next fifty years, or the next revolution in urban education.

Newcomers to Boston, strangers in our lands, will on occasion bring inadequate educational backgrounds and will face severe hostility to their language, color, religion, or mode of living. The schools will almost always try to impose solutions that worked with previous groups, but will be forced to recognize new cultures.

Governmental structures of education, considered adequate for the current time, will adjust to accommodate the newcomers. Even the appointed board and role of the mayor is subject to change, especially if black and Hispanic ministers and their congregations conclude that a regime is unresponsive to their educational aspirations. One of the newcomers will become mayor.

Citizens and philosophers will continue to debate the question of what aspects of education remain essential, how much history or literacy, science or numeracy, geography, health or wellness, art and music, physical education, occupational competence, and until what age or level of accomplishment are these skills taught, and how are these evaluated? This is the healthiest of debates, fundamental to defining the kind and quality of the civilization.

Boston, with thirty-five colleges and universities, despite its public education challenges, remains in contention for the sobriquet "Athens of America."[76] The rich cultural heritage, the profusion of universities, the high stakes for developing intellect in a region short of mineral resources, argue for a continuing commitment to developing the mental, creative, and leadership talents of young Bostonians. The Boston schools won first place for the Eli Broad prize acknowledging the most improved urban schools. Superintendent Payzant was awarded numerous national awards as "best superintendent." The Boston schools have work to do but are on the path to revival. The twenty-first century offers a new canvass for a portrait of quality education for the complex national and global challenges facing graduates of the Boston public schools. The schools will come in many forms: pilot, magnet, exam, charter, and special, they will morph into after-school programs; they will never be the same and will eventually embrace the technologies of the new century.[77]

NOTES

Introduction: Exit, Voice, and Loyalty: Leave, Speak Up, or Stay

1. Nathan Glazer and Daniel P. Moynihan, *Beyond the Melting Pot* (Cambridge, 1963).
2. Albert O. Hirschman, *Exit, Voice and Loyalty* (Cambridge, 1969), p. 49.
3. Anthony Lukas, *Common Ground* (New York, 1986).
4. Ruth Batson, *The Black Educational Movement in Boston* (Boston, 2001).

1 Boston Schools: The Height of Loyalty and Ethnic Exits (1920–40)

1. Phillip Marson, *Breeder of Democracy* (Cambridge, 1970).
2. Walter Muir Whitehill, *Boston in the Age of John Fitzgerald Kennedy* (Norman, Oklahoma, 1966).
3. Alexis de Tocqueville, *Democracy in America* (New York, 1945 edition), 95, 96.
4. David Tyack, *George Ticknor and the Boston Brahmins* (Cambridge, 1967), 205, 210.
5. Stephen and Paul Kendrick, *Sarah's Long Walk: The Free Blacks of Boston and How Their Struggle for Equality Changed America* (Boston, 2004).
6. Samuel Eliot Morison, *One Boy's Boston* (Cambridge, 1962), 41.
7. Thomas H. O'Connor, *The Boston Irish* (Boston, 1995), 188 and Jack Beatty, *The Rascal King* (Reading, 1992), 42–43, 48.
8. Beatty, *The Rascal King,* 230.
9. Joseph Dinneen, *The Purple Shamrock* (New York, 1949), 155.
10. Jonathan Sarna and Ellen Smith, *The Jews of Boston* (Boston, 1995), 215–216.
11. Theodore White, *In Search of History* (New York, 1978), 29, 34.
12. Ibid., 29.
13. Nat Hentoff, *Boston Boy* (New York, 1986), 11.
14. Ibid., 35.
15. Ibid., 34.
16. Ibid.
17. Sumner Redstone, *A Passion to Win* (New York, 2001), 44.

18. Marson, *Breeder of Democracy*, 147.
19. Ibid.
20. Ibid.
21. Harvard Alumni Association class of 1897 five-year reports, especially 1927, 1937.
22. Peter Schrag, *Village School Downtown* (Boston 1967), 51.
23. Marson, *Breeder of Democracy*, 148
24. Ibid., 174–176.
25. Joseph Gerard Brennan, *The Education of a Prejudiced Man* (New York, 1977), 16.
26. Ibid.
27. Ibid., 20–31.
28. Boston School Committee Annual Reports, 1920–35.
29. Richard Norton Smith, *The Harvard Century* (New York, 1986), 87–89 and Jerome Karabel, The *Chosen: The Hidden History of Admission and Exclusion at Harvard, Yale and Princeton* (Boston, 2005).
30. Boston Latin and High Schools, *Tercentenary Report* (Boston, 1935).
31. U.S. Census Reports for Boston, 1922 and 1942.
32. The Boston Finance Commission, *Report on Certain Phases of the Boston School System* (Boston, 1930), 214.
33. Boston Public School Document Number 16, 1952, Report of the Boston School Committee.
34. *Tercentenary Report*, 345, 360.
35. Ibid.
36. Boston Finance Commission, *Report on Certain Phases,* 110.
37. Donna Merwick, *Boston Priests 1848–1910* (Cambridge, 1959), 140 and Sanders in James W. Fraser, *From Common School to Magnet School* (Boston, 1979), 60–70.
38. William O'Connell, *Recollections of Seventy Years* (Boston, 1934), 5–8.
39. Report of the 1930 Survey (Boston: The Finance Commission, 1930). 215 and Robert Lord, Edward Sexton, and Edward Harrington, *History of the Archdiocese of Boston* (New York, 1944), Volume III, 347.
40. Boston School Committee Annual Reports 1915–40.
41. Thomas H. O' Connor, *South Boston, My Home Town* (Boston, 1988).
42. William Foote Whyte, *Street Corner Society* (Chicago, 1943), xv.
43. Ibid., 54.
44. Ibid., 56.
45. Ibid., 27.
46. Interview with Larry DiCara, June 2002.
47. Patrick Loftus, *That Old Gang of Mine* (South Boston, 1991), 35.
48. Ibid., 220 and Charles Dickens, *American Notes* (New York, 2001), 61–68.
49. Loftus, *That Old Gang of Mine,* 46 and O'Connor, South *Boston,* 120, 121.
50. Sam Bass Warner, *Street Car Suburbs* (Cambridge, 1967) and *The Way We Really Live: Social Change in Metropolitan Boston Since 1920* (Boston, 1977).
51. Henry A. Yeomans, *A. Lawrence Lowell* (Cambridge, 1948), 50.
52. Report of the 1930 Survey, 96.
53. Ibid., 215.

54. Charles H. Trout, *Boston: The Great Depression* (New York, 1977), xi
55. Ibid., 228, 241, 250, 279.
56. Beatty, *The Rascal King*, 199.
57. Ibid., 266.
58. Dinneen, *The Purple Shamrock*, 322.
59. Trout, *Boston*, 182.
60. Dinneen, *The Purple Shamrock*, 251.
61. Beatty, *The Rascal King*, 486; Trout, *Boston*, 264.
62. Trout, *Boston*, 277.
63. David Tyack, Robert Lowe, and Elisabeth Hansot, *Public Schools in Hard Times* (Cambridge, 1984), 33.
64. Tyack, *Public Schools in Hard Times*, 150, 166.
65. Boston School Committee Annual Reports 1930s.
66. Hillel Levine and Lawrence Harmon, *The Death of an American Jewish Community* (New York, 1992).
67. Gerald H. Gamm, *Urban Exodus: Why the Jews Left Boston and the Irish Stayed* (Cambridge, 1999).
68. Ibid., 195.
69. Ibid., 206.
70. Ibid., 211.
71. Glazer and Moynihan, *Beyond the Melting Pot*, 30, 31.
72. Stephan Thernstrom, *The Other Bostonians* (Cambridge, 1973), 173.
73. See Robert C. Hayden, *African Americans in Boston* (Boston, 1991) and Mark Schneider, *Boston Confronts Jim Crow* (Boston, 1997), 351–372.
74. Trout, *Boston*, 264 and Hayden, *African Americans in Boston*, 25.
75. Lord et al., *History of the Archdiocese of Boston*, Volume III, 39.

2 Boston Teachers Express Their Voices (1920–65)

1. James W. Fraser, "Agents of Democracy," in Donald Warren, editor, *American Teachers: History of a Profession at Work* (New York, 1989), 128–143.
2. Richard Freeland, *Academia's Golden Age* (New York, 1992).
3. Sam Barnes in James W. Fraser, *From Common School to Magnet School* (Boston, 1979), 100.
4. Michael Sedlak, "Let Us Go Buy a School Master," in Warren, *American Teachers*, 272.
5. Marjorie Murphey, *Blackboard Unions* (Ithaca, 1992), 34, 45 and Nancy Hoffman, *Woman's True Profession* (Westbury, NY, 1981).
6. James W. Fraser, "Mayor John F. Fitzgerald and Boston's Schools, 1905–1913," *Historical Journal of Massachusetts*, Vol. XII, June 1984, 2.
7. Murphey, *Blackboard Unions*, 227–233. The 1993 Bigelow Society Genealogy lists twenty Cora Bigelows, clearly a favorite family name. The first Bigelow arrived in the 1630s, and had 33,000 descendants.
8. Murphey, *Blackboard Unions*, 53.
9. *The Boston Teachers Newsletter*, June 1918.
10. Sarah Deutch, *Women and the City* (New York, 2000).
11. Richard Brown and Jack Tager, *Massachusetts: A Concise History* (Amherst, 2001), 256.

12. Murphey, *Blackboard Unions*, 84.
13. Ibid., 198–207.
14. Ibid., 54.
15. John Dewey, *The School in Society*, 1899 excerpted in James W. Fraser, *The School in the United States* (Boston, 2001). Also see also Raymond Callahan, *Education and the Cult of Efficiency* (Chicago, 1962).
16. Ella Flagg Young quoted in Fraser, *The School*, 194.
17. Margaret Haley, quoted in Fraser, ibid., 190, 191.
18. Cora Bigelow in Fraser, ibid., 197.
19. Ibid., 197.
20. Ibid., 198.
21. Murphey, *Blackboard Unions*, 188.
22. Boston School Committee Annual Report 1930.
23. Brown and Tager, *Massachusetts*, 246.
24. Boston Finance Commission, Report of the Committee to Investigate the Methods of Administration of the Boston Schools (Boston, 1931), 14, 15.
25. Brown and Tager, *Massachusetts*, 247.
26. Interview with Larry DiCara, former Boston city council president, quoting his mother Concetta employed in the 1930s as a music teacher.
27. *The Boston Globe* series from December 11, 1935 to January 2, 1936.
28. Lawrence W. O'Connell, "The Reform Group in Central City School Politics: The Boston Experience 1960–65," unpublished Ph.D. Dissertation, Syracuse University, June 1968, 67, 68.
29. *The Boston Globe,* January 5, 1936.
30. Boston School Committee Proceedings 1936, 2, and reported in O'Connell, "The Reform Group in Central City School Politics," 71.
31. Ibid.
32. Phillip Marson, *A Teacher Speaks* (New York, 1960), 131.
33. L. O'Connell, "The Reform Group in Central City School Politics," 103–104.
34. George D. Strayer, "Report of a Survey of the Public Schools of Boston, Massachusetts." (Boston, 1944), 76.
35. Ibid., 138–139.
36. Murphey, *Blackboard Unions,* 146.
37. Ibid., 155.
38. Ibid., 223–224.
39. Ibid., 64.
40. Ibid., 60 and John A. Farrell, *Tip O'Neil and the Democratic Century* (Boston, 1999), 102, 114.
41. *Boston Traveler,* December 8 and 9, 1923, 10.
42. Murphey, *Blackboard Unions,* 224.
43. L. O'Connell, "The Reform Group in Central City School Politics," 84.
44. Ibid., 88.
45. Boston Teachers Alliance *Bulletin,* October 1949.
46. L. O'Connell, "The Reform Group in Central City School Politics," 89.
47. Murphey, *Blackboard Unions,* 34.
48. Martha E. O'Neil, unpublished memoir of a retired Boston teacher, files of James W. Fraser, Northeastern University, 40.
49. Myron Lieberman, *The Future of Public Education* (Chicago, 1960), VIII.

50. Alan Rosenthal, "Pedagogues and Power," in Marilyn Gittell, editor, *Educating an Urban Population* (Beverly Hills, 1967), 204.

3 School Reform Postponed (1940–62)

1. Strayer, "Report of a Survey of the Public Schools of Boston," 249.
2. Ibid., 425, 432, 489, 763.
3. Ibid., 76.
4. Commonwealth of Massachusetts Vital Statistics, Live Births, Marriages by City and Town, 1940, on file, Boston Public Library.
5. Boston City Health Reports, Annual City Reports for 1920, 1930, 1940, and 1945, Boston Public Library.
6. Brown and Tager, *Massachusetts,* 277.
7. Ibid., 90.
8. Jackson, *Crabgrass Frontier* (New York, 1985), 190–211, 293–295.
9. O'Connor, *Building a New Boston: Politics and Urban Renewal 1950–1970* (Boston, 1993), 123.
10. Jackson, *Crabgrass Frontier,* 302.
11. Strayer, "Report of a Survey of the Public Schools of Boston," 439.
12. Ibid., 416.
13. Ibid., 506–07.
14. Memo to the School Committee on the Strayer Survey, copy in the Boston Public School Administration Library, Dorchester, Massachusetts.
15. Letter of Alexander Sullivan, March 1945 in Boston Public School Administration Library.
16. Boston School Committee Report, February 1945.
17. O'Connor, *Building a New Boston,* 126.
18. Beatty, *The Rascal King,* 186.
19. Ibid., 188.
20. Howard Bryant, *Shutout: A Story of Race and Baseball in Boston* (New York, 2002).
21. O' Connor, *The Boston Irish* (Boston, 1995), 221.
22. Francis Russell, *Knave of Boston* (Boston, 1967), 91.
23. Boston School Committee Proceedings, January, 1952, 2.
24. L. O'Connell, "The Reform Group in Central City Schools," 97.
25. Telephone interview with his son David Muchnick, July 23, 2002.
26. Boston School Committee Proceedings, January 1954, 2.
27. Bryant, *Shutout,* 35.
28. Strayer, "Report of a Survey of the Boston, Massachusetts Public Schools," 12.
29. O'Connor, *Boston Irish,* 226.
30. O'Connor, *Building a New Boston,* 124.
31. Herbert Gans, *The Urban Villagers* (New York, 1962), 13, 163.
32. Ibid.
33. Ibid., 132.
34. Glazer and Moynihan, *Beyond the Melting Pot,* 199–200.
35. Leonard Nimoy, *I Am Not Spock,* and a sequel *I Am Spock* (New York, 1990, 1995), 19.
36. O'Connor, *Building a New Boston,* 136–137.

37. Ibid., 65ff.
38. *The Boston Globe,* City Weekly section, January 6, 2002, 1.
39. L. O'Connell, "The Reform Group in Central City Schools," 116.
40. Cyril G. Sargent, *Boston Schools* (Cambridge, 1962), 47. See also his 1953 Harvard report on "Look to the Schoolhouses" (Boston, 1953).
41. Reports of the Harvard Graduate School of Education Center for Field Studies 1960s, especially 1963–68. The Gates and other foundation in the twenty-first century recommend smaller high schools.
42. L. O'Connell, "The Reform Group in Central City Schools," 110.
43. James B. Conant, *Slums and Suburbs* (New York, 1961).
44. Interview with James Buckley, former Boston teacher and assistant principal, later a suburban superintendent, February 21, 2004.
45. William G. Kanter, "Organized Political Reform in a Changing American City," unpublished honors thesis, Harvard College, 1962, 64, 65. O'Connell interviewed Kanter.
46. L. O'Connell, "The Reform Group in Central City Schools," 126–140.
47. Jackson, *Crabgrass Frontier,* 230–233.
48. Ibid., 183.
49. Tony Hill, "Route 128, the Baby Boomer of Highways Turns 59," *The Boston Globe,* April 19, 2001, D 1, 2. See also the U.S. Civil Rights Commission Report *Route 128: Boston's Road to Segregation,* 1968.
50. Ibid.

4   Black Voices for Equal Education, and the White Response (1960–74)

1. Ruth Batson, *The Black Educational Movement in Boston 2001,* 5, 43. Mrs. Batson kept personal notes, reports, and press clippings on her work to improve opportunities for black children in Boston schools; these documents were assembled by Northeastern University archivists.
2. Stephen and Paul Kendrick, *Sarah's Long Walk.*
3. Batson, *The Black Educational Movement in Boston.*
4. Interview with Melvin Miller, March 2002.
5. William Banks, *Black Intellectuals* (New York, 1996), 26, 103.
6. Ibid., 141, 148.
7. Ibid., 78, 101.
8. Ibid., 116 and Robert Hayden, *Boston's NAACP History* 1910–1982 (Boston Branch, 1982).
9. Melvin I. King, *Chain of Change* (Boston, 1981) and James Jennings and Melvin King, editors, *From Access to Power: Black Politics in Boston* (Cambridge, 1982). King later directed the MIT Urban Fellows Program.
10. Batson, *The Black Educational Movement in Boston,* 78.
11. Ibid., 79. Hirschman describes boycotts as a blend of voice and temporary exit, *Exit, Voice and Loyalty,* 86.
12. Batson, *The Black Educational Movement in Boston,* 80–81.
13. Ibid., 83.
14. Ibid., 84.

15. Ibid., 85b.
16. Ibid., 86 and Addendum 88a.
17. Joseph M. Cronin, "Boston Picks a Superintendent," unpublished case study for Syracuse University, 1965, documented the initiation of the search and Citizen activities.
18. Boston School Committee Minutes, May 20, 1963.
19. Interview with Herold C. Hunt, August 1965. Gartland's assistant was Gordon Ambach, later New York state commissioner of education.
20. Peter Schrag, *Village School Downtown* (Boston, 1967), 6.
21. Paul Parks's conversation with Joseph Cronin, April 2001.
22. Batson, *The Black Educational Movement in Boston*, 88a.
23. Ibid.
24. Ibid.
25. Boston *Traveler,* July 10, 1963.
26. Batson, *The Black Educational Movement in Boston*, Addendum 95a.
27. Ibid., 99.
28. Ibid., Addendum 104a.
29. *Boston Herald*, Globe August 24, 1963.
30. Cronin's interviews with William Ohrenberger, November 1965 and with Herold Hunt, July 1965.
31. Ibid.
32. Batson, *The Black Educational Movement in Boston*, 121.
33. Hunt interview, July 1965.
34. Banks, *Black Intellectuals*, 149.
35. Jonathan Kozol, *Death at an Early Age* (Boston, 1967).
36. Batson, *The Black Educational Movement in Boston*, 103a.
37. Ibid., 103a.
38. Ibid., 108a.
39. Ibid., 115.
40. Ibid., 115–117.
41. Ibid., 119a.
42. Ibid., 122.
43. Ibid., 122a.
44. Ibid., 127.
45. Ibid., 134–135.
46. Ibid., 150.
47. Ibid., 139.
48. Ibid., 141.
49. Ibid., 146, 149.
50. Ibid., 136, 154 and Ronald Formisano, *Boston against Busing* (Chapel Hill, 1991), 33.
51. Batson, *The Black Educational Movement in Boston*, 152.
52. Report of the Superintendent of Schools, Archdiocese of Boston, June 24, 1965.
53. Joseph M. Cronin, "Negroes in Catholic Schools," *Commonweal*, October, 1967.
54. Batson, *The Black Educational Movement in Boston,* 153.
55. Ibid., 163a.

56. Ibid., 164b.
57. Ibid., 176–178.
58. Ibid., 181–184.
59. Ibid., 185.
60. Owen B. Kiernan et al., *Because It Is Right, Educationally* (Boston, April, 1965).
61. Batson, *The Black Educational Movement in Boston*, 193, 195b.
62. Ibid., 202, 210.
63. Ibid., 196, 201.
64. Ibid., 194.
65. Abigail A. Cheever, "Which Home for English High? Boston Seeks a School Site," Government honors paper, Radcliffe College, 1967.
66. *The Boston Globe*, June 1, 1965, 1.
67. Batson, *The Black Educational Movement in Boston*, 207 and Frank Levy, Northern *Schools and Civil Rights* (Chicago, 1971), 137.
68. Batson, *The Black Educational Movement in Boston*, 209.
69. Kozol, *Death at an Early Age*, described Marguerite Sullivan as a formidable enforcer of conventional mediocrity. Observing a School Committee meeting, he thought Superintendent Ohrenberger not up to the job of providing school system leadership.
70. Levy, *Northern Schools and Civil Rights,* 49–56.
71. Batson, *The Black Educational Movement in Boston*, 214, 215.
72. Ibid., 259.
73. Nathaniel Young, letter published in the *Boston Herald,* October 21, 1965.
74. *Boston Herald,* November 1, 1965 and the *Jamaica Plain Citizen,* October 29, 1965.
75. L. O'Connell, "The Reform Group in Central City Schools," 234, 236.
76. Ibid., 236.
77. Ibid., 314.
78. *Bay State Banner*, September 1965–October 1967.
79. Batson, *The Black Educational Movement in Boston*, 224c and the *New York Times,* October 17, 1965.
80. Operation Exodus Report, cited in James E. Teele, Ellen Jackson, and Clara Mayo, "Family Experiences in Operation Exodus," *Community Mental Health Journal,* Monograph No. 3, 8–16, 1967.
81. *The Boston Globe,* July 1, 1966.
82. Batson, *The Black Educational Movement in Boston,* 319.
83. Ibid., 319.
84. Ibid., 303–306.
85. Hillel Levine and Lawrence Harmon, *The Death of an American Jewish Community* (New York, 1992), 61–65.
86. Ibid., 81, 105.
87. Ibid., 209.
88. Ibid., 214.
89. Interview with Boston banker Peter Blampied, October 2001.
90. Ernest Burgess on Chicago and New York City in the 1920s in Gerald Gamm, *Why the Jews Left Boston and the Catholics Stayed* (Cambridge, 1999).
91. Gerald Gamm, "In Search of Suburbs," in *The Jews of Boston*, Jonathan D. Sarna and Ellen Smith, editors (Boston, 1990), 154, 155.

92. Gamm, *Why the Jews Left Boston,* 217, 237.
93. Ibid., 226, 237.
94. Lord et al., *History of the Archdiocese of Boston*, Volume II, 681.
95. Leon Jick, "From Margin into Mainstream," in Sarna and Smith, *The Jews of Boston*, 106.

5 The Court Orders Reforms (1974–89)

1. Formisano, *Boston against Busing*, 70.
2. Jack Flannery, *The Sargent Years: Public Papers 1969–1975* (Boston, 1976) is the official record of Governor Francis Sargent. The author served in Governor Sargent's cabinet as secretary of educational affairs (1971–75).
3. Formisano, *Boston against Busing*, 61–62.
4. Ibid., 62–63.
5. Flannery, *The Sargent Years*, 263–265.
6. Formisano, *Boston against Busing*, 63.
7. *Morgan v. Hennigan*, Federal District Court, Boston, June 21, 1974, in Batson, *The Black Educational Movement in Boston,* 377 See also the case and working papers in City of Boston archives.
8. Flannery, *The Sargent Years*, 270.
9. Robert Dentler and Marvin Scott, *Schools on Trial* (Cambridge, 1981), 14, 77.
10. Formisano, *Boston against Busing*, 75.
11. Batson, *The Black Educational Movement in Boston,* 380; Formisano, *Boston against Busing,* 76.
12. Alan Lupo, *Liberty's Chosen Home* (Boston, 1977) and interview with Robert Schwartz, education aide to Mayor White, February 2004.
13. Jon Hillson, *The Battle for Boston* (New York, 1977), 21 and Formisano, *Boston against Busing,* 114.
14. Formisano, *Boston against Busing*, 82.
15. Hillson, *The Battle for Boston*, 21.
16. *Bay State Banner,* May 15, 1975.
17. Ibid., May 22, 1975.
18. *The Boston Globe,* May 31, 1975.
19. Hillson, *The Battle for Boston*, 103 and Formisano, *Boston against Busing*, 84.
20. Formisano, *Boston against Busing*, 85.
21. Pamela Bullard and Judith Stoia, *The Hardest Lesson* (Boston, 1980).
22. William Bratton, *Turnaround* (New York, 2000), 67, 76.
23. Hillson, *The Battle for Boston*, 106 and Batson, *The Black Educational Movement in Boston*, 426a.
24. Hillson, *The Battle for Boston*, 106–107.
25. Ibid., 111.
26. Formisano, *Boston against Busing*, 176.
27. Lukas, *Common Ground*, 389.
28. "Southie Is My Home Town," quoted in Dentler, op cit., 171.
29. O'Connor, *South Boston*, 227–230 and William Bulger in Formisano, *Boston against Busing*, 118
30. Formisano, *Boston against Busing*, 184–185.
31. Ibid., 186, and interview with Lawrence Di Cara, January 2002.

32. South Boston was also dangerous at times. Michael MacDonald, *All Souls* (Boston, 2000) on South Boston drugs and crime, and Richard Lehr and Gerald O'Neill, *Black Mass* (New York, 2001) on FBI collusion with South Boston criminals.
33. Formisano, *Boston against Busing*, 191.
34. Quotes from ibid., 190.
35. Robert Coles, with Carol Baldwin, *The Buses Roll* (New York, 1974), 27, 28.
36. Formisano, *Boston against Busing*, 195.
37. Ibid., 86, quoting a *Boston Globe* poll.
38. Ibid., 73.
39. Ibid., 74.
40. Dentler, op cit., 115, 235.
41. Formisano, *Boston against Busing*, 159.
42. Ibid., 196.
43. Ibid., 160, 161.
44. Ibid., 196 and Kathleen Sullivan Alioto, "Boxed In," doctoral dissertation, Harvard Graduate School of Education, 1980.
45. Joseph M. Cronin and Richard M. Hailer, *Organizing an Urban School System for Diversity,* first published in Boston October 1970 and then in 1973 Lexington, 46–51.
46. Kevin White, "Achieving Equal Education in Boston," a position paper, April 10, 1973, Boston City Hall, Office of the Mayor, 13.
47. Donald Montgomery Neill, "The Struggle of the Boston Black Community for Equality and Quality in the Boston Public Schools 1950–1987," unpublished doctoral dissertation, Harvard Graduate School of Education, 1987, 309.
48. Ibid., 321.
49. Ibid., 324, 325.
50. Ibid., 309–311.
51. Ibid., 365 and Dentler, op cit., 204, 205.
52. Neill, "The Struggle of the Boston Black Community for Equality," 344, 349.
53. Ibid., 408.
54. Ibid., 411. Fraser at the time taught at the University of Massachusetts, Boston.
55. Interview with Robert Peterkin, headmaster, December 2001.
56. Interview with William Pear, February 2002.
57. Interview with Robert Schwartz, February 2004.
58. Interviews with Sam Tyler, in 2001, 2002.
59. Robert C. Wood, "Professionals at Bay: Managing Boston's Public Schools," *Journal of Policy Analysis and Management*, Vol. 1, No. 4, 1982, 454–468.
60. Interview with Jean Sullivan McKeigue, who followed her sister Kathleen on the School Committee and served with Elvira "Pixie" Palladino, November 2002.
61. Wood, "Professionals at Bay."
62. United States Census 1980 and George V. Higgins, *Style versus Substance: Kevin White and the Politics of Illusion* (New York, 1984), 27.
63. Ibid., 27–59.
64. Dentler, op cit., 224.

65. Ibid., 226.
66. *Bay State Banner*, December 11, 1975.
67. Lukas, *Common Ground*, raises the question, 398–401
68. Interview with Kiernan, February 2002.
69. Higgins, *Style versus Substance*, 161.
70. James E. Glinski, "The Catholic Church and the Desegregation of Boston's Public Schools," *The New England Journal of Public Policy*, Vol. 4, No. 2, Summer/Fall 1988, 65–84.
71. Ibid., 69, 70.
72. Formisano, *Boston against Busing*, 210.
73. Glinski, "The Catholic Church," 71.
74. Lukas, *Common Ground*, 401.
75. Glinski, "The Catholic Church," 77 and Dentler, op cit. 226
76. Glinski, "The Catholic Church," 78.
77. Ibid., 68.
78. Boston City Documents 1980, Election Statistics 1981.
79. Interviews with Robert Spillane 1984–2003.
80. Ralph Edwards, "How Boston Selected Its First Black Superintendent," doctoral dissertation, Cambridge: Harvard Graduate School of Education, 1989, 94–105.
81. Ibid., 130, 147.
82. Ibid., 133.
83. Ibid., 171.
84. Ralph Edwards and Charles Willie, *Black Power, White Power in Public Education* (Westport, CT, 1998), 52, 53.
85. Ibid., 530.
86. Batson, *The Black Educational Movement in Boston*, 442b and U.S. Census 1980.
87. Edwards and Willie, *Black Power*, 31.
88. David Armor, "The Evidence on Busing," *The Public Interest,* Vol. 28, No. 90, 1972, and also Ruth Batson and Robert Hayden, *A History of METCO* (Boston, 1987).
89. Susan Eaton, *The Other Boston Busing Story* (New Haven, 2001), 8.
90. Ibid., 213.
91. Ibid., 180, 181.
92. Ibid., 236–238.
93. Boston College High School, Annual Reports 2002–10.
94. Dentler, op cit., 182–185. Jonathan Kozol wrote a favorable article "The Rebirth of Education in Boston" for *American Education,* The U.S. Department of Education, Washington, DC, June 1980, 7–14.
95. Dentler, op cit.
96. Dentler, op cit., 193.
97. Ibid., 227.
98. Bullard and Stoia, *The Hardest Lesson,* 17. Telephone interviews with Kevin McCluskey and Jean McKeigue, June 2003.
99. Dentler, op cit., 233.
100. Bullard and Stoia, *The Hardest Lesson*, 15.
101. Hillson, *The Battle for Boston,* 253.

102. Neill, "The Struggle of the Boston Black Community for Equality," 370.
103. "Prop 2 1/2 at 20," Boston Municipal Research Bureau, January 2002, 2.
104. Gary Orfield, *Must We Bus?* (Washington, DC, 1978), 144, 145.
105. Eric Dolin, *Political Waters* (Amherst, MA, 2004) on the court-ordered cleanup of Boston Harbor.

6   Universities Speak Up

1. James B. Conant, *My Several Lives* (New York, 1970), 385.
2. Boston School Department Reports 1968.
3. Interview with Theodore R. Sizer, November 2002, and Adam Nelson, *The Elusive Ideal; Equal Educational Opportunity and the Federal Role in Boston Public Schools, 1950–1985* (Chicago, 2005).
4. "Record of Service," Annual Report of the Superintendent of Boston Public Schools 1965–66 and 1967–68.
5. Interview with Sizer, November 2002.
6. Remarks of Chairman John J. McDonough, January 16, 1967, Boston School Committee Proceedings.
7. The $250,000 Danforth grant supported doctoral students under the supervision of Joseph Cronin, Harvard professor, and Leonard Fein, MIT political scientist.
8. Joseph M. Cronin and Richard M. Hailer, *Organizing an Urban School System for Diversity* (Lexington, MA, 1973), 3–11, survey by Jeffrey Raffel, later director of the University of Delaware public policy program. The MACE released the report on October 1970.
9. Ibid., 11.
10. Ibid., 37.
11. Vincent C. Nuccio and Richard J. Doyle, *A Study of the Promotional Policies and Procedures in the Boston Public Schools*, "The Deans' Study," in Cronin and Hailer, *Organizing an Urban School System for Diversity*, 61.
12. Strayer made similar recommendations in 1944, twenty-six years earlier, "Report of a Survey of the Boston, Massachusetts Public Schools."
13. Ibid., 61–62.
14. Ibid., 86.
15. Ibid., 137, citing Bernard Taper's study of the Arts in Boston.
16. Ibid., 140–142.
17. White, *In Search of History*, 16.
18. Interview with Kenneth Caldwell, Boston's Flexible Campus coordinator, February 2002.
19. White, *In Search of History*, 17.
20. Cronin and Hailer, *Organizing an Urban School System for Diversity*, 117.
21. Ibid., 124.
22. Ibid., 105, 108.
23. Ibid., 108. Dean Ammer of Northeastern reviewed the occupational outlook for Boston.
24. Ibid., 109.
25. Ibid., 96.

26. Larry Brown, *The Way We Go To School*, Task Force on Out of School Youth, Boston, 1970.
27. Cronin and Hailer, *Organizing an Urban School System for Diversity*, 112.
28. Ibid., 115.
29. Ibid., 115.
30. Ibid., 100.
31. Joseph M. Cronin, "Blue Collar Politics: The Political Power of School Workers," Chicago, American Educational Research Association paper, March 1969.
32. Hirschman, *Exit, Voice and Loyalty*, 58.
33. Joseph M. Cronin was the seminar instructor. Governor Francis Sargent on December 10, 1970 named the author secretary of educational affairs for the commonwealth of Massachusetts.
34. Harvard University Center for Law and Education (Cambridge, 1970).
35. Joseph M. Cronin, "The Boston Schools—Is Continuous Improvement Possible?" John Hancock Life Insurance Company, Managers Meeting, Boston, 1991.
36. Northeastern University, *The Boston Public Schools: An Assessment of Governance, Operations and Finance*, July 1991. President John A. Curry and Chief Financial Officer Robert Culver were key participants, with faculty.
37. Maureen Lumley, Boston School Ombudsperson, Letter to Cronin, February 12, 2002.
38. Harvard economist Richard Murnane worked in Boston to develop the student achievement data analysis system for Boston public schools in 2003–04.
39. Interview with Superintendent Thomas Payzant, June 2001.
40. The colleges with high percentages passing were Wellesley College and Harvard College, but with many fewer test takers than other colleges.
41. Larry Cuban, *To Make a Difference* (New York, 1970), 242–245.

7 The Organized Teacher Voice (1965 to the Present)

1. U.S. Census and the *Monthly Labor Review*, March 1975.
2. Charles Perry and Wesley Wildman, *The Impact of Negotiations on Public Education* (Worthington, Ohio, 1970) and Ronald Corwin, *Militant Professionals* (New York, 1970), 54.
3. Wayne Urban, "Teacher Activism," in Warren, *American Teacher*, 198.
4. Cronin, *The Control of Urban Schools* (New York, 1973), 103 and Martin Mayer, *Teachers Strike* (New York, 1969), 193.
5. Cronin, *The Control of Urban Schools*, 194.
6. Peter Swanson Hogness, "The Boston Teachers Union Strikes of 1970 and 1975," unpublished honors thesis, Cambridge: Harvard College, 1976.
7. Urban in Warren, *American Teacher*, 198.
8. Hogness, "The Boston Teachers Union Strikes," 74–83.
9. Ibid., 89–90.
10. Alan Rosenthal, *Pedagogues and Power* (Syracuse, 1969), 86, 87.
11. Interview with Larry DiCara 2002. DiCara's mother told him that she and many women teachers stayed home during the citywide power outage and blackout that evening.

12. Hogness, "The Boston Teachers Union Strikes," 94.
13. Boston School Committee Proceedings 1968.
14. Interview with former Boston School Committeeman Bill Spring, vice president, Federal Reserve Bank of Boston, June 2002.
15. Interview with Thomas Johnson, June 2002. Johnson later became director of personnel for the Cambridge and Needham public schools, and associate superintendent of Broward County Schools, Florida, with Bill Leary as superintendent.
16. Higgins, *Style versus Substance*, 90.
17. Hogness, "The Boston Teachers Union Strikes," 95.
18. Ibid., 96, 97 and *The Boston Herald,* November 26, 1970.
19. *The Boston Union Teacher*, April 1970, 4.
20. *Boston Traveler,* May 15, 1970, 18.
21. Hogness, "The Boston Teachers Union Strikes," 101.
22. *The Boston Globe,* May 14, 1970, 28.
23. Hogness, "The Boston Teachers Union Strikes," 103–112.
24. *Boston Globe,* May 9, 1970, 7.
25. Hogness, "The Boston Teachers Union Strikes," 114, based on his interview with Pixie Palladino, May 12, 1976.
26. *The Boston Globe, Herald*, June 1972.
27. *The Boston Union Teacher*, 1972–74 on state racial imbalance issues.
28. Ibid., January 1974.
29. Hogness, "The Boston Teachers Union Strikes," 137–139.
30. Interview with Michael K. "Kim" Marshall, November 2002, a teacher during the 1975 strike.
31. Hogness, "The Boston Teachers Union Strikes," 146, 253.
32. *The Boston Herald*, September 22, 1975, 7.
33. Hogness, "The Boston Teachers Union Strikes," 149–152.
34. *The Boston Globe*, September 23, 1975, 12.
35. Ibid., September 30, 1975, 6.
36. Hogness, "The Boston Teachers Union Strikes," 170–171.
37. *The Boston Globe*, September 23, 1975.
38. Hogness, "The Boston Teachers Union Strikes," 176, 180, 188, 193–196.
39. Ibid., 184.
40. Interview with Kathy Kelley, February 24, 2002.
41. Hogness, "The Boston Teachers Union Strikes," 208.
42. Ibid., 212.
43. *The Boston Globe*, May 17, 1970, 76.
44. Hogness, "The Boston Teachers Union Strikes," 180.
45. Robert C. Wood, "Professionals at Bay: Managing Boston's Public School," 454–468.
46. Ibid., 460.
47. Ibid., 467.
48. *The Boston Globe,* December 28, 1979. The *Globe* was a major source for the chronology, demands, and settlements following negotiations. To assure accuracy, two BTU presidents Kathy Kelly and Edward Doherty reviewed this chapter and made comments, as did Susan Moore Johnson who researches teachers and teacher unions at the Harvard Graduate School of Education.

This is the first published history of thirteen rounds of bargaining in Boston.

49. Ibid., February 27 and March 6, 1980.
50. Ibid., May 3, 30, 1980.
51. Brown and Tager, *Massachusetts*, 287.
52. *The Boston Globe*, February 5, 1981.
53. Ibid., February 24, 1981.
54. Ibid., March 12, 1981.
55. Ibid., March 27, 1981.
56. Ibid., May and June, 1981.
57. Ibid., June 16, 1981.
58. Ibid., June 12, 1981. Not until May 1983 would Judge Garrity end the veto power over teacher transfers, requested by both the BTU and the School Committee.
59. *The Boston Globe*, June 26 and July 10, 1982 after the U.S. Court of Appeals decision.
60. Ibid., February 18, 1982.
61. Ibid., July 8, 1983.
62. Ibid., August 5, 1981.
63. Ibid., September 21, 1981.
64. Interview with James W. Fraser, March 14 and May 18, 2002.
65. Kathy Kelley became the BTU lobbyist at the State House and then president of the Massachusetts Federation of Teachers.
66. *The Boston Globe*, February 25, 1982.
67. Ibid., May 10, 1982.
68. Ibid., May 12, 1982.
69. Ibid., April 26, 1983.
70. Ibid., May 25, 1984.
71. Ibid., May 23, 1982.
72. Ibid., September 19, 1983.
73. Ibid., November 24, 1983.
74. Ibid., September 4, 1985.
75. Ibid., September 12, 1986.
76. Ibid., May 14, 1986.
77. Ibid., June 1, 1986.
78. Ibid., June 9, 1987.
79. Ibid., June 29, 1986.
80. Boston School Committee Contract with the Boston Teachers Union, 2000.
81. *The Boston Globe*, August 30, 1986.
82. Ibid., November 12, 1986.
83. *A Nation at Risk*, Washington D.C., 1983 and *The Boston Globe*, July 2, 1986.
84. *Globe*, May 22, 1987.
85. U.S. Court of Appeals, story in *Boston Globe*, September 29, 1987.
86. Ibid., June 7 and 15, 1987.
87. Ibid., November 9, 1988.
88. Ibid., March 9, 1989.
89. Ibid., April 13, 1989.
90. Ibid., May 22, 24, 27, 1989.

91. Ibid., May 26, 1989.
92. Ibid., February 1, 1990.
93. Ibid., December 22, 1989 and January 27, 1990.
94. Ibid., January 13, 1990. Mansfield was also CEO of Cabot Partners, successor to the real-estate company that opened up Route 128 for development.
95. *The Boston Globe*, May 1990.
96. Ibid., October 25, 1990.
97. Ibid., June 1, 1990.
98. Ibid., May 15, 1990.
99. Ibid., November 6, 1991.
100. Ibid., June 27, 1992.
101. Ibid., September 17, 18, 21, 29, 1992.
102. Ibid., November 10, 11, 1993.
103. Ibid., March 8, 27 and June 16, 1993.
104. Ibid., June 30, 1994.
105. Ibid., August 30, 1994.
106. Ibid., June 16, 1995 article on a survey of Boston teacher payroll by community of residence.
107. Ibid.
108. Ibid., March 23 and April 3, 1998.
109. Ibid., March 7 and June 25, 1998.
110. Ibid., January 4, 1999.
111. Kenneth Rossano, *The Boston Experience* (Boston, 1986).
112. Interview with Marshall, December 2002.
113. *Boston Globe*, May 16, 1999.
114. Ibid., January 17, 2000.
115. Boston Plan for Excellence, *Towards an Open Teacher Hiring Process* (Boston 2000), with quotes in the *Boston Globe*, March 28, 30, 2000.
116. *Boston Globe*, March 30, 2000.
117. Ibid., May 11, 2000.
118. Ibid., August 3, 21, 2000.
119. Ibid., October 12, 2000. "Work to rule" meant teachers accepted no extra assignments. Bumping meant a senior teacher could claim a position held by a teacher with less seniority.
120. Bob Peterson, "Which Side Are You On?" *Rethinking Schools*, Vol. 8, No. 122, Fall 1993.
121. Boston School Committee contract with the Boston Teachers Union, Boston, 2000.
122. Boston Plan for Excellence, Annual Reports 2002–05.
123. Ibid., Boston Plan Partnership for Performance, summary report, September 2005.
124. Race to the Top was a $4.35 billion component of the American Recovery and Reinvestment (Stimulus) Act. The Massachusetts allocation was $250 million over four years, half of the funds prioritized for Title One (low-income) city schools.
125. Richard Stutman quoted in the Boston *Globe*, April 27, 2010.
126. John Mudd interview, August 9, 2010.
127. Carol Johnson quoted in the Boston *Globe*, August 25, 2010.
128. Boston Teacher Union Web site, Summer 2010.

129. Jane Hathaway and Andrew Rotherham, editors, *Collective Bargaining in Education* (Cambridge, 2006).
130. Myron Lieberman, *Education as a Profession* (Norman, Oklahoma, 1956).
131. David B. Tyack, *The One Best System* (Cambridge, 1974).

8   Business Calls for Educational Improvements

1. Henry G. Pearson, *Son of New England: James Jackson Storrow* (Boston, 1932), 43–59, 66–68.
2. Michael Porter, Rebecca Wayland, and C. Jeffrey Grogan, *Toward a Shared Economic Vision for Massachusetts*, Boston, Secretary of State, 1992.
3. Interview with Rossano, February 2002.
4. O'Connor, *Boston's Catholics* (Boston, 1998).
5. Dentler and Scott, *Schools on Trial* (Cambridge, 1981), 34.
6. Stephen M. Coan, "Uncertain Allies: Public Private Partnerships in the Boston Compact 1982- 1996," Waltham, Brandeis University Ph.D. dissertation, 1997, 19, and interview with Sam Tyler of the Municipal Research Bureau, October 2002.
7. Eleanor Farrar, "The Boston Compact," Center for Policy Research in Education, Rutgers University, New Brunswick, New Jersey, 1988 and Joseph Marr Cronin, "Corporations and Urban School Reform," Institute for Educational Leadership, Washington DC, January 1991.
8. Coan, "Uncertain Allies," 20.
9. Edwards and Willie, *Black Power,* 60, and interview with Sam Tyler, October 2002.
10. *The Boston Globe*, November 14, 1982, 1.
11. William Spring had been a policy analyst for U.S. Senator Gaylord Nelson, later vice president of the Federal Reserve Bank of Boston and a School Committee member (appointed) for more than a decade.
12. Betsy Useem, *Low Tech Education in a High Tech World* (New York, 1986) and also Coan, "Uncertain Allies," 25, 26, 29.
13. Useem, *Low Tech Education*, 132.
14. Coan, "Uncertain Allies," 30.
15. Farrar quote in ibid., 32.
16. Interviews with Kenneth Rossano and Patricia Graham, former dean of the Harvard Graduate School of Education, 2001, 2002. Rossano, in addition to being senior vice president of Bank Boston became chairman of the Greater Boston Chamber of Commerce and organized three Boston school partnerships for his bank.
17. The first Boston Plan chair was William Brown, CEO of Bank Boston. Subsequent chairs included Daniel Cheever of Wheelock College, Edward Phillips of the New England, Joseph Cronin of MHEAC, Robert Fraser of Goodwin Procter, and for many years Chad Gifford of Bank Boston-Fleet-Bank of America. Bill Boyan of the Hancock and John Hamill (several banks) were other key leadership voices.
18. Annual Reports, Boston Plan for Excellence in the Public Schools 1984–90.
19. Ibid. Robert Schwartz worked as the initial director to expand the Boston Plan, recruiting other donors. Rossano shared the same aspiration, and argued successfully against calling it the Bank Boston Plan for Excellence.

20. Annual Reports 1984–90.
21. Rossano, *The Boston Experience*.
22. For example, the Detroit Compact, discussed in Jeffrey Mirel's *The Rise and Fall of Detroit Schools 1907–1981* (Ann Arbor, 1999), 499.
23. Coan, "Uncertain Allies," 40.
24. Bill Spring, Bob Schwartz, and Bob Sperber of Boston University cast a wide net for constructive ideas while PIC staff pointed out what had not worked during the first Compact.
25. Report of the Mayor's Advisory Committee on School Reform, *The Rebirth of America's Oldest Public School System: Redefining Responsibility* (City of Boston, May 1, 1989). See its Appendix on Boston Public School performance trends.
26. Interview with Sam Tyler, November 2002.
27. Interview with Jack Delaney, former Boston Municipal Research Bureau, February 2002.
28. Edwards and Willie, *Black Power*, 63.
29. *The Rebirth*, 22–25.
30. Ibid., 31–32.
31. Edwards and Willie, *Black Power,* 64.
32. Ibid., including the public referendum as a case study; Chapter 4, 58–92.
33. Ibid., 78.
34. Useem, *Low Tech Education*, 6, 140.
35. Massachusetts Business Alliance for Education, *Every Child A Winner*, 1991.
36. Interview with Peter Finn, February 2002.
37. Interview with Thomas Payzant, February 2002.
38. Boston *Compact IV,* November 2001, Boston Public Schools.
39. *The Boston Globe,* October 6, 8, 10, and November 20, 1992 and interview with Robert Consalvo, February 2004.
40. Boston Plan for Excellence Annual Reports 1995 and 1996.
41. Boston Plan, *Partnership Report,* September 2005.
42. *The Boston Globe*, Harry Keefe obituary, March 12, 2002.
43. Interview with former Boston Latin School headmaster Michael Contompasis, March 2002.
44. M. Kimberley "Kim" Marshall was an articulate Boston school principal whose books include *Law and Order in Grade 6E: A Story of Chaos and Innovation in a Ghetto School* (Boston, 1972).
45. Edwards and Willie, *Black Power*, 83.
46. Ibid., 84, 85.
47. *Boston Globe,* December 11, 1994.
48. Boston Municipal Research Bureau, six briefing reports on urban schools, 1996.
49. Useem, *Low Tech Education*, 122, 123.
50. Coan, "Uncertain Allies," 170–184.
51. Ibid., 198.
52. Interview with Patricia Graham, 2002.
53. Coan, "Uncertain Allies."
54. MassInsight Education, "Work in Progress," 14, Boston, June 2001.
55. *Boston Globe* Section B 1, March 11, 2002.
56. U.S. Government, *No Child Left Behind* Act, 2002.
57. *Boston Globe,* May, June 2003. Also annual Boston Public School Reports 2000–03.

58. Thomas Payzant's contract as superintendent was extended to June 2006, providing Boston with more than a decade of continuous service.
59. Interview with Graham, 2002.
60. Patricia A. Graham, *SOS: Sustain Our Schools* (New York, 1993).

9 Future Choices, Disparate Voices

1. *The Boston Globe*, April 13, 2002 summary of U.S. Census report on Boston, Section B.
2. Ibid., B1.
3. Boston Private Industry Council statistical summary on the BPS Class of 2000, Boston, 2001.
4. 2000 U.S. Census for Massachusetts.
5. *The Wisdom of Our Choices*, the Boston Foundation, with Boston College and Northeastern University, 2001.
6. Ibid., 141.
7. Reports of the Boston Public School Superintendent, 1999, 2000, 2001, 2002, 2003.
8. College Entrance Examination Board test results reported by the Boston Public School evaluation office.
9. *Wisdom*, 135, 136.
10. Ibid.
11. John Portz, Lara Stein, and Robin Jones, *City Schools and City Politics: Institutions and Leadership in Pittsburgh, Boston and St. Louis* (Kansas, 1999), 19.
12. Ibid., 91–98.
13. Ibid., 155 and Annual Reports, Boston Plan, which was chaired by Boston banker Chad Gifford for eight years of the twenty-first century.
14. Payzant after five years renamed his approach Total School Improvement.
15. Paul T. Hill, Christine Campbell, James Harvey, and others, *It Takes A City: Getting Serious about School Reform* (Washington DC, 2000), 96–110, 131–142.
16. Ibid., ix and 96–103.
17. Ibid., 136–142.
18. Ibid., 110.
19. Michael Usdan and Larry Cuban, *Urban School Reforms with Shallow Roots* (New York, 2003).
20. Henry Adams, *The Education of Henry Adams* (Boston, 1918 edition), 7.
21. Alan Lupo "This Is What Politics Is," in David R. Godine, editor, *A Book for Boston* (1980), 50, 51.
22. O' Connor, *Boston's Catholics*, 289–292.
23. Harvard Center for Civil Rights, Annual Reports 2002–04.
24. Thomas Pettigrew, "The Case for Metropolitan Approaches to Public School Desegregation," in Adam Yarmolinsky, Lance Liebman, and Corinne Schelling, *Race and Schooling in the City* (Cambridge, 1981), 177, 178.
25. The Harvard Center for Civil Rights reports these decisions and the resegregation of metropolitan school systems each year.
26. *The Boston Globe,* March 2002.
27. Anthony Downs, *Opening Up the Suburbs* (New Haven, 1973), 68, 165, 180.
28. Miriam Wasserman, "The Geography of Life Chances," in *Regional Review*, Boston, Federal Reserve Bank of Boston, Q4 2001, 25–31.

29. Michael Blanding, "Suburban Brawl," in *Boston Magazine*, Vol. 94, April 2002, 136, with statistics from the Massachusetts Department of Housing and Development.

30. Orlando Patterson, *The Ordeal of Integration* (Washington, DC, 1997), 198.

31. Ibid., 199.

32. Jonathan Kozol, *Shame of the Nation* (New York, 2005), documenting the reappearance and growth of American racial apartheid in city schools.

33. Patterson, *The Ordeal of Integration*, 14, 18, and 80. He acknowledged family instability and poverty as issues not yet solved, along with church membership segregation.

34. No Child Left Behind, an act of Congress 2002 requiring higher state education standards and accountability.

35. *Clipboard*, Boston Public Schools, September 2002.

36. Ed Hayward "Marathon Man," *Commonwealth Magazine*, special issue, Boston, 2002, by MassInc a statewide advocacy group.

37. The Renaissance Charter School, e.g., provided students with free computers and a much longer school day.

38. The John Marshall public school in Dorchester. School visit and interviews with Theresa Harvey-Jackson, 1999–2002.

39. Lawrence Cremin, *Popular Education and Its Discontents* (New York, 1989), 78, 125.

40. A few Massachusetts communities and local School Committees tried to assert their right to set the graduation criteria, not the state.

41. Paul E. Barton, "Facing the Hard Facts of Education Reform," Princeton, The Educational Testing Service, 2001. The Massachusetts State Board of Education authorized an alternative evaluation for certain students with special needs, and granted dozens of appeals for other students.

42. Press conference with Mayor Menino, Chad Gifford, and Walter Simmons of the Annenberg Foundation, October 2002.

43. Jack Tager, *Boston Riots: Three Centuries of Social Violence* (Boston, 2001).

44. Hirschman, *Exit, Voice and Loyalty*, 63.

45. Chicago Economist Milton Friedman for fifty years has been the champion of school vouchers. *The School Choice Advocate*, Friedman Foundation, Vol. 9, No. 1, 22. The Clintons, Kennedys, and a bipartisan coalition support charter schools.

46. Deborah Meier, *Will Standards Save Public Education?* (Boston, 2000), with commentary by T.R. Sizer and others.

47. Jacob Ludes III "Report from the Executive Director/CEO of the New England Association of Schools and Colleges," April 2002, Issue 1.

48. Larry Cuban in Warren, *American Teacher*, in a chapter on "The Persistence of Reform in American Schools," 385.

49. Diane Ravitch, *Left Back: A Century of Failed School Reforms* (New York, 2000).

50. "Strong Foundation/Evolving Challenge: A Case Study to Support Leadership Transition in the Boston Public Schools," The Aspen Institute, with the Annenberg Institute (Boston 2006) and Paul Reville and Celine Coggins, editors, *A Decade of Urban School Reform: Persistence and Progress in the Boston Public Schools* (Cambridge, 2007).

51. Kathryn Boudette, Elizabeth City, and Richard Murnane, *Data Wise* (Cambridge, 2005).
52. Interview with Superintendent Carol Johnson, August 31, 2010.
53. *Acceleration Agenda*, The Boston School Strategic Plan, 2009–2014, Boston.
54. Interview with Neil Sullivan, Private Industry Council, August 24, 2010.
55. *Too Big to Be Seen*: The Invisible Dropout Crisis in Boston and America, Boston, Youth Transitions Task Force. May 2006.
56. *Making the Connection*, a Report of the Massachusetts Graduation and Dropout Prevention Commission, Boston, MA Executive Office of Education, October 2009.
57. Interview with Neil Sullivan, August 24, 2010.
58. Interview with John Mudd, September 9, 2010.
59. *The Boston Globe*, June 22, 2010.
60. Boston Teacher Residency Web site, Summer 2010.
61. Interview with Ellen Guiney, September 2010, and Boston Plan for Excellence in the Public Schools board reports, and 25th Anniversary Report.
62. Kelvin Ma, "Lesson Plan in Boston Schools: Don't Go It Alone," *The New York Times*, August 28, 2010.
63. *The Boston Phoenix*, "A Race Well Run," August 27, 2010.
64. Diane Ravitch, *The Death and Life of a Great American School System*. New York: Basic Books, 2010, 203–212.
65. Paul Grogan, *Comeback Cities*: A Blueprint for Urban Neighborhood Revival, Boulder, CO: Westview Press, 2000, 212.
66. Ibid., 212.
67. Ravitch, 138–145.
68. Interview with Carol Johnson, August 31, 2010, and Sam Tyler, October 29, 2010.
69. Nancy McArdle et al. *Segregation and Exposure to High Poverty Schools*, Northeastern University, Bouve School, report with Data Diversity, Boston, 2010.
70. David Kirp, "The Widest Achievement Gap," *National Affairs*, Fall 2010, 65.
71. Boston Community Profiles, *Community Profiles*, Metropolitan Area Planning Council Boston, October 1998.
72. *Clipboard*, Boston Public Schools, 2001.
73. Seymour Sarason, *Charter Schools and Vouchers* (Portsmouth, NH, 2002), 51.
74. Scott Lafee, "Beyond the Internet," *The School Administrator*, Vol. 58, No. 9, October 2001, The American Association of School Administrators, Arlington, Virginia.
75. Sheldon Berman and Elizabeth Pape, "A Schoolman's Guide to Online Courses," *The School Administrator*, Vol. 58, No. 9, 14–18.
76. Thomas H. O'Connor, *Athens of America* (Boston, 2006).
77. Boston Public Schools had been runner up three years in a row for the prestigious Eli Broad award for "the most improved" urban school in America based on recent improvements in student and school performance, winning first place just as Payzant retired after almost eleven years in Boston.

Bibliography

Adams, Henry. *The Education of Henry Adams.* Boston: Houghton Mifflin, 1918.
Alioto, Kathleen Sullivan. "Boxed In." Unpublished doctoral dissertation. Cambridge: Harvard Graduate School of Education, 1980.
Antin, Mary. *The Promised Land.* Boston: Houghton Mifflin, 1912.
Banks, William M. *Black Intellectuals.* New York: Norton, 1996.
Batson, Ruth. *The Black Educational Movement in Boston.* Boston: Northeastern University, 2001.
Batson, Ruth and Robert Hayden. *A History of Metco.* Boston: Select Publications, 1987.
Beatty, Jack. *The Rascal King: The Life and Times of James Michael Curley, 1874–1958.* Reading, MA: Addison Wesley, 1992.
Berman, Sheldon and Elizabeth Pape. "A Schoolman's Guide to Online Courses." *The School Administrator* October 2001, Vol. 58, No. 9.
Boston Finance Commission. Studies of the Boston Public Schools, 1930, 1944 (see also Strayer).
Boston Plan for Excellence in the Public Schools, Annual Reports, Boston, The Boston Plan, 1995–2006.
———. *Partnership for Performance.* Boston, The Boston Plan, September 2005.
———. "Towards an Open Teacher Hiring Process." Boston, The Boston Plan, 2000.
Boudette, Kathryn, Elizabeth City, and Richard Murnane. *Data Wise.* Cambridge: Harvard Education Press, 2005.
Bratton, William. *Turnaround.* New York: Random House, 2000.
Brennan, Joseph G. *Education of a Prejudiced Man.* New York: Scribners, 1977.
Brown, Larry. *The Way We Go To School.* Boston: The Task Force on Out of School Youth, 1971.
Brown, Richard and Jack Tager. *Massachusetts: A Concise History.* Amherst: University of Massachusetts Press, 2001.
Bryant, Howard. *Shutout: A Story of Race and Baseball in Boston.* New York: Routledge, 2002.
Bullard, Pamela and Judith Stoia. *The Hardest Lesson.* Boston: Little Brown, 1980.
Callahan, Raymond. *Education and the Cult of Efficiency.* Chicago: University of Chicago Press, 1962.
Cheever, Abigail A. "Which Home for English High? Boston Seeks a School Site." Unpublished honors paper. Cambridge, MA: Radcliffe College, 1967.

Coan, Stephen. "Uncertain Allies: Public-Private Partnerships with the Boston Compact 1982–1996." Unpublished doctoral dissertation. Waltham, MA: Brandeis University, 1997.

Coles, Robert, with Carol Baldwin. *The Buses Roll.* New York: W.W. Norton, 1974.

Corwin, Ronald. *Militant Professionals.* New York: Appleton Century Crofts, 1970.

Conant James B. *My Several Lives.* New York: Harper and Row, 1970.

——— *Slums and Suburbs.* New York: McGraw Hill, 1961.

Cottle, Thomas J. *Busing.* Boston: Beacon Press, 1976.

Cremin, Lawrence. *Popular Education and Its Discontents.* New York: Harper & Row, 1989.

Cronin, Joseph M. "Boston Picks a Superintendent (1963)." Unpublished case study for the Maxwell School. Syracuse, NY: Syracuse University, 1965.

——— *The Control of Urban Schools.* New York: The Free Press, 1973.

——— "Negroes in Catholic Schools." *Commonweal* October 1967.

———with Richard M. Hailer. *Organizing an Urban School System for Diversity.* Boston: MACE, 1970 and Lexington: D.C. Heath Books, 1973.

Cuban, Larry. *To Make a Difference.* New York: The Free Press, 1970.

Curley, James Michael. *I'd Do It Again: A Record of All My Uproarious Years.* Englewood Cliffs, NJ: Prentice Hall, 1957.

Curran, Thomas. *Xenophobia and Immigration, 1820–1930.* Boston: Twayne, 1978.

Daniels, John. *In Freedom's Birthplace.* New York: Negro University Press, 1968.

Dentler, Robert and Marvin Scott. *Schools on Trial.* Cambridge, Abt Associates, 1981.

Deutch, Sarah. *Women and the City.* New York: Oxford University Press, 2000.

Dickens, Charles. *American Notes.* First Edition. London: Chapman and Hall, 1842.

Dinneen, Joseph F. *The Purple Shamrock: The Hon. James Michael Curley of Boston.* New York: W.W. Norton, Inc., 1949.

Dolan, Jay. *In Search of American Catholicism.* New York: Oxford University Press, 2000.

Dolin, Eric. *Political Waters.* Amherst, MA: University of Massachusetts Press, 2004.

Downs, Anthony. *Opening Up the Suburbs.* New Haven: Yale University Press, 1973.

Eaton, Susan. *The Other Boston Busing Story.* New Haven: Yale University Press, 2001.

Edwards, Ralph and Charles V. Willie. *Black Power, White Power in Public Education.* Westport, CT: Praeger, 1998.

Farrell, John A. *Tip O'Neil and the Democratic Century.* Boston: Little Brown, 2001.

Finance Commission, City of Boston. Reports on Boston Schools 1930, 1944.

Flannery, Jack. *The Sargent Years: 1969–1975.* The State House Library, Boston, 1976.

Formisano, Ronald P. *Boston against Busing: Race, Class and Ethnicity in the 1960's and 1970's.* Chapel Hill, NC: University of North Carolina Press, 1991.

Fraser, James W., Editor. *From Common School to Magnet School.* Boston: Boston Public Library, 1979.

————. *The School in the United States.* New York: McGraw Hill, 2001.

Freeland, Richard. *Academia's Golden Age.* New York: Oxford University Press, 1992.

Gamm, Gerald. *Urban Exodus: Why the Jews Left Boston and the Catholics Stayed.* Cambridge: Harvard University Press, 1999.

Gans, Herbert. *The Urban Villagers: Group and Class in the Life of Italian-Americans.* New York: The Free Press, 1962.

Gittell, Marilyn. *Education and Urban Politics.* Beverly Hills: Sage, 1962.

Glazer, Nathan and Daniel P. Moynihan. *Beyond the Melting Pot.* Cambridge: MIT Press, 1997.

Glenn, Charles. *The Myth of the Common School.* Amherst: University of Massachusetts Press, 1997.

Glinski, James F. "The Catholic Church and Desegregation of the Boston Public Schools." *The New England Journal of Public Policy* Fall 1988, Vol. 4, No. 2.

Godine, David R. *A Book for Boston.* Boston: David R. Godine, 1980.

Goodwin, Doris Kearns. *The Fitzgeralds and the Kennedys.* New York: Simon and Schuster, 1987.

Graham, Patricia A. *SOS: Sustain Our Schools.* New York: Hill and Wang, 1993.

Handlin, Oscar. *Boston's Immigrants.* Cambridge: Harvard University Press, 1959.

Hathaway, Jane and Andrew Rotherham, editors. *Collective Bargaining in Education.* Cambridge: Harvard Education Press, 2006.

Hayden, Robert C. *African-Americans in Boston.* Boston: Trustees of the Public Library, 1991.

————. *Boston's NAACP History 1910–1982.* Boston: Boston Branch NAACP, 1982.

Hayward, Editor. "Marathon Man" (Thomas Payzant). *Commonwealth* Magazine, Boston: MassInc., 2002.

Hentoff, Nat. *Boston Boy.* Boston: Alfred A. Knopf, 1986.

Hess, Frederick M. *Spinning Wheels.* Washington DC: The Brookings Institution, 1999.

Higgins, George V. *Style versus Substance: Kevin White, and the Politics of Illusion.* New York: Macmillan, 1984.

Hill, Paul T., Christine Campbell, and James Harvey. *It Takes a City: Getting Serious about Urban School Reform.* Washington, DC: The Brookings Institution, 2000.

Hillson, Jon. *The Battle of Boston.* New York: Pathfinder Press, 1977.

Hirschman, Albert O. *Exit, Voice and Loyalty: Responses to Decline in Firms, Organizations and States.* Cambridge: Harvard University Press, 1969.

Hoffman, Nancy. *Women's True Profession.* Westbury, NY: The Feminist Press, 1981.

Hogness, Peter S. "The Boston Teachers Union Strikes of 1970 and 1975." Unpublished honors thesis. Cambridge, MA: Harvard College, 1978.

Jackson, Kenneth. *Crabgrass Frontier.* New York: Oxford University Press, 1985.

Jennings, James and Mel King. *From Access to Power: Black Politics in Boston.* Cambridge, MA: Schenkman Books, 1986.

Kahn, E.J. *Harvard.* New York: Norton, 1969.

Kanter, William. "Organized Political Reform in a Changing American City." Unpublished honors thesis. Cambridge, MA: Harvard College, 1982.

Karabel, Jerome. *The Choice: The Hidden History of Admissions and Exclusion at Harvard, Yale and Princeton.* Boston: Houghton Mifflin, 2005.

Kaufman, Polly *Boston Women and City School Politics.* New York: Garland, 1994.

Kendrick, Stephen and Paul. *Sarah's Long Walk: The Free Blacks of Boston and How Their Struggle for Equality Changed America.* Boston: Beacon Press, 2004.

King, Melvin. *Chain of Change: Struggles for Black Community Development.* Boston: South End Press, 1981.

Kozol, Jonathan. Death *at an Early Age.* Boston: Beacon Press, 1980.

——— "Rebirth of Education in Boston." *American Education.* Washington DC: U.S. Department of Education, June 1980.

———. *Shame of the Nation.* New York: Crown, 2005.

Lalee, Scott. "Beyond the Internet." *The School Administrator* October 2001, Vol. 58, No. 9.

Lehr, Richard and Gerald O'Neill. *Black Mass.* New York: Perennial, 2001.

Levine, Hillel and Lawrence Harmon. *The Death of an American Jewish Community: A Tragedy of Good Intentions.* New York: The Free Press, 1992.

Levy, Frank. *Northern Schools and Civil Rights.* Chicago: Markham, 1971.

Lieberman, Myron. *Education as a Profession.* Norman: University of Oklahoma Press, 1956.

———. *The Future of Public Education.* Chicago: The University of Chicago Press, 1960.

Loftus, Patrick. *That Old Gang of Mine.* South Boston: TOLGM-PJL, 1991.

Lord, Robert H., John E. Sexton, and Edward Harrington. *History of the Archdiocese of Boston.* 3 volumes. New York: Sheed and Ward, 1945.

Lukas, J. Anthony. *Common Ground: A Turbulent Decade in the Lives of Three American Families.* New York: Alfred A. Knopf, 1986.

Lupo, Alan. *Liberty's Chosen Home: The Politics of Violence in Boston.* Boston: Little Brown, 1977.

MacDonald, Michael. *All Souls.* Boston: Beacon Press, 2000.

Malloy, Iona. *Southie Won't Go: A Teacher's Diary of Desegregation at South Boston High School.* Urbana: University of Illinois Press, 1977.

Marshall, M. K *Law and Order in Grade 6E: A Story of Chaos and Innovation in a Ghetto School.* Boston: Little, Brown, 1972.

Marson, Philip. *Breeder of Democracy.* Cambridge: Schenkman, 1970.

———. *A Teacher Speaks.* New York: David McKay Co., 1960.

Mayer, Martin. *Teacher Strike.* New York: Harper & Row, 1969.

Meier, Deborah. *Will Standards Save Public Education?* Boston: Beacon Press, 2000.

Merwick, Donna. *Boston's Priests 1848–1910.* Cambridge: Harvard University Press, 1959.

Mirel, Jeffrey. *The Rise and Fall of Detroit Schools, 1907–1961.* Ann Arbor: University of Michigan Press, 1999.

Morison, Samuel Eliot. *One Boy's Boston.* Cambridge: Houghton Mifflin, 1962.

Murphey, Marjory. *Blackboard Unions.* Ithaca: Cornell University Press, 1979.

Neill, Donald Montgomery. "The Struggles of the Boston Black Community for Equality and Quality in Public Education: 1959–1987." Unpublished doctoral dissertation. Cambridge: Harvard Graduate School of Education, 1987.

Nelson, Adam. *The Elusive Ideal: Equal Educational Opportunity and the Federal Role in Boston's Public Schools, 1950–1985*. Chicago: University of Chicago Press, 2005.

Nimoy, Leonard. *I Am not Spock (and, I Am Spock)*. New York: Ballantine, 1975 and Hyperion, 1990.

Northeastern University. *An Assessment of Governance, Operations and Finance of the Boston Public Schools*. Boston: Northeastern University, 1991.

Nuccio, Vincent and Richard J. Doyle. *A Study of the Promotional Policies and Procedures in the Boston Public Schools*. Boston: Boston College, 1970.

O'Connell, Lawrence "The Reform Group in Central City Schools." Unpublished doctoral dissertation. Syracuse: Syracuse University, 1968.

O'Connell, William. *Recollections of Seventy Years*. Boston: Houghton Mifflin, 1934.

O'Connor, Thomas H. *Athens of America*. Boston: The University of Massachusetts Press, 2006.

———. *Boston's Catholics*. Boston: Northeastern University Press, 1998.

———. *Boston Irish*. Boston: Northeastern University Press, 1995.

———. *Building a New Boston: Politics and Urban Renewal 1950–1970*. Boston: Northeastern University Press, 1993.

———. *South Boston, My Home Town: The History of an Ethnic Community*. Boston: Quinlan Press, 1988.

O'Toole, James. *Militant and Triumphant: William Henry O'Connell and the Catholic Church in Boston*. Notre Dame: UND Press, 1992.

Orfield, Gary. *Must We Bus?* Washington DC: The Brookings Institution, 1978.

Patterson, Orlando. *The Ordeal of Integration*. Washington, DC: Civitas/Counterpoint, 1997.

Pearson, Henry Greenleaf. *Son of New England: James Jackson Storrow*. Boston: Thomas Todd, 1932.

Perry, Charles and Wesley Wildman. *The Impact of Negotiations on Public Education*. Worthington, OH: Charles A. Jones Publishers, 1970.

Porter. Michael, Rebecca Wayland, and C. Jeffrey Grogan. *Toward a Shared Economic Vision for Massachusetts*. Boston, Secretary of State, 1992.

Portz, John, Lara Stein, and Robin Jones. *City Schools and City Politics: Institutions and Leadership in Pittsburgh, Boston and St. Louis*. Kansas: University Press of Kansas, 1999.

Ravitch, Diane. *Left Back: A Century of Failed School Reforms*. New York: Simon and Schuster, 2000.

———. *Death and Life of the Great American School System*. New York: Basic Books, 2010.

Redstone, Sumner. *A Passion to Win*. New York: Simon and Schuster, 2001.

Rennie, Jack et al. *Every Child a Winner*. Boston: Massachusetts Business Alliance for Education, 1991.

Reville, Paul and Celine Coggins, editors. *A Decade of Urban School Reform*. Cambridge: Harvard Education Press, 2007.

Rosenthal, Alan. *Pedagogues and Power*. Syracuse: Syracuse University Press, 1969.

Rossano, Kenneth. *The Boston Experience*. Boston: The Greater Boston Chamber of Commerce, 1986.

Russell, Francis. *Knave of Boston*. Boston: Quinlan Press, 1967.

Sarason, Seymour. *Charter Schools and Vouchers*. Portsmouth, NH: Heinemann, 2002.

Sargent, Cyril. *Boston's Schools*. Cambridge: Harvard Graduate School of Education, Cambridge 1962 (and 1953) studies.

Sarna, Jonathan and Ellen Smith. *The Jews of Boston*. Boston: Northeastern University Press, 1990.

Schrag, Peter. *Village School Downtown*. Boston: Beacon Press, 1967.

Schultz, Stanley K. *The Culture Factory: Boston Public Schools, 1789–1860*. New York: Oxford University Press, 1973.

Schneider, Mark R. *Boston Confronts Jim Crow: 1890–1920*. Boston: Northeastern University Press, 1997.

Shannon, William. *The American Irish*. New York: Macmillan 1960; reprinted by the University of Massachusetts Press, 1990.

Silberman, Charles. *Crisis in the Classroom*. New York: John Wiley, 1971.

Smith, Richard Norton. *The Harvard Century*. New York: Simon and Schuster, 1986.

Solomon, Barbara. *Ancestors and Immigrants*. Cambridge: Harvard University Press, 1956.

Strayer, George D. "Report of a Survey of the Boston, Massachusetts Public Schools." Boston: Finance Commission, 1944.

Tager, Jack. *Boston Riots: Three Centuries of Social Violence*. Boston: Northeastern University Press, 2001.

Teele, James E, Ellen Jackson, and Clara Mayo. *Evaluating School Busing: A Case Study of Boston's Operation Exodus*. New York: Praeger, 1973.

———. "Family Experiences in Operation Exodus: The Busing of Negro Children." *The Community Mental Health Journal* Monograph No. 3, 1967.

Thernstrom, Stephan. *The Other Bostonians: Poverty and Progress in an American Metropolis, 1880–1970*. Cambridge, MA: Harvard University Press, 1973.

Tocqueville, Alexis de. *Democracy in America*. New York: Vintage Books, 1945.

Trout, Charles. *Boston: The Great Depression and the New Deal*. New York: Oxford University Press, 1977.

Tyack, David B. *George B. Ticknor and the Boston Brahmins*. Cambridge: Harvard University Press, 1967.

Tyack, David B. with Elisabeth Hansot. *Managers of Virtue*. New York: Basic Books, 1982.

———. *The One Best System*. Cambridge: Harvard University Press, 1974.

Tyack, David, Robert Lowe, and Elisabeth Hansot. *Public Schools in Hard Times*. Cambridge: Harvard University Press, 1984.

Usdan, Michael and Larry Cuban. *Urban School Reform with Shallow Roots*. New York: Teachers College Press, 2003.

Useem, Betsy. *Low Tech Education in a High Tech World*. New York: The Free Press, 1986.

Warner, Sam Bass, Jr. *Streetcar Suburbs: The Process of Growth in Boston, 1870–1900*. Cambridge, MA: Harvard University Press, 1962.

———. *The Way We Really Lived: Social Change in Boston since 1920*. Boston: Trustees of the Boston Public Library, 1977.

Warren, Donald. *American Teachers: History of the Teaching Profession at Work*. New York: Macmillan, 1989.

Wasserman, Miriam. "The Geography of Life Chances." *Regional Review* Federal Reserve Bank of Boston, Q4 2001.

White, Theodore H. *In Search of History.* New York: Harper & Row, 1978.

Whitehill, Walter Muir. *Boston: A Topographical History.* Cambridge, MA: Harvard University Press, 1968.

————. *Boston in the Age of John Fitzgerald Kennedy.* Norman, OK: University of Oklahoma Press, 1966.

Whyte, William. *Street Corner Society: The Social Structure of an Italian Slum.* Chicago: University of Chicago Press, 1943.

Wilson, Steven F. *Reinventing the Schools.* Boston: Pioneer Institute, 1992.

Wood, Robert C. "A Professional at Bay: Managing Boston Public Schools." *Journal of Policy Analysis and Management* 1982, Vol. 1, No. 4.

Yarmolinsky, Adam, Lance Liebman, and Corinne Schelling. *Race and Schooling in the City.* Cambridge, MA: Harvard University Press, 1981.

Yeomans, Henry A. *A. Lawrence Lowell.* Cambridge: Harvard University Press, 1948.

New Sources for Second Edition

Boston Plan for Excellence in the Public Schools, 25th Anniversary Report.

Boston Teacher Residency Web site.

Boston Youth Transitional Task Force. *Too Big To Be Seen: The Invisible Dropout Crisis in Boston and America.* Boston: Private Industry Council, 2006.

Citizens Commission on Academic Success in Boston Schools: A Blueprint for the New Superintendent. Boston: Massachusetts Advocates for Children, 2006.

Grogan, Paul. *Comeback Cities: A Blueprint for Urban Neighborhood Revival.* Boulder, CO: Westview Press, 2000.

Kane, Thomas and Joshua Angrist. *Informing the Debate: Comparing Boston's Charter, Pilot and Traditional Schools.* Boston: The Boston Foundation and Massachusetts Department of Elementary Education, January 2009.

Massachusetts Graduation and Dropout Prevention and Recovery Commission. *Making the Connection.* Boston: Executive Office of Education, October 2009.

Mauricio Gaston Institute for Latino Community Development and Public Policy, University of Massachusetts Boston. *Halting the Race to the Bottom: Urgent Intervention for the Improvement of English Language Learners in Massachusetts.* Boston, the Subcommittee on ELL, Massachusetts Board of Elementary and Secondary Education, December 2009.

McArdle, Nancy, Theresa Osypuk, and Dolores Acerdo-Garcia. *Segregation and Exposure to High Poverty Schools in Large Metropolitan Areas, 2008–2009.* Boston: Bouve College, Northeastern University, September 2010; See also the briefing paper on Boston by same authors, October 2010. DataDiversity.org.

National Council on Teacher Quality. *Human Capital in Boston Schools: Attracting and Retraining Quality Teachers.* February 2010.

INDEX

MacDougall, Rod, 197, 204, 207
Malcolm X., 64–6
Mandela, 126
Mann, Horace, 6, 30, 206
Marson, Phillip, 9, 38
Mass Advocates for Children, 180,
    232, 244
Mass. Comprehensive Assessment
    System (MCAS), 211, 223–4
Mass. Ed Reform Act (MERA), 174,
    221, 223
Massachusetts Board of Education, 70,
    75–6, 79, 111, 206, 223
Massachusetts Institute of Technology
    (MIT), 110, 137, 146, 149
McCluskey, Kevin, 117, 123, 146, 148
McCormack, Edward, 79, 93, 108,
    122, 126, 186
McDonough, John, 85, 96, 106,
    130–1
McGuire, Jean, 116, 166
McKeigue, Jean Sullivan, 112, 123
McKinnis, Hattie, 109
Meany, George, 100
Medeiros, Humberto (Cardinal), 100,
    113–14, 126
Meier, Deborah, 223–4, 227
Menino, Thomas, (Mayor), 17, 100–1,
    114, 126–7, 174, 176, 199, 205,
    217, 230
METCO, 86–7, 105, 120–2, 210,
    217, 220
Metropolitan Achievement Test,
    193–4, 199
Miller, Melvin B., 64
Milwaukee, 177
Moakley, Joseph, (Congressman),
    106–7
Mohler-Faria, Dana, 235
Monan, J. Donald SJ, 147
Morgan v. Hennigan, 75, 97–8
Morse, Thomas (Judge), 164–5
Moscovitch, Edward, 198
Muchnick, Isadore H.Y., 42, 53–8, 62

Mudd, John, 180
Murnane, Richard (My BPS), 229–30

NAACP, 25, 63–8, 70–2, 82, 97, 102,
    118, 191, 195, 217
National Education Association, 152, 199
National Science Foundation, 224
Neill, Donald Montgomery, 108–9
Nellie Mae Educational
    Foundation, 224
New Boston Committee, 57–8
New England Association of Schools
    and Colleges, 204–5, 227–8
New York City, 40, 43, 88, 109, 133,
    151–3, 161, 207, 216, 219
Nimoy, Leonard, 56
Nixon, Richard M. (President), 96
No Child Left Behind Act, 221, 226
Northeastern University, 135, 136,
    138, 145, 214
Norton, Clem, 42, 52
Noyce Foundation, 202
Nucci, John, 117

O'Bryant High School of Mathematics
    and Science (Technical High
    School), 212
O'Bryant, John, 116, 163–6
O'Connell, Lawrence, 85–6
O'Connell, William, (Cardinal), 10,
    15, 25, 40, 78
O'Connor, Thomas, 103, 199–201,
    213, 221, 223–4, 228, 230
O'Connor, William, 73, 77, 81, 84–5
O'Leary, Gerald, 112, 143
O'Sullivan, James, 100
O'Toole, Kathleen, 127
Obama, Barack, President of the
    United States, 180, 235, 238,
    241, 242
Ohrenberger, William,
    (Superintendent), 72–4, 77, 130,
    134, 137, 143, 155, 157
ombudsman, 142, 145–6, 226

ABOUT THE AUTHOR

Joseph M. Cronin was born in 1935 in Boston where his mother Mary Marr attended Boston public schools 1908–20. After seven years as a teacher and Maryland principal, he began studying Boston schools in 1964 as a research assistant to H. Thomas James at Stanford University on Carnegie Foundation and U.S. Office of Education studies of school boards and urban school decision-making. Later, as a Harvard University professor, he directed the Danforth Foundation study of Boston school decision-making between 1968 and 1971. He published *The Control of Urban Schools* on big city school boards and *Organizing an Urban School System for Diversity*, the 1970 Massachusetts Advisory Council on Education (MACE) report on Boston schools with Richard M. Hailer. His Harvard students included two future Boston Superintendents, William Leary and Thomas Payzant. Governor Francis Sargent in late 1971 named Cronin the Massachusetts Secretary of Educational Affairs during the Boston desegregation crisis. In 1975 he became Illinois State Superintendent of Education, serving until 1980.

Returning to Boston in the 1980s, he ran the state education loan corporation. At the request of Boston banker Kenneth Rossano, he chaired The Boston Plan for Excellence in the Public Schools and revived the Education Committee of the Greater Boston Chamber of Commerce. He later served as president of Bentley College, dean of the Lesley University School of Education, and senior fellow at the New England Board of Higher Education, at the Nellie Mae Education Foundation, and Eduventures. He worked between 1965 and 2006 as an occasional consultant on Boston school matters to state agencies and to Boston mayors and school officials. He was one of the founders of Boston's Higher Education Information Center and other programs that were introduced to guide more Boston students toward higher education. He served as a federal Race to the Top Reviewer in 2010.

Books by Joseph M. Cronin

The Control of Urban Schools

Organizing an Urban School System for Diversity, with Richard M. Hailer

Student Loans: Risks and Realities, edited with Sylvia Simmons

CPSIA information can be obtained at www.ICGtesting.com
Printed in the USA
BVOW030051051111

275303BV00002B/11/P